Feminism and Women's Rights Worldwide

Feminism and Women's Rights Worldwide

Volume 2
Mental and Physical Health

MICHELE A. PALUDI, EDITOR

Praeger Perspectives

Women's Psychology

Michele A. Paludi, Series Editor

PRAEGER
An Imprint of ABC-CLIO, LLC

A B C CLIO

Santa Barbara, California • Denver, Colorado • Oxford, England

Library of Congress Cataloging-in-Publication Data
Feminism and women's rights worldwide / Michele A. Paludi, editor.
    v. ; cm. — (Women's psychology)
    Includes bibliographical references and index.
    Contents: The myth of the man-hating feminist / Melinda Kanner and Kristin J. Anderson — Gender differences : the arguments regarding abilities / Jennifer L. Martin — Women in education : students and professors worldwide / Susan Basow — In women's voices / Samantha Smith — Working life as a house : a tale of floors, walls, and ceilings / Leanne Faraday-Brash — Women as religious leaders : advances and stalemates / J. Harold Ellens — The feminine political persona : Queen Victoria, Ellen Johnson Sirleaf, and Michelle Bachelet / Emily A. Haddad and William Schweinle — Women in the military : is it time to un-gender combat roles? / Breena E. Coates — Sexual minority women : sources and outcomes of stigmatization / Rhonda M. Schultz, and Kristin P. Beals — Special issues for women with disabilities / Martha E. Banks — Body dissatisfaction and disordered eating : the globalization of western appearance ideals / Jaehee Jung and Gordon B. Forbes — Sexual violence to girls and women in schools around the world / Susan Strauss.
    ISBN 978-0-313-37596-5 (set : hard copy : alk. paper) — ISBN 978-0-313-37597-2 (set : ebook) — ISBN 978-0-313-37598-9 (v.1 : hard copy : alk. paper) — ISBN 978-0-313-37599-6 (v.1 : ebook) — ISBN 978-0-313-37600-9 (v.2 : hard copy : alk. paper) — ISBN 978-0-313-37601-6 (v.2 : ebook) — ISBN 978-0-313-37602-3 (v.3 : hard copy : alk. paper) — ISBN 978-0-313-37603-0 (v.3 : ebook)
    1. Feminism. 2. Women's rights. 3. Sexual harassment of women. 4. Abused women—Psychology. 5. Women—Psychology. I. Paludi, Michele Antoinette
    HQ1180.F424   2010
    305.42—dc22   2009035343

ISBN: 978-0-313-37596-5
EISBN: 978-0-313-37597-2

14 13 12 11 10   1 2 3 4 5

This book is also available on the World Wide Web as an eBook.
Visit www.abc-clio.com for details.

Praeger
An Imprint of ABC-CLIO, LLC

ABC-CLIO, LLC
130 Cremona Drive, P.O. Box 1911
Santa Barbara, California 93116-1911

This book is printed on acid-free paper (∞)

Manufactured in the United States of America

For Rosa and Lucia, my maternal and paternal grandmothers
and for Antoinette, my mother:

"Remember, our heritage is our power; we can know ourselves and
our capacities by seeing that other women have been strong."
—Judy Chicago

Contents

Series Introduction

*Because women's work is never done and is underpaid or unpaid or boring
or repetitious and we're the first to get fired and what we look like is more
important than what we do and if we get raped it's our fault and if we get
beaten we must have provoked it and if we raise our voices we're nagging
bitches and if we enjoy sex we're nymphos and if we don't we're frigid and
if we love women it's because we can't get a "real" man and if we ask our
doctor too many questions we're neurotic and/or pushy and if we expect
childcare we're selfish and if we stand up for our rights we're aggressive
and "unfeminine" and if we don't we're typical weak females and if we
want to get married we're out to trap a man and if we don't we're unnatu-
ral and because we still can't get an adequate safe contraceptive but men
can walk on the moon and if we can't cope or don't want a pregnancy we're
made to feel guilty about abortion and . . . for lots of other reasons we are
part of the women's liberation movement.*
   —Author unknown, quoted in *The Torch*, September 14, 1987

These sentiments underlie the major goals of the Praeger Perspectives
book series, Women's Psychology. The goals are as follows:

Value women: The books in this series value women by valuing children and working for affordable child care; value women by respecting
all physiques, not just by placing value on slender women; value
women by acknowledging older women's wisdom, beauty, aging; value
women who have been sexually victimized and view them as survivors;
value women who work inside and outside of the home; and value
women by respecting their choices of careers, of whom they mentor, of
their reproductive rights, their spirituality, and their sexuality.

Treat women as the norm. Thus the books in this series make up for
women's issues typically being omitted, trivialized, or dismissed from
other books on psychology.

Take a non-Eurocentric view of women's experiences. The books in this series integrate the scholarship on race and ethnicity into women's psychology, thus providing a psychology of all women. Women typically have been described collectively; but we are diverse.

Facilitate connections between readers' experiences and psychological theories and empirical research. The books in this series offer readers opportunities to challenge their views about women, feminism, sexual victimization, gender role socialization, education, and equal rights. These texts thus encourage women readers to value themselves and others. The accounts of women's experiences as reflected through research and personal stories in the texts in this series have been included for readers to derive strength from the efforts of others who have worked for social change on the interpersonal, organizational, and societal levels. A student in one of my courses on the psychology of women once stated:

> I learned so much about women. Women face many issues: discrimination, sexism, prejudices . . . by society. Women need to work together to change how society views us. I learned so much and talked about much of the issues brought up in class to my friends and family. My attitudes have changed toward a lot of things. I got to look at myself, my life, and what I see for the future. (Paludi, 2002)

It is my hope that readers of the books in this series will also reflect on the topics and look at themselves, their own lives, and what they see for the future. This three-volume book set on Feminism and Women's Rights Worldwide provides readers with the opportunity to accomplish this goal and offers suggestions for all of us working for gender justice within our friendships and romantic relationships, in guiding institutional and social policy change in workplace and educational institutions, and in lobbying state and federal legislators on issues related to reproductive rights, pay equity, education, sexual violence, and childcare.

Michele A. Paludi
Series Editor

REFERENCE

Paludi, M. (2002). *The psychology of women.* 2nd ed. Upper Saddle River, NJ: Prentice Hall.

Acknowledgments

Teaching and writing are separate, but serve/feed one another in so many ways. Writing travels the road inward, teaching, the road out—helping OTHERS move inward—it is an honor to be with others in the spirit of writing and encouragement.

—Naomi Shihab Nye

Nye's sentiment is echoed throughout this three-volume set on feminism and women's rights. Most of the contributors have taught courses in women's studies and feminism as well as conducted research and written about feminist issues. Many contributors have been advocates on behalf of feminist principles through working with local, state and federal agencies, legislators, and the United Nations. And many of us have collaborated with students in our classes in writing chapters for this book set. These students have made us believe that all of them, in their individual ways, will continue to do what this book set intends: value feminism and work toward equality. It has been exhilarating for me to see a new generation of feminists collaborating with mentors and colleagues on the chapters for this book set.

I have been honored to have collaborated with the contributors to these volumes. Several friendships with contributors have been rekindled and strengthened, and I have met many new colleagues from around the world who taught me about their disciplines through their writing. You have all shown me the great accomplishments of feminists as well as the work we have yet to do. Thank you.

I wish to thank my sisters, Rosalie Paludi and Lucille Paludi, for their support during the preparation of this book set. I also thank Carmen Paludi, Jr. for his guidance and encouragement. Our discussions about feminism brought back wonderful memories of my mother,

Antoinette, and my father, Michael, about whom I continue to learn and continue to cherish the time I had with them.

I acknowledge several friends who encouraged me during the preparation of this set of books. Thank you to Paula Lundberg Love, Jennifer Martin, Billie Wright Dziech, Darlene C. DeFour, and Florence Denmark.

I have been fortunate to have had the opportunity to work with students throughout my career, now at Union Graduate College. I have thoroughly enjoyed learning from them. Thank you to students in the Human Resource Management Certificate Program and Management and Leadership Certificate Program. I especially acknowledge Michelle Strand, Carrie Turco, Haimanot Kelbessa, Sarah Bennett, Sarah Boggess, Kristina Hicks, James Luciano, Sarah Henderson Maneely, Abbey Massoud-Tastor, Marie Fuda, Jessica Wilmot, Katie Kelly, and Nick Salvatoriello. I am honored you have called me your professor.

I also thank Debbie Carvalko for supporting my visions for books and helping them become realities. I have enjoyed working with Debbie and her colleagues at Praeger. They are a wonderful team of caring people. They appreciate my love of writing and editing books. Debbie somehow knew that, after the publication of the three-volume set on the *Psychology of Women and Work* (2008, Praeger), which I edited, and the political climate of the 2008 presidential campaign, especially regarding women, I had to follow up those texts with books on feminism. She knows I share Sheila Bender's sentiment:

> *We write because something inside says we must and we can no longer ignore that voice.*

Introduction

Michele A. Paludi

And how do you look backward? By looking forward. And what do you see?
As they look forward, they see what they had to do before they could look
backward. And there we have it all.

—Gertrude Stein

Alyssa Zucker and Abigail Stewart (2007) reported in their study of
333 university alumnae that feminism is internalized quite differently
depending on the developmental stage in our lives. This research led
me to consider my own feminist socialization and feminist identity development as I began writing and editing these three volumes on feminism and women's rights. I was introduced to feminism by my
parents, Antoinette and Michael, at a very young age, even though the
label feminism was not used by them. Yet, as I came to realize much
later, their behavior was very much in keeping with feminist principles. They valued my sisters and me unconditionally; wanted to give
us educational opportunities that were denied to them because of the
generation into which they were born and because they were first generation Americans whose parents had other values to instill in them;
they worked for equality in relationships, politics, and health care. I
was 18 the year individuals became eligible to vote at age 18, and both
my parents took me to cast my votes that year.

They believed that, like them, I had a responsibility to make things
better for the next generation. They valued voting; I was told what the
Suffragists had endured in order to win this right for us and to remember this each year I vote. I took my first course in feminism as an
undergraduate in the early 1970s: "Sex Roles in American Society"
with Nancy Walbek. I would share the class discussions with my
mother, telling her about the experiences of students in class that were
different from my own—for example, being denied the use of certain

toys considered "sex inappropriate" for them; being tracked into different high school and college programs because of being women or men; women being told by family and friends to hide their achievements from potential dates and mates. I was unable to relate to these experiences and realized for the first time that my parents were feminists, a term to which I was introduced formally in this class and then subsequently as a graduate student when I took courses with Dee Graham and Edna Rawlings. I also learned that I had been exposed to nonstereotyped role models, and because there were all girls in our family, we were not raised to conform to stereotyped behavior.

It was in graduate school that I decided to pursue research in feminist psychology, especially in women's career development. I was fortunate to have a mentor, William Dember, who encouraged me to pursue this research, even though it was not in his area of specialization (i.e., visual perception). Bill encouraged me to take courses with faculty in departments in addition to psychology: educational leadership and family development. He told me this would help put pieces together in understanding the research I was conducting. I thank Kathy Borman and Judy Frankel for their roles in my feminist identity development.

A few years later when my father died, Charlie, who attended my father's wake, came to my mother, my sisters, and me and told us how my father had impacted his life. Charlie, an African American man, told us my father was the only coworker (both were skilled workers at General Electric) who treated him fairly, didn't talk with him in a derogatory manner, and stopped others from making racial slurs and epithets. I learned for another time what it meant to be a feminist.

I dedicated the three-volume set on the *Psychology of Women at Work* to my parents: "For Antoinette and Michael Paludi, who encouraged me to define what women's work is for myself." They wanted all their daughters to be independent thinkers and doers and to help others. They gave us no templates to follow but encouraged us to navigate our own paths. And, especially in my case, encouraged me to leave home to attend graduate school in a city that seemed, to my parents, to be very far away—but they never said "no."

My parents thus taught me that not only did they believe in the economic, educational, social, and political equality of women and men, but they favored the social and legal changes necessary to achieve equality between the sexes and among races, and they were committed to implementing these principles. Perhaps they could not effect change at the national level, but they did do so in personal relationships with their family and friends and on the local level. This is the legacy they left my sisters and me. This book set is a tribute to Antoinette and Michael.

I have been reminded of Antoinette and Michael throughout the writing and editing of these volumes on feminism and women's rights.

I am especially reminded of what my mother used to tell me: "You are there before you get there." She knew I wanted equality to happen fast and that I grew concerned when feminists didn't win political elections, when younger women didn't know the heritage of how they came to be accepted in graduate programs and in certain jobs, how the glass ceiling for women and people of color is still strong, and that worldwide, women constitute 64 percent of all adults who are illiterate (see Susan Basow's chapter in Volume 1). I have learned that she was right; that change takes time, and to measure change differently, i.e., in increments. As Secretary of State Hillary Clinton stated as she suspended her campaign for president of the United States in 2008: "Although we weren't able to shatter this highest, hardest glass ceiling this time, thanks to you, it's got about 18 million cracks in it, and the light is shining through like never before."

The chapters in these volumes show us where the light is shining through on feminism. All three volumes represent what Judith Lorber (1998) and Snelling (1999) identified: several types of feminism and feminists. Lorber (1998) categorized feminism into three major areas: gender reform, gender resistance, and gender rebellion. Gender-reform feminism emphasizes similarities between women and men rather than focusing on differences between them. Gender-resistance feminism holds that formal legal rights alone will not end gender inequality; male dominance is too ingrained into social relations. Gender-resistance feminism focuses on how men and women are different—cognitively, emotionally, and socially—and urges women to form women-centered organizations and communities. Gender-rebellion feminism looks at the interrelationships among inequalities of sex, race, ethnicity, social class, and sexual orientation. A number of years ago my text on the psychology of women displayed a quilt on its cover (Paludi, 2002). I asked for this design to highlight Gentry's (1989) image of quilt making for understanding feminism. These three volumes on feminism and women's rights also represent quilt making in understanding feminism. Each contributor has made one piece of the quilt that has been joined with pieces by other contributors. Each of the contributors has used different stitching on their piece of the quilt. No one chapter is more important than the other. We need all pieces if we are to complete the quilt that is feminism. According to Gentry (1989):

> Feminist psychology and feminism in general seem to be at the point of trying to piece together the individual parts of a quilt. The overall pattern of the quilt that we want is still emerging. No one knows what equality in a post-patriarchal world will look like. We are beginning to piece the separate parts together—to explore the kinds of stitching to use in connecting the pieces and how to place the separate pieces into the

pattern. But we have not stopped questioning the process of quilting itself.

In Volume 1, *Heritage, Roles, and Issues*, contributors have discussed efforts to integrate feminist scholarship into several disciplines, including education, work, science, military, religion, and politics. As Catherine Stimpson (1971) noted, there have been three kinds of problems in the disciplines and curriculum with respect to women: omission, distortions, and trivializations. Each of the contributors to Volume 1 notes where the sexism in the disciplines has existed and where feminist correctives have restructured the disciplines. Jennifer Martin, in her chapter concerning gender differences in abilities, noted:

> Women have made significant social, academic, and occupational gains in the past 50 years; for example, women are entering nontraditional fields with more frequency, participating in high school and college sports more than ever before, and carving out more egalitarian roles for themselves within the family. However, women have still not ultimately achieved true equity with their male counterparts. . . . The idea that women somehow possess different or inferior aptitudes when compared to their male counterparts can lead to diminished expectations for women—in terms of how they view themselves and how others view them.

In Volume 2, *Mental and Physical Health*, contributors deal with violence and discrimination against girls and women and the resulting impact on women's emotional and physical well being, interpersonal relationships, career development, and self-concept. Types of discrimination and victimization addressed are sexual harassment, sexual violence, harassment of sexual minorities, and rape and violence in the context of women's HIV risk. Contributors have addressed these issues globally. Bethany Waits and Paula Lundberg-Love offer new cutting edge evidence on neurological responses in women victims of sexual violence. Therapeutic support for women victims of violence is also addressed in this volume, including feminist therapy and ethnocultural psychotherapy.

All contributors note that sexual victimization is prevalent in the United States and globally, as is sexual harassment and sexual orientation discrimination. As Waits and Lundberg-Love note:

> Female survivors of sexual violence are everywhere. They are in universities, religious institutions, court rooms, hospitals, and the military. They are daughters, mothers, spouses, sisters, friends, next-door neighbors, and co-workers. Many differ in age, education, ethnicity, and socioeconomic status. . . . However, their lives are connected by the violence that they have experienced.

The international focus on feminism and women's rights is continued in Volume 3, *Feminism as Human Rights*. In this volume, contributors address laws on sexual harassment, pay equity, and rape. Furthermore, contributors speak to the injustices to women with disabilities. Human rights issues such as arranged and forced marriage for women, pornography, and the globalization of western appearance ideals are also presented in this volume. All contributors to this volume call for further advocacy on behalf of women. As Noorfarah Merali stated:

> It is only if arranged marriages are understood in light of their intentions, diverse forms, actual outcomes, and local or international contexts that laws, policies, and human rights advocacy can be appropriately channeled to protect and preserve women's well-being.

In addition to the scholarly reviews of research on feminism and women's rights, I have included women's personal accounts of their own feminist identity development. They are at different stages in life, in their career, and in relationships and yet they are bound by shared stories.

It is my hope that these volumes encourage individuals to self identify as feminists. Research has suggested for some time that most people reject the term "feminist" when describing themselves but support feminist principles—equal pay for equal work, for example (see Paludi et al., Volume 3). Goldner's (1994) study noted that when women who hold feminist beliefs anticipate a negative reaction from their peers to the label "feminist," they will avoid using the term to describe themselves. Goldner indicated that media is a primary source of negative images of feminists. It is common to see photos of women identified as feminists having clenched fists. These images are not representative of feminists. More recent research by Rudman and Fairchild (2007) found that the stereotype that feminists are unattractive still persists.

However, these images are rejected by individuals, especially during adolescence and young adulthood, when maintaining gender role stereotypic behavior is reinforced and is central to their self-esteem and self-concept. Paludi, Paludi, and DeFour (2004) noted that individuals reject the label feminist because they view themselves as in control, as powerful rather than as victims of gender inequality. Thus, they perceive the term "feminist" to imply a powerless position, which they reject (Rhode, 1977).

The contributors to each of the three volumes of *Feminism and Women's Rights Worldwide* encourage us to think critically about feminism, to value cultural experiences and to integrate our knowledge of theories and research about feminism with our own life experiences. The chapters encouraged me to do this in remembering my own feminist socialization. I encourage you to do the same. It is my hope these three volumes serve as a "life raft" (Klonis, Endo, Crosby, and Worell, 1997) for feminists, especially those in the millennial generation.

REFERENCES

Gentry, M. (1989). Introduction: Feminist perspectives on gender and thought: Paradox and potential. In M. Crawford & M. Gentry (Eds.), *Gender and thought.* New York: Springer-Verlag.

Goldner, M. (1994). Accounting for race and class variation in the disjuncture between feminist identity and feminist beliefs: The place of negative labels and social movements. Paper presented at the Annual Meeting of the American Sociological Association, Los Angeles.

Klonis, S., Endo, J., Crosby, F., & Worell, J. (1997). Feminism as life raft. *Psychology of Women Quarterly, 21,* 333–345.

Lorber, J. (1998). *Gender inequality: Feminist theories and politics.* Los Angeles: Roxbury.

Paludi, M. (2002). *The psychology of women.* 2nd ed. Upper Saddle River, NJ: Prentice Hall.

Paludi, M., ed. (2008). *The psychology of women at work: Challenges and solutions for our female workforce.* Westport, CT: Praeger.

Paludi, M., Paludi, C., & DeFour, D. (2004). Introduction: The more things change, the more they stay the same. In M. Paludi (Ed.), *Praeger guide to the psychology of gender.* xi–xxxi. Westport, CT: Praeger.

Rhode, D. (1997). *Speaking of sex.* Cambridge, MA: Harvard University Press.

Rudman, L., & Fairchild, K. (2007). The F word: Is feminism incompatible with beauty and romance? *Psychology of Women Quarterly, 31,* 125–136.

Snelling, S. (1999). Women's perspectives on feminism. *Psychology of Women Quarterly, 23,* 247–266.

Stimpson, C. (1971). Thy neighbor's wife, thy neighbor's servants: Women's liberation and black civil rights. In V. Gornick & B. Moran (Eds.), *Woman in sexist society: Studies in power and powerlessness.* New York: Basic Books.

Zucker, A., & Stewart, A. (2007). Growing up and growing older: Feminism as a context for women's lives. *Psychology of Women Quarterly, 31,* 137–145.

Chapter 1

International Perspectives on Women and Mental Health

Joy Rice
Nancy Felipe Russo

Women have the right to the enjoyment of the highest attainable standard of physical and mental health. The enjoyment of this right is vital to their life and well-being and their ability to participate in all areas of public and private life. Health is a state of complete physical, mental and social well-being and . . . is determined by the social, political and economic context of [women's] lives, as well as by biology. (Platform for action: Fourth World Conference on Women, Beijing China, Chapter IV. C.89, United Nations)

These words, contained in the national platform for action of the United Nations' Fourth World Conference on Women, provide a holistic vision of women's health, one in which physical and mental health are inextricably intertwined and rooted in women's social, political, and economic conditions. Understanding the links between women's social roles and circumstances and negative mental health outcomes thus becomes a key element in any global health agenda for women (Koblinsky, Timyan, & Gay, 1992).

Although this holistic view of women's health has been resisted by the biomedical establishment that dominates health care in the United States, it is congruent with how health has been perceived globally. Indeed, for more than three decades, the World Health Organization (WHO) has emphasized a social model of health that has stressed the role of complex reciprocal relationships among psychological, behavioral, social, and economic factors in determining health and illness based on this holistic definition:

> Mental health is the capacity of the individual, the group, and the environment to interact with one another in ways that promote subjective well-being, the optimal development and use of mental abilities (cognitive, affective, and relational), the achievement of the individual and collective goals consistent with justice and the attainment and preservation of fundamental equality. (Cabral & Astbury, 2000, p. 12)

In sum, women's mental health is not simply the absence of disease, and it is inseparable from a person's health well-being. A woman's mental health enables her to find meaning in her life, function effectively in her social context, adapt to change, respond to crises, establish rewarding relationships in her community, and modify her environments to meet her needs.

One outcome of the worldwide feminist movement stimulated by the Beijing Conference was an International Consensus Statement on Women's Mental Health that was passed by the World Psychiatric Association (WPA) and signed by 140 WPA member associations, the World Federation of Mental Health, and other mental health organizations, including the American Psychological Association (APA) and the American Psychiatric Association. That statement emphasized that prioritizing women's mental health was essential for the achievement of the Millennium Development Goals of the United Nations (UN, 2000; http://www.un.org/millenniumgoals/), which include the achievement of universal primary education, promotion of gender equality, reduction of child mortality, improving maternal health, and combating human immunodeficiency virus/acquired immune deficiency syndrome (HIV/AIDS), among others. It also emphasized the importance of considering the contexts of women's lives as determinants of their mental health (Stewart, 2006).

A similar holistic biopsychosocial vision of mental health has been promulgated in feminist psychologists in the United States and around the world (Russo, in press; Safir & Hill, 2008; Wyche & Rice, 1997). International issues and perspectives were important dimensions in the feminist movement in psychology from its beginnings. Indeed, the Association for Women in Psychology, established in the United States in 1969 as the first explicitly feminist organization in the field, was designated an official nongovernmental organization (NGO) for the UN in 1976 (for a more detailed history of international issues in feminist psychology, see Safir & Hill, 2008).

Today, feminist psychology in the United States is both informed by and is a contributor to the international women's movement. The field has become explicitly multicultural, emphasizing the importance of viewing mental health in its social/political context and examining power inequities and inequalities that undermine mental health in the lives of diverse women (Enns & Byars-Winston, 2009; Goodwin & Fiske, 2001; Russo, in press).

Consequently, feminist therapy is now conceptualized as having a multicultural biopsychosocial approach, one that encompasses meaning-making and spiritual concerns, considers a woman in her social context, and has her empowerment as a therapeutic goal (Brown, 2008a; Enns & Byars-Winston, 2009; McKay, Hill, Freedman, & Enright, 2007; Worell & Johnson, 2001; Wyche & Rice, 1997). This perspective is reflected in the development of international practice guidelines for counseling and therapy with girls and women described later.

WOMEN'S MENTAL HEALTH IN A CONTEXT OF INEQUALITY AND OPPRESSION

The international women's movement has emphasized that around the world, stigma, devaluation, and inequalities in power associated with women's social roles and circumstances create conditions that undermine women's mental health (Cabral & Astbury, 2000; Russo, in press; Stewart et al., 2001). These conditions include poverty—women are 70 percent of the poor around the world and earn significantly less than men (WHO, 2002). Related conditions include hunger, malnutrition, fatigue from overwork (with women's low-paid work often under dangerous conditions), prejudice and discrimination, inadequate educational and economic resources, gender-based violence (including sexual abuse, partner violence, and sexual trafficking), and social disruption leading to displaced populations (including migration due to insufficient economic opportunity, social conflict and war, and natural disaster) (Cabral & Astbury, 2000; Demyttenaere et al., 2004; Desjarlais et al., 1995; WHO, 2000, 2002).

The mental health dimensions of sexual and reproductive health have received increasing attention, partially because of the intersections of unintended pregnancies, sexually transmitted infections (STIs; including HIV), and gender-based violence, which are all known to have a negative impact on mental health (Hamilton & Russo, 2006). In addition, the high rates of pregnancy-associated depression among women in developing countries compared to women in industrialized countries (20–40 percent vs. 10–15 percent) are of concern (WHO, 2009). Mental health problems may be associated with lack of choice in sexual and reproductive decisions, STIs, infertility, unintended and unwanted pregnancy, unsafe abortion, miscarriage, and childbirth (including premature birth), among other things (WHO, 2009; see Chrisler, this volume, for more discussion of women's reproductive rights).

The critical role of lack of power and having a disadvantaged social status is manifested by the link between rates of depressive symptoms with indicators of gender inequality that has been around the world (Arrindell, Steptoe, & Wardle, 2003), and by regions (urban vs. rural) within nations, and between states within the United States (Chen, Subramanian, Acevedo-Garcia, & Kawachi, 2005). Women's higher rates of depressive disorders compared to men, the consistency of this gender gap across diverse groups and cross-nationally, and research linking depression to hopelessness (a reflection of powerlessness) and low self-esteem (a reflection of devaluation) has made theorizing the relation of gender to depression of particular interest to feminist psychologists (Hamilton & Russo, 2006; Jackson & Williams, 2006). Consequently, we will consider women's depression in more detail below.

Women have unequal access to gender-sensitive basic health and mental health services around the world (WHO, 2002). Furthermore, service delivery may be affected by bias and stereotyping of providers such that when services are available, they are inadequate or inappropriate. Given that the development and expression of mental disorder differs for women and men, the need for gender-sensitive approaches to diagnosis, treatment, and prevention is severe. Developing such services will require understanding and investigating gender as a sociocultural construct (Russo & Tartaro, 2008).

GENDER IN INTERNATIONAL PERSPECTIVE

A shift in focus from the individual's characteristics and behaviors to a gendered sociocultural view of mental health requires a more complex understanding of gender as a cultural construct. This new understanding is a necessary foundation for developing a coherent theory of how inequality becomes translated into mental health disparities. Gender can be conceptualized as a cultural package of many interconnected factors, including gendered emotions, identities, values, expectations, norms, roles, scripts, discourse, environments, and institutions. These factors can influence mental health and well-being separately, as well as in combination (Russo, in press).

Gender defines what is considered "normal" and appropriate behavioral, psychological, and social characteristics for males and females and shapes their personal and social identities. What is considered normal varies over the life cycle, over time, and across cultures. Violations of stereotypes and gender role expectations may lead to stigmatization, marginalization, and discrimination, with implications for mental health (Hamilton & Russo, 2006). When roles assigned by gender have lower power and status, structured inequalities are created that can translate into health disparities—in mental health status as well as service delivery (Russo, in press; Russo & Landrine, 2009; Russo & Tartaro, 2008).

Gender operates at psychological, social, and situational levels. For example, the relations of gender and race to mental health are affected by perceived sexism and racism (Moradi & DeBlaere, 2009; Moradi & Subich, 2003; Thomas, Witherspoon, & Speight, 2008); the relationship of sexual orientation to mental health is affected by stigma and victimization associated with homosexuality (Balsam, Rothblum, & Beauchaine, 2005; Tjaden, Thoennes, & Allison, 1999; Herek & Garnets, 2007).

Gender intersects with other social identities that may or may not be stigmatized or associated with disadvantage, including identities based on age, ethnicity, sexuality, physical disability, tribe, religion, nationality, immigrant status, occupational status, class, and caste status. There is an urgent need for work that theorizes and investigates how complex and interacting dimensions of social difference deemed important in a particular cultural context affect women's lived experiences in ways that have implications for women's mental health (Brown, Riepe, & Coffey, 2005; McCall, 2005; Russo & Vaz, 2001). More complexity in theorizing will require overcoming epistemological, methodological, and statistical challenges, however (Landrine & Corral, in press).

In particular, measurement equivalence issues will need to be addressed, as the equivalence of measures may vary by gender and culture, and measures that are equivalent across cultures for men may not be equivalent for women (Chen & West, 2007). Such issues pose construct validity problems in measuring sexist beliefs and attitudes—beliefs that maintain or foster gender inequalities—cross-nationally (for a review of the literatures and measurement issues related to the endorsement, expression, and emergence of sexism cross-nationally, see Swim, Becker, & Lee, 2009).

In summary, advancing understanding of gender's relation to mental health internationally will require investigating a complex interplay among biological, psychological, social, cultural, and contextual factors, including multiple personal and social identities, social locations and conditions, and coping strategies and resources (Russo, in press; Russo & Tartaro, 2008; Szymanski & Kashubeck-West, 2008). In considering gender-related factors that can affect diverse women's mental health internationally, we must also keep in mind that women will vary in their response to such factors, and that variance in women's responses will both reflect their position in the social structure, as well as how they integrate or engage their multiple social identities, some of which may be specific to a particular context or culture.

WOMEN'S MENTAL DISORDER: THE GLOBAL BURDEN

The priority of mental health issues globally has risen as the enormous impact of mental disorders on what has been conceptualized as the "global burden of disease." A recent WHO (2008) report provides a comprehensive picture of the global and regional state of the physical and mental health of the world's peoples. Based on extensive country governmental data from 112 member states, it provides projections of deaths and the global burden of disease to the year 2030 and is an update of WHO research first conducted in 1990. The study finds that mental disorders are among the leading causes of disability in all regions of the word. They account for approximately one-third of years lost due to disability among people older than fourteen. Four out of 10 "diseases" with the highest burden are psychiatric disorders (Kastrup, 2007).

Violence and self-inflicted injury, which are also among the leading contributors to the disease burden, have profound implications for women's mental health as well (Cabral & Astbury, 2000). Analyses of data gathered from 15 sites in 10 countries participating in the WHO multi-country study on women's health and domestic violence against women found a strong link between gender-based violence and negative health and mental health outcomes, including higher levels of emotional distress, risk of suicide ideation, and suicide attempts found across all sites (Ellsberg et al., 2008).

Although males and females are generally similar in overall rates of mental disorder around the world, the patterns and symptoms of mental disorders differ for men and men over the life cycle (Kessler, 2006; Kessler, Chiu, Demler, & Walters, 2005; Piccinelli & Homen, 1997; Silverman & Carter, 2006). For example, in the United States, based on the National Co-morbidity Survey, Kessler et al. (2005) identified gender differences in six classes or patterns of disorder. Here presented by level of severity, they included the following: (1) unaffected respondents (more likely to be male); (2) pure internalizing disorders (more likely to be female); (3) pure externalizing disorders (more likely to be male); (4) comorbid internalizing disorders (more likely to be female); (5) comorbid internalizing and/or externalizing disorders dominated by comorbid social phobia and attention-deficit/hyperactivity disorder (more likely to be male); and (6) highly comorbid major depressive episodes (more likely to be female). No gender difference was found in a seventh class, highly comorbid bipolar disorder. High comorbidity was associated with severity—classes with the highest comorbidity (4, 6, 7) included about 7 percent of the sample, but represented 43.6 percent of the serious cases.

Comorbidity of mental disorders signals greater severity of illness and disability and higher utilization of services. Women have higher rates of lifetime and 12-month comorbidity of three or more disorders (WHO, 2002). It has long been known that anxiety is comorbid with depression, particularly for women (Breslau et al., 1995), and that women have higher rates of mood and anxiety disorders (Piccinelli &

Homen, 1997; Silverman & Carter, 2006). Symptoms of anxiety disorders are correlated with other disorders, complicating diagnosis. In particular, research is needed that clarifies the origins and relationships among symptoms of anxiety and depressive disorders, which constitute the largest contributor to the gender gap in internalizing disorders.

Countrywide studies may mask within-country variations in rates of mental disorder. Women are more likely to be poor, and surveys in Brazil, Chile, India, and Zimbabwe have found that rates of common mental disorders (anxiety and depression) are higher among the poor (Patel, Araya, Ludermir, & Todd, 1999). Furthermore, in poorer areas, treatment may be more likely to be inadequate or nonexistent. In the United States, rates and predictors of mental disorder vary substantially within subpopulations. For example, a national survey of Latinos and Asian Americans (Alegría et al., 2007), revealed that among the four Latina subethnic groups studied, Mexican heritage women were less likely than Puerto Rican women to have a depressive disorder, and Puerto Rican women had the highest overall lifetime and past-year prevalence rates compared to other women.

It is important to go beyond a focus on rates and learn more about how elements of gender affect the development, course, and context of mental disorders among women internationally. In particular, more needs to be known about how gender affects comobidity of mental disorder over the life cycle. For example, depression and anxiety are more likely to be found together for women, whereas depression and substance abuse are more likely to be paired for men. The extent to which this difference reflects a gender difference in pathways to depression versus diagnostic bias requires investigation.

Research on the patterns of being depressed found in women's daily experiences suggests that women may be more likely to experience short-term depressive episodes than men, possibly reflecting their day-to-day experience with life stressors (Kessler, 2006).

WOMEN AND DEPRESSION: A GLOBAL PERSPECTIVE

Depression is identified in the WHO report as the leading global cause of years of health lost to disease for both men and women, with unipolar depression as the eighth leading cause of loss of health in low-income countries and the primary cause of loss of health in middle- and high-income countries. Depression affects around 120 million people worldwide, and the number is projected to increase. Fewer than 25 percent of those affected have access to adequate treatment and health care.

For purposes of this discussion, the outstanding fact is that compared with men, the worldwide rate of depression in women globally is *50 percent higher*, and gender is perceived to be the critical determinant and strongest correlate of risk for different categorized types of depression (WHO, 2001). The biomedical evidence across nations, cultures, and ethnicities widely documents that women are one to three times more likely than men to develop depression and anxiety disorders (Ustun, 2000), but there is great variation in the estimated total population prevalence across studies (Kessler, 2006). Although there is marked variation in the rates of depression for women in different countries, much higher rates have been found in women attending primary health care centers in developing countries. In Indian clinics, for example, it is estimated that between 25 to 33 percent of women patients are suffering from depression (Worley, 2006).

Despite three decades of research on gender identities and a wide range of identified risk factors, no particular cause or interrelated set of causes can fully explain the significant global phenomenon of gender differences in depression (Nolen-Hoeksema, 2001). Speculation continues in the literature about biological correlates for increased incidence of depression for women. Major depression clusters in families and depression in a first-degree relative is a risk factor for depression. While some studies find similar levels of heritability of depression for women and men, several others have found higher genetic loadings for females, suggesting that the impact of some genes for risk for major depression differs in women and men (Kendler, Gardner, Neale, & Prescott, 2001).

The unique biology of women may in part explain their greater propensity to depression beginning in adolescence and early puberty, and sex hormones are likely to play a role (Ge, Conger, & Elder, 1996; Zahn-Waxler, Race, & Duggal, 2004). Depression associated with postpartum and menopausal periods is being studied in relation to hormonal factors and interactions between hormones, neurotransmitters, and other biological systems (Mazure, Kieta, & Blehar, 2002). Women are also more likely than men to be prescribed mood-altering psychotropic medication and electro-convulsive therapy for depression, even where the evidence suggests that the main conditions surrounding their diagnosis have strong social origins (Busfield, 1996).

Several psychological and environmental risk factors and social causes of depression for women have been identified (Bertram, 2003; Paltiel, 1993; Zahn-Waxler et al., 2004). They include the inequitable gendered division of labor and family responsibility, women's lesser social status and gender socialization, and the effects of poverty, abuse, and violence. Hamilton and Russo (2006) also review research that links unwanted pregnancy, sexualized objectification, and stigma as contributors to the gender gap in depression. Add to these etiological factors the astounding fact that women and children represent an estimated 80 percent of 50 million people affected by violent conflicts, civil wards, disasters, and displacement (WHO, 2006).

Paltiel concludes that the key depression risk factors for women globally are simply that "everywhere women are overworked, overlooked and undervalued, and that poverty, discrimination, violence and powerlessness are pervasive features of women's lives" (p. 197). In many developed countries, women are often poorly paid for dangerous, labor-intensive jobs, and are undernourished as well (Lopez & Guarnaccia, 2005). The so-called "feminization of poverty" is also a worldwide phenomenon as our family structures and models change, with an increasingly preponderance of single-parent mother families worldwide (Rice, 2001). Clearly, it is essential to recognize how genetic, biological, social, and psychological factors all contribute to the high incidence of depression women worldwide, and guidelines for treatment need to be based on a biopsychosocial model of assessment, research, practice, and policy.

Screening and access to treatment for depression is also a very significant concern. Even in a developed, wealthy country like the United States, only 24 percent of women who suffer from depression receive treatment, with even lower rates for African American women (16 percent) and Hispanic women (20 percent) (U.S. Department of Health and Human Services, 2000). Health care providers in developing countries identify less than one-half of women with depression in those countries (WHO, 2002). A number of overwhelming challenges occur in countries with low-resource settings including the lack of facilities, trained mental health personnel, effective population-based screening, and the prevalence of high cultural stigma (Worley, 2006). Communication between health workers and women patients can be extremely authoritarian in many countries where women are still primarily viewed as inferior with low social and economic status and often stigmatized for showing negative or depressed emotion. Furthermore, when women dare to reveal mental health concerns, health workers may reflect these stereotyped gender biases, which leads them to either overtreat or undertreat women (WHO, 1996).

PSYCHOLOGICAL PRACTICE GUIDELINES FOR WOMEN AND GIRLS

International Implications and Issues

As noted in the previous section, across the world women are challenged by significant mental health risks. These risks are associated with a multitude of pernicious outcomes and implications, including depression and suicide risk, anxiety disorders, and reproductive health issues, as well as physiological and psychosomatic problems. In light of these facts, psychotherapy and other forms of psychological intervention such as early screening and risk assessment are very important treatment strategies for prevention and treatment of women's mental health problems. The development of guidelines for psychological practice for women and girls that addresses their special mental health needs and issues and is founded on a feminist perspective of gender equity and cultural sensitivity is an area of burgeoning concern not only in the Western world, but globally (Ballou, Hill, & West, 2008; Ballou & West, 2000; Comas-Diaz & Greene, 1994: Enns, 2008, 2009; Hays, 2001).

This section will address three areas related to guidelines for practice. First, some background will be presented on the APA's Resolution on Cultural and Gender Implications in International Psychology. This resolution passed in 2004 (Rice & Ballou, 2002) formed the theoretical foundation for the actual gender practice guidelines adopted in 2006 (APA, 2007). Then, the key elements in both the American and Canadian Psychological Association guidelines (CPA, 2007) will be examined with a view to how they could apply to more international and diverse cultural perspectives cross-nationally. Finally, a summary of some key issues that seem important in the development of feminist guidelines for psychological practice with women and girls in any country of the world will be presented.

Cultural and Gender Awareness in the Practice of International Psychology

The second author of this chapter became more actively involved in international psychology leadership by founding and serving as the first chair of the International Committee for Women, a very active standing committee of the APA Division of International Psychology. One of the first successful projects launched by the committee took several years to complete and involved the participation of women from many countries and organizations in drafting and passing an APA Resolution on Cultural and Gender Awareness in International Psychology. This activity embraced the collaboration and help from many women psychologists from other countries who were interested in feminist issues from an international perspective, and it also led to advocacy work about these issues in the association.

The goal of the resolution was to encourage and facilitate awareness and reflective consideration for psychology and psychologists engaged in international projects, research, teaching, and practice. Underpinning the core concepts of the resolution was the understanding that feminist, multicultural, and critical theory, among other postmodern perspectives, had raised fundamental concerns about the values and assumptions long held in the dominant paradigm of conventional psychology (Fox & Prilleltensky, 1997; Kitzinger, 1991; Martin-Baro, 1994; Unger, 1995). The mutual and collaborative model called for in the resolution is important to world psychology because it offers guidance in postmodern perspectives in theory, research, and practice and strong models of psychological practice grounded in social justice. It also assumes that psychology based on Western values could benefit significantly from the expansion of its knowledge base through an international lens that includes diverse multicultural and cross-national perspectives. The resolution encourages psychologists to commit to five principles that help us understand and overcome oppressive attitudes and practices in dominant psychology transported internationally:

1. *Understanding the experiences of individuals in diverse cultures and contexts.* This first principle is grounded in "the other's" experience. It urges us to understanding the experience of the other, which is embedded in multiple contexts and diverse social structures. Understanding and sincerely appreciating the experience of the other person also implies that we validate the other's worldview, their ways of knowing and their authority for valid information and meaning (Ballou; 1996; Flowers & Richardson, 1996). One example for psychological practice with women, among the many, might be in the realm of values. In North America, productivity and autonomy are held as strong virtues, and many of our theoretical constructs and normative standards are based on the value of independent thinking and action. The principle of valuing others' experiences is both obvious and subtle in its many applications. At its most basic application, how we define the psychological problem, diagnose the problem, and select the intervention must be based squarely in the experience of the other.

2. *Respect for pluralism based on differences.* The second and closely related principle is respect for pluralism. Respect for pluralism takes one beyond recognizing diversity to valuing diversity. As one example, feminist research on women in other disciplines and countries often employs ethnographic and narrative methodology as a legitimate and important way to document and validate the actual voices and direct experiences of women and minorities (Alcoff & Potter, 1993; Lazarus and Lykes, 2005; Naidoo, 2005). However, in psychology these efforts may still not be seen as valid or meeting the scientific test of traditional empirical investigation of best practices (Riger, 1992, 2000).

3. *Awareness and analysis of power.* This principle points out how critical it is to understand and become aware of power differentials and to analyze power asymmetries and hierarchies of power as they operate in relationships, institutions, and systems (Ballou & West, 2000; Enriquez, 1992). As an example in psychotherapy, interpersonal relationships between therapist and client are guided by this principle of reducing power asymmetries between practitioner and client. While each has different levels of power and status, both members are involved in a reciprocal learning process in which each can make valuable contributions to the other. This is particularly true when the each person in the therapeutic dyad comes from a different cultural perspective (Wyche & Rice, 1997).

4. *Critical analysis of Western perspectives.* The normative values and definitions employed in traditional Western psychology have been critiqued

extensively. These analyses are revealing of the cultural, historical, economic, and political agendas and perspectives embedded within the theory and practice of psychotherapy, particularly in relation to the treatment of women and minorities (Brown, 1994; Fox & Prilleltensky, 1997; Kitzinger, 1991; Rosenblum & Travis, 1996; Radway, 1998).

5. *Interdisciplinary social–cultural perspective.* This principle calls for an awareness of the significant impact of external and structural forces on individuals. Such factors, for example, as poverty, violence, and war, and the effects of the law, church, family, education, and the workplace, result in multiple and complex forms of privilege and/or oppression (Rice, 2001, 2007). A feminist perspective calls for an analysis of "social location" and an interdisciplinary view that recognizes how anthropological, historical, and religious factors influence and interact with one's ethnicity, class, gender, and culture (Landrine, 1995). In psychological practice, the psychologist sometimes encounters contradictions of valuing culture and actual cultural practices, for sometimes the cultural practices are oppressive to women as in inequitable marital, divorce, and reproductive rights, violence, abuse, and economic dominance (Rice, 2005).

APA and CPA Guidelines for Psychological Practice with Women and Girls

The previous five principles formed a foundation for the succeeding work of 35 feminist psychologists who over several years of collaboration drafted guidelines for psychological practice with girls and women. The chairs of the task force, Roberta Nutt, Joy Rice, and Carolyn Enns, took the guidelines through the long and extensive process of revisions and updates required by the various APA governance bodies, council, and membership. Adopted in 2006, these 11 guidelines were based on the need to articulate a model for psychotherapeutic practice that was both gender- and culturally sensitive and that employed concepts of empowerment and an understanding and appreciation of the standpoints, world views and culture specific practices of women and men as well (APA, 2007). The 11 guidelines are organized into three sections: (1) diversity, social context, and power; (2) professional responsibility; and (3) practice applications.

DIVERSITY, SOCIAL CONTEXT, AND POWER

Guideline 1: Psychologists strive to be aware of the effects of socialization, stereotyping, and unique life events on the development of girls and women across diverse cultural groups.

Guideline 2: Psychologists are encouraged to recognize and utilize information about oppression, privilege, and identity development as they may affect girls and women.

Guideline 3: Psychologists strive to understand the impact of bias and discrimination upon the physical and mental health of those with whom they work.

Professional Responsibility

Guideline 4: Psychologists strive to use gender and culturally sensitive, affirming practices in providing services to girls and women.

Guideline 5: Psychologists are encouraged to recognize how their socialization, attitudes, and knowledge about gender may affect their practice with girls and women.

Practice Applications

Guideline 6: Psychologists are encouraged to employ interventions and approaches that have been found to be effective in the treatment of issues of concern to girls and women.

Guideline 7: Psychologists strive to foster therapeutic relationships and practices that promote initiative, empowerment, and expanded alternatives and choices for girls and women.

Guideline 8: Psychologists strive to provide appropriate, unbiased assessments and diagnoses in their work with women and girls

Guideline 9: Psychologists strive to consider the problems of girls and women in their sociopolitical context.

Guideline 10: Psychologists strive to acquaint themselves with and utilize relevant mental health, education, and community resources for girls and women.

Guideline 11: Psychologists are encouraged to understand and work to change institutional and systemic bias that may impact girls and women.

Almost concurrently, in 2007, the CPA passed "Guidelines for Ethical Psychological Practice with Women" that articulates four guiding principles:

1. *Respect for the dignity of persons.* This principle urges that psychologist ensure that they do not engage in or support any gender-based discrimination and/or oppression, recognizing that there may be situations where women clients face multiple discriminations and oppressions.

2. *Responsible caring.* The main point of this principle is that psychologists strive to understand how women's lives are shaped by the interaction of gender with other modalities like culture, ethnicity, and sexual orientation, and that is important for the practitioner to understand how the multiple social contexts of their own life might influence or interfere with their attempts to help and not harm women clients.

3. *Integrity in relationships.* Psychologists are open, honest, and accurate in their communications and recognize, monitor, and manage potential biases, multiples relationships, or other conflicts of interest that could

lead to the exploitation of the client and the diminishment of trust. Psychologists honestly acknowledge differences in beliefs and values with their women clients and work collaboratively to resolve those differences in the best interest of the woman.

4. *Responsibility to society.* Psychologists acknowledge that they have responsibilities to the societies in which they live and work and their concern for the welfare of all human beings includes concern for the welfare of women in society. They accept responsibility to do what they can to change societal laws and structures that discriminate or lead to oppressions of women.

The underlying concepts and principles in the APA and CPA guidelines are similar, but the CPA principles are more general in their articulation and do not, for example, discuss specific practices of promoting empowerment and expanded alternatives for women; using unbiased assessments, diagnoses, and materials; and employing specific interventions that have been found to be helpful and effective with women clients. Their thrust is closer to the underlying ethical principles for the APA Resolution on Gender and Cultural Awareness in International Psychology. The CPA guidelines, unlike those of the APA, do not provide a developmental perspective applying to younger girls.

FEMINIST PSYCHOTHERAPY IN A GLOBAL CONTEXT

Upon the completion of these guidelines, it was quickly realized that there was a need to address and consider the potential implications, applications, and modifications of such feminist practice guidelines for use internationally and cross-nationally. As a starting point, Enns and her colleagues began a working group at the 2008 International Counseling Psychology Conference in Chicago, and their discussion provides some potential implications and modifications of the APA guidelines for use in international contexts. The major aim of the task force was to generate a critical analysis of Western feminist psychotherapeutic practice and to consider some of the features of such practice globally (Enns, 2008). APA Guideline 5 and CPA Principle 2 which state how understanding how one's own socialization shapes one's therapeutic perspectives and practices formed a basis for the dialogue.

Certainly, developing practice guidelines that would be applicable internationally is a daunting endeavor. There are enormous challenges to developing a holistic and inclusive focus to women's diverse realities across the world and their complex multiple interacting social identities and oppressions. Nonetheless, an important beginning has been made in articulating some of the ways in which Western models of psychotherapy, including feminist models of treatment for women, are ethnocentric or otherwise narrow in their geo-political-social focus.

Three important themes can be seen to have emerged from the work of this beginning task force. The first concerns our concepts of empowerment and the language of empowerment. Such concepts are often framed in individualist terms from a Western point of view. By way of contrast, for example, many Japanese women, both feminist and non-feminists, define meaningful constructs of interdependence and fulfillment that are consistent with the values of a more collective society. It is suggested that terms such as "resourcefulness" are likely to be less ethnocentric and more useful and meaningful in the treatment of mental health problems for women in other cross-national contexts (Enns, 2008).

Second, the goals and strategies of psychotherapy for women need to be framed in culturally sensitive terms. For example, although we as Western therapists and feminists tend to see and promote gender role differentiation as negative and as a barrier to achieving equity and a positive sense of self, many Muslim and Asian women have worked toward preserving and honoring difference, especially in the realm of family and personal relations (Enns, 2008; Pharaon, 2001).

Another guiding theme identified in modifying the Western guidelines for psychological practice for women and girls was the consideration that Western society is extremely goal directed. This is also reflected in the way in which we practice psychotherapy with the goal of being assertive or achieving a certain job or status. For women from other cultures, the goal orientation of such a therapeutic approach may not resonate; for example, a Japanese woman whose personality values a role-oriented approach to life and who experiences a sense of satisfaction from fulfilling and honoring that lifetime role, such as nurturing family and children to the subordination of self (Enns, 2003). Thus, the alleviation of depression associated with that role may be not to attempt to separate the women from the role or to divorce or to separate, but to help her feel and integrate the honor her culture assigns to that role.

Several of the Western guidelines are broad enough to apply to many various contexts and to diverse mental health problems of women across the world, but they would need culture-specific language, applications, interventions, and examples. In terms of language and translation of the guidelines, the particular meanings of words and connotations of concepts embedded in individualistic perspectives may vary from country to country and culture to culture, necessitating consideration of cultural relevance (Enns, 2008). Every therapeutic encounter is embedded in a multi-lingual context, and both therapist and client must be aware of the many leveled effects. There are many opportunities for misunderstandings, as well as for mutual shared learning (Espin, 2001).

Nonetheless, the overall relevance and importance of concepts like empowerment, awareness of difference, sensitivity to and avoidance of discrimination, best practices, self-examination, and education can be seen as applicable to all women clients in various geographical settings. By way of example, applying the guidelines to women from other countries reveals both direct relevance and the need for cultural modification (Enns & Kasai, 2007). A few examples will suffice.

APA Guidelines 1, 2, and 3 speak directly to the direct effects of socialization, oppression, and bias on women and girls, outlining decades of research on these issues. Japanese women, like women in many other cultures around the world, live in worlds of highly differentiated gender roles; however, this is seen in a more positive light where difference is preserved and honored and the counseling reflects that different perspective (Kawano, 1990). As Ueno (1997) writes, "Our primary goal is not to be like men, but to value what it means to be a woman." Some Asian women believe that gender role differentiation does not automatically produce greater subordination and dependency for women on men, but in contrast independence; for example, when women do not expect men to meet their emotional needs and turn to other women for nurturing relationships. "Amae" is a widespread indigenous psychological concept in Japan. It represents a healthy other-centeredness that emphasizes attunement to the needs of others and correspondingly positive reliance on others for emotional acceptance and self-esteem. However, Japanese women are often expected to shoulder the responsibility for giving *amae*, with limited opportunities to receive *amae* (Enns & Kasai, 2001; Matsuyuki, 1998).

APA Guideline 6 states that psychologists are encouraged to use interventions and practices that have been found to be most effective in the psychological treatment of girls and women. The effectiveness of particular interventions may directly vary as a function of the socio-political-economic context of the particular woman client. Ciftci (2008) and Winter (2001) have worked extensively with immigrant Arab-Muslim women. Women who are dislocated from their native support systems are at special risk for depression, but our Western mental health systems and structures that emphasize individual therapy and psychopharmacological interventions do not necessarily meet their special needs. Speedy symptom alleviation, family therapy, cultural education, and social advocacy have been found to be effective avenues for intervention and change, as well as working with local community resources and support systems. Cognitive enhancement group therapy programs have also been found to be particularly efficacious in helping Saudi Arabian women to improve self-confidence, communication skills, and self-awareness (Pharaon, 2001).

APA Guideline 9 and CPA Principle 2 state the importance of considering the psychological problems of women and girls in their socio-political and socioeconomic context. The effects of socioeconomic status have an enormous impact on the clinical issues which Mexican women face (Hinkelman, 2001). Mexican women often suffer stresses that are due to inadequate food and shelter, domestic violence, unemployment, and oppressive political policies and structures. Religion plays a large part in their family life, and some life events are attributed to luck, supernatural forces, or acts of God, a fatalism that has been linked to a high prevalence of depression and other clinical issues such as anxiety and psychosomatic symptoms. Furthermore, Mexican women, especially in rural areas, tend to have limited information and access to medical and mental health care resources and institutions and centers specializing in assisting victims of violence and abuse (Pick, Contreras, & Barker-Aguilar, 2006). All these considerations of the social context of the depressed Mexican woman need to be considered in evaluation of the intrapsychic and external sources of her distress and the appropriate interventions.

Finally, APA Guideline 11 and CPA Principle 4 speak to the need for psychologists everywhere to help better their societies by engaging and advocating for positive social change that alleviates institutional and systemic injustice and discrimination. The question that is relevant here is whether or not there can be healing without justice. The abuse of women worldwide and their resulting trauma makes explicit the link between treatment and advocacy and calls forth a model of global practice for women and girls that incorporates advocacy. If justice is indeed therapeutic, then psychologists are urged to go beyond their relatively comfortable roles and office work to publicly work for their women clients in nontherapeutic settings and venues. From this perspective, we help to forge a world in which women can live, work, and be healed from the pernicious effects of discrimination, abuse, and violence and the multiple mental health consequences of those conditions.

BEYOND CURRENT MODELS OF RESEARCH AND PRACTICE

As Aida Hurtado (2009) has articulated, feminist theorists have challenged traditional forms of knowledge production, staked out claims in knowledge production, and emphasized the roots of multicultural feminist theory in the "every day experiences of human beings who love, live, laugh, cry, and think." Part of that challenge has been the development of new methodologies, qualitative and quantitative, to produce new knowledge about women's lives and circumstances. In particular, the development of participatory and action research techniques hold promise for the development of an action-reflection dialectic or *praxis* to create an activist scholarship in international psychology (Earth, 1998; Khanna, 1996; Lykes, 1994, 2001; Lykes, Coquillon, & Rabenstein, in press).

Stigma, cultural beliefs, and cultural norms with regard to expressing psychological distress and help-seeking, diagnostic practices, treatment accessibility, and preference for alternative forms of treatment vary cross-nationally. In countries such as Uganda, where mental illness may be seen as a punishment for bad deeds or as possession by an evil spirit, the associated stigma may lead to social isolation, exclusion, and disadvantage (Ssebunnya, Kigozi, Lund, Kizza, & Okello, 2009). Barriers to help-seeking may also be found in countries where the cultural taboo of consulting in a psychiatric setting may carry the risk of marriage ineligibility or divorce. These barriers may be particularly important to women in societies where the roles of wife and mother are central to women's status. For example, a study of outpatients in the United Arab Emirates (Ouali et al., 2004) found that women were less likely to seek mental health care than men, and that when they did seek care, 70 percent were accompanied by someone else; 60 percent of the women said they could not have sought care if they had not been accompanied, and this dependence on being accompanied led to irregular attendance in follow-up appointments. They were also more likely to report feeling stigmatized than men (37.7 percent vs. 24.4 percent). In Arab Islamic societies, the fact that women represent a family's honor may make them reluctant to disclose personal issues to outsiders for fear of damaging the family's status in addition to their own. Such conditions underscore the importance of understanding the relationship of social and cultural factors to diagnosis, treatment, and delivery of mental health services to women and of developing culturally appropriate approaches to service provision.

While U.S. studies have much to contribute to international mental health efforts, the reverse is true as well. The lack of a psychiatric establishment tied to biomedical models and an infrastructure that influences mental health practices from the "top down" may provide opportunities for "bottom" up approaches reflective of the voices of consumers and tailored to their contexts. A model for such an approach is found in *Where There Is No Psychiatrist: A mental health care manual* (Patel, 2003), which states "the promotion of gender equality, by empowering women to make decisions that influence their lives and educating men about the need for equal rights, is the most important way of promoting women's mental health" (p. 220). The manual provides practical, context-based advice for community workers and primary care doctors, nurses, social workers, and doctors, particularly in developing countries. For example, it provides guidance on how to ask about stress in a domestic context, ensure regular follow-up, ask permission to speak to family members, and deal with advocacy issues such as establishing psychoeducational or support groups for women in the community.

In cultures where Western diagnostic constructs are unknown and there are no words for mental disorders, the manual's "bottom up" approach, which focuses on symptoms and avoids usage of stigmatizing labels, is particularly appropriate. The idea that it is important to recognize that people seek help from diverse sources and there is little to gain by challenging beliefs in evil spirits and witchcraft is likely to meet with substantial resistance from a Western biomedical perspective. However, the point is made that counseling approaches based on Western psychological theories may indeed be applicable across cultures—but to be effective, a counselor must find what will be acceptable. A similar "bottoms up" effort, informed by feminist principles and guidelines for therapy with women, would provide an interesting approach for "giving multicultural feminist psychology away" to community workers and service providers who seek alternatives to traditional approaches in the United States.

CONCLUSION

International perspectives on mental health offer a holistic vision of health that is congruent with the biopsychosocial perspective advocated by feminist psychologists. This perspective views understanding the relation of women's social roles and circumstances to mental health in its social/political and cultural context as necessary for the development of effective treatment and prevention. That gender has a profound impact on the development of and response to mental distress and disorder is indisputable. The goal now is to understand the factors and mechanisms that produce that impact, including the power inequalities, stigma, and devaluation associated with women's social roles and circumstances. New theories and methods, informed by multicultural and international feminist perspectives, as reflected in the guidelines for psychological practice with women and girls, hold promise as tools for achieving that goal. However, doing so will require viewing gender as a multidimensional cultural construct with elements that may interact with elements of the cultural context at multiple levels—biological, psychological, social, environmental, cultural, and contextual—and developing policies and programs aimed at eliminating the power inequities, stigma, discrimination, and gender-based violence that continue to undermine the mental health and well being of women over their life cycle.

REFERENCES

Alcoff, L., & Potter, E. (Eds.). (1993). *Feminist epistemologies.* New York: Routledge.

Alegría, A., Mulvaney-Day, N., Torres, M., Polo, A., Cao, Z., & Canino, G. (2007). Prevalence of psychiatric disorders across Latino subgroups in the United States. *American Journal of Public Health, 97,* 68–85

American Psychological Association. (2007). Guidelines for psychological practice with girls and women. *American Psychologist, 62,* 949–979.

Ballou, M. (1996). Multicultural theory and women. In D. W. Sue, A. Ivey, & P. Pederson (Eds.), A theory of multicultural counseling and therapy. Pacific Grove, CA: Brooks/Cole.

Ballou, M., Hill, M., & West, C. (Eds.). (2008). Feminist therapy theory and practice: A contemporary perspective. New York: Springer.

Ballou, M., & West, C. (2000). Feminist therapy: Turning in turning out. In M. Biaggio & M. Hersen (Eds.), Issues in the psychology of women. New York: Plenum Press.

Bertram, M. (2003). Women and mental health: A brief global analysis. International Journal of Language, Society & Culture, 12, 1–8.

Brown, L. (1994). Subversive dialogues. New York: Basic Books.

Brown, L. S., Riepe, L. E., & Coffey, R. L. (2005). Beyond color and culture: Feminist contributions to paradigms of human difference. Women & Therapy, 28, 63–92.

Busfield, J. (1996). Men, women and madness: Understanding gender and mental Disorder. London: Macmillan Press.

Cabral, M., & Astbury, J. (2000). Women's mental health: An evidence-based review. Geneva, Switzerland: Department of Mental Health and Substance Dependence, World Health Organization.

Canadian Psychological Association. (2007). Guidelines for ethical psychological practice with women. Ottawa, ON: Canadian Psychological Association.

Chen, F. F., & West, S. G. (2007). Measuring individualism and collectivism: The importance of considering differential components, reference groups, and measurement invariance. Journal of Research in Personality, 43, 259–294.

Chen, Y., Subramanian, S., Acevedo-Garcio, D., & Kawachi, I. (2005). Women's status and depressive symptoms: A multilevel analysis. Social Science and Medicine, 60, 49–60.

Ciftci, A. (2008). Clinical implications of working with Muslim American women. Presentation, August 2008, Annual Meeting of the American Psychological Association. Boston: American Psychological Association..

Comas-Diaz, L., & Greene, B. (Eds.). (1994). Women of color: Integrating ethnic and gender identities in psychotherapy. New York: Guilford.

Earth, B. (1998). Participatory research: Gender and health in rural Tanzania. Convergence, 31, 59–67.

Ellsberg, M., Jansen, H., Heise, L., Watts, C., & Garcia-Moreno, C. (2008). Intimate partner violence and women's physical and mental health in the WHO multi-country study on women's health and domestic violence: an observational study. Lancet, 371, 1165–1172.

Enns, C. Z. (2003). Hakoniwa: Japanese sandplay therapy. The Counseling Psychologist, 31, 103–112.

Enns, C. Z. (2008). Feminist psychotherapy in a global context. Presentation, August 2008, Annual Meeting of the American Psychological Association. Boston: American Psychological Association.

Enns, C. A., & Byars-Winston, A. M. (in press). Multicultural feminist therapy. In H. Landrine & N. F. Russo (Eds.), Handbook of diversity in feminist psychology. New York: Springer.

Enns, C. Z., & Kasai, M. (2001). Feminist psychological practice in Japan. San Francisco: American Psychological Association.

Enriquez, V. G. (1992). *From colonial to liberation psychology: The Philippine Experience*. Quezon: University of Philippines Press.

Espin, O. (2001). *The language of the soul: Psychotherapy with women across cultures*. San Francisco: American Psychological Association.

Flowers, B. J., & Richardson, F. C. (1996). Why is multiculturalism good? *American Psychologist, 53*, 609–621.

Fox, D., & Prilleltensky, I. (1997). *Critical psychology*. London: Sage.

Ge, X., Conger, R., & Elder, G. (1996). Coming of age too early: Pubertal influences on girls' vulnerability to psychological distress. *Child Development, 67*, 3386–4000.

Hamilton, P., & Russo, N. F. (2006). Women and depression: Research, theory and social policy. In C. L. M. Keyes & S. H. Goodman (Eds.), *Women and depression: A handbook for social, behavioral, and biomedical sciences* (pp. 479–522). New York: Cambridge University Press.

Hays, P. (2001). *Addressing cultural complexities in practice: A framework for clinicians and counselors*. Washington, DC: American Psychological Association.

Hinkelman, J. (2001). *Converging forces: Mexican culture and clinical issues of Mexican women*. Presentation, August 2008, Annual Meeting of the American Psychological Association. San Francisco: American Psychological Association.

Kastrup, M. (2007). Global mental health. *Danish Medical Bulletin, 54*, 42–43.

Kawano, K. I. (1990). Feminist therapy with Japanese women. *Journal of Social Work Practice, 4*, 44–55.

Kendler, K. S., Gardner, C. O., Neale, M. C., & Prescott, C. A. (2001). Genetic factors for major depression in men and women: Similar or different heritabilities and same or partly distinct genes? *Psychological Medicine, 31*, 605–616.

Kessler, R. (2006). Epidemiology of depression in women. In C. L. M. Keyes & S. H. Goodman (Eds.), *Women and depression: A handbook for social, behavioral, and biomedical sciences* (pp. 22–40). New York: Cambridge University Press.

Kessler, R. C., Chiu, C., Demler, W., & Walters, E. (2005). Prevalence, severity, and comorbidity of 12-month DSM-IV disorders in the National Comorbidity Survey Replication. *Archives of General Psychiatry, 62*, 617–627.

Khanna, R. (1996). Participatory action research (PAR) in women's health: SARTHI, India. In K. de Koning & M. Martin (Eds.), *Participatory research in health: Issues and experiences* (pp. 62–71). Johannesburg: Zed Books Ltd.

Kitzinger, C. (1991). Politicizing psychology. *Feminism & Psychology, 1*, 49–54.

Koblinsky, M., Timyan, J., & Gay, J. (Eds.). (1992). *The health of women: A global perspective*. Boulder, CO: Westview Press.

Landrine, H. (1995). *Bringing cultural diversity to feminist psychology*. Washington, DC: American Psychological Association.

Landrine, H., & Corral, H. (in press). In H. Landrine & N. F. Russo (Eds.), *Handbook of diversity in feminist psychology*. New York: Springer.

Lazarus, S., & Lykes, M. B. (2005). *Indigenous and Euro-American psychologies: Resources and barriers for generating knowledge and praxis*. Washington, DC: American Psychological Association.

Lopez, S. R., & Guarnaccia, P. J. (2005). Cultural dimensions of psychopathology: The social world's impact on mental illness. In J. E. Maddow &

B. A. Winstead (Eds.), *Psychopathology: Foundations for a contemporary under-standing* (pp. 21–42), London: Rutledge.

Lykes, M. B. (1994). Terror, silencing, and children: International multidiscipli-nary collaboration with Guatemalan Maya communities. *Social Science and Medicine, 38,* 543–552.

Lykes, M. B. (2001). Creative arts and photography in participatory action research in Guatemala. In P. Reason & H. Bradbury (Eds.), *Handbook of action research* (pp. 363–371). Thousand Oaks, CA: Sage.

Lykes, M., Coquillon, E., & Rabenstein, K. L. (in press). Theoretical and meth-odological challenges in participatory community-based research. In H. Landrine & N. F. Russo (Eds.), *Handbook of diversity in feminist psychol-ogy.* New York: Springer.

Martin-Baro, I. (1994). *Writing for a liberation psychology.* Cambridge, MA: Harvard University Press.

Matsuyuki, M. (1998). Japanese feminist counseling as a political act. *Women and Therapy, 21,* 28–310.

Mazure, C. M., Keita, G., & Blehar, M. C. (2002). *Summit on women and depres-sion: Proceedings and recommendations.* Washington, DC: American Psycho-logical Association.

McKay, K. M., Hill, M. S., Freedman, S. R., & Enright, R. D. (2007). Towards a feminist empowerment model of forgiveness psychotherapy. *Psychotherapy: Theory, Research, Practice, Training, 44,* 14–29.

Naidoo, A. V. (2005). *Constructing community, reconstructing psychology: Challeng-ing the hegemony of Eurocentric psychology in South Africa.* Washington, DC: American Psychological Association.

Nolen-Hoeksema, S. (2001). Gender differences in depression. *Directions in Psychological Science, 10,* 173–176.

Paltiel, F. L. (1993). Women's mental health: A global perspective. In M. Koblinsky, J. Timyan, & J. Gay (Eds.), *The health of women: A global per-spective.* Boulder, CO: Westfield Press.

Patel, V. (2003). *Where there is no psychiatrist: A mental health care manual.* London: Gaskell.

Patel, V., Araya, R., de Lima, Ludermir, A., & Todd, C. (1999). Women, pov-erty, and common mental disorders in four restructuring societies. *Social Science & Medicine, 49,* 1461–1471.

Pharaon, N. (2001). *Personal transformation: A group therapy program for Saudi women.* San Francisco: American Psychological Association.

Piccinelli, M., & Homen, F. G. (1997). *Gender differences in the epidemiology of affective disorders and schizophrenia. A report of Nations for Mental Health: An Initiative for Mental Health in Underserved Populations.* Geneva, Switzerland: World Health Organization.

Pick, S., Contreras, C., & Barker-Aguilar, A. (2006). Violence against women in Mexico: conceptualization and program application. *Annals of the New York Academy of Science, 1087,* 261–278.

Radway, J. (1998). Gender in the field of ideological production: Feminist cul-tural studies, the problem of the political subject, and the aims of knowl-edge production. In S. V. Rosser, J. Radway, & N. Fobre (Eds.), *New perspectives in gender studies: Research in the fields of economics, culture and life sciences* (pp. 37–59). Linkoping, Netherlands: Linkoping University Depart-ment of Gender Studies.

Rice, J. K. (2001). Global divorce and the feminization of poverty. *International Psychology Bulletin, 4,* 21–24.

Rice, J. K. (2005). Social and economic support for divorce internationally. In A. D. Thomas, N. Dayan, A. B. Bernardo, & R. Roth (Eds.), *Helping others grow* (pp. 107–112). Aachen, Austria: Shaker Verlag.

Rice, J. K. (2007). Global warfare, violence and the welfare of women. In S. McCarthy, S. Newstead, K. Karandashev, C. Prandini, C. Hutz, & W. Gomes. *Teaching psychology around the world* (pp. 338–345). Newcastle, United Kingdom: Cambridge Scholars Publishing.

Rice, J. K. & Ballou, M. (2003). *Cultural and gender awareness in international psychology.* Washington, DC: American Psychological Association, Division 52, International Psychology, International Committee for Women.

Riger, S. (1992). Epistemological debates, feminist voices: Science, social values, and the study of women. *American Psychologist, 47,* 730–740.

Riger, S. (2000). *Transforming psychology.* Oxford, United Kingdom: Oxford University Press.

Rosenblum, K., & Travis, T. M. (1996). *A theory of multicultural counseling and therapy.* Pacific Grove, CA: Brooks/Cole.

Russo, N. F. (in press). Diversity and mental health. In H. Landrine & N. F. Russo (Eds.), *Handbook of diversity in feminist psychology.* New York: Springer.

Russo, N. F., & Tartaro, J. (2008). Women and mental health. In F. L. Denmark & M. A. Paludi (Eds.), *Psychology of women: A handbook of issues and theories* (2nd ed., pp. 440–481). Westport, CT: Greenwood Press.

Russo, N. F., & Vaz, K. (2001). Addressing diversity in the decade of behavior: Focus on women of color. *Psychology of Women Quarterly, 25,* 280–294.

Safir, M. P., & Hill, K. (2008). International aspects of the development of the psychology of women and gender. In F. L. Denmark & M. A. Paludi (Eds.), *Psychology of women: A handbook of issues and theories* (pp. 70–90). Westport, CT: Greenwood Press.

Silverman, W. K., & Carter, R. (2006). Anxiety disturbance in girls and women. In J. Worell & C. Goodheart (Eds.), *Handbook of girls' and women's psychological health: Gender and well-being across the lifespan* (pp. 60–87). New York: Oxford University Press.

Ssebunnya, J., Kigozi, F., Lund, C., Kizza, D., & Okello, E. (2009). Stakeholder perceptions of mental health stigma and poverty in Uganda. *BMC International Health and Human Rights, 9*(5). Retrieved June 15, 2009, from http://www.biomedcentral.com/1472-698X/9/5

Stewart, D. E. (2006). The international consensus statement on women's mental health and the WPA consensus statement on interpersonal violence against women. *World Psychiatry, 5,* 61–64.

Stewart, D. E., Rondon, M., Damiani, G., & Honikman, J. (2001). International psychosocial and systemic issues in women's mental health. *Archives of Women's Mental Health, 4,* 3–7.

Swim, J. K., Becker, J., & Lee, E. (in press). Sexism reloaded: Worldwide evidence for its endorsement, expression, and emergence in multiple contexts. In H. Landrine & N. F. Russo (Eds.), *Handbook of diversity in feminist psychology.* New York: Springer.

Ueno, C. (1997). Interview/Are the Japanese feminine? Some problems of Japanese Feminism in its cultural context. In S. Buckley (Ed.), *Broken silence: Voices of Japanese feminism* (pp. 272–301), Berkeley, CA: University of California Press.

Unger, R. (1995). Cultural diversity and the future of feminist psychology. In H. Landrine (Ed.), *Bringing cultural diversity to feminist psychology* (pp. 413, 432). Washington, DC: American Psychological Association.

United Nations. (2000). *The millennium declaration.* New York: United Nations.

U.S. Department of Health and Human Services (USDHHS). (2002). *Women of color health data book.* Rockville, MD: USDHHS, National Institute of Health, Office of the Director, Office of Research on Women's Health.

Ustun, T. B. (2000). Cross-national epidemiology of depression and gender. *Journal of Gender-specific Medicine, 3,* 54–58.

Winter, A. (2001). *Women in the Arab/Muslim world: Therapeutic strategies.* San Francisco: American Psychological Association.

World Health Organization (WHO). (2001). *Violence against women information pack.* (pp. 1–25). Geneva: Department of Injuries and Violence Prevention, WHO. Retrieved romhttp://www.who.int/violence_injury_prevention.

World Health Organization (WHO). (2002). *Gender disparities in mental health.* Geneva: Author.

World Health Organization (WHO). (2004). *Prevention of mental disorders: Effective interventions and policy options.* Geneva, Switzerland: World Health Organization, Department of Mental Health and Substance Abuse.

World Health Organization (WHO). (2006). *Gender and women's mental health.* Geneva, Switzerland: Author.

World Health Organization (WHO). (2008). *The global burden of disease: 2004 update.* Geneva, Switzerland: World Health Organization.

World Health Organization (WHO). (2009). *Mental health aspects of women's reproductive health: A global review of the literature.* Geneva, Switzerland, Author.

Worley, H. (2006). *Depression: A leading contributor to global burden of disease.* Washington, DC: Population Reference Bureau. Retrieved from http://www.coa.gov.ph/gat/ articles/depression_062006.htm

Wyche, K., & Rice, J. K. (1997). Feminist therapy: From dialogue to tenets. In J. Worell & N. G. Johnson (Eds.), *Shaping the future of feminist psychology: Education, research, and practice* (pp. 57–71). Washington, DC: American Psychological Association.

Zahn-Waxler, C., Race, E., & Duggal, S. (2004). Mood disorders, syndromes and symptoms: The development of depression in girls. In D. J. Bell, S. L. Forster, & E. J. Mash (Eds.), *Behavioral and emotional problems in girls* (pp. 25–76). New York: Kluwer Academic/Plenum Publishing.

Chapter 2

Ethnocultural Psychotherapy: Women of Color's Resilience and Liberation

Lillian Comas-Diaz

Women's lives are embedded in multiple contexts. Their intersecting identities inhabit complex realities. Consider Ana, a 30-year-old Colombian American woman, who consulted a therapist upon her physician's recommendation. Ana's presenting complaint: "I'm targeted at work because I'm a black Latina immigration lawyer," highlights the intersection of her multiple identities—a combination of ethnicity, race, gender, and profession. Enmeshed in a collective matrix, female identity and well-being tend to be relational, that is, connected to others and to contexts. To heal, nurture, and sustain women's well-being, clinicians need to address female interconnecting identities.

Psychotherapy with women—in particular, women of color—offers opportunities and challenges. Indeed, the rewards of working with culturally diverse women enrich therapists' lives. Multicultural therapeutic encounters can be replete of gratification, excitement, and deeper connection. Let's examine Ana's first session. Her body language (sweating palms, fearful facial expression) suggested that she was anxious and scared. Dr. Brown, a Jewish American therapist, addressed Ana's feelings and recommended breathing exercises. Ana agreed and while engaged in the exercise, she suddenly remembered her grandmother's breathing exercises. She shared the breathing technique with Dr. Brown, who was pleasantly surprised to learn the source of Ana's grandmother's exercise—shamanism. Interested in indigenous healing, Dr. Brown added a new strategy to her clinical repertoire.

Conversely, working with culturally diverse clients can be challenging. Partly due to cultural misunderstanding, the multicultural encounter can exert a strain in therapists. Consider Judy, a Chinese American woman who presented to therapy after a romantic breakup. She saw Dr. Smith, a European American woman who explored the circumstances around the breakup. When the therapist commented on the unfulfilled quality of the relationship, Judy described the friendship between her parents and her ex-fiancée's family. Dr. Smith's reply— "You need to take care of yourself,"—reflected an individualistic worldview where separation and individuation from family are signs of adulthood. Judy's answer, "Taking care of myself means taking care of my parents," denoted a collectivistic worldview where interdependence among family members prevails. A cultural impasse resulted out of these conflictive worldviews. This situation generated difficulties with empathy. Dr. Smith persisted in encouraging Judy to individuate from her parents. After a few sessions, Judy informed Dr. Smith that she did not need therapy anymore.

What seems to be the major difference between Dr. Brown and Dr. Smith? Research has shown that culturally diverse clients identified their therapists' cultural competence as the major source of satisfaction with their treatment (Knipscheer & Kleber, 2004). Most experts agree that cultural competence involves a set of knowledge, attitudes, and skills that enables clinicians to be effective in multicultural practice (Betancourt, Green, Carrillo, & Ananch-Firempong, 2003). Moreover, the development of cultural competence requires empathy and a life-long commitment. Working within a culturally relevant therapeutic framework helps to develop cultural competence. In this chapter, I present ethnocultural psychotherapy as a gender-affirmative, culturally relevant healing approach for women of color.

ETHNOCULTURAL PSYCHOTHERAPY: CONCEPTS AND GOALS

Ethnocultural psychotherapy incorporates ethnic, cultural, and gender parameters into mental health assessment and treatment (Comas-Díaz & Jacobsen, 2004). It is a contextual healing approach that recognizes, reclaims, and recovers gender and cultural strengths. As such, ethnocultural psychotherapists examine the role of gendered ethnicity in the lives of women of color.

Gendered ethnicity refers to the interactive effects of gender, culture, ethnicity, and race. Unfortunately, dominant mental health practitioners seldom understand the profound influence of gendered ethnicity in women of color. When in treatment, women of color often find these services irrelevant and unresponsive to their life experiences. What is more, some fear psychotherapy to be an acculturation tool (Ramirez, 1991), as well as a form of cultural imperialism. To illustrate, women of color fear that psychotherapy's androcentric and ethnocentric perspective will label them as deviant and pathological. Judy's cultural impasse with Dr. Smith exemplifies this concern. Women of color experience cultural imperialism through a systematic indoctrination that the dominant cultural values are superior to their own (Said, 1994). Consequently, healing requires empowering women of color to be themselves. When in therapy, women of color frequently talk about cultural identity, emotional expression, community expectations of gender roles, mother–daughter dyad, spirituality, sexuality, relationship with other women of color, and class differences (Slater, Daniel, & Banks, 2003).

A significant number of women of color need mental health treatment. Many struggle with loss, grief, and trauma, in addition to experiencing a nefarious form of racism and sexism. Indeed, women in general, and women of color in particular, are exposed to multiple oppressions. Beyond gendered ethnicity, women of color's social class, sexual orientation, skin color, immigration status, health status, age, language, and other variables predispose them to oppression. Exposure to continuing oppression results in a psychological adaptation to domination. For instance, oppressed individuals internalize powerlessness and develop a fractured identity (Freire, 1973). To promote empowerment and reformulate identity, ethnocultural psychotherapists help women to take control of their lives, overcome their oppressed mentality, and achieve a critical knowledge of themselves. These objectives are necessary in the delivery of effective and ethical psychotherapeutic services to women of color.

EMPOWERMENT

Ethnocultural psychotherapists aim to increase women of color's sense of agency. In other words, ethnocultural psychotherapy empowers women to increase their access to resources, examine options, enhance their ability to make choices, improve self- and collective esteem, learn culturally relevant assertiveness, rescue ethnogender strengths, overcome internalized oppression, and engage in transformative actions. Ethnocultural psychotherapy promotes critical consciousness. Coined by Paulo Freire (1970), critical consciousness refers to the process of engaging in a dialectical dialogue with one's world, becoming aware of one's circumstances, and initiating transformative actions. The critical consciousness dialogue involves asking questions such as "What? Why? How? For whom? Against whom? By whom? In favor of whom? In favor of what? To what end?" (Freire & Macedo, 2000). Exploring these critical questions raises consciousness and helps to examine existential issues. In particular, a critical dialogue facilitates women's examination of "what matters" regarding power differentials.

Ethnocultural psychotherapy addresses power differentials within a liberation perspective. Unfortunately, many mainstream psychotherapists ignore the effect of power in women's realities. Consider the following vignette. Karen, a mixed race (black and white) single mother, was in therapy with a white male clinician. Dr. Cooper treated Karen with mainstream psychotherapy. After six months in treatment, Karen did not get relief from her anxiety. When she shared her experiences with her friend Carol, Karen realized that she did not feel comfortable discussing race with her therapist. "I get this unspoken message that Dr. Cooper does not want to hear about racist sexism." To resolve her dilemma, Karen terminated therapy and entered treatment with Carol's therapist—an African American woman.

IDENTITY REFORMULATION

Besides empowerment, ethnocultural psychotherapy promotes identity reformulation. In other words, therapists encourage women to reclaim their voices. This process affirms women's ethnogender values. Such affirmation is necessary because women of color tend to reconnect with their ethnic traditions during crises. Lamentably, many women of color "forget" their ethnocultural roots to accommodate to the dominant society. Through cultural amnesia, they neglect adaptive functions of their gendered ethnicity.

Along these lines, ethnocultural psychotherapists examine women's psychocultural needs. For example, lesbians of color struggle with a combined sexism, racism, and heterosexism that require attention during therapy. Likewise, working-class women of color are exposed to a mixture of sexism, racism, and classism. They may find themselves in a dilemma as their personal striving threatens their ethnoclass ties (Kuppersmith, 1987). Regardless of social class membership, class realities are pervasive in communities of color and thus affect many women of color. Therapists who recognize ethnoclass loyalty dilemmas promote female empowerment.

Healing the historical, personal, and collective wounds of women of color necessitates a gender-affirmative, culturally relevant contextual approach.

ETHNOCULTURAL PSYCHOTHERAPY APPLICATIONS

Ethnocultural psychotherapy is gender affirmative because it acknowledges the concept of self as an internal gendered-ethnocultural representation. To elaborate, female identity is embedded and constructed within diverse contexts. For instance, Catherine Batson (1990) empirically found that females frequently compose their lives by adapting to life milestones, such as coupling, motherhood, and other gender-specific events. As a result, conducting psychotherapy with women of color entails examining their adaptation to their total environment. An ethnocultural assessment facilitates such examination.

ETHNOCULTURAL ASSESSMENT

Ethnocultural assessment helps to place female realities in contexts. This assessment explores intellectual and emotional understanding of several historical stages of cultural identity development (Jacobsen, 1988). It acknowledges the influences of external and internal factors during different stages in women's lives. As both a diagnostic and treatment tool, the ethnocultural assessment helps to unfold material relevant to women's functioning. Additionally, it aids in the development of a therapeutic alliance. Certainly, when conducting ethnocultural assessments, therapists aim to convey genuine interest in their client. This approach fosters a "safe" atmosphere for treatment. The ethnocultural assessment examines the women's heritage, saga, niche, adjustment, and relationships.

Heritage relates to women's ancestry, history, genetics, biology, and sociopolitical inheritance. In this stage, therapists examine maternal and paternal cultures of origin to delineate ethnic heritage. The examination of biological factors includes illnesses, physiological, gender, and ethnic differences in drug metabolism. Of particular interest is the exploration of cultural trauma in the form of soul wounds. A legacy of pain and suffering among many minority group members, soul wounds result from socio–historical oppression, ungrieved losses, internalized oppression, and learned helplessness (Duran & Ivey, 2006). Examples of soul wounds are a history of slavery, colonization, Holocaust, genocide, and wars. In addition, therapists explore the legacy of survivors' syndromes.

Examining women's cultural legacy provides a foundation for the unearthing of the family saga. Ethnocultural assessment second stage, saga, entails the family, clan, tribe, and group story. As an illustration, the family saga reveals the circumstances that led a woman and or her multigenerational family to journey through cultural transitions. Transition could be any kind of translocation—a geographical move, migration, immigration, sojourn, or major transitions in life such as change of job, marital status, in addition to milestones like pregnancy, abortion, miscarriage, and others. It is important to discern the voluntary versus the involuntary reasons for the transition or translocation. The translocation post analysis provides a context for client's' ethnocultural transition. Relevant questions characteristic of this stage include: "How long ago was the translocation? Was it recent or generations ago? What are the thoughts and feelings regarding the events leading to the translocation?"

The next assessment stage, niche, refers to the outcome of the post transition analysis. Niche is based on the client's intellectual and emotional perception of her family's ethnocultural identity in the host society since the translocation. Succinctly put, niche is the place carved by the family after the transition. During this stage, therapists assess what happened to the family after the translocation. Moreover, therapists examine women's cognitive and emotional perception of their family ethnocultural saga. They review women's interactions with members of their own ethnocultural group. In particular, therapists explore the family status before and after the translocation. Women's internalization of their family saga provides a blueprint of their entry into the world. Exploring this stage facilitates the development of a contextual framework within which to place women's subjective experiences. Therapists ask the following questions when examining women's niche: "Have family members stayed together? Is there a sense of family unity? What is the relationship of family with the original ethnocultural group? How have they fared financially, emotionally?"

The self-adjustment stage relates to women's own perceived adaptation to the host culture (or situation) as individuals distinct from their family. Self-adjustment explores the contrasts between the woman's ethnocultural identity and that of her family, work, and social environment. This stage involves an analysis of women's coping skills. Here, therapists help women to analyze the functionality of their behaviors within diverse contexts. Women's strengths are examined, paying attention to cultural resilience. For example, among many women of color, personal survival is connected to their collective survival.

Fostering cultural resilience, ethnocultural psychotherapy helps women to reconnect with their ethnic beliefs. Cultural resilience is a host of strengths, values and practices that promote coping mechanisms and adaptive reactions to traumatic oppression (Elsass, 1992). Cultural resilience promotes resourceful responses to oppression and adversity. Therefore, it fosters creativity, reconstruction, and evolution.

The last ethnocultural assessment stage examines women's relations. Therapists examine women's self and other relationship. Besides examining women's significant connections, clinicians focus on the therapeutic relationship, including transference and countertransference. They explore their own ethnocultural background to determine specific areas of real or potential overlap with their client's. In other words, therapists complete their own ethnocultural assessment to determine areas of similarity and difference with their clients'. Above and beyond obtaining a wealth of information crucial for therapeutic interventions, performance of an ethnocultural assessment frequently opens new channels for the recognition of self in the culturally different other.

A crucial component of the ethnocultural assessment is the inclusion of gender specific issues in all stages of the evaluation. For example, during the heritage stage, historical female roles, female biological markers, female victimization, and other history of gender issues are examined. The saga stage helps to reveal the "herstory" of significant female family members. Similarly, during the niche stage clinicians examine female gender collective scripts such as family roles of women and men, wantedness of children (including the client), and gender specific family trauma. Furthermore, therapists explore the symbolic meaning of the client's name, age cohort effect on women, acculturation, personal development, and other adjustment issues as part of women's self-adjustment. Finally, therapists explore the gender aspects of intimate relations, (with men and women), physical and sexual abuse, domestic violence, incest, battered spouse syndrome, forced prostitution, sexual abduction, and other forms of gender trauma within relationships.

In conclusion, the ethnocultural assessment is especially effective when treatment issues are unclear, gender and ethnocultural concerns are presenting complaints, and when women are in a multicultural situation.

ETHNOCULTURAL THERAPEUTIC PROCESS

Therapeutic Relationship

Ethnocultural psychotherapy acknowledges the confluence of both the therapist's and the client's realities. Such convergence is accentuated within the dyadic encounter. Consequently, ethnocultural psychotherapists recognize the therapeutic relationship as an essential agent of change. They use it as a vehicle to promote critical awareness and transformation. In fact, successful psychotherapy with women of color depends on the therapist's skill in establishing and managing the therapeutic relationship (Jenkins, 1985).

In addition to cultural competence, ethnocultural psychotherapists aim to develop cultural empathy. Indeed, the development of empathy in a multicultural context facilitates an understanding of the client's experience. Empathy is an interpersonal construct referring to a clinician's intrinsic capacity to attend to the emotional experience of others. Within mainstream psychotherapy, empathy is composed of kinesthetic, affective and cognitive elements (Jordan & Surrey, 1986). The kinesthetic component relates to the nonverbal communication and body language. Empathy's affective component involves an emotional connectedness—the experience of *being like the other*. The cognitive element refers to an intellectual understanding of the other. Therapists engaged solely in cognitive empathy tend to maintain their identity differentiated from their clients' (Kaplan, 1991), and thus, do not experience *being like the other*.

As a result, therapists need to go beyond being an empathic witness when working with women of color. They need to develop cultural empathy. Cultural empathy is a learned ability that helps therapists to culturally understand the experience of women of color. Cultural empathy entails a process of perspective taking by using a cultural framework as a guide for understanding women and recognizing cultural differences between self and other (Ridley & Lingle, 1996). Indeed, therapists able to take the perspective of the other person significantly reduce their stereotypic and ethnocentric attitudes (Galinsky & Moskowitz, 2000). Therefore, cultural empathy promotes therapists' cultural responsiveness through a combination of perceptual, cognitive, affective, and communication skills. In short, cultural empathy involves therapists' attunement to women of color's life experiences. Within this context, attunement refers to the process whereby the therapist focuses on the internal world of the woman of color and in turn, she feels understood and connected (Stern, 1985). Such a state of connection facilitates the management of identification and projection during therapy.

ETHNOCULTURAL TRANSFERENCE AND COUNTERTRANSFERENCE

The multicultural therapeutic encounter can provide opportunities for projections based on ethnicity, gender, and race. These projections infuse the therapeutic relationship with complex ethnocultural and gender influences. Therapists working with women of color need to understand transference and countertransference, including their ethnocultural determinants (Varghese, 1983). Racial, gender, and ethnic factors are available targets for projection in therapy (Jones, 1984), which may be manifested in transference. Comas-Díaz and Jacobsen (1991) identified several types of ethnocultural transference and countertransference within the inter-ethnic and the intra-ethnic psychotherapeutic dyads. In brief, the inter-ethnic transferential reactions include the following: (1) overcompliance and friendliness (observed when there is a societal power differential in the client/therapist dyad); (2) denial (when the client avoids disclosing issues pertinent to gendered ethnicity and/or culture); (3) mistrust and suspiciousness (*How can this therapist understand me?*) and (4) ambivalence (a common reaction when working with socially marginalized individuals). Women of color in an interethnic psychotherapy may struggle with negative feelings toward their therapists, while simultaneously developing an attachment to them. Issues of identification and internalization within the inter-ethnic dyad may also foster ambivalence in the client.

The intra-ethnic transference may include the following: (1) omniscient/omnipotent therapist (idealization of the therapist frequently with the fantasy of the reunion with the perfect parent, promoted by the ethnic similarity); (2) traitor (client exhibits resentment and envy at therapist's successes—equated with betrayal and the selling out of his/her culture and race); (3) auto-racist (client does not want to work with a therapist of her own ethnicity, due to projection of the strong negative feelings about herself onto the therapist); and (4) ambivalent (women may feel comfortable with their shared ethnocultural background, but at the same time, they may fear too much psychological closeness).

Some countertransferential reactions within the inter-ethnic dyad include the following: (1) denial of cultural differences; (2) the clinical anthropologist's syndrome (excessive curiosity about women of color's ethnocultural backgrounds at the expense of their emotional needs); (3) guilt (emerges when societal and political realities dictate a lower status for women of color); (4) pity (a derivative of guilt or an expression of political impotence within the therapeutic hour) (5) aggression; and (6) ambivalence (it may originate from ambivalence toward therapist's own ethnoculture).

Within the intra-ethnic dyad some of the countertransferential reactions are the following: (1) overidentification; (2) *us and them* mentality (shared victimization due to gendered ethnocultural discrimination may contribute to therapist's ascribing the woman's problems as being solely due to being a person of color); (3) distancing; (4) survivor's guilt (therapists of color may have the personal experience of escaping the harsh socioeconomic circumstances of low income ethnic minorities, leaving family and friends in the process, and generating conflict and guilt); (5) cultural myopia (inability to see clearly due to ethnocultural factors that obscure therapy); (6) ambivalence (working through the therapist's own ethnic ambivalence); and (7) anger (being too ethnoculturally close to a woman of color may uncover painful, unresolved emotional issues).

The examination of ethnocultural transference and countertransference advances the psychotherapeutic process.

PHASES IN THE PSYCHOTHERAPEUTIC PROCESS

The ethnocultural psychotherapeutic process unfolds the phases of intuition, affect, cognition, and coalescence. Although these stages seem to follow a developmental path, in reality, they are fluid and permeable.

During the intuitive stage, women of color are reading the therapist's nonverbal communication. In other words, they are literally checking the therapist out. Thus, nonverbal communication such as body language, hunches, and vibes acquires central importance. Although both therapist and client follow their gut feelings, women of color tend to rely more on their intuition, while therapists are cognitively engaged in collecting data, making a diagnosis, and developing a treatment plan.

Ethnocultural therapists pay special attention to gut feelings. Partly due to being oppressed, women of color rely on nonverbal signs to decipher meanings within power differentials. At times, they communicate indirectly—a style prevalent among sociocentric individuals. When therapists overlook such communication, then empathic difficulties occur. In particular, women of color check out their therapist for the presence of racism and sexism. In other words, women of color follow their intuition. Consequently, ethnocultural psychotherapists attend to all kinds of communication—what is said and not said—throughout all phases of the therapeutic process.

The affective phase refers to feelings and emotions. It includes women's subjective experiences of being a woman, a person of color, and a woman of color. To facilitate understanding women's feelings, therapists ask: "How do you feel being a person of color?" "What does it mean to you to be a woman of color?" The affective phase unfolds women's subjective experience of being a person of color. More importantly, the woman ascertains how she feels about the therapist, and conversely, the therapist examines how he or she feels about the client. Indeed, the affective phase sets the stage for the emergence of ethnocultural transference and countertransference.

The cognitive phase involves the intellectual understanding of the therapeutic alliance. Pre-therapy expectations are expressed and discussed during this phase. The cognitive stage entails a reality testing of cultural differences and/or similarities. It signals the recognition of the presence of transference and countertransference.

Ethnogender factors influencing the psychotherapeutic process begin to come together during coalescence. For example, women's feelings regarding treatment and their clinician are articulated and negotiated during this stage. Women begin to accept their therapist as a helping person. Cultural differences are worked through, including power differentials. These processes provide a model for the reconciliation of differences. Women examine their fractured identities and begin to integrate disparate aspects of the self. For these reasons, the therapeutic restoration takes place during coalescence and the potential for growth is enhanced.

ETHNOCULTURAL PSYCHOTHERAPY TOOLS

In addition to mainstream therapeutic strategies, clinicians use ethnocultural tools. Some of these instruments include the explanatory model of distress, cultural genograms, cultural transitional maps, and ethnocultural occupational inventory. Other ethnocultural tools include narratives/storytelling, testimonies, and indigenous healing techniques. In this chapter I briefly present the explanatory model of distress, cultural genogram, and the ethnocultural occupational inventory.

The explanatory model of distress is an ethnographical clinical tool used to elicit clients' expectations and perspectives on their illness (Kleinman, 1980). Clinicians ask the following questions (Callan & Littlewood, 1998; Kleinman, 1980):

What do you call your problem (distress or illness)?

What do you think your problem (illness) does?

What do you think the natural course of your illness is?

What do you fear?

Why do you think this illness or problem has occurred?

How do you think the distress should be treated?

How do want me to help you?

Who do you turn to for help?

Who should be involved in decision-making?

Therapists who ask these questions convey respect and interest in their clients. As they earn clients' trust, clinicians foster the emergence of a healing alliance.

Another ethnocultural tool is the cultural genogram. This instrument emphasizes the role of culture in the lives of individuals and their families (Hardy & Laszloffy, 1995). Like regular genograms (McGoldrick, Gerson, & Shellenberger, 1999), cultural genograms diagram the genealogical, developmental, historical, political, economical, and sociological influences on individuals' lives. Moreover, cultural genograms place women within their collective circumstances and identify their ethnogender, spiritual, and racial contexts. Furthermore, cultural genograms emphasize the effects of skin color, hair texture, body type, phenotype, and appearance in women of color. Similarly, the cultural transitional map clarifies the information regarding family transitions. The cultural transitional map elucidates women's individual and collective history of translocation. In addition, this tool assesses personal, familial, ethnocultural, and community mappings in families undergoing sociocultural change and transition (Ho, 1987).

Finally, the ethnocultural occupational inventory assesses women's experiences within work settings. For example, Dr. Brown explored Ana's experiences as a lawyer. She used the ethnocultural occupational inventory to explore Ana's experiences as a woman, a woman of color, a mixed race woman, and a professional of color working in a predominantly white law firm. Among other areas, the ethnocultural occupational inventory explored the following:

1. Meaning of work for Ana, her family and her ethnic group
2. Family history of higher education and occupational attainment
3. Previous and current work (paid and pro bono)

4. Occupational success and failure

5. Occupational socialization

6. Discrimination in work setting

7. Sexual harassment at workplace (direct and vicarious)

8. Racial and/or ethnocultural anger and rage

9. Interaction of ethnicity, gender, race, class, and sexual orientation

10. Previous and current occupational coping skills (functional and dysfunctional)

11. Occupational fears, fantasies, family scripts, and wishes

12. Identification and challenge of irrational and dysfunctional belief systems about work

13. Projection of family, personal, and career goals

14. Racial climate at workplace

15. Assessment of gender issues at workplace

The completion of Ana's occupational inventory signaled Ana's resolve to engage in a transformative action. All of the ethnocultural psychotherapy processes, stages, and tools affirm women's empowerment and identity reformulation. The therapeutic work lays the foundation for the development of women's ethnogender consciousness.

ETHNOGENDER CONSCIOUSNESS

Ethnocultural psychotherapy aims to provide a safe forum for women's identity reformulation. It offers acceptance of the client's gendered ethnicity by conveying the relevance of identity affirmation and reformulation in healing. Ethnocultural consciousness is a pivotal factor in recovery and liberation. Due to cultural imperialism, sexist racism, and multiple forms of oppression, many women of color develop cultural amnesia. To awaken their cultural legacy and reconnect with their roots, women of color need to become ethnoculturally conscious. The process of reconnecting with ethnic, cultural and spiritual roots, ethnocultural consciousness enhances women's ability to resist oppression. In other words, ethnocultural consciousness helps women of color to rescue their gendered cultural strengths and acknowledge their multiple intersecting identities. Simply put, ethnocultural consciousness promotes women of color's ability to assert and celebrate who they are.

Therapists initiate women's consciousness during the completion of the ethnocultural assessment. However, the development of ethnocultural and feminist consciousness requires more than the delineation of heritage, legacy, and herstory. Consciousness needs to embrace women's cultural resilience, strengths, and gifts.

An important aspect in women of color's resilience is spirituality. Indeed, feminism of color is embedded in spiritual contexts. To illustrate, womanism—African American women's feminism—affirms female strengths, fights oppression, and promotes collective social justice (Walker, 1983). A womanist goal is the infusion of spirituality into women's lives (Phillips, 2006). Likewise, Latina feminism—*mujerismo*—is anchored in spirit. Based on liberation theology, *mujeristas* commit to the decolonization of all people (Isasi-Diaz, 1994). Womanism and *mujerismo* aim to empower women and their communities. Both movements are revolutionary, communal, and generative. As collective efforts, womanism and *mujerismo* foment global solidarity (Comas-Díaz, 2008). Their multidisciplinary foundation nurtures women's ethnogender and cultural consciousness. Feminism of color spiritually based awareness enhances women of color's cultural resilience. It leads women to resist the pressure to revise or to repress experience, to embrace conflict rather than conformity, and endure anger and pain rather than submitting to repression and oppression (Tal, 1996).

When women of color become conscious, they alchemize oppression into liberation (Comas-Díaz, 2008). As women reconnect with their ethnogender strengths, they rescue their gifts of power. The experience of multiple intersecting oppressions facilitates the development of gifts of power. These gifts—ethnogender intuition, prophetic abilities, and healing capacities—are spiritually based. In other words, many women of color use their spirituality to rescue their gifts of power to empower themselves and others. Since these gifts constitute a resistance against oppression, colonization, and cultural imperialism, they instill women with transformation and liberation (Comas-Díaz, 2008). The flexibility inherent in ethnocultural consciousness helps women to reformulate their identity.

Ethnocultural consciousness travels a developmental journey. As such, it is similar to Maria Harris's (1991) depiction of female spiritual evolution. She identified women's spiritual development as a rhythmic dance of awakening, discovering, creating, dwelling, nourishing, traditioning, and transforming. All of these stages are interconnected in the lives of women of color. For instance, within their traditioning process, many women of color resort to creativity. Indeed, a significant part of cultural resilience is the nurturing of creativity. Of interest, research has shown positive relationship between people's multiculturalism and their creativity (Leung, Maddux, Galinsky, & Chiu, 2008). In other words, being exposed to multicultural experiences enhances creativity. Certainly, many women of color engage in creative healing and liberation.

CONCLUSION

Ethnocultural psychotherapy acknowledges the concept of self as an internal gendered ethnocultural representation. It addresses female intersecting identities and contextual realities through the integration of diversity variables into mental health assessment and treatment. Ethnocultural psychotherapists view the therapeutic relationship as the recognition of the self in the other. Consequently, they use ethnocultural tools to empower and affirm ethnogender identity. Indeed, ethnocultural psychotherapy helps women to go back home. They are empowered to reconstruct and inhabit their place in the world. Ana, the lawyer who was discriminated against for being a black Latina, remained in therapy with Dr. Brown for a year. The completion of her ethnocultural assessment facilitated Ana's reconnection with herself and with her community. Therapy helped her to reconcile and integrate diverse aspects of her identity. Based on her responses to the occupational inventory, Ana left the law firm where she was employed. Later on, she established her own company specializing in immigration services. Six months after completing therapy, Ana sent Dr. Brown a local newspaper article announcing Ana's selection as woman of the year.

REFERENCES

Betancourt, J. R., Green, A. R., Carrillo, J. E., & Ananch-Firempong, O. (2003, July–August). Defining cultural competence: A practical framework for addressing racial/ethnic disparities in health and health care. *Public Health Reports, 118,* 293–302.

Callan, A. & Littlewood, R. (1998). Patient satisfaction: Ethnic origin or explanatory model? *International Journal of Social Psychiatry, 44,* 1–11.

Comas-Díaz, L. (2008). Spirita: Reclaiming womanist sacredness in feminism. *Psychology of Women Quarterly, 32,* 13–21.

Comas-Díaz, L., & Jacobsen, F. M. (1991). Ethnocultural transference and countertransference in the therapeutic dyad. *American Journal of Orthopsychiatry, 61,* 392–402.

Comas-Díaz, L., & Jacobsen, F. M. (2004). Ethnocultural psychotherapy. In E. Crighead & C. Nemeroff (Eds.), *The concise encyclopedia of psychology and behavioral science* (pp. 338–339). New York: Wiley.

Duran, E., & Ivey, A. E. (2006). *Healing the soul wound: counseling with American Indians and other Native People.* New York: Teachers College Press.

Elsass, P. (1992). *Strategies for survival: The psychology of cultural resilience in ethnic minorities.* New York: New York University Press.

Freire, P. (1970). *Pedagogy of the oppressed.* New York: Seabury Press.

Freire, P. (1973). *Education for critical consciousness.* New York: Seabury.

Freire, P., & Macedo, D. (2000). *The Paulo Freire reader.* New York: Continuum.

Galinsky, A. D., & Moskowitz, G. B. (2000). Perspective-taking: Decreasing stereotype expression, stereotype accessibility, and in-group favoritism. *Journal of Personality & Social Psychology, 78,* 708–724.

Hardy, K. V., & Laszloffy, T. (1995). The cultural genogram: Key to training culturally competent family therapists. *Journal of Marital and Family Therapy, 21,* 227–237.

Harris, M. (1991). *Dance of spirit. The seven steps of women's spirituality.* New York: Bantam Books.

Ho, M. H. (1987). *Family therapy with ethnic minorities.* Newbury Park, CA: Sage.

Isasi-Diaz, A. M. (1994). Mujeristas: A name of our own: *Sisters struggling in the spirit.* In N. B. Lewis (Ed.), *A women of color theological anthology* (pp. 126–138). Louisville, KY: Women's Ministries Program, Presbyterian Church.

Jacobsen, F. M. (1988). Ethnocultural assessment. In L. Comas-Díaz & E. H. Griffith (Eds.), *Clinical guidelines in cross-cultural mental health.* New York: John Wiley & Sons.

Jenkins, A. (1985, August 25). *Dialogue and dialectic: Psychotherapy in cross cultural contexts.* Paper presented at the American Psychological Association annual convention, Los Angeles.

Jones, E. (1984). Some reflections of the black patient in psychotherapy. *The Clinical Psychologist, 37,* 62–65.

Jordan, J. V., & Surrey, J. L. (1986). The self-in-relation: Empathy and the mother–daughter relationship. In T. Bernay & D. W. Cantor (Eds.), *The psychology of today's woman: New psychoanalytic visions.* Hillsdale, NJ: The Analytic Press.

Kaplan, A. (1991). The self in relation: implications for depression in women. In J. V. Jordan, A. G. Kaplan, J. B. Miller, I. P. Stiver, & J. I. Surrey (Eds.), *Women's growth in connection: Writings from the Stone Center* (pp. 206–222). New York: Guilford.

Kleinman, A. (1980). *Patients and healers in the context of culture: An exploration of the borderland between anthropology, medicine, and psychiatry.* Berkeley: University of California Press.

Knipscheer, J. W., & Kleber, R. J. (2004). A need for ethnic similarity in the therapist-patient interaction? Mediterranean Migrants in Dutch mental health care. *Journal of Clinical Psychology, 60,* 543–554.

Kuppersmith, J. (1987). The double bind of personal striving: Ethnic working class women in psychotherapy. *Journal of Contemporary Psychotherapy, 17,* 203–216.

Leung, A. K.-Y., Maddux, W., Galinsky, A., & Chiu, C.-Y. (2008). Multicultural experience enhances creativity: The when and how. *American Psychologist, 63,* 169–181.

McGoldrick, M., Gerson, R., & Shellenberger, S. (1999). *Genograms: Assessment and intervention.* New York: Norton W.W. Company.

Phillips, L. (Ed.). (2006). *The womanist reader.* New York: Routledge.

Ramirez, M. (1991). *Psychotherapy and counseling with minorities: A cognitive approach to individual and cultural differences.* New York: Pergamon.

Ridley, C., & Lingle, D. W. (1996). Cultural empathy in multicultural counseling: A multidimensional process model. In P. B. Pedersen, J. G. Draguns, W. J. Lonner, & J. E. Trimble (Eds.), *Counseling across cultures* (4th ed., pp. 21–46). Thousand Oaks, CA: Sage.

Said, E. W. (1994). *Culture and imperialism.* New York: Vintage Books.

Slater, L., Daniel, J. H., & Banks, A. (2003). *The complete guide for mental health for women.* Boston: Beacon Press.

Stern, D. N. (1985). *The interpersonal world of the infant: A view from psychoanalysis and developmental psychology.* New York: Basic Books.

Tal, K. (1996). *Words of hurt. Reading the literatures of trauma*. Cambridge, United Kingdom: Cambridge University Press.

Varghese, F. T. N. (1983). The racially-different psychiatrist: Implications for psychotherapy. *Australian and New Zealand Journal of Psychiatry 17*, 329–333.

Walker, A. (1983). *In search of our mothers' garden: Womanist prose*. New York: Harcourt Brace Jovanovich.

Chapter 3

Women and Sexual Violence: Emotional, Physical, Behavioral, and Organizational Responses

Paula Lundberg-Love
Bethany Waits

Female survivors of sexual violence are everywhere. They are in universities, religious institutions, court rooms, hospitals, and the military. They are daughters, mothers, spouses, sisters, friends, next-door neighbors, and coworkers. Many differ in age, education, ethnicity, and socioeconomic status (Klump, 2006; Koss, Bailey, & Yuan, 2003). However, their lives are connected by the violence that they have experienced. Sexual violence is a pervasive social problem, and as Koss et al. (1994) aptly noted, there is "no safe haven" for women from victimization. National epidemiological data indicates that between 17 and 25 percent of women in the United States report some form of sexual assault in their lifetime (Campbell, 2008). Results of a national telephone survey conducted in 2001 to 2003 found that approximately 2.7 million women experienced sexual violence during the last 12 months prior to the survey. The same study also reported that approximately 11.7 million women had been victimized at some point during their lives (Basile, Chen, Black, & Saltzman, 2007). Globally, at least one woman in three is beaten, coerced into sex, or otherwise abused at some point in her life (Koss et al., 2003).

Sexual violence is a comprehensive term that describes all acts of unwanted sexual activity including rape, sexual assault, and intimate partner violence (IPV). According to Hedtke et al. (2008), rape typically includes forced vaginal, oral, or anal penetration with a penis or other objects without a person's consent. For many years, the term "rape" was used to describe all acts of sexual violence. Recently, it has been abandoned in favor of the gender-neutral term "sexual assault," which is defined as nonconsensual sexual contact obtained by physical force, by threat of physical harm, or in situations where the victim is unable to give consent (Golding, 1999; Lee & Kleiner, 2003). This definition can include unwanted sexual kissing to situations involving oral, anal, or vaginal intercourse (Golding, 1999). Furthermore, IPV is defined as "threatened, attempted, or completed physical or sexual violence or emotional abuse by a current or former intimate partner" (Black & Breiding, 2008, p. 646). IPV can be committed by a spouse, an ex-spouse, a boyfriend, or a dating partner. Since the majority of sexual assaults are committed by individuals known to the victim, it is not surprising that many victims of sexual violence also experience IPV.

Prior to the early 1970s, research concerning sexual violence focused almost exclusively on characteristics of the perpetrator, and little attention was given to the distress of survivors. The women's movement was instrumental in shifting the direction of sexual assault research from the rapist to the psychological sequelae that victims experience (Neville & Heppner, 1999). Rape crisis centers established in the late 1970s and early 1980s provided immediate intervention and long-term therapy to individuals, as well as early research documenting women's psychological reactions to sexual violence, which included fear, anxiety, and depression. These studies were critical in heightening awareness concerning the severity of the trauma that survivors encountered (1999). For instance, an initial survey interviewed victims four to six years after their rape experience and found that approximately 26 percent still did not feel recovered from the crime, suggesting that the effects of sexual violence reached far beyond the initial attack (Koss et al., 1994). Since the 1980s, literature concerning the impact of victimization has extended past psychological sequelae to other reactions that victims encounter. These include various physical, neurological, behavioral, and organizational responses, which will be discussed in the following sections (Kaltman, Krupnick, Stockton, Hooper, & Green, 2005).

PSYCHOLOGICAL RESPONSES

The psychological impact of sexual violence has been extensively studied. Research has consistently documented that victims experience intense psychological distress immediately following the attack. This distress typically peaks in severity approximately three weeks post assault and continues to remain at an elevated level for several months. While initial distress may dissipate over time, longitudinal studies suggest that a significant number of victims continue to experience chronic mental health problems for many years subsequent to victimization (Neville & Heppner, 1999). Indeed, Koss et al. (2003) found that several years after their rape, approximately one-fourth of women continued to experience negative psychological effects. These typically include posttraumatic stress disorder (PTSD), major depression, sexual dysfunction, and generalized anxiety (Koss & Kilpatrick, 2001). Even when evaluated many years later, one study found that between 31 and 65 percent of victims met the diagnostic criteria for PTSD, and 43 percent met the criteria for major depression (Campbell, 2008). These studies provided evidence that psychological distress following victimization is prevalent among survivors and can cause long-term devastation to the individual's well-being and mental health (Hedtke et al., 2008).

Several researchers have documented that the most common immediate reactions following sexual violence are fear and anxiety (Bohn & Holz, 1996; Goodman, Koss, & Russo, 1993; Koss et al., 1994; Neville & Heppner, 1999; Resick, 1993). Within 72 hours of the assault, 86 percent of victims report having intense fear of their assailant and anxiety about their personal safety. By the third week, rape-induced anxiety typically reaches maximum levels, and studies suggest that it may not begin to lessen for up to three years (Koss et al., 1994). For instance, when compared to survivors of other crimes such as robbery, rape victims describe greater anxiety and fear at six months and at one year following the assault. The most frequent fears reported by victims included talking to the police, tough-looking people, being alone, blind dates, going out with new people, and making mistakes (Neville & Heppner, 1999). As with anxiety, depressive symptomatology is typically observed within a few hours to a few days following victimization (Koss et al., 1994). These symptoms consist of sad feelings about the assault, loss of interest in normal activities, suicidal thoughts, sleep disturbances, fatigue, frequent crying spells, and an inability to concentrate (Bohn & Holz, 1996; Goodman et al., 1993; Koss et al., 1994). Many victims meet diagnostic criteria for major depressive disorder only a few weeks subsequent to the attack (Koss et al., 1994). In one study, 56 percent of rape survivors reported depressive symptoms and 43 percent met the diagnostic criteria for major depression one month after the attack (Koss et al., 2003). Furthermore, women who have been raped are three times more likely to meet criteria for lifetime major depression, are two times as likely to qualify for a diagnosis of dysthymia, and are 2.5 times more likely to report recent depression when compared to nonvictims (Koss, Figueredo, & Prince, 2002). Overall, 13 percent of victims of sexual violence suffer from a major depressive disorder sometime in their lives as compared with 5 percent who never experience such abuse (Koss & Kilpatrick, 2001). As major depressive disorders become more prevalent among victims, suicidal thoughts also may increase. According to Koss and Kilpatrick (2001), victims of sexual violence are at an elevated risk for suicidal ideation when compared with nonvictims. Within the first month, suicidal ideation was reported by 33 to 50 percent of survivors, and in one study 22 percent of sexually abused women reported suicidal ideation in the previous 12-month period as compared to 7 percent of nonabused women (Koss et al., 1994). Since the frequency of suicidal thoughts is elevated, it should not be surprising that approximately 19 percent of victims report at least one suicide attempt at some point in their lifetime (Koss et al., 2003).

Victims of sexual violence are considered the largest single group that suffers from PTSD (Koss & Kilpatrick, 2001). According to Bohn and Holz (1996), a wide range of symptoms such as flashbacks, intrusive recollections about the abuse, repetitive dreams and nightmares, psychological numbing, anxiety, irritability, insomnia, hypersensitivity, and hypervigilance are frequently reported. Approximately one-third of female survivors are diagnosed with PTSD immediately following the attack (Ullman, Filipas, Townsend, & Starzynski, 2007). After three weeks, 79 percent of victims met the *Diagnostic and Statistical Manual, fourth edition* (DSM-IV) criteria for PTSD (Gilboa-Schechtman & Foa, 2001). In addition, prospective studies have demonstrated that within two weeks of the assault, 90 percent of victims met symptom criteria for PTSD while 50 percent continued to meet the criteria three months later (Koss et al., 2003). Research from community-based samples found that between 44 and 49 percent of women who experienced sexual violence were diagnosed with PTSD (Littleton & Breitkopf, 2006). According to Resnick, Acierno, Holmes, Dammeyer, and Kilpatrick (2000), the lifetime prevalence of PTSD among survivors is approximately 30 percent; however, estimates as high as 50 percent also have been reported. Finally, another study found that individuals who experienced sexual violence were 6.2 times more likely to suffer from PTSD than women who had never been victimized (Koss et al., 2003).

Typically, survivors reported feeling "dirty" and "unclean" following sexual victimization. While many of these feelings are related to visible dirt and contamination from the attack, they also may result from a sense of internal, non-visible contamination. Researchers define this phenomenon as "mental pollution," and for many, mental pollution continues despite being visibly clean (Fairbrother & Rachman, 2004). As a result, survivors may engage in excessive washing behaviors in an attempt to remove the "unclean" feelings sustained from the assault. One study conducted by Fairbrother and Rachman (2004) assessed mental pollution among a sample of sexual assault survivors and found that 70 percent of participants reported an urge to wash or clean themselves subsequent to the attack. Furthermore, 49 percent of the sample reported washing more than one time and 24 percent continued washing for several weeks. More than 25 percent of women in the sample who washed in response to mental pollution reported that they continued to wash excessively for several months and 11.8 percent persisted in this behavior for at least one year post-assault (Fairbrother & Rachman, 2004). Few studies have determined the long-term consequences of mental pollution on victims' psychological well-being. However, several case studies suggest that continued washing as a result of mental pollution might result in the onset of obsessive compulsive disorder (OCD). While this finding has been documented in several cases, further research is needed to understand fully the relationship between mental pollution and OCD (Fairbrother & Rachman, 2004).

As mentioned previously, victims of sexual violence are at an increased risk to experience fear, anxiety, depression, suicidal ideation, PTSD, and mental pollution when compared to nonvictims. Several other psychological sequelae including sexual dysfunction and eating disorders frequently also are reported by survivors. According to Koss et al. (1994), victims experience less sexual satisfaction and more sexual problems than nonvictimized women. In one study of adult survivors, 61 percent reported sexual dysfunction, especially avoidance of sex, immediately after the crime. Other frequent problems included a lack of desire, fear of sex, and difficulty becoming aroused. Even four to six years after the incident, 30 percent of women did not feel that their sexual functioning had returned to normal pre-rape levels (1994). In addition, victims of sexual violence are more likely to report eating disorders such as anorexia and bulimia nervosa than nonvictims (H. Resnick, Acierno, & Kilpatrick, 1997). In a group of bulimic patients, 23 percent had been raped, 29 percent had been sexually abused as children, and 23 percent had experienced IPV (Koss et al., 1994). Since eating disorders may have life-threatening consequences, it is important for clinicians to assess for previous trauma history in order to provide more appropriate treatments for these individuals.

According to Koss and colleagues (2003), the psychological impact associated with sexual victimization has been well established for several decades. As a result, investigators are now turning their attention from symptomatology to the moderators and mediators that translate abuse into psychological distress. A moderator is a variable that affects the relationship between two other variables (i.e., sexual violence and poor mental health), changing the direction or magnitude of the effects. A mediator, or intervening variable, acts as a link in a causal chain which mitigates the effect from the independent (i.e., sexual assault) to the dependent (i.e., mental health) variable. In cases of sexual victimization, moderators and mediators typically enhance the damaging impact of the abuse experience on victims, thereby prolonging recovery. For example, potential moderators that may exacerbate psychological distress include previous trauma history, maladaptive coping strategies, negative social reactions, and various characteristics associated with the assault. The most powerful mediators include social cognitions involving self-blame and perceived control.

Evidence suggests that women who have been sexually victimized in childhood or adolescence are more likely to be revictimized in adulthood (Koss et al., 2003). A recent meta-analysis estimated that 15 to 79 percent of female child sexual abuse (CSA) survivors experience rape as adults (Kaltman et al., 2005). According to Campbell et al. (2008), women with a history of previous sexual violence who are revictimized in adulthood have poorer mental health outcomes than victims of a single instance of sexual assault. Indeed, these individuals have significantly elevated levels of PTSD and depression as compared to those without a history of previous trauma (Campbell, Greeson, Bybee, & Raja, 2008). Kaltman and colleagues (2005) demonstrated that college sophomores who experienced CSA and were then revictimized as adults, reported more Axis I diagnoses, more comorbid diagnoses, including PTSD, depression, and general distress than other victims without a history of prior abuse. A history of CSA also has been found to prolong recovery among victims (Krause, Kaltman, Goodman, & Dutton, 2008). For instance, longitudinal studies regarding the course of depression and PTSD suggest that CSA contributes to chronic symptomatology and persistent, unremitting distress among individuals who were revictimized at some point in adulthood (Koss et al., 2003).

The coping strategies utilized by women following sexual violence are highly influential in recovery. Research suggests that there are two primary strategies an individual can employ when faced with a stressful event, approach coping and avoidance coping. Approach coping is chosen when the individual decides that she has sufficient resources to cope with her emotional reaction to the stressor (Littleton & Breitkopf, 2006). Several of these strategies involve keeping busy, thinking positively, obtaining support, and making life changes (Draucker, 2001). In contrast, avoidance coping occurs when an individual lacks the coping resources necessary to handle the stressful situation (Littleton & Breitkopf, 2006). In such cases, the victim is likely to implement strategies such as denying the existence of the stressor, avoiding thoughts about the stressor, staying home, and withdrawing from friends (Draucker, 2001; Littleton & Breitkopf, 2006). A growing body of literature suggests that avoidance coping is correlated with more severe psychological distress following sexual victimization (Krause et al., 2008). For example, trying to forget about or "block out" the assault is correlated with the prolonged recovery of survivors (Ullman et al., 2007). Avoidance coping also has been associated with increased PTSD symptom severity when compared to victims who implemented other strategies (Krause et al., 2008; Ullman et al., 2007). Although many victims employ avoidance coping, other victims who cope by keeping busy, thinking positively, and making life changes (i.e., approach coping) actually report less psychological distress and more favorable recoveries. Thus, the manner in which a victim copes (i.e., avoidance or approach) with sexual assault may substantially determine the severity of her symptoms and duration of her recovery.

Social reactions from friends and family members can mitigate or magnify the psychological effects of sexual violence (Koss et al., 2003). Several studies have documented that negative social reactions such as blaming the victim, treating the victim differently, and trying to distract the victim result in prolonged recovery and increased psychological distress. Specifically, when victims are blamed or treated differently post-assault, PTSD symptoms are significantly worse than when other reactions are present. Attempting to distract victims from their pain by telling them to "move on with their lives" or to "stop talking about the assault" is also related to PTSD severity and long-lasting distress (Ullman & Filipas, 2001). Although many people's initial reaction to rape and sexual assault is negative, research suggests that positive social responses to victimization may result in a significantly reduced risk of anxiety, depression, PTSD, and suicidal ideation among sexual assault survivors (Coker et al., 2002). Even if the victim merely perceives more positive social support from those around her, she is more likely to report fewer psychological symptoms (Klump, 2006). Therefore, interventions targeting social support and appropriate reactions toward victims are needed in order to promote more positive outcomes in survivors (Campbell et al., 2008).

Certain characteristics associated with the attack also have been linked to more negative psychological outcomes among victims (Hedtke et al., 2008). These include the use of physical force or weapons, high perceived fear of death, physical injuries sustained during the attack, and the victim's relationship to the perpetrator (Koss et al., 2003). In one study, rape victims with PTSD were more likely to have been attacked by strangers, subjected to force or weapons, and sustained physical injuries than were victims without PTSD. Among a national sample of sexual violence survivors, researchers discovered that high perceived life threat and physical injury were related to more PTSD symptoms as compared to controls (Ullman & Filipas, 2001). Finally, Abbey, BeShears, Clinton-Sherrod, and McAuslan (2004) found that women whose perpetrators used physical force as their primary modality of victimization experienced the most extreme negative psychological consequences when compared with other victims.

According to Koss and colleagues (2002), unexpected acts such as rape stimulate causal attributions, or attempts to answer the question, "Why did this happen to me?" In response to this question, victims may blame external forces, controllable features related to their own behavior, or uncontrollable and enduring aspects of their personalities. Research suggests that individuals automatically develop specific ways of processing certain events in their lives. These processes, or social cognitions, include "just world" assumptions (i.e., bad things happen to bad people) and beliefs about personal control, invulnerability, trust, self-esteem, and intimacy (Koss et al., 2002). When incongruity exists between lived experience and social cognitions, individuals become distressed and attempt to resolve the conflict by altering beliefs and modifying how the incident is interpreted. Typically, victims of sexual assault rectify this incongruence by engaging in either behavioral self-blame or characterological self-blame (2002). In order to assess the effects of both characterological and behavioral self-blame on psychological well-being, Koss et al. (2002) assessed victims' attributions of responsibility (e.g., self-blame) and maladaptive beliefs (e.g., beliefs that result in maladaptive conclusions about the self and others following a traumatic event) after sexual assault. Their findings demonstrated that blaming one's own character for rape led to maladaptive beliefs, which increased PTSD severity. Therefore, women who felt responsible for their rape developed beliefs such as "the world is not a safe place," and were in turn less likely to recover and more likely to report long-term psychological distress (Koss et al., 2002). Other studies also have documented this finding (Fraizer, 2003; Ullman et al., 2007).

In addition to self-blame and maladaptive beliefs, perceived control concerning the past, the present, and the future may be a potential mediator between sexual assault and psychological sequelae. Perceived past control refers to an individual's belief that one had control over the occurrence of a traumatic event (Frazier, 2003). While researchers have hypothesized that perceived past control may aid in recovery, several studies suggest that past control is either unassociated with distress or associated with more distress among victims. According to Frazier, past control is rarely helpful in recovery, primarily because it is generally unrelated to measures of future control. Even if victims believe that they had control over a negative event in the past, they do not necessarily believe that they will have control over the same event in the future. However, research does suggest that recovery from rape is better among victims who do believe that they can prevent or avoid a future occurrence of trauma (Koss et al., 2002). Other studies also have documented that perceived future control is associated with lower psychological distress among victims. Although future control can be beneficial, present control, which involves control over the recovery process, has been found to be the most adaptive type of perceived control. Present control allows the victim to regain a sense of control in an otherwise uncontrollable situation. Thus, focusing on control over the recovery process may yield the most positive outcomes among victims of sexual assault (Frazier, 2003).

PHYSICAL RESPONSES

The tendency to report physical health symptoms following victimization has led to an increased rate of medical service seeking among those who experience sexual violence (Ullman & Brecklin, 2003). Koss and Kilpatrick (2001) reported that medical utilization among victims increased by 31 to 56 percent approximately five years after the attack, compared to a 2 percent increase among nonvictims during the corresponding time period. Furthermore, among all female primary care patients, 25 to 28 percent have a history of sexual violence, suggesting that poor physical health is common among these individuals (Koss et al., 1994). On standardized self-report measures of health perception and functioning, victims report significantly poorer health habits and increased symptoms in all body systems except for the skin and eyes (Resnick et al., 1997). Indeed, a number of complaints are diagnosed disproportionately among survivors including physical injuries, gynecological disorders, gastrointestinal disorders, and chronic pain (Koss & Kilpatrick, 2001).

Approximately 40 percent of victims receive nongenital, physical injuries following an incident of victimization, and among those who are injured, 54 percent seek medical treatment (Koss et al., 1994). The most common injuries consist of abrasions to the head, neck, face, thorax, breasts, and abdomen (Campbell, 2002; Goodman et al., 1993). Other injuries such as bruising, contusions, bone fractures, and lacerations also have been reported (Cook, Dickens, & Thapa, 2005; Resnick et al., 1997). Data from the National Women's Study documented that only 4 percent of victims sustained serious injuries, suggesting that the majority of injuries may be minor (Resnick et al., 1997). At least 50 percent of all victims treated in emergency departments report vaginal and perineal trauma (Groer, Thomas, Evans, Helton, & Weldon, 2006). According to Resnick et al. (2000), approximately 15 percent of women who have been sexually victimized have significant vaginal tears, with 1 percent requiring surgery to repair the damage.

The incidence of sexually transmitted diseases (STDs) among victims of sexual violence is between 3.6 and 30 percent (Koss & Kilpatrick, 2001). The most prevalent STDs include gonorrhea, chlamydia, trichomonal infections, and syphilis. However, research also indicates that victims may have an increased risk for hepatitis B and human immunodeficiency virus (HIV) (Resnick et al., 2000). Although the rate of HIV transmission due to rape is unknown, it is a great concern for a majority of victims (Koss & Kilpatrick, 2001). One study found that 89 percent of women interviewed one month after their assaults mentioned fear of contracting HIV (Resnick et al., 2000). When assessed several months following the attack, between 26 and 40 percent of victims spontaneously mentioned AIDS and HIV as a concern, and for more than half of these individuals, it was their primary concern (Koss et al., 1994). Finally, studies have consistently documented that approximately 5 percent of sexual assault cases result in pregnancy (Koss & Kilpatrick, 2001; Resnick et al., 2000).

Gynecological disorders are the most frequently reported physical health problem among victims of sexual violence. At one-year post-assault, women continue to experience severe gynecological dysfunction (Campbell, Lichty, Sturza, & Raja, 2006). For instance, approximately 26 to 82 percent of victims report chronic pelvic pain subsequent to the attack (Golding, 1999). In a study by Koss et al. (1994), women who had undergone laparoscopy for chronic pelvic pain were more likely to be victims of sexual assault than women who had the procedure for other reasons. Chronic pelvic pain results in approximately 10 to 19 percent of all hysterectomies performed in the United States, which could suggest that survivors may be more likely to have this procedure than nonvictimized women (Koss et al., 1994). While chronic pelvic pain is frequently reported among victims, other gynecological disorders and symptoms also have been mentioned. These include dysmenorrhea, menorrhagia, dyspareunia, vaginal pain, premenstrual syndrome, urinary tract infections, vaginal bleeding, excessive vaginal discharge, painful intercourse, rectal bleeding, fibroids, and multiple yeast infections (Bohn & Holz, 1996; Campbell, 2002; Campbell et al., 2006; Chrisler & Ferguson, 2006; Koss et al., 1994).

While physical injuries, STDs, and gynecological disorders are commonly reported, other physical health disturbances also have been documented. For instance, in eight studies, including one general population survey, the incidence of gastrointestinal disorders among victims ranged from 30 to 64 percent (Golding, 1999). Another study found that approximately 44 percent of women evaluated at a gastroenterology clinic reported some type of sexual victimization in adulthood (Koss et al., 1994). Research suggests that nausea, vomiting, diarrhea, constipation, spastic colon, irritable bowl syndrome, abdominal pain, and indigestion are among the most common gastrointestinal problems reported by victims (Campbell 2002; Chrisler & Ferguson, 2006; Goodman et al., 1993). In addition, chronic pain disorders including headaches, back pain, facial pain, neck pain, temporal mandibular joint discomfort, and bruxism are associated with sexual violence (Campbell, 2002; Koss et al., 1994). Among women referred to a multidisciplinary pain center, 53 percent had a history of sexual abuse (Koss et al., 1994). Golding (1999) reported that approximately 45 percent of patients with chronic headaches, 69 percent of patients with facial pain, and 46 percent of patients with chronic back pain had been sexually victimized at some point in their lives. It is estimated that between 50 to 67 percent of women with fibromyalgia and other musculoskeletal disorders have a history of sexual assault (Golding, 1999). Sleep disturbances such as nightmares and insomnia, as well as cardiovascular disorders including hypertension, rapid heart rate, and chest pain are also prevalent among victims (Chrisler & Ferguson, 2006). Finally, additional research suggests that victims may be at an elevated risk for infections including influenza and colds (Campbell, 2002).

Since many of the physical symptoms associated with sexual violence have been established, researchers are now attempting to identify factors that may explain this relationship.

Classical conditioning, assault characteristics, and psychological distress all have been proposed as causal links between abuse and negative health outcomes (Bohn & Holz, 1996; Resnick et al., 1997). When an extremely distressing event (i.e., victimization) occurs, it becomes an unconditioned stimulus that elicits an unconditioned, or automatic, response (Resnick et al., 1997). This automatic response is characterized by cognitive (e.g., perception that one's life is threatened or that one's body is defiled), behavioral (e.g., screaming, kicking, running, fighting, or freezing), and physiological (e.g., alterations in respiration, heart rate, gastrointestinal functioning, digestion, and muscle tension) components. Unfortunately, a powerful form of conditioned responding occurs when automatic responses are paired with other cues associated with the attack, such as the time of day the victimization occurred, the sounds and smells present during the attack, the physical appearance of the perpetrator, and dark shadows if the assault occurred at night (Resnick et al., 1997). When this takes place, environmental cues become learned or conditioned stimuli that have the capacity to elicit the cognitive, behavioral, and physiological responses that automatically occurred during the initial trauma. Thus, physical reactions to sexual assault such as abdominal distress, pain, nausea, increased heart rate, shortness of breath, and shaking may become learned conditioned responses to environmental fear triggers (i.e., dark shadows) and cause victims to experience an increase in problematic symptoms (Resnick et al., 1997). According to Resnick and colleagues (1997), as victims continue to experience these health problems, they may be more likely to develop chronic disorders such as fibromyalgia and irritable bowel syndrome.

A dose-response relationship may exist between sexual violence and chronic health problems whereby numerous assault experiences result in exacerbated symptoms (Ullman & Brecklin 2003). In one study conducted by Ullman and Brecklin (2003), correlates of past-year chronic medical conditions were examined among women with different sexual victimization histories identified from the National Comorbidity Survey. Findings suggested that for adult victims, more lifetime traumatic sexual encounters were related to increased chronic medical conditions compared to those who experienced a single act of sexual violence (2003). Another study conducted by Campbell et al. (2006) reported that the number of vaginal assaults alone was significantly and positively associated with a higher frequency of pelvic pain, vaginal bleeding, discharge, painful intercourse, and painful urination. Those who experienced multiple oral or anal assaults were more likely to report chronic pain and gynecological disorders than those who did not repeatedly experience these types of trauma (2006). Furthermore, research has documented that victims who believed that their lives were in danger during the assault were more likely to experience severe health problems when compared to others devoid of such a history (Ullman & Brecklin, 2003).

Recent evidence suggests that psychological distress and mental health sequelae may mediate the physical health conditions associated with sexual violence. Among women recruited from a primary care clinic, sexual assault victims had higher rates of medical complaints only if they also reported psychological distress (Ullman & Brecklin, 2003). Specifically, research suggests that PTSD symptoms are positively correlated with more severe physical symptoms following victimization (Groer et al., 2006). A study conducted by Zoellner, Goodwin, and Foa (2000) assessed survivors with chronic PTSD in order to determine if PTSD symptoms were related to negative health outcomes. Results indicated that negative life events, anger, depression, and PTSD severity all were related to an increase in self-reported health symptoms. However, PTSD symptom severity predicted physical symptoms to a greater degree than the other variables. Thus, although research has repeatedly demonstrated impairment of physical health after sexual assault, it may not be the assault per se, but rather the associated psychological sequelae, such as PTSD, that are responsible for the decline in victims' well-being (Zoellner et al., 2000). Other studies also have reported a relationship between PTSD severity and physical health symptomatology (Campbell et al., 2008). For instance, Rebecca Campbell et al. (2008) found that PTSD symptom severity was more likely to be associated with persistent health conditions, especially those related to chronic pain, as compared to other factors. As studies continue to document the role of PTSD as a mediator of physical health outcomes, the need for effective treatments and interventions for PTSD becomes more apparent (Campbell et al., 2008).

NEUROLOGICAL RESPONSES

Initially, literature concerning the neurological sequelae associated with sexual violence was limited to psychogenic seizures, fainting, and convulsions (Campbell, 2002; Koss et al., 1994). In the last twenty years however, research has documented that cognitive functioning, brain structures, hypothalamic-pituitary-adrenal (HPA) axis activity, cortisol levels, and recovery from traumatic brain injury (TBI) are different among victims of sexual violence when compared to nonvictims (Campbell, 2002). Evidence suggests that victims of sexual trauma, especially those with a diagnosis of PTSD, may experience cognitive deficits in attention, learning, memory, and executive functioning (Jenkins, Langlais, Delis, & Cohen, 2000; Stein, Kennedy, & Twamley, 2002). For instance, several studies have documented that survivors exhibit impairments on neurological measures of attention including the Trail Making Test (Part B), the Digit Span and Digit Symbol subtests of the Wechsler Adult Intelligence Scale-III (WAIS-III), the Continuous Performance Test (CPT), and the Paced Auditory Serial Addition Task (PASAT) (Jenkins et al., 2000). Jenkins and colleagues (2000) found that victims who were diagnosed with rape-related PTSD were more likely to demonstrate deficits on measures of sustained and focused attention relative to non-PTSD and nontraumatized controls. One theory explaining these results suggests that factors associated with PTSD such as trying to avoid intrusive recollections, sleeping poorly, and being easily startled might result in impaired performance on tests of sustained attention. Furthermore, dissociation, which can range from daydreaming to a complete trance state, is often observed among victims with PTSD and may interfere with an individual's ability to concentrate and remain focused on a specific task (Jenkins et al., 2000). According to Stein et al. (2002), survivors who report PTSD symptoms are also likely to experience problems with learning, memory, and executive functioning. In one study, visuoconstruction, visual memory, and executive function all were impaired significantly in sexual assault victims (Stein et al., 2002). In addition, findings from three large samples using standardized memory assessments have demonstrated that rape memories are more affectively intense and negative than other memories when compared to non-rape traumatic events (Koss & Kilpatrick, 2001).

As with cognitive impairments, research investigating differences in brain structures has largely focused on the role of PTSD in mediating these effects. Studies utilizing structural magnetic resonance imaging among individuals with rape-related PTSD have consistently found smaller hippocampal volumes compared to those without histories of trauma. Among victims with recent-onset PTSD, right hippocampal volume was significantly smaller than controls (Wignall et al., 2004). Furthermore, Wignall and colleagues (2004) found that whole brain volume was significantly smaller in traumatized individuals with PTSD compared to nonvictims. Other studies have documented significantly smaller intracranial volumes, slightly larger ventricular volumes, and smaller cerebral volumes in victims who have experienced sexual violence and subsequent PTSD symptomatology (Fennema-Notestine, Stein, Kennedy, Archibald, & Jernigan, 2002). In an effort to determine the effects of PTSD on the whole brain, Fennema-Notestine and colleagues (2002) examined volumes of specific brain regions in adult women with a history of IPV, including sexual assault, compared to women without serious trauma histories. Among the IPV women, half had a current diagnosis of PTSD, and half had never reported PTSD symptoms. Their results suggest that regardless of PTSD classification, women who experienced IPV had significantly smaller supratentorial cranial vault volumes compared with controls. Additionally, frontal and occipital gray matter volumes were significantly smaller in all IPV women, which was associated to increased Trails B time performance, especially in women diagnosed with PTSD. Thus, findings from this study reveal that aspects of neuropsychological impairment in victims of sexual violence may be rooted in frontal and mesial temporal abnormalities following victimization (Fennema-Notestine et al., 2002).

The HPA axis controls the body's natural reaction to stress and has been extensively studied in relation to traumatic events including sexual victimization (Girdler et al., 2007). When an individual is exposed to a stressful situation, the hypothalamus becomes activated and begins to release corticotropin-releasing factor, or CRF. This chemical acts at the anterior pituitary gland to induce the release of adrenocorticotropic hormone, ACTH, which in turn activates the adrenal cortex. Once the adrenal cortex is activated, it stimulates the release of cortisol and other glucocorticoids into the general circulation, which enhances energy production to help the body deal with the stressful event. As the body detects higher levels of glucocorticoids in the blood, a dual negative-feedback loop is initiated that directly reduces the release of CRF in the hypothalamus while simultaneously acting on the hippocampus, which also inhibits HPA functioning (Meyer & Quenzer, 2005). Consequently, it should not be surprising that research on the neurobiology of sexual victimization has documented that abuse can result in long-term changes in the HPA axis, which may increase a victim's risk for negative psychological and physical health sequelae (Hedtke et al., 2008). Although the results of these studies have been mixed, the majority suggest that sexual violence results in lower cortisol concentrations, leading to an overall hyporesponsiveness of the HPA system (Girdler et al., 2007; Seedat, Stein, Kennedy, & Hauger, 2003). Rebecca Campbell and colleagues (2008) have proposed that stress associated with sexual violence triggers an acute response, which increases the sensitivity of the negative-feedback loop in the HPA axis. When this feedback system becomes overly sensitive to the presence of glucocorticoids in the blood, it suppresses both the hypothalamus and the hippocampus, which results in lowered cortisol levels (Campbell et al., 2008). The long-term implications for lowered cortisol levels and HPA dysfunction are alarming. For instance, researchers hypothesize that reduced activity of the HPA axis is associated with stress-related disorders such as chronic fatigue syndrome, chronic headaches, fibromyalgia, rheumatoid arthritis, and abdominal pain. Since many of these disorders are reported as common sequelae among victims, dysfunction of the HPA axis and lowered cortisol levels may be another mediator between violence and health-related outcomes (Campbell et al., 2008).

Finally, research suggests that there may be an association between sexual victimization and recovery following traumatic brain injury (TBI). According to Reeves, Beltzman, and Killu (2000), patients with a history of sexual violence who have subsequently sustained a TBI frequently report reemergence of sequelae related to the abuse. These typically include intense flashbacks, behavioral disturbances, nightmares, and hypervigilance. Indeed, such individuals who have not reported PTSD symptomatology for many years may spontaneously re-experience vivid, intrusive, and disruptive episodes of past sexual trauma following TBI. Even more disturbing, evidence suggests that victims who have made the most adaptive recoveries from the violence, experience the most disruptive PTSD-symptoms after TBI occurs (Reeves et al., 2000). One possible explanation for this effect is that traumatized individuals develop a hyperaroused limbic system that over time may be inhibited by prefrontal neural structures, especially those in the right prefrontal area. However, in many cases of TBI, particularly those involving a motor vehicle accident, bony protrusions on the interior of the skull result in neurological insult to prefrontal brain tissue. Consequently, when the prefrontal area is damaged, it is unable to govern the effects of hyperarousal in the limbic system, resulting in the reoccurrence of PTSD symptomatology. Since recovery is typically prolonged in these individuals, future research is needed to better understand the relationship of victimization on subsequent TBI (Reeves et al., 2000).

BEHAVIORAL RESPONSES

The literature reviewed thus far provides ample evidence that sexual violence against women results in long-lasting and pervasive psychological, physical, and neurological sequelae. In addition to these negative effects, research also suggests that victims experience behavioral disturbances following victimization (Koss & Kilpatrick, 2001). For example, survivors are more likely to smoke cigarettes, engage in risky sexual activities, abuse substances, and exhibit negative social behaviors than other women (Resnick et al., 1997). Victims are even less likely to wear seat belts while driving than those without a history of sexual assault (Koss & Kilpatrick, 2001). According to Resnick et al. (1997), the most significant change in behavior subsequent to victimization is cigarette smoking. One study found that nearly 40 percent of women with a history of sexual violence were current smokers, compared to 25 percent of nonvictimized women. Even when controlling for the effects of race, education, and psychopathology, the prevalence of current smoking among victims was significantly higher than controls.

In addition, studies also have documented that individuals who experience sexual violence are more likely to engage in risky sexual behaviors such as having sex without using contraceptives (Neville & Heppner, 1999). In a sample of adults selected on the basis of engaging in risk behaviors for acquiring or transmitting HIV infection, approximately 54 percent of the women surveyed reported a history of sexual assault (Koss et al., 1994). Several other studies also have found that rape victims are more likely to engage in HIV risk behaviors including prostitution, intravenous drug use, and sex with other drug users compared to nonvictims (Resnick et al., 1997).

Research suggests that survivors of sexual violence are more likely to abuse substances than nonvictimized individuals (Sturza & Campbell, 2005), although the direction of this relationship remains unclear. Substance abuse has been identified as both a precursor and a consequence of victimization, and several alternatives have been proposed to explain this relationship (Champion et al., 2004). One theory suggests that substance abuse heightens an individual's risk for subsequent sexual violence. For instance, women who abuse alcohol and drugs may have an impaired ability to detect potential assailants compared to women who do not abuse these substances. These women may be targeted by perpetrators because they are viewed as more vulnerable to attack than other people (Champion et al., 2004). Other data support these assumptions, documenting a higher prevalence of sexual victimization among substance abusers. In studies among individuals presenting to hospital emergency departments, higher rates of alcohol or drug involvement have been related to injuries associated with sexual assault and rape. Furthermore, longitudinal research has reported that women who had used drugs in the previous year were significantly more likely to experience sexual assault before the next assessment period than women who were not drug users (H. Resnick et al., 2000).

A second theory indicates that victims abuse substances as a means of coping with the negative consequences of violence (i.e., self-medication) (Sturza & Campbell, 2005). After an assault, women may increase their use of alcohol and drugs in order to reduce symptoms of fear, anxiety, and depression (Resnick et al., 1997). Prospective data from the National Women's Study has confirmed this theory, suggesting that sexual assault leads to substance abuse in previously non-using individuals. Several studies conducted in accident and emergency departments also found that severe sexual violence preceded both alcohol and drug abuse in most cases (Campbell, 2002). According to Jacquelyn Campbell (2002), women with severe PTSD also may abuse substances to cope with specific groups of symptoms that are particularly distressing such as intrusive recollections, nightmares, and hyperarousal. Indeed, high comorbidity between assault-related PTSD and substance use disorders has been consistently documented in several studies. For example, approximately 45 percent of individuals diagnosed with PTSD subsequent to victimization also met criteria for substance use or abuse disorders, with 31 percent meeting criteria for alcohol abuse or dependence (Resnick et al., 2000).

A final theory suggests that there is a reciprocal relationship between sexual violence and substance abuse, whereby victimization leads to substance abuse, which in turn leads to subsequent victimization. As mentioned, sexual assault may lead women to engage in increased consumption of alcohol and drugs in order to alleviate negative sequelae. In turn, women who abuse substances may have an impaired ability to detect potential assailants making them more vulnerable to attack. Therefore, those who abuse substances as a coping behavior may be more likely to experience revictimization later in life than other individuals (Champion et al., 2004).

According to Neville and Heppner (1999), sexual violence has a profound effect on a woman's ability to continue to function in her various life roles including partner, friend, mother, and worker. The impact of violence on work performance persists for up to eight months. In some cases, women lose their jobs or are unable to continue working because factors associated with the victimization make it too difficult for them to function at pre-assault levels. Changing phone numbers, moving, staying home, and feeling suspicious of all male strangers are other frequent behaviors exhibited by assault victims (Neville & Heppner, 1999). Moreover, surveys have demonstrated that survivors of sexual assault are less likely than other individuals to marry or to report at least weekly contact with friends and relatives (Sarkar & R. Sarkar, 2005). A study conducted by Abdulrehman and De Luca (2001) found significant differences on the Social Dysfunction Rating Scale between women with a history of sexual abuse and nonvictimized individuals. For instance, women who were sexually abused as children had significantly higher levels of social dysfunction and had a tendency to report fewer satisfying relationships, friendships, and social interactions than nonabused controls. Also, these individuals were more likely to report higher levels of disinterest and lower levels of participation in community activities and affairs (Abdulrehman & De Luca, 2001). Clearly, sexual violence can have a significant effect on victims' social functioning and behavior.

ORGANIZATIONAL RESPONSES

Despite significant organizational encouragement, formal policies and procedures to aid victims in recovery remain slow to appear in primary-care settings, especially in the legal, medical, and mental health systems (Koss et al., 2003). This is reflected in research documenting that among all victims of sexual violence only 26 to 40 percent report their assault to the police, 27 to 40 percent seek medical care and forensic examinations, and 16 to 60 percent obtain mental health services (Campbell, 2008). Furthermore, the reactions of these organizations to a victim's traumatic experience can have profound implications for recovery and healing. If women do not receive needed services and/or are treated insensitively, post-assault help-seeking may become a "second victimization" to the initial traumatic experience (Campbell, 2008). A comprehensive article by Rebecca Campbell (2008) discusses organizational reactions to sexual violence, including the legal, medical, and mental health systems, and negative sequelae that victims experience as a result of these responses. This information will be reviewed in the following section.

When a woman seeks help following sexual victimization, her first encounter with the legal system is with a patrol officer who asks her to describe the assault. She is then assigned to a detective who conducts further investigation in order to determine if the case should be referred to a prosecutor. During this stage, she is repeatedly questioned about characteristics of the crime such as penetrations, use of force, or other control tactics in order to check for consistency. Many report that this questioning strays into issues involving what they were wearing at the time of the attack, their prior sexual histories, and whether or not they responded sexually to the assault. Victims rate these questions as particularly traumatic and emotionally unsettling, as well as simultaneously reinforcing with respect to feelings of shame and guilt. Research suggests that the investigation is designed to assess the prosecutorial strength of the cases. Indeed, approximately 56 to 82 percent of all reported rape cases are dropped (i.e., not referred to prosecutors) by law enforcement.

If a case does progress past the investigation phase, prosecutors often conduct their own interviews with the victim before deciding to file criminal charges. Prosecutors who are disinclined to charge typically engage in a lengthy exploration of any discrepancies in the account of the victim, pressing for explanations and proof. Those that do press charges attempt to coach survivors to respond appropriately when faced with difficult questions in court proceedings. Either way, these women are forced consistently to relive the assault and defend their characters to law enforcement personnel. In one study, interviews were conducted among 47 victims whose cases made it to trial or plea bargaining. Findings indicated that approximately one-third of these women felt inadequately prepared by prosecutors. Although they were repeatedly questioned, they were given little information about what to expect during their hearings. For every 100 sexual assault cases reported to law enforcement, on average 33 are referred to prosecutors, 16 are charged and moved into the court system, 12 result in a successful conviction, and 7 end in a prison sentence.

Many victims describe their encounters with the legal system as a dehumanizing ordeal characterized by interrogation, intimidation, and blame. Even those who had the opportunity to go to trial described the experience as frustrating, embarrassing, and distressing. Research suggests that secondary victimization can result in negative effects on women's mental health. For instance, in self-report characterizations of their psychological well-being, survivors indicated that as a result of their contact with the legal system, 87 percent felt bad about themselves, 71 percent felt depressed, 89 percent felt violated, 53 percent felt distrustful of others, and 80 percent were reluctant to seek further help. In a series of studies assessing victim/police contact, findings suggested that insufficient legal action (i.e., the case did not progress or was dropped) was associated with increased PTSD symptomatology. Likewise, high secondary victimization was related to increased PTSD severity.

Victims of sexual violence have extensive post-assault medical needs such as treatment for physical injuries, forensic examinations, screening for STDs, pregnancy testing, and emergency contraception. Although the majority of women are not physically injured following their attacks, law enforcement personnel, rape crisis centers, and social service agencies advise them to undergo a medical forensic exam. The medical forensic exam or "rape kit" typically involves plucking head and pubic hairs, swabbing the vagina, rectum, and mouth, and obtaining fingernail scrapings in the event that the victim scratched the perpetrator. Blood samples may also be collected for DNA, toxicology, and ethanol testing. Because sexual assault is rarely life-threatening, victims often experience long waits prior to the exam and are not allowed to eat, drink, or urinate so that the physical evidence remains intact. When these individuals are finally admitted, they receive a brief explanation about the procedure and are often shocked to discover that a pelvic exam is required immediately after being sexually violated.

Although forensic exams are the primary focus of hospital emergency departments, survivors also need information on the risk of STDs, HIV, prophylaxis (i.e., preventative medication to treat any STDs contracted during the assault), and pregnancy. Several federal agencies recommend that all sexual assault victims receive STD and HIV prophylaxis on a case-by-case basis. However, meta-analyses of hospital records suggest that only 34 percent of sexually victimized individuals receive these treatments. In one study, victims who were raped by someone they knew were less likely to receive information on STD or HIV prophylaxis than those who were raped by a stranger. Another study found that Caucasian women were significantly more likely than ethnic minority women to obtain information on HIV. Post-assault pregnancy services were also inconsistently provided. Only 40 percent to 49 percent of survivors receive information about the risk of pregnancy following sexual assault and 21 percent to 43 percent of women who need emergency contraception actually receive it.

In the process of administering the forensic exam, STD services, and pregnancy care, doctors and nurses ask questions about the assault including what the victim was wearing, her sexual response, and what she did to "cause" the attack. As with law enforcement, medical professionals may view these questions as appropriate. However, many victims find them very distressing. For example, negative responses from the medical system significantly exacerbated PTSD symptomatology in one sample of survivors. Another study found that women who did not receive basic medical services rated their medical experience as more hurtful, which was associated with increased PTSD severity. Specifically, nonstranger assault victims who encountered secondary victimization and minimal services had the worst outcomes, even compared to those who did not seek medical services.

Survivors of sexual violence may obtain mental health services from treatment outcome research, community clinics, private practice, or specialized agencies. Women who receive services by participating as research subjects typically receive high-quality treatment and numerous benefits. Unfortunately, this option is only available for individuals who live in communities where research is being conducted and who fit eligibility criteria. These treatments are not intended to provide large-scale services but hope to establish empirically supported treatments that can be utilized by many mental health professionals. Indeed, the most common way that victims receive services frequently involves care provided by psychologists, psychiatrists, counselors, and social workers in private or public community settings. Several studies indicate that women tend to have positive experiences with mental health professionals and characterize the therapists' help as useful and supportive. Research also suggests that community based mental health services are especially helpful for victims who have had negative encounters with the legal and medical systems. For instance, survivors with rape-related PTSD who were unable to obtain needed services from legal and medical professionals had significantly decreased PTSD symptomatology following mental health services compared to controls. Furthermore, victims may also receive services from specialized agencies such as rape crisis centers and domestic violence shelters. Rape crisis centers help victims negotiate with the legal and medical systems and provide individual and group counseling. One study compared PTSD symptoms before and after counseling among victims receiving services at a rape crisis center and found significant reductions in distress levels and self-blame compared to other individuals.

CONCLUSIONS

Sexual violence is prevalent in the United States, with 25 percent of women reporting assault at some point in their lives (Campbell, 2008). Research has consistently documented that victims experience intense psychological distress immediately following the attack (Neville & Heppner, 1999). The most common immediate reactions include fear and anxiety. However, depression, PTSD, mental pollution, and sexual dysfunction are also frequently reported among survivors (Bohn & Holz, 1996; Fairbrother & Rachman, 2004; Koss & Kilpatrick, 2001). Moderators and mediators that explain the relationship between sexual violence and psychological sequelae have also been documented in the literature. These include previous trauma history, coping strategies, negative social reactions, and characteristics associated with the assault, as well as social cognitions involving self-blame and perceived control (Koss et al., 2003). Furthermore, a number of physical health complaints are diagnosed disproportionately among survivors of sexual violence such as physical injuries, gynecological disorders, gastrointestinal disorders, and chronic pain (Koss & Kilpatrick, 2001). Several researchers suggest that classical conditioning, assault characteristics, and psychological distress might act as causal links between abuse and negative health outcomes; however, further research is needed to fully understand this relationship (Bohn & Holz, 1996; Resnick et al., 1997).

A growing body of research has reported that sexual violence has harmful effects on neurological functioning. Studies indicate that cognitive functioning, brain structures, HPA axis activity, cortisol levels, and recovery from TBI are different among victims of sexual violence when compared to nonvictims (Campbell, 2002; Fennema-Notestine et al., 2002; Jenkins et al., 2000; Wignall et al., 2004). In addition, survivors of sexual assault experience behavioral disturbances following victimization (Koss & Kilpatrick, 2001). These individuals are more likely to smoke cigarettes, engage in risky sexual activities, abuse substances, and exhibit negative social behaviors than other women (Resnick et al., 1997). Research had documented that victims are even less likely to wear seat belts while driving than those without a history of sexual assault (Koss & Kilpatrick, 2001). The organizational impact of violence has typically focused on the legal, medical, and mental health systems' reactions to survivors. Several studies have reported that negative experiences with legal personnel and medical professionals exacerbated PTSD severity. Victims who obtained mental health services subsequent to the attack had significantly decreased PTSD symptoms compared to those who did not receive these services (Campbell, 2008). Clearly, the evidence presented demonstrates that women who are sexually victimized experience a wide range of deleterious effects after the initial violence perpetrated against them.

REFERENCES

Abbey, A., BeShears, R., Clinton-Sherrod, A. M., & McAuslan, P. (2004). Similarities and differences in women's sexual assault experiences based on tactics used by the perpetrator. *Psychology of Women Quarterly, 28,* 323–332.

Abdulrehman, R. Y., & De Luca, R. V. (2001). The implications of childhood sexual abuse on adult social behavior. *Journal of Family Violence, 16,* 193–203.

Basile, K. C., Chen, J., Black, M. C., & Saltzman, L. E. (2007). Prevalence and characteristics of sexual violence victimization among U.S. adults, 2001–2003. *Violence and Victims, 22,* 437–448.

Black, M. C., & Breiding, M. J. (2008). Adverse health conditions and health risk behaviors associated with intimate partner violence United States, 2005. *Journal of the American Medical Association, 300,* 646–649.

Bohn, D. K., & Holz, K. A. (1996). Sequelae of abuse: Health effects of childhood sexual abuse, domestic battering, and rape. *Journal of Nurse-Midwifery, 41,* 442–456.

Campbell, J. C. (2002). Health consequences of intimate partner violence. *Lancet, 359,* 1331–1336.

Campbell, R. (2008). The psychological impact of rape victims' experiences with the legal, medical, and mental health systems. *American Psychologist, 63,* 702–717.

Campbell, R., Greeson, M. R., Bybee, D., & Raja, S. (2008). The co-occurrence of childhood sexual abuse, adult sexual assault, intimate partner violence, and sexual harassment: A mediational model of posttraumatic stress disorder and physical health outcomes. *Journal of Consulting and Clinical Psychology, 76,* 194–207.

Campbell, R., Lichty, L. F., Sturza, M., & Raja, S. (2006). Gynecological health impact of sexual assault. *Research in Nursing & Health, 29,* 399–413.

Champion, H. L., Foley, K. L., DuRant, R. H., Hensberry, R., Altman, D., & Wolfson, M. (2004). Adolescent sexual victimization, use of alcohol and other substances, and other health risk behaviors. *Journal of Adolescent Health, 35,* 321–328.

Chrisler, J. C., & Ferguson, S. (2006). Violence against women as a public health issue. *Annals of the New York Academy of Sciences, 1087,* 235–249.

Coker, A. L., Smith, P. H., Thompson, M. P., McKeown, R. E., Bethea, L., & Davis, K. E. (2002). Social support protects against the negative effects of partner violence on mental health. *Journal of Women's Health & Gender-Based Medicine, 11,* 465–476.

Cook, R. J., Dickens, B. M., & Thapa, S. (2005). Caring for victims of sexual abuse. *International Journal of Gynecology and Obstetrics, 91,* 194–199.

Draucker, C. B. (2001). Learning the harsh realities of life: Sexual violence, disillusionment, and meaning. *Health Care for Women International, 22,* 67–84.

Fairbrother, N., & Rachman, S. (2004). Feelings of mental pollution subsequent to sexual assault. *Behaviour Research and Therapy, 42,* 173–189.

Fennema-Notestine, C., Stein, M. B., Kennedy, C. M., Archibald, S. L., & Jernigan, T. L. (2002). Brain morphometry in female victims of intimate partner violence with and without posttraumatic stress disorder. *Biological Psychiatry, 51,* 1089–1101.

Frazier, P. A. (2003). Perceived control and distress following sexual assault: A longitudinal test of a new model. *Journal of Personality and Social Psychology, 84,* 1257–1269.

Gilboa-Schechtman, E. & Foa, E. B. (2001). Patterns of recovery from trauma: The use of intraindividual analysis. *Journal of Abnormal Psychology, 110,* 392–400.

Girdler, S. S., Leserman, J., Bunevicius, R., Klatzkin, R., Pedersen, C. A., & Light, K. C. (2007). Persistent alterations in biological profiles in women with abuse histories: Influence of premenstrual dysphoric disorder. *Health Psychology, 26,* 201–213.

Golding, J. M. (1999). Sexual-assault history and long-term physical health problems: Evidence from clinical and population epidemiology. *Current Directions in Psychological Science, 8,* 191–194.

Goodman, L. A., Koss, M. P., & Russo, N. F. (1993). Violence against women: Physical and mental health effects. Part I: Research findings. *Applied & Preventive Psychology, 2,* 79–89.

Groer, M. W., Thomas, S. P., Evans, G. W., Helton, S. & Weldon, A. (2006). Inflammatory effects and immune system correlates of rape. *Violence and Victims, 21,* 796–808.

Hedtke, K. A., Ruggiero, K. J., Fitzgerald, M. M., Zinzow, H. M., Saunders, B. E., Resnick, H. S., et al. (2008). A longitudinal investigation of interpersonal violence in relation to mental health and substance use. *Journal of Consulting and Clinical Psychology, 76,* 633–647.

Jenkins, M. A., Langlais, P. J., Delis, D., & Cohen, R. A. (2000). Attentional dysfunction associated with posttraumatic stress disorder among rape survivors. *The Clinical Neuropsychologist, 14,* 7–12.

Kaltman, S., Krupnick, J., Stockton, P., Hooper, L., & Green, B. L. (2005). Psychological impact of types of sexual trauma among college women. *Journal of Traumatic Stress, 18,* 547–555.

Klump, M. C. (2006). Posttraumatic stress disorder and sexual assault in women. *Journal of College Student Psychotherapy, 21,* 67–83.

Koss, M. P., Bailey, J. A., & Yuan, N. P. (2003). Depression and PTSD in survivors of male violence: Research and training initiatives to facilitate recovery. *Psychology of Women Quarterly, 27,* 130–142.

Koss, M. P., Figueredo, A. J., & Prince, R. J. (2002). Cognitive mediations of rape's mental, physical, and social health impact: Tests of four models in cross-sectional data. *Journal of Consulting and Clinical Psychology, 70,* 926–941.

Koss, M. P., Goodman, L. A., Browne, A., Fitzgerald, L. F., Keita, G. P., & Russo, N. F. (1994). The physical and psychological aftermath of rape. *No safe haven: Male violence against women at home, at work, and in the community* (pp. 177–199). Washington, DC: American Psychological Association.

Koss, M. P., & Kilpatrick, D. G. (2001). Rape and sexual assault. In E. Gerrity, T. M. Keane, & F. Tuma (Eds.), *The mental health consequences of torture* (pp. 177–193). New York: Kluwer Academic Publishers.

Krause, E. D., Kaltman, S., Goodman, L. A., & Dutton, M. A. (2008). Avoidant coping and PTSD symptoms related to domestic violence exposure: A longitudinal study. *Journal of Traumatic Stress, 21,* 83–90.

Lee, E. & Kleiner, B. H. (2003). How organizations should respond to rape in the workplace. *Journal of Employment Counseling, 40,* 123–128.

Littleton, H., & Breitkopf, C. R. (2006). Coping with the experience of rape. *Psychology of Women Quarterly, 30,* 106–116.

Meyer, J. S., & Quenzer, L. F. (2005). *Psychopharmacology: Drugs, the brain and behavior.* Sunderland, MA: Sinauer Associates.

Neville, H. A., & Heppner, M. J. (1999). Contextualizing rape: Reviewing sequelae and proposing a culturally inclusive ecological model of sexual assault recovery. *Applied & Preventive Psychology, 8,* 41–62.

Reeves, R. H., Beltzman, D., & Killu, K. (2000). Implications of traumatic brain injury for survivors of sexual abuse: A preliminary report of findings. *Rehabilitation Psychology, 45,* 205–211.

Resnick, H., Acierno, R., Holmes, M., Dammeyer, M., & Kilpatrick, D. (2000). Emergency evaluation and intervention with female victims of rape and other violence. *Journal of Clinical Psychology, 56,* 1317–1333.

Resnick, H. S., Acierno, R., & Kilpatrick, D. G. (1997). Health impact of interpersonal violence II: Medical and mental health outcomes. *Behavioral Medicine, 23,* 65–78.

Resick, P. A. (1993). The psychological impact of rape. *Journal of Interpersonal Violence, 8,* 223–255.

Sarkar, N. N., & Sarkar, R. (2005). Sexual assault on woman: Its impact on her life and living in society. *Sexual and Relationship Therapy, 20,* 407–419.

Seedat, S., Stein, M. B., Kennedy, C. M., & Hauger, R. L. (2003). Plasma cortisol and neuropeptide Y in female victims of intimate partner violence. *Psychoneuroendocrinology, 28,* 796–808.

Stein, M. B., Kennedy, C. M., & Twamley, E. W. (2002). Neuropsychological function in female victims of intimate partner violence with and without posttraumatic stress disorder. *Biological Psychiatry, 52,* 1079–1088.

Sturza, M. L., & Campbell, R. (2005). An exploratory study of rape survivors' prescription drug use as a means of coping with sexual assault. *Psychology of Women Quarterly, 29,* 353–363.

Ullman, S. E., & Brecklin, L. R. (2003). Sexual assault history and health-related outcomes in a national sample of women. *Psychology of Women Quarterly, 27,* 46–57.

Ullman, S. E., & Filipas, H. H. (2001). Predictors of PTSD symptom severity and social reactions in sexual assault victims. *Journal of Traumatic Stress, 14,* 369–389.

Ullman, S. E., Filipas, H. H., Townsend, S. M., & Starzynski, L. L. (2007). Psychosocial correlates of PTSD symptom severity in sexual assault survivors. *Journal of Traumatic Stress, 20,* 821–831.

Wignall, E. L., Dickson, J. M., Vaughan, P., Farrow, T. F., Wilkinson, I. D., Hunter, M. D., et al. (2004). Smaller hippocampal volume in patients with recent-onset posttraumatic stress disorder. *Biological Psychiatry, 56,* 832–836.

Zoellner, L. A., Goodwin, M. L., & Foa, E. B. (2000). PTSD severity and health perceptions in female victims of sexual assault. *Journal of Traumatic Stress, 13,* 635–649.

Chapter 4

Cross-Cultural Violence against Women and Girls: From Dating to Intimate Partner Violence

Janet Sigal
Dorota Wnuk Novitskie

Violence against women is a worldwide problem that has generated considerable research, political, and international interest, but that has failed to be reduced or eliminated to a significant degree even in the twenty-first century. In a recent opening speech at a United Nations (UN) event during the Commission on the Status of Women in March 2009, the UN Secretary General Ban Ki Moon declared that the "time for talk is over; the time for action is now!"

In this chapter, we will consider cross-cultural research, explanatory models, and empirical research on violence against women and girls within two contexts: dating violence and intimate partner violence (IPV) or domestic violence. We conceptualize both areas on a continuum: young girls, adolescents, or young adult women, possibly after being exposed to violent interactions between parents or peers, become victims of dating violence. This experience may lead young women to visualize violence between either dating partners or intimate partners as normal or expected. Once they become involved with a man in a long-term relationship, either by marriage or partnership, the violent pattern may continue. At some point, women in these relationships may accept the violence as normal, thus exhibiting attitudes that condone and tolerate the violent interactions.

In each of our sections, first we will examine some of the definitions associated with dating violence and IPV. In the following sections, we will review models that can be used to explain these types of violence, some estimates of statistics, empirical cross-cultural studies related to each type of violence, consequences to victims, types of perpetrators, and some proposed recommendations or programs to reduce or eliminate these behaviors.

Before addressing each type of violent pattern separately, some issues relevant to both dating violence and IPV should be discussed. To begin, accurate statistics are very difficult to determine even in developed countries but particularly in developing countries. In some areas of the world, neither dating violence nor IPV are considered appropriate to discuss in public or even in private. As the World Health Organization (WHO; 2005) report on violence against women suggested, unless accurate prevalence figures are obtained, there cannot be any accountability by nations to reduce this type of violence. In addition, often dating violence and IPV victims experience the same consequences and may blame themselves for their victimization. Perpetrators also may exhibit similar characteristics in dating violence and IPV settings.

There are, however, differences in both situations. Obviously, targets of violence in dating settings are younger in general than in IPV, and also may be less educated and established in society. In some parts of the world, particularly in patriarchal societies, dating is prohibited, so that violence in relationships may not occur until a couple is engaged prior to an arranged marriage. In addition, although many countries have specific laws or statutes against IPV, whether or not these laws are enforced, dating violence often is covered under general violence and assault, or sexual assault laws. Peer influence or pressure may be considered to have more of an impact on adolescent or young adults than adults in a marriage or long-term partnership relationship, but pressure also can emanate from cultural or societal contexts.

There are some other issues that we will emphasize in this chapter. We believe that cross-cultural attitudes toward dating and IPV are important to ascertain because cultural attitudes can influence whether or not policy or laws against these types of violence are developed and enforced, and even whether victims are willing to go forward with complaints to the police or to the authorities. On a positive note, if attitudes informed by culture can be changed, then there is the possibility that laws against violence in dating and IPV may be adopted. In addition, particular care to maintain confidentiality and protect research subjects must be adopted in these cross-cultural studies to prevent harm from coming to victims who volunteer to participate. Finally, approaches to reduce or eliminate these types of violence must include men in these efforts. As Ban Ki Moon (March 2009) so strongly and clearly emphasized, it must be understood that "real men do not hit women" and also that real men do not stand by and watch other men abuse young girls and women without intervening.

DATING VIOLENCE

According to the Bureau of Justice Special Report on Intimate Partner Violence in the United States (2000), women ages 16 to 24 experience the highest per capita rates of intimate violence. This rate accounts for roughly 20 women out of 1000 (Rennision & Welchans, 2000). The report further indicates that one in three high school students will be, or already have been, in an abusive relationship, with some high schools reporting up to 50 percent of their female students having been abused by a significant other. Such statistics are echoed in a study published by the Archives of Pediatrics and Adolescent Medicine (Roberts & Klein, 2003), which reported that one-third of the 920 students surveyed experienced dating violence during high school. One out of five college-aged women experience some form of dating violence, and more than four in every ten incidents of domestic violence involves nonmarried but romantically involved individuals (Bureau of Justice Special Report: Intimate Partner Violence, May 2000). Furthermore, in 1995, 7 percent of all murder victims were young women who were killed by their boyfriends. Seventeen-year-old Heather Norris met such a fate, when she was "stabbed, dismembered and discarded in trash bags" at the hands of her boyfriend of three years after several attempts to leave the relationship (Olson, 2009).

Recent news coverage of dating abuse in the United States has become more prevalent, as illustrated by the widely circulated report of a domestic assault by her boyfriend Chris Brown that left singer Rihanna with "bruises and a scratch on her face" (Blow, 2009). While these reports fall short of offering specific details of the assault, media attention has allowed new discussions to emerge regarding the need for prevention of dating violence. Again, limited research is available regarding the link between the media and dating violence; however, Manganello (2008) suggests that the media may serve as a risk factor in a teen violence. The study further indicates that teens may be prone to spending time acting out in real life that what they see on TV or on the Internet.

DEFINITIONS

Dating violence is the physical, emotional and verbal abuse of one partner by the other partner in a romantic relationship. Abusive behavior is any act carried out by one partner aimed at hurting or controlling the other. Dating violence occurs in heterosexual and homosexual relationships. A violent relationship means more than physical aggression by a person who claims to love the other. Violence in a relationship often is about power and control (Eaton et al., 2007). Research regarding violence in dating has been limited as the focus of interpersonal violence historically has been on married persons. However, the same type of violence happens between people who are dating, and at times may even be more violent and hurtful. Teenagers are not as experienced in relationships and may feel pressured by peers to remain with a violent partner due to reasons of popularity or status or simply for the sake of having a relationship. Oftentimes teens are not aware of the potential signs of a violent relationship. Such relationships may begin with verbal and emotional abuse and control, which then may lead to physical violence (Roberts & Klein, 2003).

CLASSIC MODELS OF TEEN DATING VIOLENCE

Some experts hold that men and women are equally aggressive. They further suggest that this behavior should be seen as an extension of or part of a larger pattern of family conflict and discord. Supporters of this viewpoint generally focus only on the studies that measure the number of times a person perpetrates or experiences certain acts of violence, such as pushing, slapping, or hitting. What is of interest is that these studies tend to show that women admit to perpetrating slightly more physical violence than men (Archer, 2000). The majority of studies that investigate teen dating violence have focused mainly on using the violence "act" scales. Another school of thought in regard to dating violence is that men are more likely to cause serious injury to a woman, especially when she is his intimate partner. Experts suggest that men tend to come from patriarchal societies. Therefore, the use of violence is a means of exerting and maintaining power and control over women (Dobash & Dobash, 1980). This line of research tends to avoid "act" scales, as "act" scales are not believed to accurately portray the nature of violence in intimate relationships. This criticism is based on the lack of consideration of the degree of injury inflicted, coercion and controlling behaviors in these measures. "Act" scale studies do not consider the fear experienced by the victim, or the circumstances under which the acts occurred (Kimmel, 2002). These arguments further state that studies using "act" scales lack information on the effects of power and control and generally focus on more common and relatively minor forms of aggression. The more severe, albeit relatively rare, forms of violence in dating and intimate partner relationships tend to be overlooked (Dobash & Dobash, 1980). Researchers from this perspective use data related to severe injuries, and generally conduct in-depth interviews with victims and perpetrators (Archer, 2000). While the above views are classic theories of dating violence, historically they stem from adult perspectives. Application to adolescent relationships may be problematic and also not appropriate. Although these views of adult IPV can be informative and helpful in understanding some dynamics of teen dating violence, they cannot be relied on to answer all questions. Therefore, there is a need to better understand how teen dating relationships differ from adult romantic relationships.

THEORETICAL MODEL OF DATING VIOLENCE

Riggs and O'Leary (1989) proposed a model of dating violence. This model offered a comprehensive background situational perspective that drew on social learning theory. The model stipulated that behaviors are learned by watching and imitating others, and then are maintained through various forms of reinforcement. The following situational variables were examined in this model: alcohol or drug use, use of aggression by the partner, skills in resolving conflict, and length of relationship. This model also included the following contextual factors: presence of aggression in dating relationship, exposure to aggression by parent, view of aggression as an appropriate response to problems, and prior aggression. Therefore the effect of situational and contextual factors on teenage relationships was examined.

Luthra and Gidycz (2006) evaluated the Riggs and O'Leary model of dating violence using a number of surveys and measures. Their results indicated that specific constructs can be useful in prediction of future dating violence. However, they also found the model to be more predictive of females (83 percent) rather than males (30 percent). It should be noted that the most significant predictor of female violence was presence of aggression by a male partner. These women were 108 times more likely to act out violently against their partner, compared to those women who were not physically assaulted. For men, however, the most significant predictor of perpetration of violence found was the length of relationship. For every six months that the man was in the relationship, his likelihood of aggression doubled.

FACTORS AFFECTING DATING VIOLENCE

Gender Power Differential

One striking difference between teen and adult romantic relationships is the power differential between the man and the woman. Teen relationships tend to lack the elements traditionally associated with greater male power in adult relationships (Wekerle & Wolfe, 1999). This lack of power is a result of several factors. One factor is that unless there are extenuating circumstances, teenage girls are not financially dependent on romantic partners. Unless there are children involved, and there is a need to provide and protect, adolescent girls tend to be more dependent on their parents. One study of seventh, ninth and eleventh graders in Toledo (Giordano, 2007) interviewed boys and girls to investigate the power dynamics in these relationships. The majority of the boys and girls interviewed said they had a relatively "equal balanced" relationship in regard to power. However, in cases where a power imbalance was noted, the female students were more likely to admit to having the power over the boyfriend. The boys surveyed agreed, indicating that they had less power than the girls did in the relationship. Furthermore, boys who reported a presence of physical aggression felt even less empowered than the boys who were not in physically aggressive relationships. The presence or lack of aggression did not make a difference in the girls' perception of power; girls reported no perceived difference in power regardless of whether or not their relationships included physical aggression (Giordano, 2007).

LACK OF EXPERIENCE

Another major difference between violent adult and violent adolescent relationships is the lack of experience teens have in maneuvering through their romantic relationships. If the teens in the relationships do not know how to negotiate, communicate, and relate to their romantic partner, that can lead to reinforcement of poor coping strategies, such as verbal and physical aggression (Dutton, 1995). A teen who has not had much experience in romantic relationships may struggle to express affection and may act out aggressively when he or she experiences frustration or jealousy toward the romantic partner. This concept was supported by a study in which boys and girls participated in focus groups on dating. The results found that physical aggression can stem from an inability to communicate feelings and a deficit in skills that ordinarily lead to constructive methods of dealing with frustration (Laursen & Collins, 1994).

As adolescents get older, their idealist view of a romantic relationship becomes more grounded in reality. In addition, with age, their ability to experience closeness and intimacy increases (Montgomery, 2005). This change is positive, as adolescents who hold on to idealistic beliefs about dating relationships can at times feel disillusioned and may not be able to cope effectively with interpersonal conflict (Kerpelman, 2007). In addition, many adolescents express themselves through aggression as they have not yet learned how to appropriately express and experience intimacy and communication.

INFLUENCE OF PEERS

Friends are extremely important during the adolescent years. During this time, friends exert more influence on each other than at any other time in their development. (Giordano, 2007). Research shows that peer interactions and behaviors have a great impact on adolescents' attitudes and behaviors, especially in relation to dating violence (Adelman & Kil, 2007). In addition to this influence, friends during the teen years are present in day to day activities and can be very involved in a teenage couple's social life, as teens tend to date in groups or double date more than twice as much as they go on one-on-one dates (Molidor & Tolman, 1998). Therefore, relationship dynamics tend to be very public, and often are witnessed in groups of friends or during school time hours. Boys and girls tend to act very differently when surrounded by peers, to fit into the expected norms. One study found that boys would respond with physical aggression when hit by their girlfriend, just to save themselves the embarrassment of being hit in front of peers (Fredland et al., 2005).

Teens also argue about various issues. For example, many teens argue about jealousy, how much time is dedicated to one another, and threats of a new significant other (Fredland et al. 2005). Although these conflicts can be viewed as normal and almost appropriate for this age group, dealing with such issues when they are not emotionally and developmentally ready can lead teens to experience conflict, physical aggression, and other problematic coping strategies, such as efforts to gain control, stalking, and psychological or verbal abuse.

INTERNATIONAL STUDIES ON DATING VIOLENCE

Cross-cultural research on dating violence is limited. Much of the data regarding this type of IPV comes from the International Dating Violence Study, which although comprehensive in scope, is limited to just one study (Straus, 2007). The countries involved in this study include two African nations: South Africa and Tanzania; seven Asian countries: China, Hong Kong, Taiwan, India, Japan, South Korea, and Singapore; Australia and New Zealand; thirteen European countries: Belgium (Flemish and French sites), Germany, Great Britain, Greece, Hungary, Lithuania, Malta, Netherlands, Portugal, Romania, Russia, Sweden, Switzerland (French and German sites); four Latin American countries: Brazil, Guatemala, Mexico, and Venezuela; two Middle Eastern countries: Iran and Israel; and two North American countries: Canada (Anglo and French sites) and the United States (Mexican American, historically black colleges, and other sites) (Straus, 2007).

Straus (2007) investigated the widely held beliefs that interpersonal physical violence is almost entirely perpetrated by men, and that the major risk factor for interpersonal violence is male dominance in the relationship. Straus tested his hypothesis across the aforementioned 32 countries and surveyed 13,601 university students. The results showed that almost one-third of the female as well as male students physically assaulted a dating partner in the previous 12 months, and that the most frequent pattern was bidirectional where both partners were violent, followed by "female-only" violence. Violence by only the male partner was the least frequent pattern according to both male and female participants. Straus also investigated whether dominance by one partner is a crucial aspect of the etiology of partner violence. The results showed that dominance by either the male or the female partner is associated with an increased probability of violence. These results question the assumption that interpersonal violence is primarily a male crime and that women are only violent at times of self-defense (Straus, 2007).

Using the information from the above study, Hines and Straus (2007) also evaluated the relationship between binge drinking and aggression in dating relationship. The study sampled 7,921 students at 32 universities worldwide. The strongest positive association between binge drinking and violence was found in Pune, India. Similar findings also emerged in Mississippi, United States, and Leicester, England. No gender differences were found.

Another focus of the data from the International Dating Violence Study was an evaluation of gender in the prevalence and chronic nature of dating aggression (Straus & Ramirez, 2007), with a focus on participants from universities in Mexico and America. Findings indicated that students, across the four universities surveyed, experienced dating violence anywhere from 29.7 percent to 46 percent in the last 12 months, with students in Juarez, Mexico, reporting the highest percentage. Chronicity of severity of assaults was consistent across the four universities. Another interesting finding was that when only one partner was violent, the female was almost twice as likely (19 percent) as the male (9.8 percent) to perpetrate the violence.

Lysova and Douglas (2008) also utilized the data from the International Dating Violence Study to focus on dating violence among Russian college students. Their findings indicated no gender difference regarding victimization (females: 23.1 percent; males: 28.6 percent). However, statistical significance was found between the genders regarding reporting having assaulted an intimate partner, with 35.6 percent of females reporting acts of aggression and 20.6 percent of males. Although not statistically significant, women reported higher rates of psychological aggression (66.7 percent) compared to men (56.5 percent). The authors suggested that men in Russian universities either report or commit lower rates of dating violence due to fear of expulsion from universities or forced enlistment in the military.

Doroszewicz and Forbes (2008) also utilized the same data pool and focused on physical aggression and injury among college age students in Poland. The findings indicated that 15 percent of men and 25 percent of women reported having perpetrated physical violence against a partner at least once. Few other gender differences were noted; however, women did report engaging in more frequent psychological aggression than men. The authors attributed the findings to high rates of domestic violence in Poland, suggesting that violence is a learned behavior. In addition, recent and rapid changes in women's role in the home and in the workplace are believed to have contributed to these rates.

Wang and Petula (2007) conducted interviews and focus groups to explore men's and women's views of physical aggression by women in dating relationships. The sample was limited to 20 participants (13 women and 7 men) and offered insight into women's identification with an aggressive female character in a popular Asian movie "Sassy Girl." Female participants identified with the aggressive character, and to some extent were reported to appreciate the aggression perpetrated by this character, often justifying and defending her behavior. Men on the other hand, in an attempt to maintain levels of masculinity, reported the woman's aggression to be playful and not hostile. Furthermore, the men surveyed reported that men cannot be hurt by such physical contact and "cannot be defeated by such challenges" (p. 628).

In another cross-cultural study, Sherer (2009) focused on dating violence in Jewish and Arab male and female teens in Israel. The study examined the effect of sociodemographic variables on male and female behavior. The sample consisted of 1,357 Arab and Jewish youths who were surveyed on measures of threatening, relational, physical, sexual and verbal abuse. Dating violence was found to be high among teens in Israel, with the highest rates found among Arab youths. Although girls were involved in every type of dating violence, boys exhibited higher scores. The author explained that such prevalence can be understood in terms of cultural norms and expectations of roles of men and women in society.

VIOLENCE IN ENGAGED COUPLES

Halford, Sanders, and Behrens (2004) studied the relationship between physical aggression in engaged couples and the presence of violence in the family of origin in Australia. The researchers surveyed 71 engaged couples. Men exposed to parental violence experienced more negative emotions and thoughts, and found it difficult to participate in subsequent focus group discussions. Couples in which only the woman was exposed to parental violence did not appear to have concerns regarding negative affect or conflict between the two engaged people.

Haj-Yahia (2006) also examined violence perpetrated against Arab women in Israel who were engaged. Of 1,111 engaged Arab women in the sample, between 1 and 11 percent of the women reported experiencing physical aggression, and between 8 and 48 percent reported experiencing psychological aggression. When conflicts with their partner were not discussed or worked through, these women were more likely to suffer from low self-esteem, depression, stress and anxiety.

Haj-Yahia and Edleson (1994), in an earlier related study, surveyed Arab-Palestinian men living in Israel as to their means of working through conflict with their fiancées. The research focused on the following three frameworks: male dominance, intergenerational learning, and interpersonal skills deficits to determine the role played by these factors in men's relationships. Haj-Yahia and Edleson found that men who did not come from violent homes were more likely to engage in discussion and reasoning as a means of resolving conflict, and were more open to an egalitarian household. On the other hand, men who grew up in violent homes were more likely to be verbally and physically abusive toward their fiancées, were less likely to see what was wrong with their actions, and were more likely to hold patriarchal views.

OUTCOMES

Effects on Mental Health

Chan, Straus, Brownridge, Tiwari, and Leung (2008) evaluated the prevalence of dating violence and suicidal ideation among male and female university students. Information also was obtained from the International Dating Violence Study, with a focus on the prevalence of physical assault, sexual coercion, and suicidal ideation among these students. The authors sampled 16,000 students from 22 universities in 21 countries. The results showed that although there were large differences among countries, even the lowest rates of dating violence were quite high. Male and female students had similar rates regarding the proportion of having physically assaulted a partner, and having been a victim of sexual coercion. An increased rate of suicidal ideation was found among both perpetrators and victims of physical assault. This finding was linked to the occurrence of depression. This study highlighted a need for universal screening and targeted services for violence, depression and suicide prevention.

Effects of Abusive and Neglectful Childhood

Straus and Savage (2005) investigated the relationship between neglectful parents and the child becoming involved in a violent dating relationship. The study was conducted with university students from 17 countries, and the data was once again collected through the International Dating Violence Study. Students in Pusan, Korea, reported experiencing the highest level of childhood neglect (34.4 percent) followed by 28.6 percent of students in Hong Kong. The lowest reported prevalence of neglect was in New Hampshire (3.2 percent). Straus and Savage also found that the more neglectful behaviors that the student had experienced, the more likely they were to have assaulted a dating partner. The link between neglect experienced as a child and dating violence was strongest at universities where dating violence was more prevalent.

TYPOLOGIES OF ADOLESCENT DATING VIOLENCE PERPETRATION

Foshee et al. (2007) interviewed 116 boys and girls who were previously identified to have been perpetrators of dating violence. Using narrative descriptions, the authors developed typologies of dating violence perpetration that were context specific. Most of the boys' acts of violence were attributed to "escalation prevention," or attempts to stop a girlfriend from inflicting further violence. Female perpetration was identified by motive, preceding events, and abuse by parents. From these reports, the following four types of perpetrators were proposed: patriarchal terrorism response, anger response, ethic enforcement, and first-time aggression response.

Patriarchal terrorism response was created from responses that girls offered indicating that the boyfriends attempted to control them through physical or psychological means. Acts committed by the girls that were coded in this typology included the following: described physical violence against a boyfriend who had historically been psychologically or physically abusive, or acting violently against a boyfriend immediately after he was physically or psychologically abusive. It should be noted that 38.5 percent of females met the criteria for patriarchal terrorism response.

Anger response differed from the type listed above in motive, precipitating events, and history of violence. For an act to be labeled as "anger response," the description given by the female had to meet the following criteria: no indicated history of past physical abuse by the boyfriend, no report of immediately precipitating violence by the boyfriend before the violent act, or the girl needed to report that the reason for such violence was motivated by a desire to be violent. Twenty-five percent of females met the criteria for anger response.

Ethic enforcement was reported in 19.2 percent of female participants. For ethic enforcement to be coded, the female had to report the following: violence was used to communicate to the boyfriend that he had done something wrong and she was not going to accept it, no evidence of history of abuse by boyfriend was noted, and there was no report of violence being used against the girl immediately before her violent act. Some common "wrongs" that resulted in the girls' violence included the following: cheating, flirting with another girl, indulging in too much alcohol or drugs, "talking ugly" to her, removing himself from an argument, pressuring her to have sex, and ruining prom night.

First time aggression response was reported in 17.3 percent of the females surveyed. For the act to be labeled as first time aggression, the following had to be reported: there was a report of the boy using physical violence against the girl immediately before the act, and there was no history of physical aggression by the boy prior to this incident. In these instances, most of the girls surveyed reported their aggression to be attributed to self-defense, while others reported retaliation against the boy for wronging them.

For boys, most of their acts were identified as "escalation prevention" or attempts to stop the escalation of violence by their female counterparts. For the acts to be labeled as such, a male had to report the following: he used restraint while the girlfriend was being violent against him, he attempted to stop her from harming him with a weapon, or stop the possibility of having violence against him. Other acts were noted by the authors; however no commonalities were noted to offer additional specific typologies.

RECOMMENDATIONS AND PROGRAMS

Black et al. (2008) evaluated factors that resulted in teenaged victims of dating seeking help. The authors found a large risk factor for not seeking help was when the violence occurred in isolation, with no witnesses. However, when the violence was witnessed or observed by a third party, the victim was more likely to begin to speak about the violence, become open to the possibility of intervention, and seek help. In addition, boys were less likely than girls to seek help. In light of such findings, "Safe Dates" programs have gained greater popularity. After a four-year study, participants in safe date programs have seen a decrease in physical, serious physical, and sexual dating violence perpetration and victimization (Foshee et al., 2007).

Wekerle and Wolfe (1999) conducted a literature review of six relationship violence prevention programs designed for and practiced with teenage students. One of the programs discussed was in a larger community, while the remaining five programs were school-based. Prevention of dating violence was targeted on two levels: toward all high school students, as well as toward selected adolescent populations, such as youths with histories of maltreatment, or problems with peer violence. These programs addressed specific skills and knowledge that opposed the use of violent and abusive behavior toward intimate partners. In addition, one program addressed interpersonal violence more generally, and was also included in this review because of its implications for dating violence initiatives. Positive changes were found across studies in violence-related attitudes and knowledge. In addition, positive gains were noted in self-reported decreases in perpetration of dating violence, with less consistent evidence in self-reported victimization. Limited follow-up and generalizability was noted; therefore the possibility of greater application is questionable.

Foshee et al. (2001) studied predictors of dating violence. The study focused on eighth and ninth graders in one county in a U.S. school. These participants were asked to complete baseline questionnaires and were again evaluated 18 months later. Some risk factors found for males being abused by females in a dating relationship included having friends who were victims of dating violence, using alcohol, and being of a race other than white. However, risk factors for males perpetrating the violence included attitudes that condoned dating violence. The researchers also suggested that any interventions that are implemented for school-aged children should be separate and specific for males and females. In addition, those found to be at greater risk should be targets for intervention first, with other interventions becoming more available only when there is funding.

Valls, Puigvert, and Duque (2008) reported that schools in Spain are working to implement preventive socialization in the field of education. The authors proposed that a correlation exists between prevention of dating violence measures and promotion of power equality in relationships. They suggested that the current presentation of violence in the media is glorified and made attractive to young teens. Therefore, work should be done to make nonviolent movies, videos, and games just as attractive and normative. The authors suggested that this approach also would undermine double standards in relationships, and healthy care and passion could be viewed as a possible replacement for aggression.

IPV: A CROSS-CULTURAL PERSPECTIVE

The WHO's (2005) Summary Report on its multi-country study on IPV and violence against women, stated that "Since the World Conference on Human Rights held in Vienna in 1993, and the Declaration on the Elimination of Violence Against Women in the same year, civil society and governments have acknowledged that violence against women is a public policy and human rights concern" (p. vii). The Foreword of the Report further stated that "Violence against women is both a consequence and a cause of gender inequality (p. viii). CEDAW, or the Convention on the Elimination of Discrimination against Women, is a UN tool designed to address this issue.

DEFINITIONS

In 1993, the UN General Assembly adopted the following definition of violence against women: "Any act of gender-based violence that results in, or is likely to result in, physical, sexual, or psychological harm or suffering to women, including threats of such acts, coercion, or arbitrary deprivation of liberty, whether occurring in public or private life" (UN, 1993, Article 1).

Although recently, considerable research attention has been focused on whether IPV or domestic violence is perpetrated only by men against women, or can be identified with either partner in a marriage or relationship (Archer, 2000; Frieze, 2005), for the purposes of this chapter, we will restrict our discussion to IPV perpetrated solely by men against women.

MODELS OF IPV

Feminist Power Model

In this classic model, male-dominated societies are viewed as reinforcing traditional gender roles in which men are the wage earners and make all the decisions, and women stay at home and take care of the husband and the family. As a result, men have more power and status than women (Sigal & Annan, 2008). As described above, the WHO Report (2005) emphasized inequality between men and women as a cause of IPV.

Sexist attitudes also can provide a foundation for gender-based violence that is related to the inequality between men and women. For example, the Ambivalent Sexism Inventory (ASI) which was developed by Glick and Fiske (1997) distinguished between Hostile Sexism, measuring hostility toward the equality of women and men, and Benevolent Sexism, which is rather paternalistic and implies that women are weak and fragile and must be protected. In each case, women are seen as having inferior status. It was established in cross-cultural studies using the ASI, that higher scores on this measure were associated with more gender inequality in the countries sampled.

The Gender Equity Index (2008) has compiled a list of gender equity in many countries around the world and will be referred to again later in this chapter.

Hypermasculinity

This model is an extension of the feminist power model. According to this approach, "macho men" often see violence as an acceptable way to achieve and maintain power over women. In addition, these individuals may associate violence against women with being more "masculine" (Kilmartin & Allison, 2007).

Patriarchal Culture and Culture of Honor Models

Both of these models stem from an extension of the feminist power model's conception of women having inferior status.

Patriarchal Culture

As Haj Yahia (2002) describes in his article, the patriarch, or male head of the family, has complete control over the family including making all the decisions for the family. In particular, since patriarchal societies often view men as sexual predators (although without the condemnation that this behavior would produce in other types of cultures), their women must be protected at all times. Therefore, they cannot go food shopping without a male relative or even seek medical help unless their husband allows them to do so. In fact, after the birth of a child, many women lose their lives because of their inability to access emergency medical help.

Culture of Honor

This type of culture is an extreme version of a patriarchal society. As described by Vandello and Cohen (2003), in these cultures, the "honor" of the male head of the family is directly related to the purity or "chastity" of the women in his family. If a woman strays, either by committing adultery, being raped, or being seen in the company of men who are not relatives, the patriarch is required to punish her, often violently. The patriarch must "wash the honor with blood" to restore his honor and that of his family (p. 999). In many culture of honor societies, the women in the family are under the control of their fathers until they are married, under the control of their husbands when they are wives, and under the control of their sons when they are widows. In extreme forms, the punishment may take the form of an "honor killing." As a result of increased punishment for honor killings in some countries (for example, Jordan), some young women in rural areas have been locked in a room with a gun until they kill themselves, an act which is now termed "honor suicides."

There have been many egregious examples of violence against women in honor cultures, but we will just mention a few to illustrate our description of these models.

A few years ago, in Saudi Arabia, a girl was in a car with her boyfriend when she was raped by a number of men. She was sentenced to 160 lashings and possibly a jail term, but after the case attracted media attention worldwide, the King pardoned her. More recently, in 2009, a woman in her seventies in Saudi Arabia walked outside her house with two workmen and also was sentenced to several lashings. Media attention so far has not been successful in this case.

Another example was in the fall of 2008 in Pakistan. Three girls refused to marry older men chosen for them by their fathers (they were teenagers and the men were in their 40s and 50s), because they wanted to choose their own husbands. These young girls, and two older women who supported them, were all buried alive. Finally, in the spring of 2009, a 17-year-old girl was repeatedly lashed by several men in a rural area of Pakistan for an unknown "crime" which many suggested was fraudulent. However, after cell phone photographs were sent all over Pakistan, the incident caused a tremendous outcry, both in Pakistan and throughout the world. The Pakistan chief judge was not satisfied with the legal response to this outrageous violent behavior and sent a government official to the area to report on what actually occurred.

INTERNATIONAL STUDIES ON IPV

In this section, we will review a selective number of cross-cultural research investigations on the prevalence of IPV and attitudes toward IPV. We will relate these studies to models and explanations described in an earlier section. Clearly, all cross-cultural researchers agree that estimates of IPV most likely represent underreporting worldwide. In addition, comparison of prevalence figures is extremely difficult and any conclusions must be made with caution, due to the variability of the methods used in these estimates.

In some of the studies that we will review, the focus has been on attitudes toward IPV rather than on the prevalence of IPV. However, IPV prevalence estimates tend to be highly correlated with attitudes condoning or even supporting IPV. If attitudes are positive toward violence against women, it is likely that women in these cultures will experience IPV to a higher degree than women in cultures that disapprove of and punish perpetrators of IPV.

One of the most significant investigations of IPV cross-culturally was sponsored by the WHO in 2005. This study encompassed data from women residing in several countries, and in 15 locations within these countries. Interviewers obtained data from countries representing a widely diverse sampling including 24,000 respondents from Bangladesh, Brazil, Ethiopia, Japan, Namibia, Peru, Samoa, Serbia and Montenegro, Thailand, and the United Republic of Tanzania. Lifetime prevalence of IPV ranged from 15 percent (Japan) to just over 70 percent. Prevalence in the year before the study again revealed large variability among samples. The lowest IPV rate was in Japan, with just under 5 percent, and the highest was in Ethiopia, which had a rate of almost 55 percent.

There were many advantages of this worldwide study of IPV including the sponsorship of this major international health organization, WHO, the collaboration of a wide variety of experts and women's organizations, the very large sample size, the variety of countries involved in the project, and the use of standardized measures and intensive training of female interviewers because of the sensitivity of the topic. However, there were several criteria that were used to determine which countries would be included in the study that may limit the generalization of the results. Prior to sampling women in a particular country, the researchers determined if there was a positive political atmosphere in the country which would suggest that the government would respond positively to the survey, there had to be a lack of information on the amount of IPV in the country, and women's groups had to be active in the country in order to turn the data-collecting phase into the stage of implementation of the recommendations stemming from the report. Although these criteria were reasonable, the question of whether the results may generalize to other countries which may not exhibit these same characteristics is at issue. A further question related to the methods of the study, is that the emphasis was placed on physical and sexual IPV, despite the suggestion in the report that emotional or psychological abuse often is associated with physical abuse, and can have long-lasting negative consequences. However, despite these considerations, the study is one of the best in terms of careful planning, training and collection of data in so many countries using standardized measures.

ASIAN STUDIES

Hong Kong and Mainland China

Prevalence of figures from Hong Kong and mainland China vary. Xu et al. (2005) sampled about 600 women (with close to a 90 percent acceptance and return rate) at a clinic in Fuzhou, China. Face-to-face measures modified from the WHO multi-country study were administered to determine the percentage of IPV in the sample. Results indicated that 43 percent of women from a sample in mainland China reported having experienced IPV in the lifetime of their marriage, and 26 percent had been abused in the last year. Marital conflict and financial control by husbands were two of the factors associated with IPV. Attitudes were supportive of wife beating: 36 percent of the women surveyed believed that wife-beating was appropriate and approved of if the wife had committed adultery. Although the large sample supports the validity of the conclusions, limitations of the study include the self-report nature of the methodology and the lack of participation of men. One other interesting conclusion stemmed from the research. Xu et al. suggested that although the Chinese society supposedly now supports more economic equality between men and women (women should "hold up half of the sky," p. 84), their respondents did not appear to have internalized or accepted this concept.

Another recent investigation by Chan, Brownridge, Tiwari, Fong, and Leung (2008) concluded that IPV still is a significant problem in

Hong Kong and Chinese societies. As part of a larger study employing face-to-face interviews in Hong Kong (there was a very high response rate of about 70 percent), the authors selected a sample of 1,870 women and included an additional question on the effect of in-law conflict on IPV. The larger study utilized the Revised Conflict Tactics Scale (CTS2), an often-used standardized measure, to investigate prevalence of IPV. Prevalence figures in this study were lower than in the Xu et al. investigation (lifetime figures were approximately 8.5 percent, and the previous year figures were about 4.5 percent). Since the Chan et al. study was conducted in Hong Kong and the Xu et al. study in mainland China, it is difficult to directly compare these figures. Although Hong Kong has experienced more of a Western influence than mainland China, it still is questionable whether either self-report figure is accurate.

In the article, Chan et al. suggested that common risk factors that have been discovered in other countries also may be important in the explanation of IPV victimization in China. The main risk markers in the Chan et al. study included a younger age of the wife, and financial situations being unfavorable in the home, as well as the partner's alcohol abuse. An interesting finding was that if the wife had a higher income she was more at risk for abuse. The authors offered the explanation that a financially successful wife might demand more equality in the home, and that might cause increased conflict with her husband. Other studies have produced conflicting results regarding the relationship between the wife's education and income and prevalence of IPV.

The major contribution of the Chan et al. research was to investigate the role of in-law conflict in IPV. The authors found that this type of conflict, particularly the involvement of the mother-in-law, was an important risk factor in predicting increased IPV in these families. Although this result may seem inconsistent with the stereotyped view of the Chinese culture as a patriarchal society, the authors suggested a complex interpretation of this relationship. According to Chan et al., Chinese women's status in the family does not change when their sons get married; they are still under the domination of their husbands to a large extent and of their sons as well. However, since Chinese women may be assumed to identify with the men in their family, if their sons are engaging in IPV, the mother-in-law may feel constrained to participate or at least to condone and encourage her son to continue abusing his wife. Another suggested explanation of the complex role that in-law conflict may play in Chinese marriages, is that if there is conflict with the husband's family, then the wife can be accused of disrespecting her husband's family, which can be used as a justification for IPV. However, conflict between the husband and the wife's family may lead to a diminished amount of time spent with that family, which can reduce the amount of support the wife can experience from her own family.

Although this study is quite recent, and the sampling procedure and return rate were excellent, as the authors pointed out, the examination of the role of in-law conflict was based on one question which could be interpreted in different ways. As in all these cross-cultural studies, self-report measures were used, and only women were sampled.

Japan

Weingourt, Maryama, Sawada, and Yoshino (2001) conducted a self-report survey in Japan, which was completed by approximately 180 women with a relatively low response rate (close to 25 percent). As an explanation of this low response rate, the authors pointed out that to avoid offending respondents by pressuring them to participate in a study on such a sensitive issue, the researchers avoided contacting individuals who did not send back the survey. The results of the survey indicated that in this middle-class sample in Sapporo in the north of Japan, close to 60 percent were psychologically abused by their partners, around 30 percent were physically battered, and about 25 percent were sexually abused. Very few of these women told anyone about their experienced abuse. The authors explained this lack of disclosure by theorizing that IPV is viewed as the fault of the woman who thinks she has been a bad wife, and therefore she is fearful about disclosing the abuse to anyone. In addition, the wife is considered a "property" of the husband and thus he is permitted to do anything to punish her if she has not been a good wife. This explanation fits within the framework of the patriarchal society discussed earlier.

In addition to the lack of follow-up mailings which contributed to the relatively low response rate in the Weingourt et al. survey study, the authors indicated that the survey which was developed for use in a study in Tokyo, has not been tested for reliability and validity. Therefore, it is unclear how valid these results would be in comparison to studies that utilize standardized measures such as the CTS.

India

Wilson-Williams, Stephenson, Juvekar, and Andes (2008) investigated 64 women's attitudes toward domestic violence through focus groups in Gangadhar, which is a small community south of Mumbai. The community was described as patriarchal in nature, and the women strongly supported the traditional gender roles associated with the patriarchal culture. Women in this sample were basically from poor households and many were illiterate. Respondents indicated that they viewed physical and psychological abuse as normal within the culture, and suggested that a man has the right to beat a wife in order for her to learn the correct behavior. At times, it was suggested that mothers-in-law could be involved in the process, as was found in the Chan et al. study described earlier. Women were expected to be sexually available to their husbands at all times, and were not expected to use contraceptives as a means of preventing pregnancy. If a woman began using contraceptives, that was seen as a precursor to domestic violence. Once again, the authors took particular care to protect their respondents from any adverse effects of participating in this study. Prior to the focus groups convening, a discussion was held with the entire village, and participants were recruited following this meeting.

Although the Wilson-Williams et al. investigation revealed several interesting findings that fit within the framework of the effect of the patriarchal culture on domestic violence, the authors mentioned that it was difficult to get women to speak out on this sensitive topic. Since it was self-selected, there clearly is a concern about the representativeness of the sample. In addition, it is difficult to compare attitudes in a qualitative study using focus groups with more quantitative investigations. However, this study was one of the first in this type of small community, and the authors also attempted to connect the desire to use contraceptives with the consequences of subsequently becoming a victim of IPV.

Another study conducted in a rural area of India (Jejeebhoy, 1998) found that 40 percent of the sample of about 1,800 women reported having experienced IPV. Many of the respondents again believed that IPV was "justified" because she engaged in the wrong behaviors. However, Jejeebhoy reiterated the point that we have been stating, that this figure is most likely an underestimation of the actual level of IPV in India.

Turkey

Ozcakir, Bayram, Ergin, Selimoglu, and Bilget (2008) stated that there were no large scale studies of the prevalence of IPV in Turkey. If IPV occurs, it is supposed to be kept within the family, and even if some women actually call the police, only a very few ever prepare a complaint. Turkey is an unusual combination of eastern and western influences, but according to the authors, "Turkish law endorses a patriarchal family model in which the husband is named the head of the family" (p. 636). Therefore, the patriarchal model would suggest that men and women in Turkey might condone and accept physical punishment of women by their partners.

In their study, the authors examined attitudes of men toward "wife beating." Almost 1,200 married men in the city of Bursa, Turkey, were recruited at medical centers and interviewed in a face-to-face setting. Several demographic questions were asked, along with a number of questions about the conduct of marital partners and attitudes toward wife beating. Respondents also were asked "have you ever beaten your wife?'' (p. 633) and ''have you ever yelled, shouted or used abusive language to your wife?'' (p. 633). A relatively lower rate of physical abuse (29 percent) than in previous regional Turkish studies was determined from respondents' self-report, and close to 60 percent acknowledged that they had verbally abused their spouses. Risk factors included the wife's lack of education or poor educational background, the husband's alcohol problems, and if the husband had been physically abused as a child. Economic issues played a role in marital conflict as well. In addition, close to 20 percent of the men surveyed believed that men had the ''right'' to engage in IPV.

This study was a significant contribution to the literature because it is important to ascertain what men believe is appropriate and acceptable to be able to attempt to eliminate IPV in Turkey. Many studies only sample women's attitudes and experiences, but including men in these studies will be useful in determining the extent of the problem. In addition, the finding that childhood physical abuse was related to whether or not men engaged in IPV suggested to the authors that men began to see IPV as a normal part of family life. However, although the sample was large and the response rate was over 80 percent in this large Turkish city, only self-report data was obtained, and two of the significant measures consisted of one question each concerning physical and verbal IPV. These factors, in addition to the issue of only sampling men, possibly could have led to a considerable underreporting of IPV. In fact, the authors reported several regional studies based on women's self-reports, which estimated very much higher levels of IPV. Despite the patriarchal structure of the Turkish society, men may have been reluctant to report engaging in IPV.

AFRICA

Nigeria

Antai and Antai (2008) examined rural women's attitudes toward domestic violence in Nigeria. The authors indicated that rural Nigerian communities embody the ideals of the patriarchal culture. Men hold all the power and women accept their subordinate position in the family and the community. Once again, in accord with our contention, Antai and Antai suggest that it is important to determine women's attitudes toward IPV because if ''the victim perceives IPV to be an integral part of male supremacy'' (p. 2), and that the culture supports and condones violence against marital partners, she is unlikely to report this behavior and will see it as a normal part of the marriage. In support of this contention, at a UN symposium in 2007 a woman from Africa asked how she could report her husband's violence against her when her marriage vows ordered her to obey him?

In a manner similar to several other national studies, the authors utilized data from the 2003 Demographic and Health Survey conducted in Nigeria. An unusually high response rate of more than 90 percent enabled the researchers to investigate attitudes toward IPV among more than 3900 rural women. Data were collected in face-to-face interviews. More than 40 percent of the rural sample suggested that IPV was acceptable under certain conditions, including arguing with the husband, and not agreeing to sex. Interestingly, there were several variations in condoning IPV related to the specific communities in various geographical locations in the country. Similar to other studies, women with poorer educational backgrounds, Muslim women, and women living in economic hardship, were more likely to justify IPV. However, the authors also found other risk factors. Of particular interest to this chapter, women with little say in the family and those without the ability to read about the news or to be exposed to other media tended to approve of IPV. Antai and Antai suggested that empowerment consists of three components; "autonomy in domestic decisions," "access to media," and "literacy level" (p. 4).

This study was important for a number of reasons. First, the methodology employed a standardized national face-to-face interview process which had a very high response rate. Second, the authors focused on rural women, an often-overlooked type of sample. Third, the questions included significant categories including specification of empowerment, a concept very much associated with prevention and reduction of IPV. Fourth, the authors identified variations among women respondents that can lead to more complex and possibly more valid interpretations of data. Finally, the interpretations were related to the concept of a patriarchal society, which is support for one of the most common explanations of IPV worldwide. Of course, Antai and Antai's study is subject to the limitations of self-report measures as well as the focus only on women's attitudes toward IPV.

Kenya and Zambia

A study similar to the Antai and Antai study described above was conducted by Lawoko (2008) in Kenya and Zambia. Lawoko suggested that there might be varied interpretations of a man's positive attitude toward IPV depending on conditions in the country. In general, he indicated that Kenya has a more favorable economic and social climate than Zambia. However, both countries embody the traditional gender role approach suggesting that deviations from the female gender role may have adverse consequences for the wife.

Prevalence of IPV in Kenya and Zambia appear to be comparable to other African countries, and are somewhere between 20 and 30 percent. Lawoko indicated that there are no comparative studies of attitudes toward IPV among men in these two countries. In both countries, interview data were obtained through a national Demographic and Health Survey (DHS) of men in many households. High response rates (close to 90 percent in each country) increased the validity of the study's findings. Scenarios were constructed to measure men's attitudes toward IPV following hypothetical transgressions by women. For example, if the woman neglects her household duties or refuses to have sex with her husband, men were asked if she "deserved to be punished."

In general, men from both countries demonstrated a high and similar rate of acceptance of wife beating ranging from 65 to 71 percent. Most of the justifications for the IPV revolved around the wife's deviating from normative gender-role expectations, but the correlations and interpretations differed for the two countries. In Kenya, younger marriage partners and living outside of cities predicted higher support for wife beating, but that was not the case in Zambia. Conversely, lower educational levels were associated with higher tolerance of IPV in Kenya but not in Zambia. It was suggested by Lawoko that the educational material in each country might differ. Perhaps part of the educational information in Kenya might lead to a change in patriarchal ideals but not in Zambia. Similarly, access to the media was associated with a lower justification of IPV in Zambia but not in Kenya. Perhaps, as Lawoko indicated, the media in Zambia may support empowering women. Along the same lines of reasoning but in the opposite direction, Lawoko found that men's positive attitudes toward sharing in decision-making in the home predicted a lower acceptance of IPV in Kenya but not in Zambia.

Once again, this comparative study of men's attitudes toward IPV in two African countries was illuminating and important in identifying certain possible causes of IPV. In addition, by showing that predisposing factors may work differently in various countries, Lawoko made the case for developing culture and country-specific interventions. However attitudes relating to IPV were examined only for men, and both these countries were described as relatively peaceful. Therefore, the results cannot be generalized to African countries experiencing a great deal of conflict. Lawoko described other limitations of his study including the questionable validity of the DHS measures, the plausibility of extensive underreporting because of the face-to-face interviews, and the lack of consideration of alternative factors affecting men's attitudes toward IPV in addition to issues related to patriarchy.

MIDDLE EAST

Haj-Yahia (2002) conducted a study in Jordan investigating attitudes of approximately 350 married Jordanian women toward IPV. This convenience sample of women (with a response rate of more than 80 percent) was recruited from several clinics in a variety of locations including a city, a village, and a refugee encampment. Participants completed surveys in private, since interviews would be considered to be difficult to conduct on such a sensitive subject. Several measures were included such as the Beliefs about Wife Beating and Sex-Role Stereotyping, a measure of attitudes toward women, and the Familial Patriarchal Beliefs scale. All measures were translated and adjusted for cultural appropriateness. Haj-Yahia's findings suggested that a high proportion of the Jordanian respondents (ranging from about 35 percent to 65 percent depending on the "offense") justified IPV, felt that wives would become "better wives" as a result, blamed the women for their behavior, did not think that violent partners should be punished ("men will be men") and thought that the problem should stay in the family and not be dealt with by the government in any form. As in studies described previously, factors associated with increased wife blaming included poor educational levels, more traditional gender-role attitudes and patriarchal beliefs. This study strongly supported our contention that patriarchal belief structures will support and condone, and possibly even demand punishment of "bad wives." Haj-Yahia pointed out some difficulties with his study including questions about the generalizability of his findings to all women even in Jordan, the use of self-report questionnaires, and the lack of a measure of whether or not the respondents had experienced IPV. In addition, only women were surveyed in Haj-Yahia's research report. However, the study remains one of the few to examine attitudes toward IPV in the Middle East. In fact, in a meta-analysis, by Boy and Kulczycki (2008), the authors reported that only 21 studies contained statistics on occurrence of IPV in the Middle East and North Africa even though the abuse is known to be extensive and widely condoned and accepted both by men and women.

LATIN AMERICA

Peru

Flake's study (2005) of IPV in Peru surveyed more than 15,000 women and revealed that about 40 percent had experienced physical abuse. Several factors were related to the abuse, including poor educational background for the woman, forced early marriages, and alcoholic excesses of the husband. Once again, effects of the woman's status were unpredictable. Under certain circumstances higher status protected the woman from IPV, but if her status was superior to her partner, it exposed her to more IPV. Flake's interpretation of these results revolved around the concept of the frequency of patriarchal family relationships in Peru. If a man feels threatened by a woman's status or achievements, he may use violence to emphasize his control over his partner. Although this study supports our emphasis on the importance of the effects of a patriarchal culture on IPV, and the large sample is very positive, the measure of IPV was based on one question and self-reports of the prevalence of IPV are questionable especially in cultures where the issue is sensitive and is not discussed very much in public.

Another study in Latin America was conducted by Ceballo, Ramirez, Castillo, Caballero, and Lozoff (2004) using the Conflict Tactics Scale (Strauss, 1979). Thirty percent of the more than 200 poor women sampled in Chile said they had been physically abused, and approximately 80 percent had been verbally abused by their partners. Ceballo et al. identified Chile as a patriarchal society and indicated that IPV is not discussed outside the family. The authors also revealed that until 1989 a husband was considered to "own his wife" and therefore he could do anything he liked with his "property." Although the Ceballo et al. study surveyed an unusual sample of poor women, and used the CTS which is a standardized measure of IPV, the authors indicated that problems existed in their study including the use of self-report measures which most often underestimate the extent of IPV and the fact that not all types of violence were measured. The advantage of an unusual sample of poor women also is undercut by the fact that the results may not be representative of married women in Chile.

Both of these Latin American studies support our contention that patriarchal societies are key elements in the perpetration of physical and verbal abuse particularly in developing nations in Latin America, the Middle East and Africa.

CANADA

Brownridge (2003) investigated the differences in prevalence in IPV between Aboriginal and non-Aboriginal Canadian women. Brownridge's data were based on a large national study, Statistics Canada, conducted in 1999. He analyzed the data from interviews conducted by telephone, sampling close to 150 Aboriginal and close to 7,000 non-Aboriginal women. The survey suggested that Aboriginal women were likely to be abused at least three times as much as non-Aboriginal women. On all risk markers, including younger age, living in rural areas, having a partner with a strong belief in patriarchal power, and having a partner abusing alcohol, Aboriginal women were more likely to exhibit these markers than non-Aboriginal Canadian women. However, again illustrating the inconsistency of findings related to the educational level of women and the connection to IPV victimization, as Aboriginal women became more highly educated their chances of experiencing IPV actually increased. Brownridge suggested that Aboriginal men may be reacting against their low status in Canadian society, on the one hand, but also may be internalizing the negative views of women characterizing some views of non-Aboriginal men. In addition, if Aboriginal men have low status they may resent the higher status and educational level of Aboriginal women which may lead to increased levels of IPV.

Although this study utilized data from a representative Canadian sample, it still is subject to the limitations of a self-reported interview and a relatively small number of Aboriginal women participants. It also is unclear as to how participants were protected from the consequences of participating in this type of study. In addition, only women respondents' data were considered by Brownridge.

OUTCOMES FOR IPV VICTIMS

Cwikel, Lev-Weisel, and Al-Krenawi (2003) questioned Bedouin Arab women living in Israel in the Negev area, about the physical and psychological consequences of IPV victimization. The authors described the Bedouin society as highly collectivistic and as exhibiting a patriarchal structure, although there have been some changes as the Bedouins move from a nomadic life to living in a more settled manner in towns. The society also may be termed a "culture of honor" and women are punished for "straying" in order to preserve the honor of the family. Based on a revision of a national Israeli measure that was translated and back translated from the Hebrew, prevalence of physical abuse and consequences of the abuse were investigated. The outcome measures included the shortened form of the CES-D, the Center for Epidemiological Studies-Depression Scale (Sherbourne, Dwight-Johnson, & Klap, 2001). About 200 Bedouin women visiting a medical center were interviewed in person by an Arab nurse. Since the women knew the nurse and trusted her, she obtained cooperation from all the women she approached.

Results indicated that Bedouin women were very fertile until about age 40, and that they experienced increased IPV during their fertile years. As a consequence, women who had experienced IPV exhibited "symptoms of depression, low self-esteem, hopelessness and/or helplessness, low social support . . ." (p. 250). One other finding that adds to our discussion of the effect of educational level on IPV experiences, showed that women with a higher educational attainment experienced higher levels of IPV. The authors used an interpretation that we have observed in other studies suggesting that women who have been educated apparently are more likely to challenge their partners' dominance and the restrictions placed on them by their husbands and the culture. The authors acknowledge the limitations of self-report measures which most probably underestimated the extent of the IPV problem. In addition, they suggested that it will be very difficult to develop culturally appropriate interventions because IPV is closely connected to the heart of patriarchal societies such as the Bedouin culture in Israel.

A study in Kenya utilizing the previously mentioned Demographic and Health Survey of 2003, was conducted by Emenike, Lowoko, and Dalal (2008). In examining the relationship between IPV and physical consequences to women, the authors looked at data from more than 4,000 respondents. IPV was correlated with a higher rate of a pregnancy ending before term, and a greater chance of the baby not surviving. As indicated by the authors there obviously is no causal link but just suggestions that IPV in Kenya might make women more susceptible to problems in childbirth and infants to possible death.

Another cross-cultural study by Weingourt et al. (2001), described in an earlier section of the chapter, examined the consequences of IPV using the General Health questionnaire which was translated into Japanese. A higher percentage of women exposed to IPV expressed symptoms of depression and anxiety, and somatic symptoms, as well as sleep problems, than women who had not experienced domestic violence.

Finally, in the previously discussed study by Ceballo et al., the authors reported on the psychological symptoms experienced by their relatively small sample of poor women in suburbs of Santiago, Chile. The CES-D (Center for Epidemiological Studies Depression Scale) and a measure of women's experiences of posttraumatic stress disorder (PTSD) revealed severe levels of depression and PTSD-type symptoms.

All of these studies confirm predictions from researchers that victims of both physical and emotional abuse will demonstrate high levels of psychological distress as a result. Therefore, it is crucial for professionals in countries worldwide to develop prevention and intervention programs to combat this prevalent physical and mental health problem.

TYPES OF PERPETRATORS

Recently, some attempts have been made to classify IPV perpetrators. One of the most popular categorizations was developed by Holtzworth-Munroe and Stuart (1994). The different types of possible perpetrators included:

1. "Family-only" batterers who have poor social and conflict resolution skills, may belong to a peer group which is supportive of IPV, and tend to be violent only toward their spouses;

2. "Dysphoric-borderline" batterers have severe psychological problems, may exhibit borderline characteristics, may abuse substances and may be violent toward people outside their family;

3. "Violent antisocial" batterers are violent in every setting, may be criminals and are characterized by antisocial personality disorder diagnoses.

Although these categories have proved useful in identifying which types of perpetrators may respond to an intervention to reduce or eliminate IPV in America, and possibly in other Westernized countries, it is unclear how well the categories will apply cross-culturally. For example, in a "culture of honor" country such as Jordan, if a patriarch violently punishes his wife, or even engages in an "honor killing" according to westernized views, and the perpetrator categories described above, he definitely would be classified at least as a family-only batterer, or more likely as a spouse murderer. In his country, however, this type of individual would be perceived as following the dictates of the culture of the country, at least until recently. Therefore, it is important to develop categories of abusers which would apply cross-culturally to determine what types of interventions would work best in different cultures.

RECOMMENDATIONS TO ELIMINATE OR REDUCE IPV WORLDWIDE

WHO (2005) developed a series of recommendations to eliminate IPV across the world. We will briefly review some of these recommendations, suggest that there are issues and problems with implementing these recommendations, and describe some intervention programs.

The first major recommendation in the WHO report was to enforce adherence to international agreements protecting human rights of women around the world. In particular, patriarchal cultures that subordinate women and place women under men's control must be changed. If women are to be treated as equals, with the same rights as men, and if these patriarchal cultures stop condoning and even demanding that women be harshly punished for "straying" then violence may no longer be a viable means of gaining control over women by men. Particularly if men and boys are punished for engaging in violence against women, then the behavior will decrease.

Although this recommendation is the most important suggestion, it is also true that it will be the most difficult to implement. Individuals in countries where patriarchy and "culture of honor" principles are deeply ingrained will resist these changes even if the government does sign onto international agreements. For example, in 2004 the UN General Assembly passed a resolution prohibiting honor-related violence against women (Women's UN Report Network, April 25, 2009). However, in countries such as Saudi Arabia and Pakistan, as our previous examples illustrated, the practices still continue. Key government officials as well as community and religious leaders, particularly men, must be enlisted in the fight to change the violence-supportive patriarchal cultures. From a social psychological perspective, it is clear that attitudes that are based on strongly held values are the most difficult to change. Therefore, there must be a concerted effort by many individuals, at the government, local, community and religious levels to engage the populace in a discussion of the harm that is being done, to the women who are victims, to the children who observe and possibly imitate the violence, and to the male perpetrators themselves.

Even though many countries where violence is endemic espouse the patriarchal structure of societies, it also is clear that there are other viable explanations and models of IPV which may fit other societies. It is important that researchers, as well as academic and community agents of change recognize that IPV is a complex issue that may be related to a number of different risk factors. It also is crucial to understand that although some risk factors are common across the world, others are specific to individual countries.

A related recommendation is that all countries begin to collect data on the prevalence of all types of violence against women, including IPV. These data should be available to international organizations, and the UN should send a special rapporteur around the world to determine whether countries are adhering to the agreements and if in fact, violence against women has decreased.

Creating safe environments for women is an essential part of the recommendations. Shelters for battered women should be established with safeguards to prevent men from invading the shelters. Women in the shelters should be provided with treatment for physical and psychological injuries as well as skill-building to permit the women to reduce their dependence on their abusive spouses. The WHO report suggests that women may be identified as victims through clinics associated with reproduction, since many women visit these clinics. Other venues and professionals including primary health care workers should be involved in identifying and protecting women.

Education for women and girls is emphasized all through the cross-cultural research on IPV. However, since the findings are inconsistent, unless the patriarchal culture is changed, if women receive a high level of education and achieve a high status, it is possible that this situation may become a risk factor for IPV.

Even if laws are changed to punish perpetrators of violence against women, law enforcement officials' attitudes must be changed as well. Women must be encouraged to report IPV, and police and other authorities must provide women with sympathetic and helpful officers who do not identify with and embody patriarchal values.

Both primary and secondary prevention programs should be implemented to reduce violence against women. In particular, the media may be useful in primary prevention programs designed to reach many individuals within the country. In Turkey for example, at one point, all the media outlets in Istanbul were owned by women who decided to begin a primary and secondary prevention effort to stop violence against women. Television ads were produced including one showing a young child dressing up in her mother's clothes and shoes, and putting a black eye on as well since she had seen her mother in that condition so many times. In addition, ads stated that the "shame is not yours" while showing an abused women. Other interventions, including training individuals to engage couples in improving their conflict resolution and communication skills, as well as instituting hotlines in the Istanbul area, were designed to attack the problem. Therefore, the media can be used as a positive force to combat this worldwide problem. What also should be included in any of these programs is an evaluation component. The WHO report stated that there should be additional cross-cultural research on the causes of violence and programs to prevent or eliminate violence against women.

The WHO report also emphasized the importance of involving men and boys in the effort to eliminate violence against women. Until men who do not engage in violence against women and oppose it speak out and intervene when they see violence occurring, perpetrators will continue to engage in this behavior. Once again the media can act as a forum for nonviolent men to speak out, and these men may become good role models for spousal interactions.

Flood (2001) discussed three different ways in which men can become involved in the efforts to stop violence against women.

1. Men can join groups which emphasize that "men must take responsibility for stopping men's violence," (p. 3) possibly though public action such as protests. Flood describes the "White Ribbon campaign" in which men wear white ribbons to show the world that not only will they avoid violence but they will speak out and intervene if they observe violence. Flood emphasized the importance of reaching out to boys and young males to try and change fundamental attitudes which condone and support violence against women. These men also can act as proactive role models to teach young men how to interact with women in a positive way. However, Flood contends that men's groups must work in cooperation with women's groups in the same effort.

2. Men can become involved in educational media campaigns based on the same concept espoused by Ban Ki Moon: "Real men don't bash or rape women." Flood described some programs in Australia which serve this educational function. Sports figures were recruited for advertisements in one of the Australian programs to target men who identify with athletes. Once the athletes define violence against women as wrong, it is hoped that men identifying with these athletes will internalize their new views. However, it is difficult for these programs to succeed because of the violence-supportive culture of many types of sports. Another type of Australian program which targeted violent males found that one of the most effective approaches was to connect men's violence against women to the negative effects on the children in their family.

3. Men can become directly involved in programs treating violent men, or even men incarcerated for violence against women. However, Flood

argues that many of these programs have not been rigorously evaluated. In addition, even if these programs were effective, unless the culture and attitudes of members of society are changed to oppose violence against women, single programs will not eradicate the problem.

As a conclusion to this section, we will present an overall program that was instituted in Romania. Wimmer and Harrington (2008) described a comprehensive program, "Floare de Colt," (p. 623) developed to address IPV in Sighisoara, Romania. This grant-funded project involved international partners who traveled to Sighisoara to hold a three-day conference with community individuals, trained local participants, and provided social work students with the means to live in the town for a brief period to assist in the program. Wimmer and Harrington emphasized that the first step was to achieve community involvement and sensitize the community to the existence of IPV and the need for services for victims. An overall evaluation of the program indicated that as a result, a wide range of services for victims had been established, and utilized by various types of individuals, not just IPV victims. However, the authors reported that several years after the creation of the project, the need for shelters and programs which focus on changing perpetrators' behavior, as well as access to public funding, still remains.

The article by Wimmer and Harrington was an important stage in illuminating the complex nature of any type of IPV prevention and intervention program. The emphasis on involving community leaders and representatives from the beginning of the project, the role that outside international experts can play as partners, and the significance of grants and funding to at least begin a program cannot be overestimated. Despite the success of the initial program, this article also illustrated the difficulty of maintaining a program once the funding and international partnerships are no longer involved.

One of the issues associated with this project was the viability of the evaluation process. The authors defended the involvement of the original international partners in the evaluation by suggesting that a sufficient distance between these professionals and the on-site program had been established to enable the researchers to maintain their objectivity. That involvement still may be seen as a barrier to an objective evaluation of the effectiveness of the project. In addition, the lack of direct interviews with victims and the lack of any input of victims in the process of evaluation other than documentation of the use of the services, also may be viewed as a serious drawback of the evaluation process. However, since many programs do not include essential evaluations in their descriptions, the Wimmer and Harrington article represents a significant contribution to the literature.

COMPARISONS BETWEEN IPV AND
DATING VIOLENCE STUDIES

As we predicted in the opening section of this chapter, there is a considerably larger volume of cross-cultural studies on IPV than on dating violence. One of the issues is that IPV is more prevalent world-wide, since in some cultures dating is not permitted. However, it also seems clear that dating violence most often is subsumed under a more general category of violence or sexual assault, whereas IPV is conceptualized as a separate form of violence. As a result, there are many more studies on IPV and more estimates of the prevalence than there are for dating violence.

Similarities still exist in terms of the estimates of both types of violence. As a result of underreporting which occurs even in countries where these behaviors are discussed publicly, accurate prevalence figures are impossible to obtain. Women victims of IPV and dating violence are reluctant to report because of feelings of self-blame, shame and fear of retaliation. Even in cross-cultural research where considerable efforts have been made to protect participants from retaliation from partners, these individuals still are fearful to give accurate responses. Another issue relates to the variations in methodology among the different studies. Methods range from randomly sampling women from large Demographic and Health Surveys, or WHO surveys, where the response rate is quite high, to individual surveys designed specifically for one country and which are completed by as few as 25 percent of those sampled. As a result, it is impossible to compare estimates of IPV and dating violence among countries when the methods of obtaining these data are so diverse. The situation is even more complex when investigating IPV and dating violence in countries where these issues are "kept within the family" or "under the veil" (in Arab countries). Even women in many of these countries condone IPV and believe that women deserve the abuse to help them become "better wives" (Haj-Yahia, 2002).

We also hypothesized that the prevalence of both IPV and dating violence would be more expected and would occur to a more extreme degree in patriarchal and culture of honor societies than in countries with higher gender equity. In addition to the strong support that our contention received in our selective review of cross-cultural studies, this pattern is relevant to our ongoing multicultural investigation of undergraduate students' perceptions of IPV. In our study, we constructed a scenario describing a domestic violence incident in which a husband abused his wife either after finding out that she had been unfaithful or had been visiting her friend rather than taking care of his dinner. This scenario was followed by a series of measures based on the domestic violence incident. The study has been conducted in Spain, the United States, the United Kingdom, Croatia, Israel, Romania, Greece, Georgia, Ghana, Malaysia, Lebanon, and India, and has been translated into seven languages. Based on the Gender Equity Index of 2008 which ranks countries in terms of gender equity (the rankings are a summary of the "Education Gap", Economic Activity Gap" and the "Empowerment Gap"), students from countries higher in gender equity (the first six of the countries listed above) were more sympathetic toward the wife and more negative toward the husband, whereas undergraduate participants in the latter six countries showed the reverse reactions to the scenario.

Since gender equity showed such a strong relationship with prevalence of violence against women worldwide, the recommendation of the WHO that patriarchal attitudes and culture of honor norms be changed is a reasonable approach to the issue. However, as we described earlier, it will be extremely difficult to change such ingrained attitudes and customs which have been characteristic of some cultures for centuries. It is most important that the impetus for change emanates from the top down: male leaders of these societies, both in government and in the religious community, must be at the forefront of these efforts. Men and boys definitely must be involved in the change approach. International organizations should act as models and also pressure member nations to act according to international agreements and eliminate this aversive behavior. The media also can play a role in creating the image that wife-beating and dating violence is wrong and has severe negative consequences. In addition, law enforcement officials also must be involved in the process.

Although the type of culture clearly has been implicated in IPV and dating violence, patriarchy is not the sole reason or even the most plausible explanation of these types of violence in all countries. Since IPV and dating violence also occur in countries where gender equity is high, other models and theories must be established to fully comprehend this complex behavior. One other point is important for us to emphasize. In addition to involving men in the effort to eliminate violence against women worldwide, we must focus more attention on types of perpetrators and treatment and punishment for violent men. If we only propose treatment and shelters for women, we may be engaging in an implicit type of "blaming the victim."

Different trends in reports of violence are noted in dating relationships than what is seen in domestic disputes. These discrepancies can be attributed to the following factors: teens generally do not cohabitate with romantic partners, and therefore stereotypical relationship and power dynamics that are seen in marriages have not yet had a chance to develop; adolescent girls are more likely to report abuse and assault, regardless of who the perpetrator was, whereas married women may find such disclosure shameful; adolescent boys, on the other hand, may be prone to underreporting or not be willing to accept the blame for assault, and therefore the numbers are lower; and some cultures are in fact changing and shifting, as was noted in the Wang and Ho article (2007), which results in young women feeling more empowered and able to stand up for themselves, even if their actions are not always appropriate, or respected by their romantic counterparts.

In conclusion, IPV and dating violence are pervasive and complex behaviors which adversely affect women all around the world. It is important to conduct more cross-cultural comparisons, using standardized measures, in order to obtain accurate figures, as well as to develop models to understand and eliminate the violent behaviors.

REFERENCES

Adelman, M., & Kil, S. H. (2007). Dating conflicts: Rethinking dating violence and youth conflict. *Violence Against Women, 13,* 1296–1318.

American Psychological Association. (1996). *APA Presidential Task Force on Violence and the Family Report.* Washington, DC: American Psychological Association.

Antai, D. E., & Antai, J. B. (2008). Attitudes of women toward intimate partner violence: A study of rural women in Nigeria. *The International Electronic Journal of Rural Remote Health Research, Education, Practice, and Policy, 8,* 1–12.

Archer, J. (2000). Sex differences in aggression between heterosexual partners: A meta-analytic review. *Psychological Bulletin, 126,* 651–680.

Black, B. M., Tolman, R. M., Callahan, M., Saunders, D. G., & Weisz, A. N. (2008). When will adolescents tell someone about dating violence victimization? *Violence Against Women, 14,* 741–758.

Blow, C. (2009). Editorial: *Love shouldn't hurt.* New York Times, February 12, 2009.

Boy, A., & Kulczycki, A. (2008). What we know about intimate partner violence in the Middle East and North Africa. *Violence Against Women, 14,* 53–70.

Brownridge, D. A. (2003). Male partner violence against Aboriginal women in Canada. *Journal of Interpersonal Violence, 18,* 65–83.

Ceballo, R., Ramirez, C., Castillo, M., Caballero, G. A., & Lozoff, B. (2004). Domestic violence and women's mental health in Chile. *Psychology of Women Quarterly, 28,* 298–308.

Chan, K. L., Brownridge, D. A., Leung, W. C., Tiwari, A., & Ho, H. W. Y. (2008). Mental health profile of sexual violence perpetrators among university students in Hong Kong. In J. K. Quinn & I. G. Zambini (Eds.), *Family relations: 21st century issues and challenges.* Hauppauge, NY: Nova Science.

Chan, K. L., Brownridge, D. A., Tiwari, A., Fong, D. Y., & Leung, W.-C. (2008). Understanding violence against Chinese women in Hong Kong: An analysis of risk factors with a special emphasis on the role of in-law conflict. *Violence Against Women, 14,* 1295–1312.

Cwikel, J., Lev-Wiesel, R., & Al-Krenawi, A. (2003). The physical and psychosocial health of Bedouin Arab women of the Negev area of Israel. *Violence Against Women, 9,* 240–257.

Dobash, R. E., & Dobash, R. P. (1980). *Violence against wives: A case against the patriarchy.* London: Open Books.

Doroszewicz, K., & Forbes, G. B. (2008). Experiences with dating aggression and sexual coercion among Polish college students. *Journal of Interpersonal Violence, 23,* 58–73.

Douglas, E. M., & Straus, M. A. (2006). Assault and injury of dating partners by university students in 19 countries and its relation to corporal punishment experienced as a child. *European Journal of Criminology, 3,* 293–318.

Dutton, D. G. (1995). Intimate abusiveness. *Clinical Psychology: Science and Practice, 2,* 207–224.

Eaton, D. K., Davis, K. S., Barrios, L., Brenner, N. D., & Noonan, R. K. (2007). Associations of dating violence victimization with lifetime participation, co-occurrence, and early initiation of risk behaviors among U.S. high school students. *Journal of Interpersonal Violence, 22,* 585–602.

Emenike, E., Lawoko, S., & Dalal, K. (2008). Intimate partner violence and reproductive health of women in Kenya. *International Nursing Review, 55,* 97–102.

Flake, D. F. (2005). Individual, family, and community risk markers for domestic violence in Peru. *Violence Against Women, 11,* 353–373.

Flood, M. (2001). Men's collective anti-violence activism and the struggle for gender justice. *Development* (Special Issue: Violence Against Women and the Culture of Masculinity), *44,* 42–27.

Foshee, V. A., Bauman, K. E., Ennett, S. T., Linder, G. F., Benefield, T., & Suchindran, C. (2004). Assessing the long-term effects of the safe dates program and a booster in preventing and reducing adolescent dating violence victimization and perpetration. *American Journal of Public Health, 94,* 619–624.

Foshee, V. A., Bauman, K. E., Linder, F., Rice, J., & Wilcher, R. (2007). Typologies of adolescent dating violence: Identifying typologies of adolescent dating violence perpetration. *Journal of Interpersonal Violence, 22, 498–519.*

Foshee, V. A., Linder, F., MacDougall, J. E., & Bangdiwala, S. (2001). Gender differences in the longitudinal predictors of adolescent dating violence. *Preventative Medicine, 32, 128–141.*

Foshee, V. A., Lindner, F., Rice, J., & Wilcher, R. (2007). Typologies of adolescent dating violence: Identifying typologies of adolescent dating violence perpetration. *Journal of Interpersonal Violence, 22, 498–519.*

Fredland, N. M., Ricardo, I. B., Campbell, J. C., Sharps, P.W., Kub, J. K., & Yonas, M. (2005). The meaning of dating violence in the lives of middle school adolescents: A report of a focus group study. *Journal of School Violence, 4,* 95–114.

Frieze, I. H. (2005). Female violence against intimate partners: An introduction. *Psychology of Women Quarterly, 29,* 229–237.

Gender Equity Index. (2008). Retrieved March 10, 2009, from http://www. socialwatch/org/en/avncesyRetrocesos/IEG_2008/tablas/SWG EI.htm

Giordano, P. (2007). *Recent research on gender and adolescent relationships: Implications for teen dating violence research/prevention.* Presentation at U.S. Departments of Health and Human Services and Justice Workshop on Teen Dating Violence: Developing a Research Agenda to Meet Practice Needs, December 4, 2007, Crystal City, VA.

Glick, P., & Fiske, S.T. (1997). Hostile and benevolent sexism: Measuring ambivalent sexist attitudes toward women. *Psychology of Women Quarterly, 21*, 119–135.

Haj-Yahia, M. M. (2002). Beliefs of Jordanian women about wife beating. *Psychology of Women Quarterly, 24*, 209–219.

Haj-Yahia, M. M. (2006). Patterns of violence against engaged Arab women from Israel and some psychological implications. *Psychology of Women Quarterly, 24*, 209–219.

Haj-Yahia, M. M., & Edleson, J. L. (1994). Predicting the use of conflict resolution tactics among engaged Arab-Palestinian men in Israel. *Journal of Family Violence, 9*, 47–62.

Halford, W. K., Sanders, M. R., & Behrens, B. C. (2004). Repeating the errors of our parents? Family-of-origin spouse violence and observed conflict management in engaged couples. *Family Process, 39*, 219–235.

Hines, D. A., & Straus, M. A. (2007). Binge drinking and violence against dating partners: The mediating effect of antisocial traits and behaviors in a multinational perspective. *Aggressive Behavior, 33*, 441–457.

Holtzworth-Munroe, A., & Stuart, G. L. (1994). Typologies of male batterers: The subtypes and the differences among them. *Psychological Bulleting, 116*, 426–497.

Jejeebhoy, S. J. (1998). Wife beating in rural India: A husband's right? Evidence from survey data. *Economic and Political Weekly, 33*, 855–862.

Kerpelman, J. L. (2007). Youth focused relationships and marriage education. The Forum for Family and Consumer Issues, *12*, 37–46.

Kilmartin, C., & Allison, J. (2007). *Men's violence against women: Theory, research, and activism.* Mahwah, NJ: Lawrence Erlbaum.

Kimmel, M. S. (2002). Gender symmetry in domestic violence: A substantive and methodological research review. *Violence Against Women, 8*, 1332–1363.

Laursen, B., & Collins, W. A. (1994). Interpersonal conflict during adolescence. *Psychological Bulletin, 115*, 197–209.

Lawoko, S. (2008). Predictors of attitudes toward intimate partner violence: A comparative study of men in Zambia and Kenya. *Journal of Interpersonal Violence, 23*, 1056–1074.

Luthra, R., & Gidycz, C. (2006). Dating violence among college men and women: Evaluation of a theoretical model. *Journal of Interpersonal Violence, 21*, 717–731.

Lysova, A. V., & Douglas, E. M. (2008). Intimate partner violence among male and female Russian university students. *Journal of Interpersonal Violence, 23*, 1579–1599.

Manganello, J. A. (2008). Teens, dating violence, and media use: A review of the literature and conceptual model for future research. *Trauma, Violence, & Abuse, 9*, 3–18.

Molidor, C., & Tolman, R. M. (1998). Gender and contextual factors in adolescent dating violence. *Violence Against Women, 4*, 180–194.

Montgomery, M. J. (2005). Psychosocial intimacy and identity: From early adolescence to emerging adulthood. *Journal of Adolescent Research, 20*, 346–374.

Olson, E. (2009, January 4). A rise in efforts to spot abuse in youth dating. *The New York Times*, p. A12.

Ozcakir, A., Bayram, N., Ergin, N., Selimoglu, K., & Bilgel, N. (2008). Attitudes of Turkish men toward wife beating: A study from Bursa, Turkey. *Journal of Family Violence, 23*, 631–638.

Rennison, C. M., & Welchans, S. (2000). *Bureau of Justice Statistics Special Report: Intimate partner violence, National Crime Victimization Survey.* Washington, DC: Rennison & Welchans.

Riggs, D., & O'Leary, K. (1989). A theoretical model of courtship aggression. In M. A. Pirog-Good & J.E. Stets (Eds.), *Violence in dating relationships* (pp. 53–71). New York: Praeger.

Roberts, T.A., & Klein, J. (2003). Intimate partner abuse and high-risk behavior in adolescents. *Archives of Pediatrics and Adolescent Medicine, 157*, 375–380.

Sherer, M. (2009). The nature and correlates of dating violence among Jewish and Arab youths in Israel. *Journal of Family Violence, 24*, 11–26.

Sigal, J., & Annan, V. (2008). Violence against women: International workplace sexual harassment and domestic violence. In F. L. Denmark & M. A. Paludi (Eds.), *Psychology of women: A handbook of issues and theories* (pp. 590–622). Westport, CT: Praeger.

Straus, M. A. (1979). Measuring intrafamily conflict and violence: The conflict scales. *Journal of Marriage and the Family, 41*, 75–88.

Straus, M. A. (2007). Validity of cross-national research based on convenience samples: The case of the international dating violence study data. In *Violence against dating partners in world perspective: The International Dating Violence Study.* Durham, NH: Family Research Laboratory, University of New Hampshire.

Straus, M. A., & Ramirez, I. L. (2007). Gender symmetry in prevalence, severity, and chronicity of physical aggression against dating partners by university students in Mexico and USA. *Aggressive Behavior, 33*, 281–90.

Straus, M. A., & Savage, S. A. (2005). Neglectful behavior by parents in the life history of university students in 17 countries and its relation to violence against dating partners. *Child Maltreatment, 10*, 124–135.

United Nations. (1993). Declaration on the elimination of violence against women. General Assembly Resolution 48/104, December 20, 1993. Retrieved September 29, 2006, from http://www.ohchr.org/english/law/elimination.vaw.

United Nations General Assembly Resolution A/C.3/59/L.25:15 (2004, October). *Crimes of honor.* Retrieved April 25, 2009, from http://www.wurn.com.

Valls, R., Puigvert, L., & Duque, E. (2008). Gender violence among teenagers: Socialization and prevention. *Violence Against Women, 14*, 759–785.

Vandello, J. A., & Cohen, D. (2003). Male honor and female fidelity: Implicit cultural scripts that perpetuate domestic violence. *Journal of Personality and Social Psychology, 84*, 997–1010.

Wang, X., & Ho, P. S. K. (2007). My sassy girl: A qualitative study of women's aggression in dating relationships in Beijing. *Journal of Interpersonal Violence, 22*, 623–638.

Weingourt, R., Maruyama, T., Sawada, I., & Yoshino, J. (2001). Domestic violence and women's mental health in Japan. *International Nursing Review, 48*, 102–108.

Wekerle, C., & Wolfe, D.A. (1999). Dating violence in mid-adolescence: Theory, significance, and emerging prevention initiatives. *Clinical Psychology Review, 19,* 435–456.

Wilson-Williams, L., Stephenson, R., Juvekar, S., & Andes, K. (2008). Domestic violence and contraceptive use in a rural Indian village. *Violence Against Women, 14,* 1181–1198.

Wimmer, J. S., & Harrington, P. A. (2008). Domestic violence services in Romania: A longitudinal case study. *International Social Work, 51,* 623–633.

Xu, X., Zhu, F., O'Campo, P., Koenig, M. A., Mock, V., & Campbell, J. (2005). Prevalence of and risk factors for intimate partner violence in China. *American Journal of Public Health, 95,* 78–85.

Chapter 5

Intimate Partner Violence as a Workplace Concern: Impact on Women's Emotional and Physical Well-Being and Careers

Michele A. Paludi
Jessica Wilmot
Lindsey Speach

Barbara Cavalier had been married to her husband, Chris Cavalier, for seven years. During the course of their marriage, Chris had been abusive toward Barbara. When he put a gun to her head, she decided to leave him. For six months her living arrangements were kept secret. One day Chris walked into the Elmwood siding supply business and saw Barbara where she was working as a data-entry clerk. Subsequently, Chris walked into the store, armed with two guns, a .45 caliber automatic pistol and a .357 caliber Magnum revolver. Chris killed Barbara and her co-worker, Stephanie Revolta, who had tried to defuse the situation. Stephanie had placed a 911 call, but by the time assistance arrived, Barbara and Stephanie were dead. Chris also took his own life. Barbara's coworkers reported that Chris had been harassing Barbara all day, calling her at work, and stealing her truck. Authorities had found a note in Chris's house in which he assigned power of attorney and listed valuables that he wanted to give away. This behavior led police to believe that Chris had planned the murders that day (cited in Paludi, Nydegger, & Paludi, 2006).

Ellen works for a small shipping company in the western Canada city of Vancouver. She has been unhappily married to Paul for more than

20 years, and she and her two daughters bear the brunt of Paul's verbal taunts and controlling behavior. Though he has never physically abused the children, he often beats Ellen so severely that vicious bruises cover her arms and legs, and she regularly lies to her coworkers about their origin, claiming clumsiness, embarrassed by their true cause. At least once a month Ellen is so badly hurt that she must call out of work. In the past two years alone, she has lost 22 days of work, and thousands of dollars in wages.

One night, Paul angrily smacks Ellen's younger daughter, and she falls down the stairs, cutting open her knee. After years of abuse, Ellen has finally had enough, and leaves. She moves in with a friend, and changes her phone number and personal email address. For a while things are fine. But soon Ellen begins receiving threatening prank phone calls at the office, and nasty emails to her work email account. She thinks it might be Paul, and her suspicions are confirmed when one evening she discovers him waiting for her in the office parking lot. In a dark and menacing tone Paul threatens to kill her—and their children—unless she returns to him.

She doesn't know who to turn to or where to go. For years she has been hiding her abuse from her friends, family, coworkers and employers, and the threats continue to escalate . . . (cited in Soroptimist International of the Americas, 2007).

The experiences of Barbara and Ellen are not unique; approximately 2,600,000 women are victims of intimate partner violence each year (Swanberg & Logan, 2005). Homicide is the leading cause of occupational death for women in the United States (National Institute for Occupational Safety and Health, 2009; Reeves & O'Leary-Kelly, 2007; Swanberg & Logan, 2007; Swanberg, Macke, & Logan, 2006). Furthermore, women who are victims perpetrated by their mates/spouses account for one-fourth of all women who are murdered in a given year (McHugh & Frieze, 2006; Rathus & Feindler, 2004). Swanberg et al. (2005) reported that more women in the United States are victimized by their spouses/mates than are harmed because of reported automobile accidents, muggings, and rapes combined.

Straus, Gelles, and Steinmetz (1980) noted that one out of every six couples engage in at least one violent act each year. Over the course of a marriage, just over one-fourth of couples will experience intimate partner violence. Intimate partner violence is not confined to marriage. Research suggests that violence in dating relationships and among unmarried couples who live together is even greater than among married couples. Ryan, Frieze, and Sinclair (1999) noted that approximately one-third of U.S. college students reported using or being victims of intimate partner violence. Abuse in relationships includes intense criticisms and put-downs, verbal harassment, sexual coercion and assault, pushing, grabbing, shoving, physical attacks and intimidation, stalking, choking, striking a partner with an object, restraint of normal activities and free-doms, and denial of access to resources (Butts Stahly, 1999; McHugh, Livingston, & Frieze, 2008; Ryan et al., 1999). Straus et al. (1980) con-cluded: "The American family and American home are perhaps as or more violent than any other American institution or setting (with the exception of the military, and only then in time of war" (p. 4).

The Fourth United Nations (UN) International Conference on Women concluded that "in all societies . . . women and girls are sub-jected to physical, sexual and psychological abuse that cuts across lines of income, class and culture" (Walker, 1999, p. 21). Tran and Des Jardins (2000) reported that the incidence of intimate partner violence experienced by Vietnamese and Korean communities is similar to U.S. incidence rates. Horne (1999) noted that intimate partner violence rates in Russia exceed United States rates by four to five times.

Intimate partner violence is prevalent in all races and ethnic groups and among women in urban, rural, and suburban areas and in lesbian, gay, and heterosexual relationships (Coleman, 1991; McHugh & Frieze, 2006; Paludi, Nydegger & Paludi, 2006; Potocziak, Murot, Crosbie-Burnett, & Potoczni, 2003). In addition, while women are more likely to be victims of intimate partner violence, men may be battered (Heise, 1998; McHugh & Frieze, 2006). Men batter because they want control in the relationship. Women, however, batter in self-defense because of fear of being murdered. Heise (1998) found that more women are seri-ously injured and killed by male partners each year than men are by female partners. Tjaden and Thoennes (2000) reported that over a life-time, the prevalence of intimate partner violence for women is triple the prevalence for men. In addition, research suggested that the incidence of same-sex intimate partner violence is similar to that of het-erosexual intimate partner violence (McHugh & Frieze, 2006; Potocziak et al., 2003).

INTIMATE PARTNER VIOLENCE SPILLS OVER INTO WORKPLACES

Swanberg and Logan (2005) asked U.S. women about the ways in which intimate partner violence spilled over into their workplace. Women's responses indicated that batterers interfered with women's employment before, during, and after work. Pre-work interference pre-vented 56 percent of the women in this study from going to work, including physical restraint, having clothes cut up, being beaten, and being denied access to the car. Swanberg and Logan (2005) and Wetterstein et al. (2004) noted that women reported experiencing pre-work incidents of violence at least once a week. Interference with wom-en's employment at the workplace included the following behaviors:

phone harassment, harassment of the women's supervisors, threatening comments, stalking, and being physically forced to leave work.

Thus, the workplace is not a safe haven for women victims of intimate partner violence; the violence spills over into the workplace. The workplace provides a site where batterers, like Chris Cavalier, can find their victims. And, as Swanberg et al. (2006) noted:

> When partner violence traverses the boundaries of women's jobs, the victimized partner is no longer the only victim. Other people on the workplace premises, including supervisors, other workers, and customers, are at risk for injury or some other form of trauma. (p. 573)

Intimate partner violence costs employers more than $727.9 million annually on costs related to lost productivity, including 7.9 million paid workdays each year. In addition, there are additional costs related to health care costs associated with intimate partner violence. Intimate partner violence is thus a workplace issue.

In this chapter we review the empirical research on the impact of intimate partner violence on women's emotional and physical health, self-concept, interpersonal relationships with coworkers and supervisors, and career goals. We offer recommendations for employers in exercising "reasonable care" in responding to women employees who are victims of intimate partner violence, including developing and enforcing an effective policy and investigatory procedures and training programs on intimate partner violence awareness and the organization's policy.

IMPACT OF INTIMATE PARTNER VIOLENCE ON EMPLOYEES

The biggest challenge is to convince a woman that it's not her fault. My daughter is 25; my stepdaughter is 22. As a mother, I want them to know that if a boyfriend is abusive, you cannot ignore it—"Oh, he's been drinking," or "He had a bad day." There is no excuse for a man hitting a woman. Ever.

—Sen. Debbie Stabenow, Michigan

Research on intimate partner violence has documented impact on several areas of functioning, including emotional/psychological, physiological or health related, career, interpersonal, and self-perception (Lundberg-Love & Marmion, 2006; McHugh et al., 2008; O'Leary & Maiuro, 2001; Reeves & O'Leary, 2007; Swanberg et al., 2006). Examples of emotional/psychological effects of intimate partner violence include, but are not limited to, guilt, denial, withdrawal from social settings, shame, depression, fear, anger, anxiety, phobias, isolation, fear of crime, helplessness, frustration, shock, and decreased self-esteem (Cunradi, Ames, & Moore, 2008; Swanberg et al., 2006).

The following are reported physical/health-related effects of intimate partner violence: headaches, tiredness, respiratory problems, substance abuse, sleep disturbances, eating disorders, lethargy, gastrointestinal disorders, post traumatic stress disorder, the hostage syndrome, and inability to concentrate (Lundberg-Love & Wilkerson, 2006; McHugh & Frieze, 2006; Walker, 2006; Zorza, 2002). In addition, battered women experience injuries including bruises, cuts, concussions, black eyes, broken bones, scars from burns, knife wounds, loss of hearing and/or vision, and joint damage (Felblinger, 2008; Lundberg-Love & Wilkerson, 2006). Pregnant women who experience intimate partner violence face the risk of severe outcomes for their fetus as well as themselves (Sagrestano, Carroll, Rodriguez, & Nuwayhid, 2004).

The impact intimate partner violence has on social and interpersonal relationships includes the following: withdrawal, fear of new people, lack of trust, and changes in social network patterns at work (Lundberg-Love & Wilkerson, 2006; Swanberg et al., 2006).

Research by Swanberg (e.g., Swanberg et al., 2006; Swanberg & Logan, 2007) suggested that the impact of intimate partner violence on women employees contributed to women victims' inability to (a) concentrate and solve problems at work, (b) perform their job, (c) go to work, (d) stay at work, and (e) keep their jobs. In addition, women victims of intimate partner violence may receive threatening emails, calls, and/or faxes at work. This has implications for women employee's mental state and contributes to their inability to concentrate and failure to follow their job responsibilities and thus be fired.

Similar results were obtained by Lloyd and Taluc (1999), who found that out of the 824 women in their sample, 18 percent indicated that they had experienced intimate partner violence, 11.9 percent had incurred more severe violence at the hand of their mate/spouse and 40.3 percent said they had been coerced and threatened by their mate/spouse. In addition, 28.4 percent had experienced abuse at the criminal assault level. These women reported experiencing unemployment, emotional and physical health problems, and higher welfare rates than women who did not experience intimate partner violence.

Ridley's (2004) research with the Maine Department of Labor and Family Crisis Services indicated that 74 percent of batterers reported having easy access to their partner's workplace. Twenty-one percent of these men had contacted their partner at the company in violation of a restraining order, and 48 percent indicated they could not concentrate at their own job because of their preoccupation with their partner. Of these men, 19 percent had a workplace accident; 42 percent were late for work because of engaging in battering.

Intimate partner violence also has direct implications for a mother's effectiveness to parent. The dysfunction and disorganization of the home offer little or no support, structure, nurturance, or supervision for children (Walker, 1999). Children are often neglected by mothers who are too emotionally and physically abused to care for them (Black & Newman, 2000).

IMPACT OF INTIMATE PARTNER ABUSE ON CHILDREN

Furthermore, the impact of intimate partner violence on children is significant. Children are in the middle of domestic violence in a number of ways, including arguments about child rearing practices and children's behavior. Children blame themselves for the violence as a consequence of their stage of cognitive development even though they are not the cause (Paludi, 2002). Walker (1999) and Graham and Rawlings (1999) estimated that each year approximately 3.3 million children in the United States between the ages of 3 and 17 years are at risk of exposure to their mothers being battered by a male spouse/mate. Children learn to become part of a conspiracy of silence. They lie to prevent inappropriate behavior; they learn to suspend fulfillment of their needs rather than risk a confrontation with the batterer. Thus, as Paludi (2002) stated, "they live in a world of make-believe" (p. 351). They themselves are at greater risk for physical abuse than children whose mothers are not battered (Black & Newman, 2000). Homicide is currently one of the five leading causes of child mortality in the United States (Paludi & Paludi, 2000).

WOMEN'S FEAR OF LEAVING THE VIOLENT RELATIONSHIP

According to Lundberg-Love and Wilkerson (2006):

> Being a victim of domestic violence can result in serious and long-lasting psychological consequences. The initial emotion reported after a battering incident tends to be helplessness. Over time, most women become fearful, anxious, angry, and depressed . . . many battered women develop PTSD. The duration of the abuse and the victim's history of prior abuse impact the severity of the symptoms she may experience. (p. 40)

Most battered women remain in the violent relationship because they believe their situation is inescapable. They feel helpless about changing their lives and fear that any action they take will contribute to additional violence, which is justified (Butts Stahly, 1999; Zorza, 2002). Furthermore, cultural factors contribute to remaining silent to protect the family's honor (Marmion & Faulkner, 2006). Battered women remain in violent relationships for several well-founded reasons (McHugh & Frieze, 2006; Paludi, 2002; Butts Stahly, 1996) including:

a. Threats to her life and the lives of her children if she leaves the home
b. Fear of not getting custody of her children

c. Financial dependence

d. Feeling of responsibility for keeping the relationship together

e. Love for the batterer

f. The batterer is not always violent

Grothues and Marmion (2006) noted that women victims of intimate partner violence frequently attempt to leave the relationship; their attempts are thwarted by their partners who exercise more control and coercion with threats. Furthermore, it has been reported that economic issues must be taken into consideration when understanding women remaining in a violent relationship:

> Women who leave their spouse often have no good alternatives for housing or support for themselves or their children. Because of the nature of the abuse, which often involves increasing isolation from others, victims tend to have a very small support system. Shelters are not readily available in all communities, and even this option has limitations and has an impact on the children. It is not simply a case of not wanting to leave; most women do wish to do so. However, the costs of leaving are significant. (Grothues & Marmion, 2006, p. 11)

We note that Butts Stahly's (1999) review of the National Crime Survey of the Department of Justice indicated that 70 percent of intimate partner violence occurs after the relationship has ended. Similar findings were reported by Walker (1995) and Birns (1999), who reported that women are at an increased risk for homicide following the break up of a relationship, more so than women who remain in the relationship.

EMPLOYEE ASSISTANCE PROGRAM (EAP) ASSISTING WOMEN VICTIMS OF INTIMATE PARTNER VIOLENCE

An EAP assists employees with dealing with non-work-related issues that interfere with their ability to perform their job (Smith & Mazin, 2004). EAPs provide short-term counseling on the telephone or in-person, as well as refer employees for help in the community. An EAP can be utilized to help women employees deal with the symptomatology of intimate partner violence reviewed above (Paludi & Paludi, 2000; Rothman, Hathaway, Stidsen, & deVries, 2007). Recommendations for EAPs include: (a) helping women to develop a sense of trust and safety in the current environment, (b) helping women foster relationships with appropriate nonviolent male models, (c) understanding women's insecurity about their future, (d) countering any sense of guilt about having caused the violence and/or not being able to prevent the battering, and (e) increasing women's self-esteem.

An EAP can also assist children of battered women through play assessment and play therapy to encourage preschool children to express feelings about the trauma, individual counseling for children, and women-children support groups (Paludi & Paludi, 2000).

Most importantly, women who have left a battering relationship often report that they had learned about intimate partner violence and the impact of this violence on themselves and their children from listening to an EAP counselor discuss the issue at a noon-time seminar. Such programs facilitated by an EAP should include information about local domestic violence shelters, the importance of considering psychological abuse as a form of intimate partner violence, emotional responses to intimate partner violence, consequences of intimate partner violence, religious beliefs and remaining in a battering relationship, and cultural issues involved in reporting the abuse (e.g., Bostock, Plupton, & Pratt, 2009; Mitchell et al., 2006; Watlington & Murphy, 2006).

We discuss subsequently in this chapter the role the EAP can play in training supervisors to recognize changes in employees' behavior as a consequence of intimate partner violence and to refer them to the EAP in a confidential manner (DeCenzo & Robbins, 2007; Paludi & Paludi, 2000).

IMPACT OF INTIMATE PARTNER VIOLENCE ON THE WORKPLACE

As we have previously discussed, intimate partner violence impacts the primary employed individual, coworkers, clients, vendors, and customers. Intimate partner violence thus contributes to stress for all in the workplace. This stress consequently results in lost productivity, decreased morale, increased absenteeism, and increased employee turnover. In addition, Gurchiek (2005) reported that intimate partner violence has a "sweeping effect—on employee safety, work performance and even the employer's bottom line" (p. 1). As we noted earlier, intimate partner violence costs employers more than $727.9 million annually on costs related to lost productivity.

The health-related costs of intimate partner violence, including stalking, rape, and murder, exceed $5.8 billion per year. In addition, approximately $4.1 billion of this cost is for employees who require physical and mental health care, both paid for by the employer. Direct costs also include ambulance transport, paramedic assistance, physical therapists' assistance, and emergency department visits (Swanberg et al., 2005). It is important to note that mental health care may continue for several years after the victimization. Thus, the estimated costs of intimate partner violence are an underestimate in any year (Centers for Disease Control and Prevention, 2009).

The American Institute on Domestic Violence (2009) reports that victims of intimate partner violence lose approximately 8 million days of paid workdays each year. The average absenteeism rate of victims of intimate partner violence is approximately 30 percent higher than the average employee absenteeism rate (Urban, 2000). In addition, the Centers for Disease Control and Prevention (2009) measured expected value of lost earnings that victims of intimate partner violence who were murdered would have contributed to society if they had lived out their full life expectancies. The Centers for Disease Control and Prevention estimated this figure to be $892.7 million, approximately $713,000 per woman.

Willman's (2007) review of Fortune 1000 companies indicated that 49 percent of corporate leaders indicated intimate partner violence had harmful effects on the organization's productivity. In addition, 47 percent indicated the violence had a harmful impact on attendance. Forty-four percent said the violence was harmful to their health care costs and therefore, intimate partner violence impacts their bottom lines.

ORGANIZATIONS' USE OF "REASONABLE CARE" IN DEALING WITH INTIMATE PARTNER VIOLENCE AS A WORKPLACE ISSUE

"Reasonable care," adapted from rulings in *Burlington Industries, Inc. v. Ellerth* (1998) and *Faragher v. City of Boca Raton* (1998) includes the following at a minimum:

1. Establish and enforce an effective policy.
2. Establish and enforce effective investigative procedures.
3. Facilitate training in intimate partner violence as a workplace issue in general and in the organization's policy and procedures specifically.

These cases focused on sexual harassment; however, the Equal Employment Opportunity Commission (1999) has maintained that these basic standards apply to "all types of prohibited harassment."

We pursue an institutional level of analysis to explain the prevalence of intimate partner violence as a workplace issue. We thus focus on educational, psychotherapeutic, legal, management, and sociocultural factors in understanding intimate partner violence that spills over to the workplace. We also discuss the importance of social science research in helping organizations understand why intimate partner violence exists, including issues of power and control (also see McHugh & Frieze, 2006). We thus integrate management theory, case law, and social science research to effectively enforce policies and procedures in an atmosphere of trust that encourages individuals to come forth with their experiences of intimate partner violence.

EMPLOYERS BEING PUT ON NOTICE ABOUT INTIMATE PARTNER VIOLENCE

In Swanberg and Logan's (2005) research, 46 percent of women in their sample informed their supervisors or managers about the intimate partner violence they were experiencing. Thus, 54 percent of the women decided not to disclose the abuse. Furthermore, 43 percent of the women informed one of their coworkers about the battering; 57 percent did not do so. Swanberg and Logan also reported that those women who did inform their coworkers or managers received support with having their phone calls screened and physical protection from their batterer.

We note that women who did not disclose their victimization at work did so because they feared losing their job, were ashamed of being battered, wanted to deal with the battering themselves, were ashamed of their appearance, and were frightened (Paludi & Paludi, 2000). In addition, women who received support from their employer did eventually resign because they were forced by their mate/spouse to stop working and/or because of the stress of fearing their mate/spouse would come to their workplace (Swanberg & Logan, 2005).

We discuss the following prevention strategies to assist organizations in assisting employees who are victims of intimate partner violence: primary; secondary; and tertiary. Primary prevention strategies include the development and enforcement of policies, investigatory procedures, and training programs on intimate partner violence awareness and the organization's policy. Secondary prevention strategies include facilitating individualized training with employees who are at high risk for being victims. Finally, tertiary prevention includes working with victims of violence, providing counseling services for them. Each of these strategies is addressed in the following sections.

PRIMARY PREVENTION STRATEGIES

Policies and Procedures

Policies that establish a zero-tolerance for workplace violence and intimate partner violence in the workplace require more than a general statement against the behavior (Barling, Rogers, & Kelloway, 2001; Paludi, Nydegger, & Paludi, 2006; Swanberg, Macke, & Logan, 2007). They require the efforts and support of management at all levels and continual training of all employees (to be discussed later in this chapter), as well as procedures that encourage employees to disclose their victimization to the organization (Kelly & Mullen, 2006). All employees would benefit from a workplace climate of respect and cooperation.

COMPONENTS OF POLICIES AND PROCEDURES

The Centers for Disease Control and Prevention (2009) and Society for Human Resource Management (2009) recommend an explicit policy statement and investigatory procedures for assisting victims of intimate partner violence. Components of effective policy statements are the following (Paludi, Nydegger & Paludi, 2006):

a. Statement of Purpose
b. Legal Definition
c. Behavioral Examples
d. Statement Concerning Impact of Intimate Partner Violence on Individuals and Workplace
e. Statement of Individual's Responsibility in Notifying Employer
f. Statement of Workplace's Responsibility in Assisting Employee
g. Statement Concerning Confidentiality of Complaint Procedures
h. Statement Concerning Sanctions Available
i. Statement Regarding Retaliation
j. Statement of Sanctions for Retaliation
k. Statement Concerning False Complaints
l. Identification and Background of Individual(s)

DEALING WITH INTIMATE PARTNER VIOLENCE IN THE WORKPLACE

An important consideration for the policy is whether it sets a tone of appropriate seriousness and concern for employees' rights. Thus, the policy needs to specify the types of behaviors that are prohibited in the workplace and the potential consequences of these behaviors should they occur. Paludi, Nydegger and Paludi (2006) and Occupational Safety and Health Association (OSHA; 2009) recommend the policy including a Personalized Safety Plan for victims of intimate partner violence that outlines the employers' responsibility in assisting victims. Components to include in this Personalized Safety Plan include the following:

a. Providing receptionists and the building's security officer with a photograph and description of the batterer.
b. Screening the employee's visitors and phone calls.
c. Accompanying the employee to and from their cars.
d. Permitting the employee to park close to the office building.
e. Having a formal notification letter be sent to the batterer by the president of the organization that indicates their presence on the company premises will result in an arrest since the employee has a restraining order on the batterer.
f. Providing referrals for individual counseling.

A sample policy statement and personalized safety plan are presented in Appendix 1 and Appendix 2. Additional suggestions for safety plans may be found in Lundberg-Love and Marmion (2006).

We caution employers however, to be careful in implementing these procedures since they may put employees' safety at risk. As Wilman (2007) discussed:

> Abusers, who have anger and control problems, often perceive such efforts as a conspiracy between the employer and the victim. They become frustrated, angry, and feel out of control when employers make it difficult for them to access their victims. (p. 7)

Paludi, Nydegger, and Paludi (2006) have identified components for effective complaint procedures for organizations. Empirical research has indicated that employees will feel more encouraged to discuss their experiences with intimate partner violence when they understand what the process entails (Swanberg et al., 2006). Thus, employees must be given accurate and adequate information about disclosing their victimization, written in understandable language and terms. Failure to provide such information makes the policy statement inhibitive.

Components of effective procedures include all of the following at a minimum:

a. Informing employees that the workplace will not ignore any disclosure of intimate partner violence.
b. Informing employees that the employer will not make determinations about the employee victim based on the reputations or organizational status of the employee involved.
c. Informing employees that they will respond promptly to any incident of intimate partner violence.
d. Informing employees that witnesses to incidents and/or to changes in the employee's behavior will be interviewed.

Paludi and Paludi also recommended that:

a. The policy statement should be made available in languages in addition to English for individuals and their support systems for whom English is not their first language.
b. The policy statement must be made available in Braille and in large type as well as be made available on audio tape.

TRAINING PROGRAMS

For Managers

Paludi and Paludi recommended that human resource specialists facilitate training programs for managers in two sections: (a) to provide information on intimate partner violence awareness, e.g. definitions, incidence, impact on victims and the workplace and (b) the organization's policy and procedures so that managers know their rights and responsibilities with respect to assisting employees who are victims of intimate partner violence. Lee (cited in Gurchiek, 2005) noted that "employers should provide an atmosphere for disclosure" since victims feel ashamed, embarrassed, and are fearful of losing their job.

Results from research by Swanberg et al. (2006) indicated that women who chose not to disclose the intimate partner violence to their employer did so because of stigma associated with the violence (e.g., embarrassed, ashamed, fear of being judged), safety related (e.g., threatened by the abuser not to tell anyone about the violence, didn't want coworkers to become involved) and work-environment-related (e.g., didn't know anyone to tell about the violence, couldn't trust co-workers and supervisors with the disclosure, and the abuser also worked for the same organization). We recommend these findings be made part of the training for managers so they can understand reasons for silence and reasons why the employer must be supportive to victims of intimate partner violence.

We also believe it is important to train managers about why victims of intimate partner violence do disclose the abuse at work. Women in Swanberg et al. (2006)'s research who did report the intimate partner violence at work indicated doing so because they needed to talk about the abuse and because their coworker in whom they confided was also a friend. Women who disclosed at work also did so as a way to explain absences and tardiness, to request time off from work to attend court proceedings or to answer a supervisor or coworker who inquired about any potential abuse. Furthermore, some women disclosed at work because they feared for their lives and wanted a coworker or supervisor to know about the abuse in case of their death. These findings can assist managers in setting up a welcoming and safe environment for all employees so they feel encouraged to report abuse.

Swanberg et al. (2006) noted that women victims of intimate partner violence who disclosed the abuse at work fared better in terms of having longer job tenure, low job-quitting rates, and higher wages. Thus, it is important to inform managers (and employee victims) that disclosing the intimate partner violence at work does not translate into employees losing their jobs.

Paludi, Nydegger, and Paludi (2006) identified the following components of effective training program for managers:

a. Ways to encourage employees to report problems.
b. Skills in behaving compassionately and supportively to employees who disclose intimate partner violence.

   c. Skills in handling crises.

   d. Basic emergency procedures.

In addition, Paludi and Paludi (2000) recommended including a unit in the training programs for managers that deal with stereotypes, what Grothues and Marmion (2006) refer to as "dismantling the myths" about intimate partner violence, including blaming women for their victimization, believing intimate partner violence is a rare occurrence, that women are masochistic and ask for the victimization, that intimate partner violence is about sex, not power, and that intimate partner violence only occurs among poor families.

Paludi and Paludi also recommended that training programs on intimate partner violence be separate from training on workplace violence in general. Examples of policies, procedures, and training programs may be found in Paludi, Nydegger, and Paludi (2006) and on OSHA's Web page, www.osha.gov.

For Threat Assessment Team

OSHA (2009) has recommended the use of threat assessment teams or crisis intervention teams that receive, evaluate, and respond to threats in the workplace. Members of these teams include management and labor as well as security, human resources, legal, and operations personnel. The teams are trained to implement policies of the company. They must not intervene inappropriately or endanger employees by their responses. As Paludi, Nydegger, and Paludi (2006) noted, these teams may be feared by employees as "secret police" spying on employees to try to get them fired:

> The following steps can be implemented to insure that these teams are effective and appropriate: (1) an inclusive group of employees to represent the organization should be selected and (2) training that offers legal, management, and psychological perspectives should be provided to the team on a periodic basis. (p. 92)

OSHA (2009) also recommends training for the company's threat assessment team to deal with situations as they emerge. These teams must receive continuing training on issues related to intimate partner violence. Their training is identical to the components identified for managerial training. In addition, OSHA recommends that:

   a. These teams need to be professionally competent and know what to do and when to call for help.

   b. All members need to know the other team members and their individual jobs very well.

   c. They should role-play and practice a wide variety of potential problem situations.

   d. They should have frequent meetings and ongoing training.

For Employees

Paludi and Paludi recommend the same components of the training program for managers be provided to employees as well. In addition, employee training should include a discussion about the personalized safety plans and the role of the EAP in assisting victims of intimate partner violence. Emphasis should be placed on ensuring the employer will take each victim seriously and will provide assistance to the victimized employee.

We also recommend including in the training program for employees a discussion on ways they can assist coworkers who are victims of intimate partner violence, including being alerted to changes in the individuals' behavior. In addition, training in how to respond to a coworker who confides in employees should be provided, including listening without judging, recognizing the difficulty it took for an individual to discuss the topic of intimate partner violence, and being an advocate for the employee by referring them to human resources, a manager, or the EAP. We also advise that intimate partner violence be part of all new employee orientations. As Swanberg et al. (2006) noted:

> Educating employees about partner violence could help to demystify the disgrace associated with this social problem and consequently help reduce or eliminate the risk of partner violence entering into the workplace. (p. 574)

PEDAGOGICAL TECHNIQUES

The pedagogical techniques that have been recommended in the literature (e.g., Paludi & Paludi, 2000) for training programs are ones that:

1. Empower employees.
2. Encourage employees to think strategically.
3. Assist employees in communicating effectively with employees.
4. Manage conflict in the workplace.

The interactive pedagogy encompasses adult learning principles. Research in educational psychology (Slavin, 2008) has identified that adults prefer learning situations that:

   a. Are practical and problem-centered.

   b. Promote their positive self esteem.

   c. Integrate new ideas with existing knowledge.

   d. Show respect for the individual learner.

   e. Capitalize on their experience.

   f. Allow choice and self-direction.

We recommend facilitating the training in the following ways:

   a. Provide overviews, summaries, case studies, and behavioral rehearsals to link research to practice.

   b. Use collaborative, authentic problem-solving activities.

   c. Assist individuals in becoming more effective and confident through guided practice and establishing routines.

   d. Ask individuals what they would like to know about the training topic.

   e. Provide a quality, well-organized, differentiated experience that uses time effectively and efficiently.

The major objective of the training modules and pedagogical techniques is to facilitate transference to the workplace. We recommend accomplishing this goal by:

   a. Association: having participants associate the new information with something with which they are already knowledgeable.

   b. Similarity: presenting information that is similar to material that participants already know; i.e., it revisits a logical framework or pattern.

   c. Degree of original learning: the degree of original learning for the participants was high.

   d. Critical attribute element: the information learned by the participants contains elements that are extremely beneficial and/or critical on the job.

We do not recommend Web-based training programs for teaching employees about intimate partner violence. This pedagogy generates high levels of employees' acquisition and retention of the material presented (Frisbie, 2002; Goldstein & Ford, 2002) as well as offers fast-paced learning. However, Web-based training can create frustration in employees who are not computer literate, who would prefer learning from an individual, not a computer, and because the issue is emotionally laden and therefore sensitive (Dessler, 2009). We do recommend the use of behavioral rehearsal with case studies with managers, asking their input on how to handle an incident presented to them. Discussion of their responses must include providing critical evaluation of their behavior, including whether or not they are following the organization's policy.

NEEDS ASSESSMENTS

In keeping with the literature in human resource management (e.g., Barbazette, 2006; DeCenzo & Robbins, 2007) we recommend conducting a needs assessment with employees to identify additional issues they expect to be covered in a training session. Brown (2002) identified four reasons why needs assessments must be conducted prior to facilitating training programs: (1) identify problem areas in the company, (2) obtain management support, (3) develop data for measuring the effectiveness of the training program, and (4) determine the costs and benefits of the training program. Needs assessments may be conducted through anonymous surveys and/or focus groups (Lucier, 2008; Tyler, 2002). We recommend the following process (also see Levy & Paludi, 2002):

1. Ask individuals to provide answers to questions regarding discrimination in the workplace via an anonymous mail survey.
2. Facilitate 2-hour focus groups with self-identified employees (no more than 15-20 per session) to elicit in-depth responses. Structured interview questions for individuals who participate in the focus groups center around employees' goals for training, including their needs with regard to better understanding intimate partner violence and individuals with viewpoints different from their own.
3. Analyze responses from the previous steps using qualitative and quantitative analyses.
4. Prepare a written report that summarizes the needs assessment, including suggestions for the following:

   • How to increase awareness

   • Ways to examine attitudes

   • Alternatives to stereotyping

   • Methods of supportive action

5. Make recommendations for post-training evaluations (to be discussed subsequently in this chapter).

The main goal of the needs assessment therefore is to obtain information concerning the manner in which intimate partner violence is addressed in the organizational climate of the company, including topics such as empowerment, the establishment of mutual trust and respect, methods of inclusion or exclusion, and verbal and nonverbal communication. The process of the assessment will be consistent with the goal of the training programs in which the employees will subsequently participate.

POSTTRAINING EVALUATIONS

In further keeping with the human resource management literature, we highlight the necessity of conducting posttraining evaluations.

Measuring the effectiveness of training programs in intimate partner violence as a workplace issue is an important aspect of the training program so that the organization may determine if the training delivered or failed to deliver the expected organizational benefits. The measures of success for the training programs in intimate partner violence are ones identified in the needs assessment phase. Issues in the measurement phase can be discussed in two phases: types of information about which to measure and ways to measure whether or not the training effort achieved its goals. It is not enough to merely assume that any training an organization offers, even if it is legally mandated, is effective. The transfer of knowledge from the training room to the workplace is the most important measure of success.

The most wellknown model for determining the effectiveness of training programs is the Kirkpatrick Model (1959, 1998) that is comprised of four levels: reaction, learning, behavior, and results. Results concerns the benefits resulted from training. Behavior taps into what extent trainees change their behavior, back in the workplace as a result of this training. The learning level asks to what extent trainees improved their knowledge and skills and changed their attitudes as a result of the training programs. Finally, the reaction component determines trainees' opinions about the structure of the training program, location of the program, trainer effectiveness, and so on.

The most commonly used level of the Kirkpatrick Model is the reactions level. However, this is the least valid evaluation technique (Tan, Hall, & Boyce, 2003). Individuals' opinions are heavily influenced by factors that may have little to do with the training effectiveness. By measuring reactions, organizations do not obtain information regarding employees' learning, how well they are integrating the new knowledge and skills on their job, or whether there has been increased disclosure of intimate partner violence posttraining.

Common performance-based evaluations that incorporate any of the Kirkpatrick Model levels are posttraining, pre-post training, pre-post training performance with control group, and the Solomon Four Group Design. We encourage the reader to review Graziano and Raulin, 1996, for additional information.

We recommend using an "ecological approach" for conducting training programs on intimate partner violence (Paludi & Paludi, 2003). This approach stresses that training be facilitated in a sequence that ensures optimum assistance for all parties. The sequence is as follows:

Individuals hearing reports of intimate partner violence

Counselors in EAP

President and administrators

Managers and supervisors

Employees

We suggest report persons and counselors be trained initially so that employees will have an outlet for disclosing intimate partner violence and receiving emotional support. Typically flashbacks can occur during training programs; we want to ensure employees have trained individuals who can assist them with these experiences.

ADDITIONAL HUMAN RESOURCE RESPONSIBILITIES

We note the importance of ensuring that victims of intimate partner violence not be retaliated against on other human resource functions (Lemon, 2001; Randel & Wells, 2003). For example, employee victims should not be identified as "tardy" or absent if they have to go to counseling, court, physicians' appointments, and so on. In addition, performance appraisals should not penalize employee victims on time management, absenteeism, and so on. While managers may not fully be aware of the employees' situation, the human resource department must ensure protection for employee victims.

Furthermore, employers must abide by the General Duty Clause of OSHA, which states that the employer has to provide a safe and healthy workplace free from violence for all its employees. Employers should also provide family and medical leave to employee victims. Organizations that recognize the need and adapt work to employees' lives will assist employee victims as well as win all employees' loyalty and thus have a competitive edge (Eastman, 1998, Paludi, et al., volume 3 of this book set). Organizations with family-friendly policies report less stress for employees, lower absenteeism, higher morale, positive publicity, improved work satisfaction, lower turnover rate, staffing over a wide range of hours, child care hours that conform to work hours, and access to quality infant, child, and elder care (Frone & Yardley, 1996; Paludi & Neidermeyer, 2006).

Examples of family friendly policies for victims of intimate partner violence include flexible work hours, on-site health services, time off/career break, and workplace relocation that provide employees with the opportunity to continue working for their employer at a safer and anonymous job site (Paludi, Vaccariello, Graham, Smith, Allen-Dicker, & Kasprzak, 2006; Swanberg et al., 2006). Examples of such policies are found in Paludi and Paludi (2006).

In addition, educational materials may be developed for distribution and posting throughout the workplace, including posters with tear-off tabs containing hotline phone numbers.

We also note that an intimate batterer may be a coworker of the employee victim. We recommend employers consider adopting a consensual relationship policy (also see Paludi, Nydegger, & Paludi, 2006).

We recognize that consensual relationships are not illegal, but they do cause difficulties for organizations because:

a. The situation involves one person exerting power over another.

b. The seduction of a much younger individual is usually involved.

c. Conflict of interest issues arise, e.g. how can a supervisor fairly evaluate an employee with whom she/he is having a sexual relationship?

d. The potential for exploitation and abuse is high.

e. The potential for retaliatory harassment is high when the sexual relationship ceases.

f. Other individuals may be affected and make accusations of favoritism (Paludi, Nydegger & Paludi, 2006, pp. 79-80).

Sample consensual relationship policies may be found in Paludi and Barickman (1998).

We recommend the implementation of engineering solutions to assist with intimate partner violence as well as workplace violence in general (Middelkoop, Gilhooley, Ruepp, Polikoski, & Paludi, 2008). Examples of engineering solutions include:

Controlling or limiting access to work areas after dark

Creating clear escape routes

Installing locks on doors that lead to "staff only" areas like break or lunch rooms

Employee identification badges

Increased lighting

Video surveillance

Alarm systems

Buddy system

On-site guard services

Weapons policy

Coded card keys for access

Equip field staff with cellular phones and daily work plans

Providing a portable "panic button" for each employee

Providing handheld alarms.

Security staff are also important in prevention strategies, including:

a. Working with administrators to improve the security level of the buildings, grounds, and parking lots.

b. Serving as the liaison with local law enforcement.

c. Serving as the company's security experts, providing administrators with a risk management analysis.

d. Serving as the company's technologies experts with respect to engineering solutions.

e. Assisting with conducting effective background checks as part of the employment process.

f. Coordinate electronic surveillance, building security with global positioning, communications, etc. with local law enforcement to provide quicker response times.

g. Install voice activated and Braille security call boxes.

h. Ensure a company-wide emergency notification system in the event of violence on site, including the parking lot.

THE EAP

EAPs can offer the following services in primary prevention of intimate partner violence as well as workplace violence in general (see Paludi, Nydegger, & Paludi, 2006):

a. Providing short term counseling to managers and employees.

b. Providing referrals for counseling outside of the workplace.

c. Consulting with and training Threat Assessment Team.

d. Training managers to deal with employee victims without diagnosing the employee.

e. Providing referrals for legal counseling.

f. Providing referrals for financial counseling.

g. Determining whether the employee has sought and/or obtained a protective order against the abusive partner.

h. Working closely with human resources to monitor the employee victim in order to protect their safety.

Paludi, Nydegger, and Paludi (2006) outlined steps companies should take for emergency action plans, including:

a. Procedures for getting help.

b. Emergency escape procedures and routes for every person and for every place in the company.

c. Identification of personnel with training needed to perform medical duties.

d. Training for employees on how to deal with violence and how to use the emergency action plan.

e. Procedures for calling for medical assistance.

f. Procedures for notifying law enforcement.

g. Procedures for securing the area after a violent event.

h. Procedures for accounting for all employees after a violent event.

We thus take the approach that intimate partner violence that spills over into the workplace is the responsibility of all members of an organization.

SECONDARY AND TERTIARY PREVENTION

Relying on the symptomatology of victims of intimate partner violence reviewed in this chapter we can assist employees we believe are at risk for violence as well as those who have disclosed the abuse. The American Bar Association Commission on Domestic Violence (1999) also noted the following observable behavior that may suggest possible intimate partner abuse that may be helpful for secondary prevention measures (p. 16). We recommend providing this listing to managers as well during training on intimate partner violence as a workplace issue:

a. Unexplained tardiness and absences.

b. Unplanned use of leave time.

c. Lack of concentration.

d. A tendency to remain isolated from coworkers or reluctance to participate in social events.

e. Discomfort when communicating with others.

f. Disruptive phone calls or e-mail.

g. Frequent financial problems indicating lack of access to money.

h. Unexplained bruises or injuries.

i. Noticeable change in use of makeup (to cover up injuries).

j. Inappropriate clothes (e.g., sunglasses worn inside the building, turtleneck worn in the summer).

k. Sudden changes of address or reluctance to divulge where she is staying.

l. Court appearances.

The EAP counselor can assist employee victims with conflict resolution, providing guidance about options and procedures, e.g., domestic violence shelter, providing emotional support for concerns about disclosing victim status to the employer, short term counseling, referral services, and countering myths about causes of violence with realities.

We also recommend EAP counselors discussing the cycle of violence with employee victims (Walker, 1979). The three phases of the cycle of violence are as follows: In the tension-building phase, there are battering incidents. The victim attempts to avoid escalation of the battering by calming her mate and by staying away from him. However, the tension builds too high to be controlled by these efforts and the batterer responds with an acute battering incident in the second phase of the cycle. In the final phase, the tension from the first two phases has ceased and the batterer becomes apologetic and charming toward the victim. The level of violence increases both in frequency and severity as the relationship continues.

CONCLUSION

Sexual, racial, gender violence and other forms of discrimination and violence in a culture cannot be eliminated without changing culture.
—Charlotte Bunch

The Partnership for Prevention (2002) reported that most employers do not have a defined policy and procedures for dealing with intimate partner violence that spills over into the workplace. Smaller companies are less likely to include a policy on intimate partner violence than larger ones. Services that are most commonly offered by companies have included victim referral services, security precautions, and educational materials, e.g., posters, brochures. Roper's (2002) study of the Liz Claiborne survey of Fortune 1000 senior executives and managers indicated that victim resources were the only focus of these employers' attention to intimate partner violence, including emergency counseling services, employee benefits that covered the costs of medical assistance, and referrals to organizations that deal with intimate partner violence.

We have offered recommendations in this chapter to assist workplaces in implementing effective interventions in intimate partner violence. We borrow from the Higher Education Center's (Langford, 2006, p. 5) suggestions for campus violence in that workplace interventions must be:

Prevention-focused

Comprehensive

Planned and evaluated

Strategic and targeted, using results from a risk assessment of the vulnerability of the workplace

Research-based

Multicomponent

Coordinated and synergistic, ensuring all prevention and response efforts complement and reinforce each other

Multisectoral and collaborative, involving campus stakeholders, including counselors and advisors

Supported by infrastructure and institutional commitment

In order for these recommendations for primary, secondary, and tertiary prevention strategies to be successful, there must be support and initiative from the president of the organization. Without this commitment, the prevention strategies will not be effectively implemented, contributing to employees believing the organization is not seriously committed to the issue of intimate partner violence and thus being silenced about their experiences with this abuse. Furthermore, as we have suggested in this chapter, dealing with intimate partner violence as a workplace issue must be based on a multidisciplinary team approach, including human resources, EAP, security, managers, law enforcement, attorneys, and employees themselves. Unions may also assist by supporting the company's intimate partner violence policy, facilitating training on intimate partner violence for new stewards/delegates, and ensuring all employees have received the company's policy and have been trained on intimate partner violence.

We also recommend organizations conducting a safety audit to determine whether the prevention strategies are working effectively (Smith & Mazin, 2004), including conducting anonymous organization climate surveys to inquire about employees' perceptions of the company's commitment to dealing with intimate partner violence. A safety audit would include:

a. Building security (e.g., automatic locked doors? Security guards on duty for all shifts?)
b. Visitors (e.g., sign in guests with guard?)
c. Health services (e.g., EAP, wellness center?)

The audit will uncover disconnects between the workplaces policies, procedures, and practices and what the workplace wants to achieve in terms of meeting the needs of victims of intimate partner violence. Results from the audit and climate survey must be used to understand the reason for employees' perceptions and to correct the policies, procedures, and training, and ensure employees feel safe disclosing the abuse. Recommendations can be prioritized based upon the risk level assigned to each item: high (required immediate attention), medium (required to be dealt with in a short time frame), and low (suggestions to make the practices more efficient). From this risk matrix, a workplace security plan can be developed to address the most pressing issues first (Crouhy, Galai, & Mark, 2005). We hope workplaces will find the recommendations in this chapter useful in meeting their goal of helping victims of intimate partner violence so Jerry Moran's sentiment becomes a reality:

> Through education, improved funding and support, we can continue to work together to provide safe environments for victims and end the cycle of domestic violence.

Additional resources to assist organizations meeting this goal are presented in Appendix 4.

APPENDIX 1: SAMPLE POLICY ON INTIMATE PARTNER VIOLENCE AS A WORKPLACE CONCERN

Employees of _____ must be able to work in an atmosphere of mutual respect and trust. As a place of work, _____ should be free of violence and all forms of intimidation and exploitation. _____ is concerned and committed to our employees' safety and health. The Firm refuses to tolerate violence in our workplace.

_____ has issued a policy prohibiting violence in the workplace. We have a zero tolerance for workplace violence.

_____ also will make every effort to prevent violent acts in this workplace perpetrated by spouses, mates, or lovers. The Firm is committed to dealing with intimate partner violence as a workplace issue.

_____ has a zero tolerance for intimate partner violence.

Intimate Partner Violence: Definition

Intimate partner violence—also referred to as domestic violence, battering, spouse abuse, spousal assault, and intimate partner abuse—is a global health problem. This victimization is defined as violence between adults who are intimates, regardless of their marital status, living arrangements, or sexual orientations. Such violence includes throwing, shoving, and slapping as well as beatings, forced sex, threats with a deadly weapon, and homicide.

Intimate Partner Violence: Myths and Realities

Myth: Intimate partner violence affects a small percentage of employees.

Reality: Approximately 5 million employees are battered each year in the United States. Intimate partner violence is the leading cause of injury and workplace death to women in the United States.

Myth: People must enjoy the battering since they rarely leave the abusive relationship.

Reality: Very often victims of battering do leave the relationship. Women and men remain in a battering relationship not because they are masochistic, but for several well-founded reasons, e.g.,

- Threats to their lives and the lives of their children, especially after they have tried to leave the batterer
- Fear of not getting custody of their children
- Financial dependence
- Feeling of responsibility for keeping the relationship together
- Lack of support from family and friends
- The batterer is not always violent
- They still love the batterer

Myth: Individuals who batter abuse their partners because they are under a great deal of stress, including being unemployed.

Reality: Stress does not cause individuals to batter their partners. Society condones partner abuse. In addition, individuals who batter learn they can achieve their goals through the use of force without facing consequences.

Myth: Children are not affected by watching their parents in a battering relationship.

Reality: Children are often in the middle of domestic violence. They may be abused by the violent parent. Children may also grow up to repeat the same behavior patterns they witnessed in their parents.

Myth: There are no long-term consequences of battering.

Reality: There are significant long-term consequences of battering, including depression, anger, fear, anxiety, irritability, loss of self-esteem, feelings of humiliation and alienation, and a sense of vulnerability.

Myth: Intimate partner violence only occurs in poor and minority families.

Reality: Intimate partner violence occurs among all socioeconomic classes and all racial and ethnic groups.

Services Offered by _____ for Employees who are Victims of Intimate Partner Violence

_____ will offer the following services for our employees who are victims of intimate partner violence:

- Provide receptionists and building security officer with a photograph of the batterer and a description of the batterer
- Screen employee's calls
- Screen employee's visitors
- Accompany the employee to her/his car, subway, bus stop
- Permit the employee to park close to the office building if required
- When there is a restraining order, _____ will send a formal notification to the batterer that indicates that his/her presence on the Firm's premises will result in arrest
- Referrals for individual counseling

Training programs dealing with intimate partner violence will be facilitated annually for managers and employees.

Members of the Threat Assessment Team you may contact to discuss intimate partner violence are:

Name _____ Phone Number _____

APPENDIX 2: SAMPLE PERSONALIZED SAFETY PLAN

Name:
Date Completed:

1. I can inform my immediate supervisor, security, human resources and _____ at work that I am a victim of intimate partner violence.
2. I can ask _____ to help me screen my telephone calls at work.
3. When leaving work, I can walk with _____ to my car or the bus stop. I can park my car where I will feel safest getting in and out of the car.
4. If I have problems while driving home, I can_____.
5. If I use public transit, I can _____.
6. I can go to different grocery stores and shopping malls to conduct my business and shop at hours that are different from those I kept when residing with my battering partner.
7. I can use a different bank and go at hours that are different from those I kept when residing with my battering partner.
8. I can use _____ as my code word to alert my coworkers when I am in danger so they will call for help.

Important Telephone Numbers
Police: 911 and _____
Domestic Violence Shelter:
District Attorney's Office:
My Supervisor's Home Phone Number:
My Clergy Contact's Phone Number:
Human Resources:
Security:
Other:

_____

_____

APPENDIX 3: SAMPLE TRAINING PROGRAM FOR MANAGERS

Goals of Training
    To:

a. Provide information about the incidence and psychological dimensions of intimate partner violence.
b. Discuss the impact of intimate partner violence on individuals and the workplace.
c. Distinguish between myths and realities regarding intimate partner violence.
d. Discuss reasons employees will disclose and not disclose intimate partner violence at work.

e. Provide information on ways the workplace can encourage disclosure regarding intimate partner violence.

f. Discuss workplace's policy statement on intimate partner violence.

g. Discuss the role of the EAP, security, unions in assisting victims of intimate partner violence.

h. Discuss characteristics of perpetrators of intimate partner violence.

At the conclusion of the training program, managers will be able to:

a. Assess their own stereotypes and hidden biases regarding intimate partner violence.

b. Adequately label emotional, physical, interpersonal, and career impacts of intimate partner violence on individuals and the workplace.

c. Identify employees' rights and responsibilities to disclose intimate partner violence at the workplace.

d. Adequately assist employees who wish to disclose intimate partner violence.

Topics for Presentation and Discussion
Introduction to training session and goals of training
Case presented to managers, managers offer opinions related to case
Discussion of case
Myths related to intimate partner violence:

Intimate partner violence is a rare event.

Intimate partner violence is about sex.

Women are masochistic and ask to be abused.

Intimate partner violence only includes physical assault.

Intimate partner violence only occurs in poor families.

Intimate partner violence only occurs in heterosexual couples.

Myths vs. realities

Definition of intimate partner violence.

Incidence of intimate partner violence.

Sex vs. power in intimate partner violence.

Reasons why women remain in battering relationships.

Verbal and physical examples of intimate partner violence.

Sex, ethnic, racial, and socioeconomic status related to intimate partner violence.

Sexual orientation and intimate partner violence.

Psychological issues in disclosing or not disclosing intimate partner violence in the workplace.

Pre-work, during work and after work threats by perpetrators.
Impact of intimate partner violence on victims.

> Emotional symptoms
> Physical symptoms
> Behavioral symptoms
> Organizational symptoms

Impact of intimate partner violence on coworkers.
Impact of intimate partner violence on workplace.
Factors contributing to intimate partner violence.

> Behavioral risk factors
> Social and cultural factors
> Personal and psychological factors

Characteristics of perpetrators of intimate partner violence.
Managing intimate partner violence in the workplace.

> Workplace's policy and procedures
> Workplace's role in responding to disclosure of intimate partner violence
> Identifying security procedures
> Personalized safety plans
> Referring employees to the EAP
> Ensuring victims are not discriminated against on performance appraisals, etc.
> Encouraging disclosure: Keeping stereotypes and biases in check

Discussion of case
General discussion

APPENDIX 4: RESOURCES ON INTIMATE PARTNER VIOLENCE AS A WORKPLACE ISSUE

Abusive Men Exploring New Directions
    www.amendinc.org

American Bar Association Commission on Domestic Violence
    www.abanet.org/domviol/home.html

American Domestic Violence Crisis Line
    www.awoscentral.com

American Psychological Association
    www.apa.org

Asian and Pacific Islander Institute on Domestic Violence
    www.apiahf.org/apidvinstitute

Battered Women's Justice Project
    www.bwjp.org

Centers for Disease Control and Prevention
www.cdc.gov

Department of Justice Violence Against Women Office
www.ojp.usdoj.gov/vawo

Domestic Violence Clearinghouse and Legal Hotline
www.stoptheviolence.org

Equal Employment Opportunity Commission
www.eeoc.org

Family Violence Prevention Fund
Endabuse.org

Institute on Domestic Violence in the African American Community
www.dvinstitute.org

National Center for Victims of Crime
www.ncvc.org

National Center on Domestic and Sexual Violence
www.ncdsv.org

National Coalition Against Domestic Violence
www.ncadv.org

National Domestic Violence Hotline
www.ndvh.org

National Institute for Occupational Safety and Health
www.niosh.gov

National Latino Alliance for the Elimination of Domestic Violence
www.dvalianza.org

National Organization for Women
www.now.org

National Resource Center on Domestic Violence
www.nrcdv.org

Occupational Safety and Health Association
www.osha.gov

Safe at Work Coalition
www.safeatworkcoalition.org

Society for Human Resource Management
www.shrm.org

U.S. Department of Health and Human Services
www.4woman.gov/violence/index.cfm

Violence Against Women Office
www.ovw.usdoj.gov

Violence Prevention
www.ama-assn.org/ama/pub/category/3242.html

REFERENCES

American Bar Association Commission on Domestic Violence. (1999). *A guide for employees: Domestic violence in the workplace.* Washington, DC: Author.

American Institute on Domestic Violence. (2009). Domestic violence in the workplace statistics. Retrieved July 8, 2009 from http://www.aidv-usa.com/statistics.htm

Barbazette, J. (2006). *Training needs assessment: Methods, tools and techniques.* New York: John Wiley & Sons.

Barling, J., Rogers, A., & Kelloway, E. (2001). Behind closed doors: In-home workers' experience of sexual harassment and workplace violence. *Journal of Occupational Health Psychology, 6*, 225–269.

Birns, B. (1999). Battered wives: Causes, effects and social change. In C. Forden, A. Hunter, & B. Birns (Eds.), *Readings in the psychology of women: Dimensions of the female experience.* Boston: Allyn & Bacon.

Black, D., & Newman, M. (2000). Children: Secondary victims of domestic violence. In A. Shalev, R. Yehuda, & A. McFarlane. (Eds.), *International handbook of human responses to trauma.* New York: Plenum.

Bostock, J., Plumpton, M., & Pratt, R. (2009). Domestic violence against women: Understanding social processes and women's experiences. *Journal of Community and Applied Social Psychology, 19*, 95–110.

Brown, J. (2002). Training needs assessment: A must for developing an effective training program. *Public Personnel Management, 31*, 569–578.

Burlington Industries v. Ellerth, 524 U.S. 742 (1998).

Butts Stahly, G. (1999). Violence against women by male partners: Prevalence, outcomes and policy implications. *American Psychologist, 48*, 1077–1087.

Centers for Disease Control and Prevention. (2009). Retrieved July 8, 2009 from http://www.cdc.gov/ncipc/ub-res/ipv

Coleman, V. (1991). Violence in lesbian couples: A between groups comparison. Doctoral dissertation, California School of Professional Psychology, Los Angeles, 1990. *Dissertation Abstracts International, 51*, 5634B.

Crouhy, M., Galai, D., & Mark, R. (2005). *The essentials of risk management.* New York: McGraw Hill.

Cunradi, C., Ames, G., & Moore, R. (2008). Prevalence and correlates of intimate partner violence among a sample of construction industry workers. *Journal of Family Violence, 23*, 101–112.

DeCenzo, D., & Robbins, S. (2007). *Fundamentals of human resource management.* New York: Wiley.

Dessler, G. (2009). *Fundamentals of human resource management.* Upper Saddle River, NJ: Prentice Hall.

Eastman, W. (1998). Working for position: Women, men and managerial work hours. *Industrial Relations, 37*, 51–66.

Equal Employment Opportunity Commission. (1999). Enforcement guidance: Vicarious employer liability for unlawful harassment by supervisors. Washington, DC: Equal Employment Opportunity Commission.

Faragher v. City of Boca Raton, 524 U.S. 725 (1998).

Frisbie, S. (2002). *Sexual harassment: A comparison of on-line versus traditional training methods.* Unpublished doctoral dissertation, Texas Tech University, Lubbock, TX.

Frone, M., & Yardley, J. (1996). Workplace family-supportive programmes: Predictors of employed parents' importance ratings. *Journal of Occupational and Organizational Psychology, 69,* 351–366.

Goldstein, I., & Ford, J. (2002). *Training in organizations: Needs assessment, development and evaluation* (4th ed.). Belmont, CA: Wadsworth.

Graham, D., & Rawlings, E. (1999). Observers' blaming of battered wives: Who, what, when, and why (pp. 55–94). In M. Paludi (Ed.), *The psychology of sexual victimization: A handbook.* Westport, CT: Greenwood Press.

Graziano, A., & Raulin, M. (1996). *Research methods: A process of inquiry.* White Plains, NY: Longman.

Grothues, C., & Marmion, S. (2006). Dismantling the myths about intimate violence against women. In P. Lundberg-Love & S. Marmion (Eds.), *Intimate violence against women* (pp. 9–14). Westport, CT: Praeger.

Gurchiek, K. (2005, March). Study: Domestic violence spills over into workplace. *HR Magazine.* Retrieved July 9, 2009 from http://findarticles.com/p/articles/mi_m34950/ai_n13247058.

Horne, S. (1999). Domestic violence in Russia. *American Psychologist, 54,* 55–61.

Kelly, E., & Mullen, J. (2006). Organizational response to workplace violence. In K. Kelloway, J. Barling, & J. Hurrell (Eds.), *Handbook of workplace violence.* New York: Sage.

Kirkpatrick, D. (1959). Techniques for evaluating training programs. *Journal of the American Society for Training Development, 13,* 3–9.

Kirkpatrick, D. (1998). *Evaluating training programs: The four levels.* San Francisco, CA: Berrett-Koehler.

Langford, L. (2006). *Preventing violence and promoting safety in higher education settings: Overview of a comprehensive approach.* Newton, MA: Higher Education Center for Alcohol and Other Drug Abuse and Violence Prevention.

Lemon, N. (2001). *Domestic violence law.* St. Paul, MN: West Group.

Levy, A., & Paludi, M. (2001). *Workplace sexual harassment* (2nd ed.). Englewood Cliffs, NJ: Prentice Hall.

Lloyd, S., & Taluc, N. (1999). The effects of male violence on female employment. *Violence Against Women, 5,* 370–392.

Lucier, K. (2008). A consultative training program: Collateral effect of a needs assessment. *Communication Education, 57,* 482–489.

Lundberg-Love, P., & Marmion, S. (2006). *Intimate violence against women.* Westport, CT: Praeger.

Lundberg-Love, P., & Wilkerson, D. (2006). Battered women. In P. Lundberg-Love & S. Marmion (Eds.), *Intimate violence against women* (pp. 31–45). Westport, CT: Praeger.

Marmion, S., & Faulkner, D. (2006). Effects of class and culture on intimate partner violence. In P. Lundberg-Love & S. Marmion (Eds.), *Intimate violence against women* (pp. 131–143). Westport, CT: Praeger.

McHugh, M., & Frieze, I. (2006). Intimate partner violence. In F. Denmark, H. Krauss, E. Halpern, & J. Sechzer (Eds.), *Violence and exploitation against women and girls* (pp. 121–141). Boston: Blackwell Publishing.

McHugh, M., Livingston, N., & Frieze, I. (2008). Intimate partner violence: Perspectives on research and intervention. In F. Denmark & M. Paludi (Eds.), *Psychology of women: A handbook of issues and theories,* Westport, CT: Praeger (pp. 555–589).

Middelkoop, J., Gilhooley, J., Ruepp, N., Polikoski, R., & Paludi, M. (2008). Campus security recommendations for administrators to help prevent and deal with violence. In M. Paludi (Ed.), *Understanding and preventing campus violence* (pp. 234–235). Westport, CT: Praeger.

Mitchell, M., Hargrove, G., Collins, M., Thompson, M., Reddick, T., & Kaslow, N. (2006). Coping variables that mediate the relation between intimate partner violence and mental health outcomes among low-income African American women. *Journal of Clinical Psychology, 62,* 1503–1520.

National Institute for Occupational Safety and Health. (2009). www.niosh.gov

Occupational Health and Safety Administration. (2009). www.osha.org

O'Leary, K., & Maiuro, R. (Eds.). (2001). *Psychological abuse in violent domestic relations.* New York: Springer.

Paludi, M. (2002). *The psychology of women* (2nd ed.). Upper Saddle River, NJ: Prentice Hall.

Paludi, M., & Barickman, R. (1998). *Sexual harassment, work, and education: A resource manual for prevention.* Albany: State University of New York Press.

Paludi, M., & Neidermeyer, P. (Eds.). (2006). *Work, life and family imbalance: How to level the playing field.* Westport, CT: Praeger.

Paludi, M., Nydegger, R., & Paludi, C. (2006). *Understanding workplace violence: A guide for managers and employees.* Westport, CT: Praeger.

Paludi, C., & Paludi, M. (2000, October). *Developing and enforcing an effective workplace policy statement, procedures, and training programs on domestic violence.* Paper presented at the conference on domestic violence as a workplace concern: Legal, psychological, management, and law enforcement perspectives, Nashua, NH.

Paludi, M., & Paludi, C. (Eds.). (2003). *Academic and workplace sexual harassment.* Westport, CT: Praeger.

Paludi, M., & Paludi, C. (2006). Integrating work/life: Resources for employees, employers, and human resource specialists. In M. Paludi & P. Neidermeyer (Eds.), (2006). *Work, life and family imbalance: How to level the playing field* (pp. 122–154). Westport, CT: Praeger.

Paludi, M., Vaccariello, R., Graham, T., Smith, M., Allen-Dicker, K., Kasprzak, H., et al. (2006). Work/life integration: Impact on women's career, employment and family. In M. Paludi & P. Neidermeyer (Eds.), *Work, life and family imbalance: How to level the playing field* (pp. 21–36). Westport, CT: Praeger.

Partnership for Prevention. (2002). *Domestic violence and the workplace.* Washington, DC: Author.

Potoczniak, M., Murot, J., Crosbie-Burnett, M., & Potoczni, A. (2003). Legal and psychological perspectives on same-sex domestic violence. *Journal of Family Psychology, 17,* 252–259.

Randel, J., & Wells, K. (2003). Corporate approaches to reducing intimate partner violence through workplace initiatives. *Clinical Occupation and Environmental Medicine, 3,* 821–841.

Rathus, J., & Feindler, E. (2004). *Assessment of partner violence: A handbook for researchers and practitioners.* Washington, DC: American Psychological Association.

Reeves, C., & O'Leary-Kelly, A. (2007). The effects and costs of intimate partner violence for work organizations. *Journal of Interpersonal Violence, 22,* 327–344.

Ridley, E. (2004). *Impact of domestic violence offenders on occupational safety and health: A pilot study.* Augusta, ME: Family Crisis Services, Maine Department of Labor.

Roper, A. (2002). *Corporate leaders on domestic violence awareness of the problem, how it's affecting their business, and what they're doing to address it.* New York: Liz Claiborne, Inc.

Rothman, E., Hathaway, J., Stidsen, A., & deVries, H. (2007). How employment helps female victims of intimate partner violence: A qualitative study. *Journal of Occupational Health Psychology, 12,* 136–143.

Ryan, K., Frieze, I., & Sinclair, H. C. (1999). Physical violence in dating relationships. In M. Paludi (Ed.), *The psychology of sexual victimization: A handbook* (pp. 33–54). Westport, CT: Greenwood.

Sagrestano, L., Carroll, D., Rodriguez, A., & Nuwayhid, B. (2004). Demographic, psychological and relationship factors in domestic violence during pregnancy in a sample of low-income women of color. *Psychology of Women Quarterly, 28,* 309–322.

Slavin, R. (2008). *Educational psychology: Theory and practice* (9th ed.). Boston: Allyn & Bacon.

Smith, S., & Mazin, R. (2004). *The HR answer book.* New York: AMACOM.

Society for Human Resource Management. (2009). www.shrm.org

Soroptimist International of the Americas. (2007). *White paper: Domestic violence as a workplace concern.* Retrieved June 22, 2009, from http://staging.soroptimist.org/whitepapers/wp_dv.html

Straus, M., Gelles, R., & Steinmetz, S. (1980). *Behind closed doors: Violence in the American family.* Garden City, NY: Anchor Books.

Swanberg, J., & Logan, T. (2005). Domestic violence and employment: A qualitative study of the effects of domestic violence on women's employment. *Journal of Occupational and Health Psychology, 10,* 3–17.

Swanberg, J., & Logan, T. (2007). Intimate partner violence, employment and the workplaces: An interdisciplinary perspective. *Journal of Interpersonal Violence, 22,* 263–267.

Swanberg, J., Logan, T., & Macke, C. (2005). Intimate partner violence, employment and the workplace: Consequences and future directions. *Trauma, Violence and Abuse, 6,* 286–312.

Swanberg, J., Macke, C., & Logan, T. (2006). Intimate partner violence, women, and work: Coping on the job. *Violence and Victims, 21,* 561–578.

Swanberg, J., Macke, C., & Logan, T. (2007). Working women making it work: Intimate partner violence, employment, and workplace support. *Journal of Interpersonal Violence, 22,* 292–391.

Tan, J., Hall, R., & Boyce, C. (2003). The role of employee reactions in predicting training effectiveness. *Human Resource Development Quarterly, 14,* 397–411.

Tjaden, P., & Thoennes, N. (2000). *Full report of the prevalence, incidence and consequences of violence against women: Findings from the National Violence Against Women Survey, NIJ/CDC.* Washington, DC: U.S. Department of Justice. (NCJ 183781).

Tran, C., & DesJardins, K. (2000). Domestic violence in Vietnamese refugee and Korean immigrant communities. In J. Chin (Ed.), *Relationships among Asian American women.* Washington, DC: American Psychological Association.

Tyler, K. (2002). Evaluating evaluations. *HR Magazine, 47.*

Urban, B. (2000). *Anonymous foundation domestic abuse prevention program evaluation: Final client survey report.* Chicago, IL: The University of Illinois at Chicago.

Walker, L. (1979). *The battered woman.* New York: Harper & Row.

Walker, L. (1995). Foreword. In L. Adler & F. Denmark (Eds.), *Violence and the prevention of violence* (pp. ix–xii). Westport, CT: Praeger.

Walker, L. (1999). Psychology and domestic violence around the world. *American Psychologist, 54,* 21–29.

Walker, L. (2006). Battered woman syndrome: Empirical findings. In F. Denmark, H. Krauss, E. Halpern, & J. Sechzer (Eds.), *Violence and exploitation against women and girls* (pp. 142–157). Boston: Blackwell Publishing.

Watlington, C., & Murphy, C. (2006). The roles of religion and spirituality among African American survivors of domestic violence. *Journal of Clinical Psychology, 62,* 837–857.

Wetterstein, K., Rudolph, S., Paul, K., Gallagher, K., Trang, B., Adams, K., et al. (2004). Freedom through self-sufficiency: A qualitative examination of the impact of violence on the working lives of women in shelter. *Journal of Counseling Psychology, 51,* 447–462.

Willman, S. (2007). *Too much, too long? Domestic violence in the workplace.* Testimony before the U.S. Senate Subcommittee on Employment and Workplace Safety.

Zorza, J. (2002). Battering. In J. Zorza (Ed.), *Violence against women.* Kingston, NJ: Civic Research Institute.

Chapter 6

From Victim to Empowered Survivor: Feminist Therapy with Survivors of Rape and Sexual Assault

Avigail Moor

Sexual violence against women is a widespread phenomenon affecting a large percentage of women. According to available data, approximately 20 to 40 percent of all women will experience some form of sexual assault during their lifetime (Casey & Nurius, 2006; Koss, 1983; Koss & Harvey, 1991; Moor, 2009). Rape and other forms of sexual violence are traumatic experiences that commonly result in severe psychological sequelae. These include posttraumatic stress disorder (PTSD), depression, anxiety, loss of meaning, self-devaluation, shame, and impaired sexual functioning (Angell, 1994; Burnam, Stein, Golding, & Siegel, 1988; Foa & Rothbaum, 1998; Gilbert, 1994; Herman, 1992; Jaycox, Zoellner, & Foa, 2002; Lebowitz & Roth, 1994).

While the posttraumatic aspects of the clinical presentation of rape survivors are similar to those noted in the aftermath of other types of trauma (Foa & Rothbaum, 1998; Jaycox et al, 2002; Meadows & Foa, 1998), many of the additional symptoms observed are rape-specific and socially determined (Koss & Harvey, 1991; Lebowitz & Roth, 1994; Moor, 2007). Sexual violence against women occurs in a very particular social context, characterized by prejudiced, victim-blaming attitudes toward survivors that fault, shame, and isolate the victim of the assault. Thus, rather than receiving social support and comfort, as is typical in the case of most other forms of trauma, victims of sexual violence are often scorned and abandoned. This can lead to extreme levels of self-blame, guilt, and shame, which incessantly torment victims of sexual violence.

Although some form of self-blame is common to the experience of trauma in general, the particularly insidious rape-specific self-disdain is incremental to the more customary self-blame, and a serious complication to recovery. Yet this reality is frequently overlooked in therapies uninformed by the social analysis of the aftermath of rape to the detriment of survivors; hence the necessity for a therapeutic model that incorporates this understanding on a most fundamental level.

Feminist therapy is such an approach. Rooted in a contextual conceptualization of female psychological distress, it is the optimal perspective from which to treat survivors of rape. This chapter is intended to delineate the principles of feminist therapy that are expected to augment all forms of treatment for rape survivors, regardless of theoretical orientation. It is a philosophy of treatment and shared principles that are meant to accompany all theoretical orientations and approaches to treatment. It should be stated that while the focus of this chapter is on the treatment of rape and sexual assault survivors, much of its content applies equally to victims of other forms of sexual violence such as sexual harassment and child sexual abuse, although each of these has its unique elements that must be addressed as well.

Having worked extensively with rape and sexual assault survivors for more than two decades at two regional rape crisis centers and in private practice, I have come to believe that it is the feminist aspects of the treatment, particularly the social analysis and the egalitarian stance of the therapist that benefit these clients most. This holds true in my experience for the majority of victims. The population that I have worked with over the years has been highly variable in age, ethnic background, socioeconomic status, and preassault psychological functioning, as well as in previous exposure to trauma. Their clinical presentations generally fit the typical rape survivors' profile, with the majority exhibiting PTSD symptoms along with rape-specific symptomatology. Yet all have responded favorably above all else to the feminist tenets of the treatment.

This is not to negate the importance, and even the necessity, of specific trauma resolution interventions such as eye movement desensitization and reprocessing (EMDR; Power et al., 2002; Rogers & Silver, 2002; Shapiro & Maxfield, 2002), cognitive–behavioral therapy (CBT; Foa & Rothbaum, 1998; Jaycox et al, 2002; Meadows & Foa, 1998), prolonged exposure (Foa, Zoellner, Feeny, Hembree, & Alvarez-Conrad, 2002; Lee, Gavriel, Drummond, & Greenwald, 2002; Pitman, Altman, Greenwald, Longpre, Machlin, Poire, & Steketee, 1991), and other modalities. All of these techniques are positively effective in treating the PTSD aspects of the presenting problem. However, there is also extensive evidence that these interventions alone may not suffice in relieving survivors' sense of disempowerment and guilt, which often persist after PTSD symptoms have subsided if not targeted directly.

For example, Pitman et al. reported that while survivors treated with flooding showed considerable decrease in anxiety, their feelings of shame and blame did not respond to further exposure to the narrative. A similar account is provided in Meadows and Foa's case study of a survivor whose anxiety symptoms responded well to prolonged exposure, while her tendency to berate herself for having been at the bar where she was assaulted actually increased. They report that these feelings of guilt and shame were not alleviated by further exposure to the assault narrative. The integration of feminist principles, with their contextual and egalitarian emphases, into the therapeutic process offers us the chance to provide our clients with the ultimate empowerment needed for recovery. These principles are outlined next.

FEMINIST PSYCHOTHERAPY

Feminist therapy is a philosophy of psychotherapy rather than a distinct orientation (Hill & Ballou, 1998; Moradi, Fischer, Hill, Jome, & Blum, 2000; Rader & Gilbert, 2005). Being woman-centered, it underscores the social context of women's distress, maintaining that women's pain cannot be fully understood outside of social context. Social norms, values, and attitudes are seen as greatly contributing to the creation and maintenance of many of the problems and issues that are brought into therapy (Feminist Therapy Institute, 1990; Hill & Ballou, 1998; Kaschak, 1992; Worell & Remer, 1992; Worell & Johnson, 2001). Each individual's personal experiences and situations are viewed as reflective of and influenced by society's attitudes and values. Therefore, one of the goals of therapy is to afford the clients an awareness of these influences so as to bring about change in perspective and an understanding of the interactions between the various social factors and the client's internal experiences (Brown & Brodsky, 1992; Hill & Ballou, 1998; Rader & Gilbert, 2005). Although feminist therapists are trained in a variety of disciplines and theoretical orientations, they are united amid this diversity by their feminist analyses and perspectives regarding the interactive effects of the client's internal and external worlds.

Another central tenet of feminist therapy stemming from feminist philosophy is a commitment to the empowerment of women and the validation and valuing of their experience and viewpoint. Caring, compassion and respect are, accordingly, the foundation of this approach to treatment (Brown & Brodsky; 1992; Moradi et al., 2000; Rader & Gilbert, 2005; Worell & Remer, 1992). It is a relationship in which clients are empowered to find their strengths and strivings, a practice in which growth-promoting reframing of social realities allows for new ways of thinking and being. It is a process of connectedness in which each client is made to feel worthy of respect, affection, tenderness, and judgment-free acceptance, an endeavor of caring that identifies each client's unique and positive qualities so as to enhance her self esteem.

In addition, the principles of feminist therapy call for an egalitarian therapeutic relationship, which is considered a core tenet of this approach to treatment. Recognizing the negative impact of the gender-based power imbalance in the lives of most women, feminist therapy is intent on maintaining an egalitarian structure within its bounds (Feminist Therapy Institute, 1990; Hill & Ballou, 1998; Jordan, Kaplan, Miller, Stiver, & Surrey, 1991; Rader & Gilbert, 2005). Accordingly, feminist therapists are committed to maximizing the equality between therapist and client by exercising power-sharing behaviors of various kinds. These include refraining from placing themselves in the one-up position, working collaboratively with the client, viewing the client as her own expert, treating her with complete respect and belief in her strengths and knowledge, informing the client of the therapy process, allowing the client to guide the sessions, and so on (Hill, 1990; Gilbert, 1980; Hill & Ballou, 1998; Rader & Gilbert, 2005; Worell & Remer, 1992). Equalizing the relationship with the client is seen as a primary responsibility of the therapist, who routinely evaluates her ongoing interactions with her clients for any evidence of hierarchy, biases or discriminatory attitudes and practices. Moreover, she accepts responsibility for taking action to confront and change any interfering, oppressing, or devaluing biases she may have.

Feminist therapy is also devoted to the creation of social change and the valuing of the female perspective. Therapy from this perspective is intended to bring about individual as well as social change through raising awareness to the oppressive social forces impacting the client's wellbeing and offering new ways of being and perceiving. This process reverberates beyond the bounds of therapy into ever-growing circles of awareness and action. In order to increase the social impact of their practice, feminist therapists attempt to reach out to large segments of the population. They also may engage in broadly defined social activism in addition to their professional work.

It is suggested that the principles of feminist therapy offer the best conceptual framework for understanding the myriad of symptoms exhibited by survivors of sexual aggression. Treatment from this perspective is likely to deliver optimally suited interventions to this population, while providing the kind of empowering interpersonal experiences that can counteract the utter disregard sustained in rape. We therefore turn next to a discussion of the application of feminist therapy to the treatment of survivors of rape and sexual assault. The discussion begins with a feminist analysis of the social context of the sexual victimization of women, so as to provide a conceptual foundation for the therapy. Application to treatment of each tenet of feminist therapy is considered thereafter.

APPLICATION OF FEMINIST THERAPY TO THE TREATMENT OF SURVIVORS OF RAPE AND SEXUAL ASSAULT

Feminist Analysis of Sexual Violence against Women

In accordance with the focus of feminist therapy on the social context of individual psychological distress, the treatment of victims of sexual violence is rooted in an analysis of the interplay between social factors and internal responses to the events. In this analysis, sexual violence against women is considered to be an integral part of the social oppression of women. Similarly, societal attitudes toward the victims of this aggression are viewed as constituting one of the central public forces to negatively impact women's lives and wellbeing subsequent to rape. Following is an analysis of the social context of rape followed by an application of feminist therapy guidelines to the treatment of its aftermath.

Social Context of Rape

Rape and other forms of sexual violence epitomize the social oppression of women. In fact, from the feminist standpoint, sexual violence against women is one of the primary means by which patriarchy aims to keep women in their place (McKinnon, 2005). The astronomical prevalence rates of all forms of sexual violence directed at women, coupled with the utter failure of the system to combat this menace, suggest that society is bent, at best, on regulating rather than eliminating it. Katherine McKinnon refers to this social order as the "Rape Culture." According to her, sexual violence against women is rooted in a discriminatory social hierarchy, which both mobilizes and perpetuates the abuse of women. The ideology of this system amounts to an eroticization of women's oppression and domination, thereby turning this type of violence into conceivable and even appealing for many individual males, while abandoning the victims in the process. Feminist therapy, anchored in such a conceptualization of sexual violence against women, can empower victims greatly by helping them to realize that their victimization was not due to any contribution of their own, but was rather part of the systematic victimization of women in patriarchy.

Consistent with the social function of sexual violence as a means of keeping women in line, social attitudes toward victims of these crimes are oppressive and damaging as well. In fact, the present social environment is extremely detrimental for rape survivors, with societal victim-blaming and revictimization being rampant (Campbell, 1998; Campbell & Raja, 1999; Campbell, Wasco, Ahrens, Sefl, & Barnes, 2001). As a consequence, rape survivors are commonly burdened with an external, societal assault of prejudiced collective attitudes that blame and shame them for being raped (Ardovini-Brooker & Caringella-MacDonald, 2002; Burt,

1980). These stereotyped attitudes, generally subsumed in the term "rape myths" (Lonsway & Fitzgerald, 1994), amount to a second victimization, and are frequently internalized by survivors, often generating an array of severe self-denigrating cognitions and emotional suffering.

VICTIM-BLAMING AND SECONDARY VICTIMIZATION

Present society is laden with a wide array of detrimental rape myths. Typical myths revolve around the notion that victims somehow contributed to their own victimization and are responsible for its occurrence (Koss & Harvey, 1991). Victim precipitation is the most common and well-known rape myth, which directly holds the victim responsible for the rape (Cowan, 2000). It is founded on a belief that the victim in some way provoked the rape. It claims that she asked to be raped by engaging in "unsafe" behavior, such as drinking or hitchhiking; by placing herself in "unsafe" situations, such as bars or dark streets; by wearing revealing clothes, or by behaving "promiscuously" ("nice" girls don't get raped). Rape myths further proclaim that women can prevent rape if they truly want to, and that no woman can be forced to have sex against her will. Hence, if a woman is raped, she obviously did not mind it or worse yet, secretly desired it. She may also be viewed as having been dishonored by the rape (e.g., rape is shameful, it only happens to certain types of women), particularly, but not solely, if she belongs to an ethnic minority or to a low SES (Alvidrez, 1999; Wyatt, 1992).

Finally, there are two related rape myths regarding acquaintance rape (the most prevalent form of rape); that victims of such rapes precipitate the event by leading the perpetrators on, and that women say "no" to sexual advances when they actually mean "yes," and hence there was no rape at all.

There are many indications that endorsement of rape myths is fairly pervasive within the legal, law enforcement, and medical establishment (Campbell, 1998; Ullman & Filipas, 2001). This has been referred to as secondary victimization or second rape. There is also evidence that responses of formal support providers may vary in relation to the victim's ethnicity, such that minority women may encounter even harsher reactions than do their majority counterparts (Ullman & Filipas, 2001; Ullman & Brecklin, 2002; Wyatt, 1992).

Some evidence points to similar revictimization of rape victims within the mental health profession (Campbell, 1998; Campbell, Wasco, Ahrens, Sefl, & Barnes, 2001). In a survey of licensed mental health professionals who work extensively with rape survivors, Campbell and Raja (1999) found that 58 percent of the therapists surveyed expressed the view that mental health professionals may carry out some harmful counseling practices when treating this population. Entirely unaware at times of their own prejudices regarding rape and rape survivors, some clinicians may be inclined to view survivors as contributing in some way to the occurrence of the rape. Consequently, they may engage fairly regularly in the interpretation of survivors' motives and behaviors in matters related to the assault. For example, analyzing a survivor's motives for accompanying a romantic partner to his place, where she was then raped, is a case in point. This multitude of adverse social factors can inflict serious psychological harm on survivors.

THE PSYCHOLOGICAL SEQUELAE OF THE SOCIAL CONTEXT OF RAPE

The socially contextual elements of rape and other forms of sexual violence seriously complicate the post-assault clinical presentation of many survivors. This appears to hold true across varied cultural and ethnic backgrounds. Not only must survivors deal with the aftereffects of the humiliating violation that is rape, but also with the devastation of the collective victim-blaming and its internalization. Together, these factors inflict severe agony and pain upon survivors, causing them unbearable levels of self-blame and shame (Koss & Harvey, 1991; Moor, 2007; Ullman, 1996).

The all too common accusation that the rape victim precipitated the assault can exacerbate her self-accusation and contempt, heightening her already strong tendency to berate herself for her "carelessness" (e.g., "How could I have been so stupid . . . putting myself in such a situation and allowing this to happen"). The belief that she is to blame for being attacked can make the survivor doubt her own perceptions, invalidating her lived experience. While hurting to the core, she may nonetheless consequently feel that she got exactly what she deserved (e.g., "I decided to hitchhike home so I deserve what I got. . . . there can be no sympathy towards me"). The pain and despair that result are massive. The charge that the rape occurred because of the type of woman she is coupled with the widespread notion that rape is dishonoring, routinely leads to extreme shame and self-disdain (e.g., "I am so ashamed; no one can ever know of this"). The dehumanizing nature of rape, intended to denigrate and demean, typically creates a sense of humiliation, desecration, and helplessness, all of which tend to lead to intolerable shame, disgrace, and self-disgust (e.g., "I am utterly disgusting").

While the brunt of the post-assault self-blame is socially driven, it is important to keep in mind that blaming the self also has a function in dealing with trauma (Koss & Harvey, 1991). It provides survivors with some (albeit illusionary) sense of control over the traumatic events designed to counteract the experience of helplessness. If a rape survivor believes that her behavior contributed to the assault in some way, she can believe that changing this particular behavior in the future will prevent a reoccurrence of the event. It is important to be aware of this protective function of self-blame and guilt when treating this population.

Encountering victim-blaming often discourages survivors from disclosing the incident, thereby reducing their likelihood of obtaining social support that could facilitate their recovery (Botta & Pingree, 1997). For example, some stereotypes may cause survivors to doubt that their experience qualifies as "real rape," which may keep them, in turn, from seeking help. This problem appears to be especially, although not uniquely, common among survivors of date rape (Alvidrez, 1999; Ullman & Brecklin, 2002).

Similarly, accusatory and demeaning social attitudes may drive a sizeable proportion of survivors to isolate themselves from loved ones, friends, and family for on many occasions rape myths are actually accepted and believed by survivors' close social and familial environment (Sheldon & Parent, 2002; Ullman, 1999). It is not uncommon to encounter victim-blaming on the part of those closest to the victim, in the form of dismay that she behaved in a certain way or failed to do one thing or another. Shame among family members is also common. It may take the form of urging the survivor to keep quiet about the assault and pretend it never happened or of outright disgracing her for having been violated. This can be devastating.

Survivors may be further harmed if upon turning to the system for help they meet with second victimization and rape myth endorsement by members of the helping professions. This can increase their feelings of culpability and shame, as well as cause them to feel completely invalidated, misunderstood, and judged. Moreover, survivors are likely to become distrustful of others, making them reluctant to seek further help (Campbell & Raja, 1999; Ullman & Filipas, 2001). In fact, a majority of the therapists surveyed in Campbell & Raja's (1999) study voiced a concern that interaction with community professionals can actually, at times, worsen the state of survivors' mental health. In comparison, less than half (48 percent) of the clinicians surveyed believed that contacting community professionals had positive outcomes for rape victims. For this reason, 85 percent of therapists expressed a belief that clinicians must be made more aware of the risks of secondary victimization and its repercussions for the effectiveness of treatment, to avoid inflicting further harm on survivors and to fully maximize the efficacy of therapy. Feminist therapy incorporates such awareness, and in view of that can offer specific treatment principles for working with rape survivors as delineated next.

TREATMENT PRINCIPLES

In light of the socially contextual aspects of much of the pain experienced by survivors of rape and other sexual assaults, there can be little doubt that their treatment must be rooted in a feminist conceptualization and analysis if the correction of the effects of the social factors is to take place. In the absence of a thorough comprehension of the combined impact of rape and related victim-blaming rape myths on survivors' wellbeing, therapy stands the risk of lacking in effectiveness. Even the direct reprocessing of the traumatic events will be augmented by approaching it from a socially contextual viewpoint. In this process, each tenet of feminist therapy has a particularly healing function as delineated next.

EGALITARIAN THERAPEUTIC RELATIONSHIP

Being predicated on nonjudgmental respect and genuine belief in every woman's innate value and strength, feminist therapy offers survivors the opportunity to restore their sense of dignity and self-worth so brutally shattered by the sexual assault. At its core, this treatment aims to counter the humiliation and dehumanization sustained in the attack, while restoring a sense of dignity and self-worth. The type of non-hierarchical, genuinely caring and compassionate empathy that this approach to treatment is built upon plays a crucial, curative role in the recovery from rape, as it imparts a sense of complete validation of every aspect of each survivor's experience. The kind of therapeutic relationship in which each woman is made to feel worthy in all respects, aims to foster a sense of trust, as it communicates a true acceptance of all of her feelings and thoughts, her choices and needs. Through these interventions, the therapist aims to convey an accurate appraisal of the suffering endured by survivors, provide support, and relief; and at the same time, affirm survivors' emotional reality (Paivio & Laurent, 2001; Ullman, 1999).

Out of respect for our clients who have been sexually victimized, we aspire to gain comprehensive familiarity with all aspects of the reaction to rape and sexual assault in order to be able to unequivocally validate their experience and help them to put it into words. Imparting our knowledge of what rape survivors have been known to experience provides each individual survivor with a sense of safety and trust, as well as being understood. Her experience is normalized as she is assured that it is a shared one, typical of other women who have been through similar horror. This is usually highly comforting and reassuring, as it gives survivors reassurance that their reactions are not unusual or pathologic, as they often fear, but rather normal reactions to an abnormal situation (Herman, 1992; Koss & Harvey, 1992). In essence we strive to use our expertise and experience to benefit the client, without taking control or power that rightfully belong to her (Feminist Therapy Institute, 1990; Hill & Ballou, 1998; Rader & Gilbert, 2005). In the process, the survivor begins to regain a sense of control that she was robbed of during the assault.

By viewing the survivor as an equal, we approach therapy with the idea that we are on this journey together, jointly aiming for her full recovery. Our true and genuine presence gives her a sense that she matters, that she is not alone. It counteracts social isolation and loss of trust, as it restores her self-dignity and worth. We give her strength to withstand the devastation, as we believe in her innate coping skills. We also commit to standing by her every step of the way. A survivor expressed the feelings that arise, "Even though the pain is unbearable almost all of the time, knowing that you are truly with me, I don't feel so alone and actually am starting to believe that I might actually make it."

We believe in her strengths and her ability to help herself. As she feels powerless, helpless, and despondent, we offer her hope by reframing her position as survivor rather than victim. She may find this view hard to accept at first, and so we stand by her with full respect, hoping that as we gently point to those aspects of her experience that make her a survivor in our mind, she joins us in this view before long.

The egalitarian position translates into genuine solidarity with the survivors that we treat. While assisting them to process the traumatic events, we share in their pain and permit ourselves to be touched by it, without being overwhelmed or derailed from our therapeutic stance. Recognizing how devastating the experience of sexual violence can be, we validate all aspects of the emotional reality that ensues. We believe in each survivor's inner wisdom, and we let her know it. We guide her to that place of authentic knowledge, so that she may come to believe in herself and in her own perceptions and thoughts. Where she doubts her own experience, we stand by her conveying our belief in her ability to find all the answers within herself. We never doubt her account of the assault, thus helping her to not question it herself. Nor do we impose our conceptualization or formulation on her, but rather attune ourselves most empathically to hers.

From our respectful view of survivors as blame-free in every way, we never pass judgment on their conduct and do our utmost to help ease their sense of blameworthiness and shame, so often contextually heightened. In communicating nonjudgmental acceptance and respect, we aim to counteract the widespread social judgment and reproach (e.g., "It is so heartbreaking to hear you berating and devaluing yourself so"). This mirrors a different perspective on the self—that of the one who has been wronged, not the one to be blamed—while conveying supportive caring at the same time. Self-empathy and compassion are expected to follow, and to give way, in turn, to affirming views of self in place of the existing self-loathing and guilt.

As survivors deal with their sense of self-disgust and defilement, desecration and shame, our genuine belief that they have not been damaged in any way, can help survivors attend to and verbalize their internal experience regarding the sense of self as defiled and shameful. Empathetic mirroring of their feelings of violation and humiliation can help contain these emotions. Insisting that they are shame-free (e.g., "It sounds like your self-disgust is so impossible to bear . . . we will not rest until we find a way to completely free you of it") can help alleviate her shame and foster the emergence of a valued and worthy sense of self.

Treating the survivor as an equal and endowing her with the right to determine the pace and direction of the therapy, can also play a major role in enabling the reprocessing of the traumatic memories. While attuning to the survivor's levels of arousal, voicing our genuine confidence in her ability to sustain the process can afford her a sense of safety, emotional modulation, reassurance, and support, all needed to withstand the painful process of remembering and reliving the traumatic events (Moor, 2007; Paivio & Laurent, 2001). Moreover, experiencing our true caring for her through our soothing and containing responses can help nurture the development of self-soothing capacities and true hope.

As the process progresses, the therapist's belief in the client's strengths is steadily internalized. We enthusiastically share her cautious optimism, while validating and strengthening her new perceptions of self (e.g., "Sounds like you're not blaming yourself anymore . . . how exciting"). Feedback from many survivors allows us to view the egalitarian stance as instrumental in consolidating a new outlook of the self and the future.

EMPOWERMENT

The experience of rape and other forms of sexual violence can be utterly disempowering to most victims, shattering their sense of self-worth, control, and dignity (Herman, 1992; Koss & Harvey, 1991; Moor, 2007). It is the role of therapy to counter this devastating experience by helping survivors to regain a sense of personal power and control. A central goal of feminist therapy, empowerment of the client and advocacy for women (Brown & Brodsky; 1992; Feminist Therapy Institute, 1990; Hill & Ballou, 1998; Moradi et al, 2000; Rader & Gilbert, 2005; Worell & Remer, 1992), thus has a major role to play.

Beyond the empowerment inherent in the egalitarian nature of feminist therapy, contextual reframing of various aspects of the ordeal and reconstruction of self-devaluing cognitions based on the analysis of their social roots are employed to bring about a corrective perceptual shift. Feminist therapy aims to provide clients with novel ways of seeing, along with helpful information that can facilitate this shift (Rader & Gilbert, 2005). Realizing the degree to which survivors' self-loathing cognitions are rooted in internalized societal victim-blaming myths, the feminist therapist thus suggests new ways of perceiving intended to bring about meaningful cognitive shifts. Any internalized prejudiced attitudes that may underlie the demeaning perception of the self are recognized and subject to reconstruction. Clearly, all unfounded cognitions are fully processed, including those related to safety and ability to tolerate stress (Foa & Rothbaum, 1998; Foa & Jaycox, 1999). However, rebuilding a positive and empowered sense of self is at the very heart of the healing process.

Our main objective is restructuring the unfounded views of self as culpable and shameful. The entire array of distorted cognitions regarding precipitation of the assault is targeted. In this process, we encourage the survivor to assess the rationality of these beliefs, so that she can recognize their false nature and their roots in societal victim-blaming rape myths. To increase her sense of mastery, self-conviction, and empowerment, we aim to help the survivor absolve herself of culpability on her own, rather than through our insistence. Reaching this conviction from within makes it more meaningful and lasting. A shift to a more realistic blame-free viewpoint should ensue, allowing her to appropriately place fault where it belongs, namely, with the assailant. For example, a survivor who had held on to the notion that she was to blame for being raped because she did not fight back was helped to see that she stood no chance against her assailant who was considerably bigger and stronger than herself. Gentle probes such as "How big was he? How strong? Now consider your relative size and strength . . . what could you have done?" should facilitate the hoped-for shift.

To further validate survivors, it is useful point to the contextual origin of much of their self-blame and shame, while letting them know that their response is entirely typical of most rape survivors, who generally feel responsible for their plight (e.g., "Like you, almost every rape survivor blames herself mercilessly for the ordeal she had endured. . . . and all too often this is because of common, accusatory social attitudes towards rape victims that absolutely cannot be ignored"). Survivors frequently experience great relief upon realizing that their self-denigration is a characteristic response to the trauma of rape, especially in the current social context.

At this stage it is also important to acknowledge and work through the protective function of the self-blame. Following rape, many victims worry that if none of what happened was due to their actions, they may not have any control over future safety either (Koss & Harvey, 1991). Thus, they hold onto self-accusation and are reluctant to let go of it in order to maintain the sense of control it provides. Helping them to distinguish between liability and ill-advised behavior can promote the complete relinquishment of this self-blame. For example, a survivor raped while hitchhiking was unable to stop berating herself for her "stupid" behavior, which "caused" the rape until she could feel that she would be able to keep herself safe in the future. Interventions such as "while you now realize that hitchhiking isn't safe for you, the fact that you hitchhiked in the past in no way makes you guilty of precipitating the rape" eventually enabled her to replace the self-accusation with a more realistic appraisal of her ability to recognize and to minimize danger in the future, while not having to hold herself responsible for being raped.

Cognitive restructuring can also be used to target the shame and the beliefs, common to many survivors, which they are disgraceful, disgusting, and defiled for having been raped. These beliefs appear to show up in one of two ways; a direct expression of shame in oneself (i.e., "I am so disgusting and damaged") or an indirect, masked manifestation (i.e., "No one must ever know that I have been raped"). Interventions aimed at this aspect of the injured self can gently encourage survivors to examine the rationality of their shame (e.g., "Did you hurt anyone or were you the one being hurt . . . Who should be ashamed, then?"), which should help them to realize that in reality, they have nothing to be ashamed of, and that, in fact, it is the assailant, as well as society and its prejudiced attitudes that are shameful. A positive sense of self is the expected outcome.

Finally, much of the empowerment afforded to survivors stems simply from raising their awareness of the social roots of their distress. The notion of the personal being political underlies all interventions aimed at freeing the survivor from internalized victim-blaming and shame. It also provides answers to the questions regarding the reasons for the assault that trouble them so. "Why did it happen?" "Why to me?" "If I am not to blame then how can I explain what happened?" Helping a survivor to realize that rape generally does not occur because of any individual woman's behavior, but rather is systematically embedded in patriarchal culture, offers her an alternative explanation for her plight. Redefining male abusive behavior as conformation to society's promotion of male violence can help her make further sense of the events. Along the way, the changed perspective of each individual survivor is quite likely to reverberate beyond the therapeutic process, contributing in some way to social change in line with this particular tenet of feminist therapy.

In essence, by presenting survivors with a social analysis of male violence against women, by shifting much of what they endured from the personal domain into the shared collective one, by reframing their experience in growth-promoting terms, all coupled with trauma reprocessing and cognitive restructuring, feminist therapy stands a rather good chance of freeing rape victims from the agonizing sequelae of rape and sexual assault and turning them into empowered survivors.

REFERENCES

Alvidrez, J. (1999). Ethnic variations in mental health attitudes and service use among low-income African American, Latina, and European American young women. *Community Mental Health, 35,* 515–530.

Alvidrez, J., & Azocar, F. (1999). Distressed women's clinic patients: Preference for mental health treatment and perceived obstacles. *General Hospital Psychiatry, 21,* 340–347.

Angell, S. A. (1994). Acute and chronic symptomatology of sexual trauma: Treatment issues. *National Center for PTSD Clinical Quarterly, 4,* 9–11.

Ardovini-Brooker, J., & Caringella-MacDonald, S. (2002). Media attributions of blame and sympathy in ten rape cases. *The Justice Professional, 15,* 3–18.

Botta, R. A., & Pingree, S. (1997). Interpersonal communication and rape: Women acknowledging their assaults. *Journal of Health Communication, 2,* 197–212.

Brown, L., & Brodsky, A. (1992). The future of feminist therapy. *Psychotherapy, 29,* 51–57.

Buddie, A. M., & Miller, A. G. (2002). Beyond rape myths: A more complex view of perceptions of rape victims. *Sex Roles, 45,* 139–160.

Burnam, M. A., Stein, J. A., Golding, J. M., & Siegel, J. M. (1988). Sexual assault and mental disorders in a community population. *Journal of Consulting and Clinical Psychology, 56,* 843–850.

Burt, M. R. (1980). Cultural myths and support for rape. *Journal of Personality and Social Psychology, 38,* 217–230.

Campbell, R. (1998). The community response to rape: Victims' experiences with the legal, medical, and mental health systems. *American Journal of Community Psychology, 26,* 355–379.

Campbell, R., & Raja, S. (1999). Secondary victimization of rape victims: Insights from mental health professionals who treat survivors of violence. *Violence and Victims, 14,* 261–274.

Campbell, R., Sefl, T., Barnes, H.E., Ahrens, C. E., Wasco, S. M., & Zaragoza-Diesfeld, Y. (1999). Community services for rape survivors: Enhancing psychological well-being or increasing trauma? *Journal of Consulting and Clinical Psychology, 67,* 847–858.

Campbell, R., Wasco, S. M., Ahrens, C. E., Sefl, T., & Barnes, H. E. (2001). Preventing the "second rape": Rape survivors' experiences with community service providers. *Journal of Interpersonal Violence, 16,* 1239–1259.

Casey, E. A., & Nurius, P. S. (2006). Trends in the prevalence and characteristics of sexual violence: A cohort analysis. *Violence and Victims, 21,* 629–644.

Cowan, G. (2000). Beliefs about the causes of four types of rape. *Sex Roles, 42,* 807–823.

Feminist Therapy Institute. (1990). Feminist therapy code of ethics. In H. Lerman & M. Porter (Eds.), *Feminist ethics in psychotherapy* (pp. 37–40). New York: Springer.

Foa, E. B., & Rothbaum, B. O. (1998). *Treating the trauma of rape: Cognitive-behavioral therapy for PTSD.* New York: Guilford.

Foa, E. B., Zoellner, L.A., Feeny, N.C., Hembree, E.A., & Alvarez-Conrad, J. (2002). Does imaginal exposure exacerbate PTSD symptoms? *Journal of Consulting and Clinical Psychology, 70,* 1022–1028.

Gilbert, L. A. (1980). Feminist therapy. In A. M. Brodsky & R. T. Hare-Mustin (Eds.), *Women and psychotherapy* (pp. 245–266). New York: Guilford.

Gilbert, B. J. (1994). Treatment of adult victims of rape. *New directions for mental health services, 64,* 67–78.

Herman, J. (1992). *Trauma and recovery.* New York: Basic Books.

Hill, M. (1990). On creating a theory of feminist therapy. In L. S. Brown & M. P. Root (Eds.), *Diversity and complexity in feminist therapy* (pp. 53–66). New York: The Haworth Press, Inc.

Hill, M., & Ballou, M. (1998). Making therapy feminist: A practice survey. *Women and Therapy, 21,* 2–16

Jaycox, L. H., Zoellner, L., & Foa, E. B. (2002). Cognitive–behavior therapy for PTSD in rape survivors. *Journal of Clinical Psychology, 58,* 891–906.

Jordan, J., Kaplan, A., Miller, J. B., Stiver, I., & Surrey, J. (1991). *Women's growth in connection.* New York: Guilford.

Kaschak, E. (1992). *Engendered lives: A new psychology of women's experience.* New York: Basic Books.

Koss, M. P. (1983). The scope of rape: Implications for the clinical treatment of victims. *The Clinical Psychologist, 38,* 88–91.

Koss, M. P., & Harvey, M. R. (1991). *The rape victim: Clinical and community interventions.* Newbury Park, CA: Sage.

Lebowitz, L., & Roth, S. (1994). "I felt like a slut": The cultural context and women's response to being raped. *Journal of Traumatic Stress, 7,* 363–390.

Lee, C., Gavriel, H., Drummond, P., Richards, J., & Greenwald, R. (2002). Treatment of PTSD: Stress inoculation training with prolonged exposure compared to EMDR. *Journal of Clinical Psychology, 58,* 1071–1089.

Lonsway, K. A., & Fitzgerald, L. F. (1994). Rape myths: In review. *Psychology of Women Quarterly, 18,* 133–164.

MacKinnon, C. A. (2005). Defining rape internationally. *Columbia Journal of Cross National Law, 44,* 940.

Meadows, E. A., & Foa, E. B. (1998). Intrusion, arousal, and avoidance: Sexual trauma survivors. In V. M. Follette, J. I. Ruzek, & F. R. Abueg (Eds.), *Cognitive-behavioral therapies for trauma* (pp. 100–123). New York: Guilford.

Moor, A. (2007). When recounting the traumatic memories is not enough: Treating persistent self-devaluation associated with rape and victim-blaming rape myths. *Women & Therapy, 30,* 19–35.

Moor, A. (2009). A preliminary assessment of the prevalence and nature of sexual violence against women in Israel (in Hebrew). *Social Issues in Israel, 7,* 46–65.

Moradi, B., Fischer, A. R., Hill, M. S., Jome, L. M., & Blum, S. A. (2000). Does feminist plus therapist equal "feminist therapist"? *Psychology of Women Quarterly, 24,* 285–296.

Paivio, S. C., & Laurent, C. (2001). Empathy and emotion regulation: reprocessing memories of childhood abuse. *Journal of Clinical Psychology, 57,* 213–226.

Pitman, R. K., Altman, B., Greenwald, E., Longpre, R. E., Machlin, M. L., Poire, R. E., & Steketee, G. S. (1991). Psychiatric complications during flooding therapy for posttraumatic stress disorder. *Journal of Clinical Psychiatry, 52,* 17–20.

Power, K., McGoldrick, T., Brown, K., Buchanan, R., Sharp, D., Swanson, V., et al. (2002). A controlled comparison of eye movement desensitization and reprocessing versus exposure plus cognitive restructuring versus waiting list in the treatment of post-traumatic stress disorder. *Clinical Psychology & Psychotherapy, 9,* 299–318.

Rader, J., & Gilbert, L. A. (2005). The egalitarian relationship in feminist therapy. *Psychology of Women Quarterly, 29,* 427–435.

Rogers, S., & Silver, S. M. (2002). Is EMDR an exposure therapy? A review of trauma protocols. *Journal of Clinical Psychology, 58,* 43–59.

Shapiro, F., & Maxfield, L. (2002). Eye movement desensitization and reprocessing (EMDR): Information processing in the treatment of trauma. *Journal of Clinical Psychology, 58,* 933–946.

Sheldon, J. P., & Parent, S. L. (2002). Clergy's attitudes and attributions of blame toward female rape victims. *Violence Against Women, 8,* 233–256.

Ullman, S. E. (1996). Social reactions, coping strategies, and self-blame attributions in adjustment to sexual assault. *Psychology of Women Quarterly, 20,* 505–526.

Ullman, S. E. (1999). Social support and recovery from sexual assault: A review. *Aggression and Violent Behavior, 4,* 343–358.

Ullman, S. E., & Filipas, H. H. (2001). Correlates of formal and informal support seeking in sexual assault victims. *Journal of Interpersonal Violence, 16,* 1028–1047.

Ullman, S. E., & Brecklin, L. R. (2002). Sexual assault history, PTSD, and mental health service seeking in a national sample of women. *Journal of Community Psychology, 30,* 261–279.

Worell, J., & Johnson, D. (2001). Therapy with women: Feminist frameworks. In R.K. Unger (Ed.), *Handbook of the psychology of women and gender* (pp. 317–329). New York: Wiley.

Worell, J., & Remer, P. (1992). *Feminist perspectives in therapy: An empowerment model for women.* New York: Wiley.

Wyatt, G. E. (1992). The sociocultural context of African American and White American women's rape. *Journal of Social Issues, 48,* 77–91.

Chapter 7

Gender Microaggressions: Implications for Mental Health

Kevin L. Nadal

For the past 40 years, psychologists, educators, and other social scientists have advocated for an increase in multicultural knowledge and awareness in training, practice, and research. For example, the American Psychological Association (APA) has published the "Guidelines on multicultural education, training, research, practice, and organizational change for psychologists" (2003), which focus primarily on ways of being culturally competent toward oppressed racial and ethnic minority groups, with minimal focus on other multicultural subgroups (e.g., gender, sexual orientation, etc.). So while such guidelines recognize the intersections of other identities with race/ethnicity (e.g., the impacts of gender on race and racial identity), the emphasis is primarily on race and ethnicity. And while there is a definite need for the advocacy of racial and ethnic minority issues, several other culturally oppressed groups are often viewed as afterthoughts when discussing multiculturalism. Some of these groups include women, lesbian/gay/bisexual/transgender (LGBT) persons, disabled persons, elderly, and religious minority groups.

Research studies on multicultural competence models in psychology tend to follow this pattern of emphasizing race and/or ethnicity exclusively. Writings involving culturally competent counseling methods, counselor biases, identity development, and other multicultural issues are predisposed to concentrate primarily on race (and sometimes ethnicity). This can be exemplified by the newest line of multicultural research involving racial microaggressions, which are defined as "brief and commonplace daily verbal, behavioral, or environmental indignities, whether intentional or unintentional, that communicate hostile, derogatory, or negative racial slights and insults toward people of color" (Sue & Capodilupo, 2007, p. 271). These authors cite that because the United States is more "politically correct" today than it was twenty or thirty years ago, racism takes more subtle and covert forms. However, because of the cumulative nature of these subtle forms of discrimination, persons of color may experience an array of emotions, including belittlement, anger, rage, frustration, sadness, and alienation (Sue, Bucceri et al., 2007; Sue, Nadal et al., 2008), which consequently may lead to depression, anxiety, trauma, and other mental health problems.

While the introduction of microaggressions into the forefront of psychology is necessary and eliciting a range of positive and negative reactions in the field, it is important to recognize that previous research with microaggressions focuses primarily on race, following the trend that other social identity groups are ignored or minimized in multicultural discourses. Accordingly, research on microaggressions fails to take into account experiences involving gender, sexual orientation, ability, age, religion, and ethnicity. The purpose of this chapter is to advocate for the expansion of research on microaggressions to encompass other cultural groups. Specifically, this chapter will concentrate on microaggressions involving gender, hypothesizing the various types of gender microaggressions that may impact women in everyday life and in therapy settings. Utilizing the major tenets in the taxonomy of racial microaggressions, this chapter will define gender microaggressions and conjecture numerous categories of gender microaggressions that women may experience.

DEFINITIONS OF MICROAGGRESSIONS

To understand microaggressions in general, it becomes important to recognize the literature on racial microaggressions. Racial microaggressions consist of brief statements or behaviors that send denigrating and hurtful messages to people of color. By this definition, microaggressions can occur between any two parties (individuals or groups or both), in which the member(s) from a privileged/dominant group communicates a denigrating and hurtful message toward the member(s) from an oppressed group. For example, a man can commit a gender microaggression toward a woman; a heterosexual person can be responsible for a sexual orientation microaggression toward a LGBT person; and an able-bodied person can perpetrate an ability microaggression toward a disabled person (Nadal, 2008).

Studies have also indicated there are three forms of racial microaggressions: microassaults, microinsults, and microinvalidations. Microassaults are what are closest to overt, "old-fashioned" racism, with examples ranging from calling a black American the "N word" or yelling at an Asian American or Latin American person to "go back where you came from." However, microinsults and microinvalidations are less obvious, more subtle, and often well intentioned. Microinvalidations are defined as actions that negate or nullify a person of color's experiences or realities, while microinsults refer to actions that convey insensitivity and are belittling to a person's racial identity. These are the types of microaggressions that may be more harmful because the perpetrator may not even realize that she/he is insulting or invalidating the individual. Unlike microassaults, that are often conscious and purposefully hurtful, microinsults and microinvalidations may be more unconscious and may have several potential impacts on the recipient.

For example, the experience of being treated as an intellectual inferior is a common experience for African Americans, in which many individuals are consistently told that they are "smart" or "articulate" (Sue, Nadal et al., 2008). This would be considered a microinsult because the perpetrator is conveying that because the individual is African American, she or he would not be expected to be smart or would not be expected to speak well. While the statement may have been well intentioned or meant to be a compliment, the recipient may have a negative reaction, with subsequent emotions such as anger, frustration, or hurt. An example of a racial microinsult that may occur toward Asian Americans includes the experience of being exocitized, which is demonstrated by a male individual telling an Asian that he has an "Asian fetish" or that Asian women have "beautiful skin" or "silky hair" (Sue, Bucceri, et al., 2007). Again, while the statement might be meant to be a compliment, the Asian American recipient may feel objectified, hurt, and insulted by the comment. Because such a statement might occur regularly for the recipient, the cumulative impact of similar statements might lead to emotional distress.

Some racial microaggressions may be more intentional, in that the perpetrator might be more conscious of her/his behavior. For example, many African American individuals report being treated as criminals on a regular basis; this message is conveyed in situations where store-owners follow African American individuals around while they shop. This microinsult sends the messages that black individuals are criminals who are likely to steal or damage their stores (Sue, Nadal, et al., 2008). However, if the perpetrator in this case would be confronted with her/his behavior, it is possible that the individual would deny that race was involved in their decision making, because she/he is a "good person" who does not "see race" and treats people of all racial groups the same (Sue, 2005). So even when perpetrators of microaggressions may be aware of their behaviors toward persons of color, it is less likely that they would be able to admit to it.

A common form of a racial microinvalidation is one where an individual is denied her/his racial reality, often occurring when a person of color is told that her/his experience with racism is invalid and that she/he should stop complaining about racial stressors (Sue, Bucceri et al., 2007). In this case, the perpetrator may not realize the impact that such a statement may have on the recipient; the individual may believe that she/he is simply stating one's opinion and assumes that the recipient should be able to agree with her or his statement. However, the recipient may instead feel misunderstood because the perpetrator is not accounting for her/his experiences with race, leading to potential distress at the clash of their "racial realities" and feelings of belittling, frustration, or sadness.

Given these three categories of racial microaggressions, it is likely that similar experiences can occur across different social identities. For example, a sexual orientation microassault may include a heterosexual person calling a gay man a "faggot" or calling a lesbian a "dyke." An ability microinsult might include an able-bodied person speaking to a disabled person slowly and condescendingly, assuming that she/he would not be able to understand the person. A religious microinvalidation might include a Christian telling a Jewish person that "You complain about the Holocaust too much" (Nadal, 2008). All of these types of statements or behaviors convey a negative and derogatory message toward the member of the oppressed group. And again, the cumulative nature of these statements and behaviors may have lasting impacts on the member(s) of the oppressed group.

Given the definitions of racial microaggressions and the ability to apply the experiences of microaggressions to interactions between different social groups, it is now possible to define microaggressions that may occur as a result of gender. Gender microaggressions are brief and commonplace daily verbal, behavioral, or environmental indignities (whether intentional or unintentional) that communicate hostile, derogatory, or negative sexist slights and insults toward women. These microaggressions are often unconscious in that the perpetrator of the microaggressions may not realize that he is being hurtful in his statements or behaviors. Gender microaggressions are different from other forms of sexism in that they may manifest in various forms: microassaults, microinvalidations, and microinsults; they may be subtle and covert, in that the recipient may often question whether the microaggression would even have a lasting impact on her psychological well being. However, similar to racial microaggressions, the cumulative nature of these gender microaggressions may lead to mental health problems, including depression, anxiety, trauma, or issues with self-esteem.

GENDER MICROAGGRESSIONS

Sexism in Everyday Life

Little research has been written on the term "gender microaggressions" in psychology, education, and social sciences, but rather describes sexism in different forms. The vast range of literature on sexism reveals that sexism, much like racism, has become more concealed than it is open and obvious (Sue & Capodilupo, 2008). Some authors contend that sexism takes three major forms: overt, covert, and subtle (Swim & Cohen, 1997). Overt sexism could be comparable to "old-fashioned" sexism toward women, in which women are directly discriminated against and/or treated unfairly and unequally than men. This can be exemplified by a man blatantly telling a woman that he would not hire her for a position because of her gender, or a man directly insulting a woman by calling her a derogatory term. Covert sexism would include discrimination that is less direct and less revealed. This can be exemplified by some men who might claim to be "liberal" and "gender-neutral," yet would never vote for women president of the United States. Finally, subtle sexism is defined as "unequal and unfair treatment of women that is not recognized by many people because it is perceived to be normative, and therefore does not appear unusual" (Swim, Mallett, & Stagnor, 2004, p. 117). This can be exemplified by someone assuming that an authority figure or professional (e.g., employer, author, professor, or doctor) is a "he" without knowing the gender of the said person. While covert and overt sexism might be conscious processes, it is likely that subtle sexism is unconscious and/or not maliciously intended (Sue & Capodilupo, 2008).

One study conducted on "everyday sexism" or the discriminatory or prejudicial experiences with gender (Swim, Hyers, Cohen, & Ferguson, 2001) found that female participants encounter about one to two impactful sexual incidents per week. Participants reported three major categories of everyday sexism: (1) traditional gender role stereotypes and prejudice, (2) demeaning and degrading comments and behaviors, and (3) sexual objectification. Examples of traditional gender role stereotypes and privilege include a man telling a woman to fold laundry or do the dishes, while illustrations of demeaning and degrading comments and behaviors include men using labels (e.g., "bitch," "slut," or "chick") to describe women. Examples of sexual objectification include men making comments about women's body parts, as well as behaviors like unwanted staring or touching. In these studies, women reported psychological impacts, including a decrease in comfort and self-esteem and feelings of anger and depression. Another study highlighted experiences with sexism with adolescent girls (Leaper & Brown, 2008). The authors found the majority of the participants reported sexism related to academics (e.g., being discouraged about their computer, math, or science abilities) and/or athletics (e.g., being teased about their athletic ability). The majority of these female adolescents also reported several incidents of gender harassment, namely receiving unwanted romantic attention, being teased with an embarrassing or mean joke or a demeaning name, and being teased about physical appearance. These two studies on sexism exemplify types of gender microaggressions and the negative psychological effects these experiences may cause. While they may seem like trivial everyday occurrences, these slights may influence a woman or girl's self-esteem, worldview, motivation to achieve, and mental health.

Understanding various measures that assess different types of sexist slights can be helpful in understanding examples of everyday sexist experiences. The Schedule of Sexist Events (SSE) is a measure that assesses perceived frequencies of sexist discrimination (Klonoff & Landrine, 1995). Recent studies have supported three subscales of the SSE, including sexist degradation and its consequences (e.g., been called a sexist name), unfair sexist events at work/school (e.g., denied a raise, promotion, or tenure at work), and unfair treatment in distant and close relationships (e.g., being treated unfairly by people in helping jobs; Matteson & Moradi, 2005). In the initial use of the SSE, it was found that 99 percent of a given sample of women (n = 633) experienced sexism at some point in their life, while 97 percent of the sample experienced sexism in the past year (Klonoff & Landrine, 1995). Since then, the SSE has been used in several empirical studies which have provided support that daily sexist experiences are prevalent in women's lives (Matteson & Moradi, 2005). However, some research has found that most women may not respond to these sexist events, with majority ignoring the incident (Lott, Aquith, & Doyon2001), instead of confronting the perpetrator. This experience of dealing with sexist incidents is comparable to previous research on racial microaggressions, which state that people of color often find themselves in a "catch 22" when they experience such racist events (Sue, Capodilupo et al., 2007). If the recipient of the racist or sexist incident says something to the perpetrator, she/he runs the risk of being invalidated, ridiculed, or even physically assaulted; if she/he doesn't say something, she/he may become distressed and regret not standing up for oneself.

Sexual Harassment

The research on sexual harassment is also important to review when discussing gender microaggressions, as it may explain the impacts of sexist experiences at the workplace on individual mental health. There has been much research in the field of psychology that has documented the psychological impact of sexual harassment on both women and men (Schneider, Swann, & Fitzgerald, 1997). It is imperative to recognize how sexual harassment may relate to gender microaggressions, but how it may also differ. Sexual harassment has been defined as:

"unwelcome sexual advances, requests for sexual favors, and other verbal or physical conduct of a sexual nature constitutes sexual harassment when submission to or rejection of this conduct explicitly or implicitly affects an individual's employment, unreasonably interferes with an individual's work performance or creates an intimidating, hostile or offensive work environment." (U.S. Equal Employment Opportunity Commission, 2008)

It is reported that in 2007, that the Equal Employment Opportunity Commission (EEOC) received 12,510 charges of sexual harassment (with 16.0 percent of those charges filed by males), and that EEOC resolved 11,592 of these sexual harassment charges (U.S. Equal Employment Opportunity Commission, 2008). However, some experts have reported that between 40 to 60 percent of all women in the United States have experienced some form of harassing behavior at work, but that many of these experiences did not meet the legal criteria for sexual harassment and may often go unreported (Murray, 1998).

Understanding measurements for sexual harassment can be valuable in recognizing specific examples of sexist experiences in the workplace, leading to further understandings of gender microaggressions. The Sexual Experiences Questionnaire (SEQ) was developed to examine the experiences of women with sexual harassment in the workplace (Fitzgerald, Gelfand, & Drasgow, 1995) and has been used frequently over the past two decades. According to this measure, there are three major components used to define sexual harassment: gender harassment, unwanted sexual attention, and sexual coercion. Gender harassment refers to verbal and nonverbal behaviors that convey insulting, hostile, and degrading attitudes about women. Unwanted sexual attention includes a range of verbal and nonverbal behavior that is offensive, unwanted, and unreciprocated. Sexual coercion refers to the extortion of sexual cooperation for job-related considerations.

Given these three categories, one can observe the similarities between different types of sexual harassment and gender microaggressions. Gender harassment seems to be most parallel to unconscious microaggressions, in which the perpetrator of these microaggressions may not even be aware that his statements/behaviors convey a negative message to the recipient. Concurrently, unwanted sexual attention and sexual coercion are likely to be more conscious processes, in which the individual may be more aware of the intentions behind his statements and/or behaviors. As a result, unwanted sexual attention and sexual coercion can be compared to "microassaults," in that these behaviors are more obvious and noticeable by both the perpetrator and recipient. These microassaults would likely represent the types of behaviors that would qualify for sexual harassment charges. However, it appears that gender harassment is less obvious and is likely to be in line with "microinsults" and/or "microinvalidations." These types of unconscious statements/behaviors are likely not obvious enough to meet the legal requirements for sexual harassment, yet send insulting and invalidating messages to the women that receive them.

OBJECTIFICATION THEORY

The literature on objectification theory is also important to review in order to further understand illustrations of gender microaggressions and negative psychological effects. Objectification theory can be defined as "a framework for understanding the experiential consequences of being female in a culture that sexually objectifies the female body" (Fredrickson & Roberts, 1997, p. 173). It further explains that sexual objectification can occur through an array of interpersonal interactions including romantic partners, family members, friends, acquaintances, strangers, and even media outlets that depict interpersonal and social interactions. Accordingly, women and girls in an objectifying society may experience various mental health risks, including depression, sexual dysfunction, eating disorders, and body image issues.

Through examining current measures of objectification, it can be beneficial to understand how specific experiences of being objectified are interrelated with gender microaggressions. The Interpersonal Sexual Objectification Scale (ISOS) was created to understand how sexual objectification occurred interpersonally and how it related to psychological distress (Kozee, Tylka, Augustus-Horvath, & Denchik, 2007). Exploratory and confirmatory factor analyses revealed two factors: body evaluation and unwanted explicit sexual advances. Examples of body evaluation include: "How often have you been whistled at while walking down a street?" or "How often have you noticed someone staring at your breasts when you are talking to them?" Examples of unwanted explicit sexual advances include "How often have you been touched or fondled against your will?" or "How often has someone grabbed or pinched one of your private body areas against your will?" Scores on the ISOS were strongly related to sexist degradation and slightly to moderately related to other sexist events, self-objectification (e.g., internalization of the thin-ideal) and body shame. These findings support that the experiences of being interpersonally sexualized and/or feeling judged about one's body can lead to psychological distress, including a lower self-esteem and an impaired body image. Similarly to previous research on microaggressions, the cumulative nature of these events increases psychological distress over time.

HOSTILE AND BENEVOLENT SEXISM

There has been some research that has conceptualized two additional forms of sexism: benevolent sexism and hostile sexism. Benevolent sexism is defined as "a subjectively favorable, chivalrous ideology that offers protection and affection to women who embrace conventional roles" (Glick & Fiske, 2001, p. 109) while hostile sexism is defined as "antipathy toward women who are viewed as usurping men's power" (Glick & Fiske, 2001, p. 109). With benevolent sexism, men may believe that they are nonsexist and that they believe in gender equality. However, in reality these men may endorse traditional gender roles that actually promote female inferiority. For example, men may believe that it is their responsibility to protect and provide for women, which may seem favorable and innocuous, but demonstrates the belief that women need to be taken care of. On the other hand, men may exhibit hostile sexism and feel threatened by women who are empowered, independent, and/or assertive. These men may be averse to feminists or female authority figures and may express this discomfort or disgust in blatant and subtle ways. For example, a man may belittle a female supervisor by referring to her with sexist labels when talking to his male coworkers.

Benevolent and hostile sexism are unique to other forms of sexism in that they are personal ideologies that promote male dominance and female inferiority. At the same time, they are related to gender microaggressions because they may be unconscious and may manifest in an array of hurtful behaviors or statements. For example, when a man desires for a woman to uphold traditional gender roles, his behaviors may include asking a woman to cook or clean for him, or treating a woman as if she was not intelligent. He may or may not be consciously aware of the sexist message he is portraying, and he may not recognize the impact such behaviors/statements may have on the recipient. Depending on the consciousness and intent of his actions, these may be considered microassaults or microinsults. Similarly hostile sexism may also take microassaultive, microinsulting, or microinvalidating forms. For example, a man calling a woman in power a "bitch" or "aggressive" may be considered a microassault. A man who unconsciously ignores a woman's ideas (because he feels threatened by her power or intelligence) may be an example of a microinsult, and a man who tells a woman (particularly an outspoken or assertive woman) to stop playing the "gender card" would be an example of a microinvalidation.

GENDER MICROAGGRESSIONS

Sue and Capodilupo discuss microaggressions that are related to race, gender, and sexual orientation. Several categories of gender microaggressions are introduced, citing the behaviors/statements and the messages that are being communicated to the recipient. In the theme of "sexual objectification," men may conduct behaviors that send the message that a woman's body is a sexual object. Examples may include a male stranger putting his hands on a woman's hips to pass her, or a man whistling or "catcalling" as a woman walks down the street. The theme of "denial of individual racism/sexism/hetero-sexism" occurs when an individual denies one's own potential bias or prejudice. An example can include a statement where a male says "I always treat men and women equally," sending the message that he is incapable of gender bias or sexism. The theme of "traditional gender role prejudicing and stereotyping" takes place when individuals assume that others should hold traditional gender roles or stereotypes. An example may include a person looking at a thirty-year-old woman's ring finger, sending the message that she should be married because being a wife should be a woman's main purpose in life. The theme of "second-class citizen" occurs when an oppressed group member receives less preferential treatment than a dominant group member. For example, if a woman is not invited to a social gathering by her coworkers, when clearly all of the male coworkers are, she may feel left out because of her gender. Finally, the theme of "use of sexist/hetero-sexist language" speaks to the aforementioned subtle sexism (i.e., using the pronoun "he" to refer to all people), but also includes other degrading language (i.e., labeling a woman a "whore"). The first of these two examples communicates that the experience of men is universal, while the second imparts that women are meant to be passive and/or are allowed to be sexualized. While these themes of gender microaggressions illustrate the types of behaviors and statements that can convey denigrating messages toward women, they are merely a few samples of types of gender microaggressions that may occur. Therefore, it is important for psychologists to be aware that gender microaggressions exist, how they may impact the psychological processes of women, how they affect women's mental health, and how they may occur in therapeutic settings.

On the basis of the previous literature involving microaggressions, everyday sexism, objectification theory, hostile and benevolent sexism, and sexual harassment, this chapter will provide a hypothesis to the major types of gender microaggressions that may occur in everyday life and in therapeutic settings. This hypothesis is based on several empirical studies that have revealed that women experience various forms of gender discrimination in their everyday lives (see Swim et al., 2001, for a review), in school systems (see Leaper & Brown, 2008, for a review) and in the workplace (see Fitzgerald, Hulin, & Drasgow, 1994, for a review). The hypothesis of these gender microaggression categories is also based on several writings involving gender and experiences of women from a feminist therapy perspective, which focuses on providing culturally-competent therapy toward women (Brabeck & Brown, 1997; Collins, 1998; Enns, 1992; Espin, 1993; McNamara & Rickard, 1998). These empirical studies, theoretical models, social justice movements, and personal narratives all provide evidence that gender microaggressions do exist and may have a negative impact on mental health.

In understanding these various types of gender microaggressions, it is expected that individuals become aware of their own experiences as perpetrators or recipients of these microaggressions, while understanding the psychological impact that these microaggressions may have. It is also expected that psychologists become more culturally competent in understanding these microaggressions: gaining knowledge about the impact of these microaggressions, increasing awareness of how they may enact these microaggressions in psychological and therapeutic settings, and learning the skills to be able to deal with these microaggressions as they occur in their lives and in the lives of their clients.

FORMS OF GENDER MICROAGGRESSIONS

Based on the previous literature on microaggressions (Nadal, 2008; Sue, Bucceri, et al., 2007; Sue, Capodilupo, et al., 2007; Sue, Nadal, et al., 2008), sexism (Klonoff & Landrine, 1995), gender harassment (Fitzgerald et al., 1995), interpersonal objectification (Kozee et al., 2007), and benevolent and hostile sexism (Glick & Fiske, 2001), there are eight proposed themes of microaggressions that may occur toward women. Five of these themes are originally conceived in Sue and Capodilupo (2008) and include the following: *sexual objectification, assumptions of inferiority, assumptions of traditional gender roles, use of sexist language*, and *denial of individual sexism*. One of the themes is a reconceptualization of Sue and Capodilupo's (2008) second-class citizen and is described as *invisibility*. Two of these themes are new microaggression categories that are derived from previous literature on microaggressions, and they include *denial of reality of sexism* and *environmental gender microaggressions*. Table 7.1 provides examples of situations involving these microaggressions and the messages that are conveyed to the recipient.

These themes of gender microaggressions align with the previous literature with racial microaggressions, citing that (a) many of these microaggressions may be unconscious, in that the perpetrator may not realize the impact on the recipient, (b) these microaggressions (whether conscious or not) communicate various oppressive messages to the women who receive them, and (c) the various themes these microaggressions represent a spectrum of microassaults, microinvalidations, or microinsults. In fact, one of the main ways that gender microaggression is different than other forms of sexism (e.g., everyday sexism, objectification theory, and hostile and benevolent sexism) is that they are clearly categorized into these three subcategories. For example, with the theme of sexual objectification, the example of a man "catcalling" a woman as she walks down the street might be considered a

Table 7.1
Examples of Gender Microaggressions in Everyday Life

Theme	Example	Message
Sexual Objectification: Occurs when a woman is treated as a sexual object.	A man glances at a woman's breasts while he compliments her shirt.	Your body is not yours; I have a right to stare at you without your permission
	A construction worker catcalls a woman while she walks down the street	You are a sexual object; you are meant to entertain men.
	A male stranger places his hands on a woman's hips or the small of her back as he passes her	Your body is not yours; I have a right to touch you without your permission.
Invisibility: Occurs when a woman is overlooked and/or when men are given preferential treatment.	A female employee is passed up for a job promotion.	Your service is not as valuable as a man's.
	A woman is waiting to order a drink at a bar; the bartender serves the male customers before her.	You deserve to wait. Men are valued more than you.
	The male head of a company does not know the names of his female employees but knows the names of the male employees.	You are not valuable.
Assumptions of Inferiority: Occurs when a woman is assumed to be less competent than men (e.g., physically or intellectually).	A woman is carrying boxes; without permission, a man grabs the boxes and says "Let me do it."	You are not physically capable of doing things.
	A woman demonstrates leadership skills at her workplace; a man is surprised and says "I didn't know you had it in you!"	You are not expected to have intellectual or leadership capacities.
	A female student is told "I didn't know that women were good at math."	You are not expected to be smart in math or sciences.
	A man says "I don't think a woman could ever be president because women are too emotional."	Women should know their place.

166

Category	Examples	Messages
Denial of Reality of Sexism: Occurs when a woman is told that sexism does not exist.	A man tells a woman that she is exaggerating about how many times a day she gets "catcalled" on the street.	You complain too much.
	A woman is told that she didn't get the job because she wasn't qualified, not because of her gender.	You are to blame, not your gender.
Assumptions of Traditional Gender Roles: Occurs when an individual assumes that a woman should maintain traditional gender roles.	A woman is put in charge of the office party (without volunteering), when there are other lower-ranking males at the company.	Women should know their place.
	A forty-year-old woman with a successful career is asked why she never had any children.	You are not serving your primary purpose in life.
Denial of Individual Sexism: Occurs when a man denies his gender biases or prejudice.	"I'm not sexist. I have a wife and daughters!"	I am incapable of sexism.
	"I treat men and women the same all the time."	I have no gender biases.
	"As a person of color, I'm offended that you would imply that I'm sexist."	Because I belong to another oppressed group, I am allowed to have biases.
Use of sexist language: Occurs when language is used to degrade a woman.	A male coworker calls his female coworker "sweetie," "honey," or "shorty."	You are inferior to men/I have a right to patronize you.
	A male news correspondent calls a female politician a "shrew" or a "bitch."	Women should know their place.
Environmental Invalidations: Macro-level aggressions that occur on a systemic and environmental level.	Women make less money than men.	You are not as important or valuable as men.
	Majority of university professors in a department are men.	You are an outsider/You do not belong.
	A corporation has pictures of the "Board of Directors" of the company featuring all men.	You as a woman will never break the "glass ceiling."

Adapted from Sue & Capodilupo (2008)

microassault in that the man is likely more conscious of how he is demeaning the woman and making her feel uncomfortable. While he may not realize the impact of his behavior on her, it is an experience that both parties would be aware. In the same theme, a man may compliment a woman on her shirt, while also glancing at her breasts. This may be considered a microinsult in that the man is drawing attention to a woman's body, without her permission, and is objectifying her in the process. At the same time, this microaggression may be more unconscious or well intended by the man. He may be conscious that he is looking at her breasts; yet, if he was confronted, he might be defensive and say that he was simply paying her a compliment. However, this "compliment" is actually insulting and objectifying to the woman and may end up causing her distress, frustration, and feelings of objectification.

There are also some themes of microaggressions that would be considered microinvalidations, which can also be conscious or unconscious. For example, in the theme of use of sexist language, a male individual may call his female coworker "honey" or "sweetie" when he would never refer to a male coworker in the same way. This may be well intended in that he may believe that he is trying to be personable and cordial with the female coworker, but he may not realize that the recipient may feel dehumanized or belittled. This behavior may not even be conscious by the perpetrator, in that this male individual may call all women some form of a "pet name" and may not realize the impact he has on others. Concurrently, in the same theme, the example of a news correspondent calling a female politician a "bitch" or a "shrew" might be a behavior that is more conscious. However, despite awareness of the comment, it is possible that the perpetrator would deny the invalidating messages that are conveyed if/when he is confronted. This may be supported through many anecdotes of news correspondents who dismissed allegations of sexism when referring to Senator Hillary Clinton with such sexist terms during the U.S. presidential election of 2008.

INTERSECTIONS OF GENDER MICROAGGRESSIONS WITH OTHER MICROAGGRESSIONS

It is important to recognize that gender microaggressions cannot occur independently from other social identity groups (namely race, ethnicity, social class, age, ability, or religion). In fact, previous authors have written about the impact of identity and experiences based upon the intersection of race and gender (Bowman et al., 2001). Accordingly, the manifestation of these microaggressions is likely to be heavily influenced by a woman's other reference groups, especially her race and age. For example, with the theme of invisibility, it is likely that a woman of color would be viewed as more invisible than a white woman and would likely receive substandard service or recognition. Similarly, with the theme of inferiority, a woman of color (namely a black American or Latina American) woman would likely be treated as less intelligent than her white counterparts, which may even speak to the notion that black and Latina women make significantly less money than white women (National Women's Law Center, 2008). Finally, with the theme of sexual objectification, a woman's race would influence the type of microaggression that she receives. For example, black women are stereotyped to be "independent, assertive, and aggressive" (Bowman et al., 2001), while Asian American women are stereotyped to be "passive" and "exotic" (Sue, Bucceri, et al., 2007). As a result, it is important to notice two trends: (1) the ways that women of different racial groups are objectified sexually may be different because of their race, and (2) a woman's race may always have some impact on her experiences with gender microaggressions. So while it is important to not discount the experiences that white women may experience with sexual objectification, it is necessary to recognize that women of all racial groups may experience gender microaggressions differently.

Age may also impact gender microaggressions in many ways. This can be demonstrated through the dehumanizing of women through language. Perhaps women who are called "honey" or "dear" by their male coworkers might be younger, which may contribute to such patronizing language. At the same time, perhaps younger women may struggle more with microaggressions dealing with assumptions of inferiority, in that the combination of their age and gender may contribute to others' perceptions that they would not be capable. This is not to discount that women of all ages deal with microaggressions involving inferiority, but rather to illuminate how the impact of age may influence one's general experiences with microaggressions. Accordingly, it is important for research to be conducted to understand these experiences with gender microaggressions more empirically.

GENDER MICROAGGRESSIONS IN CLINICAL PRACTICE, EDUCATION, AND OTHER SETTINGS

Given these proposed themes with gender microaggressions, there are several implications for clinical practice (e.g., counseling/psychotherapy) and education (e.g., training, classroom settings). First, it is important to recognize that these microaggressions may be enacted in counseling/psychotherapy settings, just as microaggressions may occur in everyday life. As a result, it is important for psychologists, educators, and other practitioners to recognize different ways that microaggressions may manifest in their professional relationships and on different levels (e.g., counselor–client, client–counselor, supervisor–supervisee, supervisee–supervisor, professor–student, or student–professor). This type of awareness is one that may be communicated directly (e.g., a client or supervisee points out a microaggression to a therapist or supervisor); however, it is likely that many microaggressions are unconscious and may go unnoticed. Therefore by understanding different types of microaggressions that may exist, psychologists and other clinicians can pay extra attention to their own behaviors and interpersonal dynamics. Table 7.2 describes various examples of gender microaggressions that may occur in clinical and educational settings, as well as other work environments.

For clinical settings specifically, there are many ways that microaggressions can be integrated into therapeutic relationships by utilizing the two major principles of feminist psychology and feminist therapy: (1) the personal is political and (2) relationships must be egalitarian (Collins, 1998). In understanding that the personal is political, a counselor/psychotherapist (either female or male) must recognize that she/ he is an agent of social change that can challenge the status quo and advocate for the well-being of all women. Thus, this individual must be aware that she/he has a responsibility to educate her/his clients about gender microaggressions, while also encouraging the elimination of gender microaggressions in everyday life. This would be an advocacy that can be promoted toward both female and male clients who may be either perpetrators or recipients of gender microaggressions. For example, a feminist counselor/psychotherapist might gently point out to a male client that his sexist behaviors send denigrating messages to women, or a feminist counselor/psychotherapist might assist a female client in understanding how her internalized sexism causes her to enact gender microaggressions onto other women. In both of these cases, the counselor/psychotherapist is confronting her/his clients and pushing for individual change, while addressing the impact of microaggressions on both individual and societal levels.

Furthermore, in understanding that all relationships are egalitarian, the feminist therapist must be willing to accept client's feedback about her/his experiences with gender microaggressions (or any other type of microaggression) that may occur in the therapeutic relationship. The counselor/psychotherapist must not become defensive if she/he is provided feedback about enacting potential microaggressions in the room. Rather the counselor/psychotherapist must be open-minded and respect the client's right for empowerment. This is an incident that can give power to the client, in that she/he will have learned how to communicate her/his feelings with an authority figure, which can be symbolic of a client's ability to speak her/his voice in an oppressive world.

It is also important for psychologists and other practitioners to recognize gender microaggressions, as a way of maintaining the APA Ethical Guidelines and increasing their multicultural competence (Nadal, 2008). In thoroughly understanding the proposed eight microaggressions (and

Examples of Gender Microaggressions in Clinical Practice and Other Settings

Theme	Example	Message
Sexual Objectification: Occurs when a woman is treated as a sexual object.	A male therapist tells a female that he likes her pants, while glancing at her body.	Your body is not yours; I have a right to stare at you without your permission
Invisibility: Occurs when a woman is overlooked and/or when men are given preferential treatment.	A male psychologist at a staff meeting is credited for a similar comment that a female psychologist made earlier.	Women's opinions are not as valuable as men's opinions.
Assumptions of Inferiority: Occurs when a woman is assumed to be less competent than men (e.g., physically or intellectually).	A male client challenges a female therapist's competence. A female therapist is not hired for a position working with male sex offenders.	Women should know their place. Women are not capable of defending themselves.
Denial of Reality of Sexism: Occurs when a woman is told that sexism does not exist.	A therapist tells a client "I think you spend too much time blaming your problem on sexism."	You are to blame, not your gender.
Assumptions of Traditional Gender Roles: Occurs when an individual assumes that a woman should maintain traditional gender roles.	A career counselor encourages a student to pursue social sciences or humanities instead of math or sciences. A therapist focuses sessions on why a middle-aged woman is not married.	Women are not smart enough. Women should know their primary purpose in life is to be a wife and mother.
Denial of Individual Sexism: Occurs when a man denies his gender biases or prejudice.	A male therapist says: "Your gender doesn't affect the way that I view you."	I have no gender biases and am incapable of sexism.
Use of sexist language: Occurs when language is used to degrade a woman.	A male therapist calls his female client "dear."	You are inferior to men/I have a right to patronize you.
Environmental Invalidations: Macro-level aggressions that occur on a systemic and environmental level.	In the waiting room of a mental health clinic, there are all pictures of historical male psychologists.	Men are intellectually superior to women.

Adapted from Sue & Capodilupo (2008)

171

many other potential categories of gender microaggressions that may exist), it is expected that therapists will enhance their multicultural competence by increasing their (a) knowledge, (b) awareness, and (c) skills, that are described in multicultural competence models (see Sue & Sue, 2008). Knowledge of gender microaggressions can be increased by understanding the presence and process of microaggressions as well as the psychological impacts of microaggressions on both perpetrators and recipients. Awareness of gender microaggressions can be strengthened by learning how these microaggressions may occur in therapeutic settings and how they as therapists might serve as perpetrators or recipients of microaggressions. Finally, therapists can gain the skills to deal with gender microaggressions—learning how to confront microaggressions when they occur in therapy, assisting clients in coping with microaggressions in their everyday lives, and healing from microaggressions themselves.

It is important to recognize that while it has been discussed that gender microaggressions occur from male perpetrators to female recipients that it is possible for microaggressions to occur from female perpetrator to female recipient and even male perpetrator to male recipient. For example, a married woman may enact a microaggression involving gender roles onto a single woman, by asking her why she is not married or why she doesn't have any children. An example of sexual objectification that may occur between women is when a woman makes demeaning, unwelcomed comments about another woman's body (i.e., commenting on her breasts) or if a lesbian woman catcalls another woman as she walks down the street.

In addition, men may enact microaggressions onto other men as well. For example, a man may use degrading language toward another man, by referring to him as a "pussy," a "queer," or a "wimp" (regardless of the male recipient's sexual orientation). Given this, it is also important to recognize how sexual orientation microaggressions may exist, how they may be very similar to gender microaggressions, and how they may often be labeled interchangeably. For example, in the aforementioned incident of the man calling another man a "queer," it might be considered a gender microaggression because the perpetrator is sending a hurtful, denigrating message to the recipient; however, if the recipient identifies as gay, then it could also be considered a sexual orientation microaggression because the man is receiving this hateful message primarily because of his sexual orientation. Furthermore, gender microaggressions in this context did not focus explicitly on transgender persons and those who identify as non-gender-conforming. Accordingly, it is important to recognize that microaggressions may impact transgender women and men in unique ways, in which they may receive denigrating messages about their transgender identity, their gender presentation, or their transgender way of life.

Research may be beneficial in further exploring the psychological impact of gender microaggressions, sexual orientation microaggressions, transgender microaggressions, and other microaggressions involving religion, ability, age, or size. Future research involving the intersections of these identities (as well as the experiences of microaggressions based on these intersections) would have significant implications for counseling/ psychotherapy. While previous literature demonstrates that women may cope with sexism in various ways (Lott et al., 2001) or that experiences of sexism objectification may lead to various mental health problems (Fredrickson & Roberts, 1997; Kozee et al., 2007), it is unclear how women deal with gender microaggressions and how they may impact one's psychological health. What is clear is that microaggressions need to be further studied and exposed in the field of psychology, in order to improve the lives of women and of all oppressed and disenfranchised individuals.

ACKNOWLEDGMENTS

I would like to acknowledge Kendra Brewster, Kate Krontris, and Silvia Mazzula Roman for their assistance in conceptualizing and editing this paper. I also would like to acknowledge my mother, aunts, cousins, and grandmothers, for being such amazing female role models in my life.

REFERENCES

American Psychological Association. (2003). Guidelines on multicultural education, training, research, practice, and organizational change for psychologists. *American Psychologist, 58*, 377–402.

Brabeck, M., & Brown, L. (1997). Feminist theory and psychological practice. In J. Worell & N. G. Johnson (Eds.), *Shaping the future of feminist psychology: Education, research, and practice* (pp. 15–35). Washington, DC: American Psychological Association.

Bowman, S. L., Rasheed, S., Ferris, J., Thompson, D. A., McRae, M., & Weitzman, L. (2001). Interface of feminism and multiculturalism: Where are the women of color? In J. G. Ponterotto, J. M. Casas, L. A. Suzuki, & C. M. Alexander (Eds.), *Handbook of multicultural counseling* (2nd ed., pp. 779–798). Thousand Oaks, CA: Sage.

Collins, L. H. (1998). Illustrating feminist theory: Power and psychopathology. *Psychology of Women Quarterly, 22*, 97–112.

Enns, C. Z. (1992). Toward integrating feminist psychotherapy and feminist philosophy. *Professional Psychology: Research and Practice, 23*, 453–466.

Espin, O. M. (1993). Feminist therapy: Not for White women only. *The Counseling Psychologist, 21*, 103–108.

Fitzgerald, L. F., Gelfand, M. J., & Drasgow, F. (1995). Measuring sexual harassment: Theoretical and psychometric advances. *Basic and Applied Social Psychology, 17*, 425–445.

Fitzgerald, L. F., Hulin, C. L., & Drasgow, F. (1994). The antecedents and consequences of sexual harassment in organizations: An integrated model. In G. P. Keita & J. J. Hurell, Jr. (Eds.), *Job stress in a changing workforce: Investigating gender, diversity, and family issues* (pp. 55–74). Washington, DC: American Psychological Association.

Fredrickson, B. L., & Roberts, T. (1997). Objectification theory: Toward understanding women's lived experiences and mental health risks. *Psychology of Women Quarterly, 21,* 173–206.

Glick, P., & Fiske, S. T. (2001) An ambivalent alliance: Hostile and benevolent sexism as complementary justifications for gender inequality. *The American Psychologist, 56,* 109–118.

Klonoff, E. A., & Landrine, H. (1995). The schedule of sexist events: A measure of lifetime and recent sexist discrimination in women's lives. *Psychology of Women Quarterly, 19,* 439–472.

Kozee, H. B., Tylka, T. L., Augustus-Horvath, C. L., & Denchik, A. (2007). Development of psychometric evaluation of the Interpersonal Sexual Objectification Scale. *Psychology of Women Quarterly, 31,* 176–189.

Leaper, C., & Brown, C. S. (2008). Perceived experiences with sexism among adolescent girls. *Child Development, 79,* 685–704.

Lott, B., Aquith, K., & Doyon, T. (2001). Relationship of ethnicity and age to women's responses to personal experiences of sexist discrimination in the United States. *The Journal of Social Psychology, 141,* 309–315.

Matteson, A. V., & Moradi, B. (2005). Examining the structure of the Schedule of Sexist Events: Replication and extension. *Psychology of Women Quarterly, 29,* 47–57.

McNamara, K., & Rickard, K. M. (1998). Feminist identity development: Implications for feminist therapy with women. In D. R. Atkinson & G. Hackett (Eds.), *Counseling diverse populations* (2nd ed., pp. 271–282). Boston: McGraw-Hill.

Murray, B. (1998). Psychology's voice in sexual harassment law: A psychologist casts light on the murky area of sexual harassment. *APA Monitor, 29.*

Nadal, K. L. (2008). Preventing racial, ethnic, gender, sexual minority, disability, and religious microaggressions: Recommendations for promoting positive mental health. *Prevention in Counseling Psychology: Theory, Research, Practice and Training, 2,* 22–27.

National Women's Law Center. (2008). The Fair Pay Campaign. Retrieved September 15, 2008, from http://www.nwlc.org/fairpay/

Schneider, K. T., Swann, S., & Fitzgerald, L. F. (1997). Job-related and psychological effects of sexual harassment in the workplace: Empirical evidence from two organizations. *Journal of Applied Psychology, 82,* 401–415.

Sue, D. W. (2005). Racism and the conspiracy of silence. *Counseling Psychologist, 33,* 100–114.

Sue, D. W., Arredondo, P., & McDavis, R. J. (1992). Multicultural counseling competencies and standards: A call to the profession. *Journal of Counseling & Development, 70,* 477–486.

Sue, D. W., Bucceri, J. M., Lin, A. I., Nadal, K. L., & Torino, G. C. (2007). Racial microaggressions and the Asian American experience. *Cultural Diversity and Ethnic Minority Psychology, 13,* 72–81.

Sue, D. W., & Capodilupo, C. M. (2008). Racial, gender, and sexual orientation microaggressions: Implications for counseling and psychotherapy. In D. W. Sue & D. Sue (Eds.), *Counseling the culturally diverse* (5th ed.). New York: John Wiley & Sons.

Sue, D. W., Capodilupo, C. M., Nadal, K. L., & Torino, G. C. (2008). Racial microaggressions and the power to define reality. *The American Psychologist, 63,* 277–279.

Sue, D. W., Capodilupo, C. M., Torino, G. C., Bucceri, J. M., Holder, A. M., Nadal, K. L., et al. (2007). Racial microaggressions in everyday life: Implications for counseling. *The American Psychologist, 62,* 271–286.

Sue, D. W., Nadal, K. L., Capodilupo, C. M., Lin, A. I., Rivera, D. P., & Torino, G. C. (2008). Racial microaggressions against Black Americans: Implications for counseling. *Journal of Counseling and Development, 86,* 330–338.

Sue, D. W., & Sue, D. (2008). *Counseling the culturally diverse* (5th ed.). New York: John Wiley & Sons, Inc.

Swim, J. K., & Cohen, L. L. (1997). Overt, covert, and subtle sexism: A comparison between the attitudes toward women and modern sexism scales. *Psychology of Women Quarterly, 21,* 103–118.

Swim, J. K., Hyers, L. L., Cohen, L. L., & Ferguson, M. J. (2001). Everyday sexism: Evidence for its incidence, nature, and psychological impact from three daily diary studies. *Journal of Social Issues, 57,* 31–53.

Swim, J. K., Mallett, R., & Stangor, C. (2004) Understanding subtle sexism: Detection and use of sexist language. *Sex Roles, 51,* 117–128.

U.S. Equal Employment Opportunity Commission. (2008). Sexual harassment. Retrieved August 28, 2008, from http://www.eeoc.gov/types/sexual_harassment.

Chapter 8

Prejudice and Discrimination against Sexual Minorities: A Brazilian Perspective

Eros DeSouza
Elder Cerqueira-Santos

This chapter focuses on a neglected population—sexual minorities (lesbian, gay, bisexual, transgender, and questioning [LGBTQ] individuals) in Brazil, a developing country, which is relevant to U.S. researchers, clinicians, and policy makers interested in sexual minorities of color who often face similar challenges. We begin by defining some basic concepts concerning gender, sexual orientation, and transsexualism. Next, we briefly discuss prejudice and discrimination, including subtle discrimination toward LGBT individuals. We also discuss pertinent material published in English or Portuguese concerning prejudice, discrimination, and violence toward sexual minorities in Brazil. Moreover, we give a voice to such population by inserting excerpts from interviews that we conducted during 2009 with Brazilian LGBTQ individuals from Porto Alegre (southern Brazil), São Paulo, Rio de Janeiro (both in southeastern Brazil), and Aracaju (northeastern Brazil).

Brazil is the largest Latin American country and is ranked eighth in the world economy. It is slightly smaller than the United States, with a population of about 200 million (54 percent white; Central Intelligence Agency, 2009). Brazilian society differs greatly from region to region, from rural to urban life, with industrialization and urbanization widespread in some regions (e.g., south and southeast) and not as much in others (e.g., north and the interior). Moreover, sexuality and gender norms have been changing substantially in contemporary Brazil (DeSouza, Baldwin, Koller, & Narvaz, 2004). According to Parker (1999), Brazil has "the largest and most visible gay subculture . . . anywhere outside the fully industrialized West" (p. 45). Gay and lesbian sexuality are increasingly visible in Brazil, with an emergent gay and lesbian as well as mainstream press discussing gay and lesbian cultural and political issues and a growing commercialization of the Brazilian gay culture, which has been influenced by North American and Western European gay cultures (Klein, 1999; Parker, 1999).

It is impossible to discuss homosexuality in Brazil without also discussing how Brazilian society views gender and sexuality in general. Brazil is a *machista* society (DeSouza et al., 2004); thus, gender relations, as well as relations across different sexual orientations must be viewed in that context as well.

BASIC CONCEPTS

Sex versus Gender

These terms are often used interchangeably, but they carry different connotations. Sex is a biological category used to differentiate human males (individuals with XY chromosomes and male genitalia) from human females (individuals with XX chromosomes and female genitalia). There is a small percentage of humans who are inter-sexed (hermaphrodite), having ambiguous components of their biological sex; however, the overwhelming majority of humans can be unambiguously classified as male or female (Faust-Sterling, 2000). Gender is a socially constructed term that describes social interpretations of what it means to be a man or a woman in a given society; gender stereotypes are beliefs shared by people in a given society about how men and women differ or should differ (Larsen & Buss, 2008).

Sexual Identity versus Sexual Orientation

Sexual identity refers to one's sexual attraction (wanting) and pattern of sexual behavior (doing), having both personal and political meanings (Starks, Gilbert, Fischer, Weston, & DiLalla, 2009). Such meanings are interpersonally constructed; thus, they are fluid, changing over time and throughout one's life. Researchers often categorize sexual identity based on one's self-assessment (labeling) at a given time (e.g., lesbian, gay, bisexual, heterosexual). One's sexual identity (how one views oneself as a sexual being) may not always coincide with one's sexual orientation, which includes one's physical (sexual) and affectional (emotional) attraction toward another person. Like sexual identity, sexual orientation is fluid and is best conceptualized on a continuum, from exclusively homosexual to exclusively heterosexual; it is also complex, including one's sexual identity, desires, behaviors, disclosures, and experiences (Horowitz & Newcomb, 2001). Research suggests that women, compared to men, are more likely to show variability and transitions throughout their lifetimes for both sexual orientation and identity, probably due to women's more fluid and less narrow attractions than men's (e.g., Diamond & Savin-Williams, 2000).

Transvestism versus Transsexualism

Transvestism refers to obtaining pleasure or sexual fulfillment by adopting the clothes, mannerisms, or gender roles of the opposite sex (e.g., during Brazilian Carnival, many men dress up as women; Cardoso, 2005). According to Cardoso, transvestism is also related to cross-dressing; for example, when gay men dress up as drag queens for entertainment purposes. Cardoso explains transsexualism as a longing to look, feel, and be like the opposite sex from the one with which an individual was born. Some transsexuals opt for permanent sex reassignment through surgery. Transgender is the umbrella term that encompasses both transvestites and transsexuals.

PREJUDICE AND DISCRIMINATION

Although human sexuality is diverse, with same-sex attraction, desire, and behavior being normal reflections of such diversity, there is resistance in developed and developing countries alike to extend universal principles of equality, justice, freedom, and dignity to LGBTQ individuals (Kitzinger & Wilkinson, 2004; Klein, 1999). Such resistance may be related to sexual prejudice, which Herek (2000) defines as all negative attitudes toward a person because of his or her homosexuality. According to Herek, sexually prejudiced individuals are usually male, report being exclusively heterosexual, and have limited contact with LGBTQ individuals.

A recent Brazilian study conducted with 200 students from a public university corroborates the above findings, including the contact hypothesis, which states that heterosexuals who interact with LGBTQ individuals seem to develop more positive attitudes toward sexual minorities than those with limited contact with LGBTQ individuals (Cerqueira-Santos, Winter, Salles, Longo, & Teodoro, 2007). However, Cerqueira-Santos et al. found that the contact hypothesis worked better among heterosexual women, who showed significantly less sexual prejudice, especially toward lesbians, than among heterosexual men. These findings suggest that Brazilian men fear being perceived as not masculine enough if they associate with sexual minorities, which is similar to how U.S. masculinity is construed (e.g., Kimmel, 1997). Moreover, in order for the contact hypothesis to work, others must know about one's sexual orientation.

Unlike women and ethnic/racial minorities who have visible phenotypic characteristics, homosexuality is often invisible, dependent on revelation to become known to others (Sedgwick, 1990); thus, Fassinger (1991) refers to their status as an invisible minority in society. Sexual prejudice (i.e., antipathy toward LGBTQ individuals) may lead to discrimination, which is an act, either physical or verbal, as well as avoidance or social exclusion (i.e., not associating with LGBTQ individuals; Crocker, Major, & Steele, 1998).

DeSouza and Showalter (in press) recently examined micro-aggressions (e.g., social exclusion and spreading malicious rumors) directed at sexual minorities that are subtle, yet detrimental. DeSouza and Showalter sampled 133 LGBTQ college students in the United States. After controlling for negative affectivity, they found that LGBTQ students who experienced at least one act of subtle sexual orientation harassment during the past year were significantly more likely to state intention to leave their institution and have a lower GPA than non-harassed students. In addition, DeSouza and Showalter found that LGBTQ students who were open about their sexual orientation reported higher levels of self-esteem and life satisfaction and lower levels of anxiety and depression than those less committed to their sexual identity, suggesting significant benefits for coming out to others.

HOMOSEXUALITY IN BRAZIL

In the Brazilian sexual script, there is a hegemonic distinction between masculine *atividade* (activity) and feminine *passividade* (passivity), in which sexuality is subjected to male desire, reflecting widespread machismo (Parker, 1993). According to Parker, such a distinction is reflected in the daily language Brazilians use to describe sexual relations, in which the role of the macho is to *comer* (literally to eat, but loosely translated as to fuck) and the role assigned to women, effeminate gay men, and transvestites is to *dar* (to give). In the Brazilian sexual universe, *comer* is synonymous with *vencer* (to win, to conquer) and *possuir* (to own, to possess). Such a vocabulary of sexual meanings suggests that women, effeminate gay men, and transvestites are socialized to be passive, receptive sexual partners, while macho men are socialized to pursue, to penetrate, and to dominate. Thus, in Brazil, a macho man continues to exercise the power of his virility with any feminine individual, including a *bicha* or effeminate male homosexual (Mendes-Leite, 1993). In other words, as long as the macho maintains his *atividade* (i.e., be the active person or penetrator, not the penetrated), he is typically not viewed as a homosexual by society. There is also an internalization of such sexual script by some gay men, creating a sexual hierarchy in Brazil, with macho men at the top and feminine individuals (i.e., heterosexual women, effeminate gay men, and transgendered individuals) on the bottom.

> *Here I have to be macho. It does not matter what one does within four walls; it is our secret. As long as you act like a macho in public, everything is fine. Even among other gay men, the idea of being macho [active or penetrator] is strong. If a gay man wants to offend another, just call him a "passive" [or penetrated] queer.*
>
> —thirty-six-year-old gay man from Aracaju

> *People talk bad about transvestites . . . they say we are the scummiest subgroup of all homosexuals, but nobody questions macho homosexual men who go out with us and pay to have sex with us. They continue to be honorable gentlemen in the eyes of society, because they live an anonymous life and often pass as heterosexual. They think they are the most macho men in the world. They are macho because they eat [have sex with] anyone!*
>
> —twenty-four-year-old transvestite from Aracaju

According to Prado and Machado (2008), the distinction between masculine *atividade* (activity) and feminine *passividade* (passivity) is reflected in same-sex and other-sex relations throughout Latin America. Thus, to be active during sexual intercourse is viewed as dominant, aggressive, and masculine, whereas to be passive is viewed as weak, submissive, and feminine.

In the Brazilian culture, the above distinction also applies to one's public image or persona and interfaces with one's appearance and socioeconomic status. Thus, certain terms (e.g., being called *bofe* or macho gay man) carry a more positive connotation than others (e.g., being called *frutinha* or little fruit, which means to be a delicate or effeminate gay man).

> *It is different to be gay in the wealthy parts of Rio than in the poor sections. There is prejudice everywhere, but in the wealthy areas we have some protection. It is our beach! Besides, gays are a part of the social culture and the way of life in Ipanema. If we are gone, half of the bars will close down!*
>
> —thirty-eight-year-old gay man from Rio de Janeiro

> *In public, people think I am a heterosexual. It is funny; women flirt with me a lot. I think it is because I take care of myself . . . I am fit, well-dressed, etc. I am sure that if I were a mal-nourished poor queer it would be another story. They would laugh at me instead. One's appearance makes a big difference, even among other gays who think I am a dominant top, but nobody knows what people do in bed.*
>
> —twenty-five-year-old gay man from São Paulo

Moreover, homosexuals seem to be the most oppressed group in Brazil—much more than women, racial minorities, and people with disabilities (Almeida & Crillanovick, 1999)—even though open displays of homosexuality are common and widely accepted. For example, former Brazilian President Fernando Henrique Cardoso was often photographed kissing drag queens; one of Brazil's top female models was once a man; and crowds cheer nearly naked gay men every year during Carnival (Goering, 1997). Based on historical analyses of events in Rio de Janeiro and São Paulo, Green (1999) reported a growing male homosexual appropriation and transformation of Carnival during the twentieth century, which opened up a more accepting view of male homosexuality, at least in large cities. Green documented a paradox of permissive same-sex eroticism during the four days of Carnival with accounts of intolerance toward homosexuals during the rest of the year.

> *Everybody thinks that being gay is fantastic in Rio, but only if you are good-looking and rich. Poor gays only show up during Carnival or during the LGBT [Pride] parade. Afterwards we should become invisible and quiet. There are two worlds in this city. It is not easy to be a queer from the slums.*
>
> —twenty-eight-year-old gay man from a *favela* (*slum*)
> in Rio de Janeiro

> *When I am dressed up as a Drag Queen I am a goddess of Carnival, but afterwards everything changes. In their eyes, I am a queer with AIDS whom nobody wants to see or employ! The only path to survive is prostitution. There are plenty of clients. Who are they? The same ones who deny me legal employment and do not want to see me around.*
>
> —thirty-year-old transgendered person from Rio de Janeiro

A national poll revealed a similar ambivalence toward homosexuality among a cross-section of Brazilian men and women. Fifty percent of those surveyed indicated daily contact with homosexuals at work or in the neighborhood; however, 56 percent said they would change their behavior toward a colleague if they discovered he or she was a homosexual, with 20 percent avoiding contact with such colleague and 36 percent indicating they would not hire a homosexual, even if he or she were the best-qualified candidate for the position; 58 percent reported being opposed to homosexual couples adopting a child even if they had lived in a committed relationship for a long time; and 79 percent said they would be disappointed if they had a homosexual child (O mundo gay rasga as fantasias, 1993).

A survey study conducted in the city of São Paulo (Instituto de Pesquisa e Cultura GLS, 2000) revealed that 67 percent of the LGBT sample reported being discriminated against due to their sexual orientation by family members, friends, and neighbors, as well as in work, school, public, and health services settings. In addition, victims of such discrimination were re-victimized when filing complaints in police stations.

A study conducted with 220 college students in northeast Brazil indicated that only 24 percent of those sampled were not prejudiced toward homosexuals, with 38 percent being mildly prejudiced and an additional 38 percent being blatantly so (Lacerda, Pereira, & Camino, 2002). As in the United States, Lacerda et al. found that heterosexual Brazilian men had more negative attitudes toward gay men and lesbians than heterosexual Brazilian women did.

In addition, a recent study with 891 U.S. and Brazilian college students revealed that in both countries, bystanders often witnessed harassment of homosexuals (DeSouza & Scheinder, 2009). Overall, 77 percent of all respondents reported having experienced at least one act of being a bystander verbal harassment of homosexuals, whereas only 25 percent of the participants reported having experienced at least one act of bystander to exclusion of homosexuals during the past 12 months. Note that these types of bystander experiences are not mutually exclusive. Being a bystander to verbal harassment of homosexuals had negative consequences to bystanders, especially in Brazil. Specifically, being a bystander to verbal harassment of homosexuals was a significant predictor of multiple negative consequences (i.e., physical illness and drug-alcohol use) in Brazil, but this may also be a source of concern in the United States as well (via a link with drug and alcohol use). These findings extend past research on the negative outcomes of being a bystander to sexual (Glomb, Richman, Hulin, & Drasgow, 1997) or ethnic (Low, Radhakrishnan, Schneider, & Rounds, 2007) harassment.

Violence against Sexual Minorities

As in the United States, violence against sexual minorities is not a new problem in Brazil. In fact, transgendered individuals are the main victims of discrimination and violence based on sexual orientation (Carrara & Vianna, 2006). According to Carrara and Vianna, the police are indifferent to crimes committed against poor transgendered individuals who turn to prostitution to survive. Even their murder is viewed as a "normal" consequence of an illegal way of earning a living. In fact, police officers often look the other way when confronted with hate crimes against homosexuals (Goering, 1997).

According to Mott (2002), Brazil ranks number one in the world for hate crimes based on sexual orientation. A recent study by Grupo Gay da Bahia (2009) reports that 190 homosexuals were killed during 2008, with gay men (96 percent) being by far more likely to be killed than lesbians (4 percent). According to Grupo Gay da Bahia, northeastern Brazil, which makes up 30 percent of the Brazilian population, has the deepest anti-gay attitudes and the highest percentage (48 percent) of homosexuals murdered compared to the south/southeast (28 percent), midwest (14 percent), and north (10 percent).

A study conducted in 2001 in the state of Rio de Janeiro revealed that during an eighteen-month period, the police received 500 reports of violence against LGBT individuals. Of these, 6.3 percent consisted of murder, 10.3 percent were extortion cases, 18.7 percent were of physical assault, and 20.2 percent were of discrimination based on sexual orientation (cited in Conselho Nacional de Combate à Discriminação, 2004). Every three days a person is murdered in Brazil because of his or her sexual orientation (Rios, 2002). Note that these statistics reflect crimes that were reported, representing an underestimation of the true prevalence of crimes against LGBT individuals. Thus, it is important to conduct survey studies that tap victimization, potentially revealing crimes committed against LGBT persons that may otherwise go unreported.

A survey study conducted in Rio de Janeiro with 416 gay men, lesbians, and transgendered individuals revealed that 60 percent of the respondents reported being victims of violence/discrimination (Carrara, Ramos, & Caetano, 2002). Specifically, 16.6 percent reported experiencing physical assault (the rate almost tripled for transgendered individuals, with 42.3 percent), 18 percent bribery or extortion (the rate almost doubled for transgendered individuals, with 30.8 percent), 56.3 percent experienced verbal insults or threats due to their sexual orientation, and 58.5 percent were discriminated against because of their sexual orientation. This study also revealed that 22.4 percent of the lesbians surveyed were victimized by family members because they were women and lesbian.

The above findings suggest that many Brazilian sexual minorities live in silence, secrecy, threat of rejection, and marginality. In addition, these somber statistics require consciousness of the violence against sexual minorities that goes on in their own family of origin.

The Brazilian family usually does not accept a homosexual child, especially a transgendered adolescent whose "inappropriate" gender expression is used as an excuse for family-inflicted violence; such a child is eventually expelled from home and often survives through prostitution (Conselho Nacional de Combate à Discriminação, 2004). There is a gendered violence in many Brazilian families that "submit individuals, physically and/or emotionally, consciously and/or unconsciously as a function of their sex" (Werba & Strey, 2001, p. 72). According to DeFrancisco (1997), as gender roles play out in Brazilian society and in the family, they are linked to violence, especially physical and sexual abuse; such abuse is aggravated by secrecy and denial of family-inflicted violence. Machismo is often present in the typical family scenery of abusive systems to the extent that these systems reflect more rigid gender roles that correspond to patriarchal systems that are institutionalized in society (DeSouza et al., 2004). Thus, it is easy to see that transgendered people, like women, are often victims of family and social violence.

Prejudice against homosexuals is everywhere, even inside us. I don't feel accepted by my family and cannot even mention my partner at work. What is left is a [gay] ghetto. I only befriend other gay men and sometimes they too show machismo. I have dated a transgendered individual and they spoke badly of this relationship.

—thirty-one-year-old gay man from Porto Alegre

I ended up moving to the big city to escape. Here nobody knows me or my life. I had to bury my past and my life began when I moved here. Now I am myself!

—thirty-six-year-old lesbian from São Paulo

When my father found out that I am a transvestite and do shows at night, he told me not to return home. In order to see my mother, she has to come to my house. I do not have a family anymore, you know. I had no choice. It was me or them.

—thirty-five-year-old transgendered person from Porto Alegre

Recently, Rocha et al. (2009) interviewed eight transsexuals to find out their perceptions of the Brazilian public health system, which provides universal and free health services to all Brazilian nationals. The findings revealed stereotypes about transsexuals and sexual prejudice by health providers at all levels (e.g., clerical staff, nurses, and doctors), especially toward transgender sex workers. For instance, these participants experienced humiliation from health care providers when they voiced a desire to be called by their chosen names rather than by their birth names, even though by law transsexuals are allowed to have their chosen names in all their medical files. One participant said, "When they call me [in the health clinic] by my birth name . . . the name written in the identification file, I stand up and go in order not to lose the consultation with the doctor. I walk with my head down, cause I feel embarrassed" (p. 14). Another participant recalled a similar experience: "They [health officials] don't call you by your chosen name, you know. They are not sensible. On top of that, you can hear the comments and laughs as soon as you leave" (p. 14). Rocha et al. reported that staff members simply refused to call transgendered individuals by their chosen name even when explicitly asked to do so: "A receptionist treated me really bad. She said simply, 'I will call you R (masculine name)'. I said I would really like to be called by my chosen name G (feminine). The receptionist said, 'No, I will call you R'" (p. 15).

The interviews also showed a lack of sensitivity and training to deal with transgendered individuals. "I reckon there is no preparation to deal with us, from those who work in the reception desk up to the doctors. I believe they don't have a minimum of training" (p. 16). Another said: "How can you develop any rapport with your doctor if, upon arrival, the doctor starts treating you as a 'he.' How can I develop rapport with someone who calls me 'sir'? How can I be open enough to talk about my life, to expose myself or talk about intimate stuff with the doctor? There is no rapport! I may need a doctor in the future and not go" (pp. 16–17).

Another participant brings up the important topic of how public stigma, stereotype, prejudice, and discrimination against transgendered individuals negatively affect treatment seeking, yielding significant harm to this population: "When they [transvestites] seek health services, they face discrimination instead, and they no longer go back . . . the public perceptions of prejudice and hatred don't change. Many of them get really bad [with their health] . . . only when their condition worsens significantly, then they seek help" (p. 19). Another participant described how physicians stereotype and prejudge transgendered individuals as automatically being HIV positive: "When you report any health symptom, and they realize you're a transvestite or transsexual, most [health care professionals] believe that you are infected with HIV straight away . . ." (p. 17).

Rocha et al.'s interviews support the notion that there is widespread public stigma against sexual minorities, especially against transgendered individuals, even by well-educated professionals. There is a hopeful trend though: Whitam, Daskalos, Sobolewski, and Padilla (1998) suggest that there is increasing public support for the civil rights of sexual minorities in Brazil.

IMPORTANT LAWS AND RESOLUTIONS TOWARD EQUALITY

Historically, homosexuality has been viewed as pathological and deviant both in the United States and Brazil. Though sodomy was decriminalized in 1830 throughout Brazil (Rios, 2002), it remained a crime in some states in the United States until the Supreme Court's decision in 2003, which overturned state same-sex sodomy laws (*Lawrence v. Texas*, 2003).

It was only in 1985 that homosexuality was removed as a mental disorder from the Brazilian Federal Association of Medicine (cited in Conselho Nacional de Combate à Discriminação, 2004), compared to its removal from the second edition of the Diagnostic and Statistical Manual of Mental Disorders in 1973 in the United States (American Psychiatric Association, 1973). On March 22, 1999, the Brazilian Federal Association of Psychology passed a resolution stating that no professional who provides therapeutic services to sexual minority clients can act in a way that reinforces the notion of homoerotic behaviors or practices as pathological (Resolução CFP # 001/99, 1999). Such resolution is similar to the U.S. resolution on appropriate therapeutic responses to sexual orientation passed by the American Psychological Association council of representatives on August 14, 1997 (American Psychological Association, 1998). There is an important difference, however. In Brazil, such a resolution refers to actual standards that are mandatory, whereas in the United States it refers to guidelines or recommendations aimed at motivating psychologists to act ethically toward sexual minority clients without enforcement mechanisms.

On May 13, 2002, former Brazilian President Fernando Henrique Cardoso proposed a program to amend the Brazilian Constitution of 1988—which does not include sexual orientation as a protected group—that would explicitly make sexual orientation a human rights issue, prohibiting discrimination based on sexual orientation (Leis, 2002). Such an amendment has not yet passed. Currently, Brazil has a patchwork of legal protection, with three states protecting LGBT individuals from discrimination, whereas the remaining 24 states lack such protection (Conselho Nacional de Combate à Discriminação, 2004). Such a patchwork of legal protection parallels the situation found in the U.S., where only 20 states ban discrimination based on sexual orientation (National Gay and Lesbian Task Force, 2008).

Unlike in the United States, Brazilian federal laws have extended many rights to same-sex domestic partners, including social security and inheritance (Rios, 2002). In addition, legislation was passed on December 3, 2003, extending immigration rights to foreign homosexuals who wish to join their Brazilian partners (Silva & Barbi, 2005).

Laws against sexual harassment are relatively recent in Brazil. The first such law was enacted in the state of Rio de Janeiro in 1991, where organizations could be fined and the perpetrator dismissed (Noviski, Davoli, & Castro, 2000). On May 15, 2001, a national law passed that criminalizes sexual harassment and provides for up to two years in jail for perpetrators found guilty (Código Penal Brasileiro, 2001). Such law defines sexual harassment only as sexual coercion by a superior in order to obtain sexual favors; it does not include a hostile environment created by peers or subordinates. It emphasizes an abuse of power by a superior. These laws are gender neutral. Pastore and Robortella (2003) found that 9 percent of reported cases involve same-sex sexual harassment.

According to the Brazilian Health Ministry (Conselho Nacional de Combate à Discriminação, 2004), the government needs to take several steps to reduce prejudice, discrimination, and violence based on sexual orientation. We highlight the first four because they are of interest to U.S. researchers, clinicians, and decision makers as well. First, there is a need for action by disseminating among all levels of society the notion that homosexual citizenship is a human rights issue. Second, the constitution must be amended in order to protect sexual minorities from discrimination in employment, education, housing, mental and health care, and the military in all Brazilian states, territories, cities, municipalities, and public institutions. Third, it is necessary to cooperate with international organizations to ensure that human rights are extended to all sexual minorities worldwide. Fourth, LGBTQ individuals have the right to live in a society free of violence; when crime based on sexual orientation occurs, punishment needs to be swift and just.

SEXISM

The Brazilian Health Ministry (Conselho Nacional de Combate à Discriminação, 2004) also suggested that prejudice based on sexual orientation must be reduced alongside other types of prejudice, such as sexism. Research has shown that sexism is related to negative attitudes toward sexual minorities. Glick and Fiske (1996) differentiated between two types of sexist ideologies. The first is a subjectively positive, but patronizing, orientation of protection, idealization, and affection toward women (benevolent sexism), whereas the second reflects men's violence against women and exploitation of women as sex objects (hostile sexism). These two types of sexism are complementary. They reinforce and justify patriarchy, including heterosexuals' hostility toward women who deviate from traditional gender roles (e.g., lesbians; Glick & Fiske, 1997). Research across six U.S. samples showed that men consistently scored significantly higher than did women on both hostile and benevolent sexism; however, the gender gap was greater for hostile sexism than for benevolent sexism (Glick & Fiske, 1996).

Moreover, benevolent and hostile sexism have been found to be widespread across 19 nations, including Brazil, reflecting and maintaining the oppression of women (Glick et al., 2000), including lesbians. For instance, in a study across three British samples of high school students, college students, and full-time employees, Masser and Abrams (1999) found that benevolent sexism, hostile sexism, and neosexism were negatively related to support for lesbians' and gay men's rights. In addition, in a study of college students at a medium-sized Midwestern U.S. public university, Whitley (2001) found that the best predictors of attitudes toward homosexuality were gender, benevolent sexism, endorsement of the traditional masculine role, and attitudes toward women.

DeSouza, Solberg, and Elder (2007) examined the influence of one's attitudes toward women in general and lesbians in particular on perceptions of woman-to-woman sexual harassment among 952 U.S. and Brazilian college students. The authors found significant relationships between negative attitudes toward lesbians with both benevolent and hostile sexism. Thus, sexist individuals also have anti-lesbian attitudes. The authors also found some support for the contact hypothesis, as there was a significant relationship between associating with homosexuals and having positive attitudes toward lesbians. There were interesting cross-cultural differences. Overall, college students in Brazil viewed hypothetical cases involving woman-to-woman sexual harassment as significantly more harassing and more likely to require an investigation than did college students in the United States. There were significant gender differences, but only between U.S. men and women, suggesting that Brazilian men and women are alike in the perceptions of woman-to-woman sexual harassment. Finally, hostile sexism and perceptions of what behaviors constitute woman-to-woman sexual harassment significantly predicted views of the hypothetical case as sexual harassment and in need of an investigation. These findings generally supported Fiske and Glick's (1995) argument that sexist attitudes predict judgments about unwanted social-sexual behaviors.

CONCLUSION

The picture of Brazil portrayed by the media is of Carnival, where nudity is the norm, but most Brazilians remain conservative underneath the mask of a sensual and seductive society, where there is no sin below the equator or within four walls everything is permitted (Parker, 1991, 1993, 1999). In fact, machismo is alive and well. However, like its views toward women, Brazilian society has been changing its views toward LGBTQ individuals, with a significant shift toward acceptance of sexual minorities.

There are many lenses to understand Brazil. On the one hand, sexual minorities in Brazil experience dehumanization in the form of public stigma, stereotyping, prejudice, discrimination, and violence. On the other hand, Brazilians are discussing homosexuality more openly, which is changing morality from a rigid hegemonic heterosexual viewpoint toward a more accepting view of differences and diversity as desirable. According to Prado and Machado (2008), homosexuality in Brazil has been through a political transformation: from criminalizing and pathologizing homosexuality toward fighting for human rights and dignity of LGBTQ individuals.

Increasing numbers of sexual minority individuals in Brazil are coming out of the closet and slowly are being accepted by family members, friends, neighbors, and co-workers. For instance, on June 14, 2009, the city of São Paulo held its 13th Gay Pride parade, the largest in the world with an estimated 3.5 million people in attendance (Parada Gay, 2009). The process is not uniform though. Acceptance is more common in large urban centers, such as São Paulo and Rio de Janeiro, than in rural areas or in the northeast of Brazil. In addition, sexual minority individuals who publicly conform to traditional gender role expectations are more easily accepted than their less gender-typical counterparts, especially transgendered individuals who totally break away from traditional gender expressions and are the most marginalized and the most victimized sexual minority subgroup in Brazil.

REFERENCES

Almeida, L. M., & Crillanovick, Q. (1999). A cidadania e os direitos humanos de gays, lésbicas e travestis no Brasil [Citizenship and human rights of gays, lesbians and transvestites in Brazil]. In D. D. Oliveira, R. B. Lima, S. A. Santos, & T. L. D. Tosta (Eds.), *50 anos depois: Relações raciais e grupos socialmente segregados* [50 years later: Race relations and socially segregated groups] (pp. 167–183). Goiânia, Brazil: MNDH.

American Psychiatric Association. (1973). *Diagnostic and statistical manual of mental disorders* (2nd ed.). Washington, DC: American Psychiatric Association.

American Psychological Association. (1998). Appropriate therapeutic responses to sexual orientation in the proceedings of the American Psychological Association, Incorporated, for the legislative year 1997. *American Psychologist, 53,* 882–939.

Cardoso, F. L. (2005). Inversões do papel de gênero: "Drag queens," travestismo e transexualismo [Gender identity divergence: "Drag queens," transvestism, and transexualism]. *Psicologia: Reflexão e Crítica, 18,* 421–430.

Carrara, S., & Vianna, A. R. B. (2006). "Tá lá o corpo estendido no chão": a violência letal contra travestis no município do Rio de Janeiro ["Over there the body lies on the ground": Deadly violence against transvestites in the municipality of Rio de Janeiro]. *Physis: Rev Saúde Pública—Rio de Janeiro, 16,* 233–249.

Carrara, S., Ramos, S., & Caetano, M. (2002). *Política, direitos, violência e homossexualidade* [Politics, rights, violence and homosexuality]. Rio de Janeiro: Pallas.

Central Intelligence Agency. (2009, May 14). *The world fact-book—Brazil.* Retrieved June 2, 2009, from https://www.cia.gov/library/publications/the-world-factbook/geos/br.html

Cerqueira-Santos, E., Winter, F., Salles, A., Longo, J., & Teodoro, M. (2007). Contato interpessoal e crenças sobre homossexualidade: Desenvolvimento de uma escala [Interpersonal contact and beliefs about homosexuality: A scale construction]. *Interação em Psicologia, 11,* 221–229.

Código Penal Brasileiro [Brazilian Penal Code]. (2001). *Lei 10.224, Art. 216-A.* Brasília.

Conselho Nacional de Combate à Discriminação [National Committee to Combat Discrimination]. (2004). *Brasil sem homofobia: Programa de combate a violência e à discriminação contra GLTB e promoção da cidadania homosexual* [Brazil without homophobia: Program to combat violence and discrimination against GLTB and promote homosexual citizenship]. Brasília: Ministério da Saúde.

Crocker, J., Major, B., & Steele, C. (1998). Social stigma. In D. T. Gilbert, S. Fiske, & G. Lindzey (Eds.), *The handbook of social psychology* (4th ed., pp. 504–553). New York: McGraw Hill.

DeFrancisco, V. (1997). Gender, power and practice: Or, putting your money (and your research) where your mouth is. In R. Wodak (Ed.), *Gender and discourse* (pp. 37–56). London: Sage.

DeSouza, E. R., Baldwin, J., Koller, S. H., & Narvaz, M. (2004). A Latin American perspective in the study of gender. In M. A. Paludi (Ed.), *Praeger guide to the psychology of gender* (pp. 41–67). Westport, CT: Praeger.

DeSouza, E. R., & Schneider, K. T. (2009). *Incivility based on sexual orientation: The impact on North American and Brazilian bystanders*. Manuscript in preparation.

DeSouza, E. R., Solberg, J., & Elder, C. (2007). A cross-cultural perspective on judgments of woman-to-woman sexual harassment: Does sexual orientation matter? *Sex Roles, 56,* 457–471.

DeSouza, E., & Showalter, B. In M. Paludi & F. Denmark (Eds.), *Victims of sexual assault and abuse: Resources and responses for individuals and families*. Westport, CT: Praeger.

Diamond, L. M., & Savin-Williams, R. C. (2000). Explaining diversity in the development of same-sex sexuality among young women. In L. D. Garnets (Ed.), *Psychological perspectives on lesbian, gay, and bisexual experiences* (pp. 130–148). New York: Columbia University Press.

Fassinger, R. E. (1991). The hidden minority: Issues and challenges in working with lesbian women and gay men. *The Counseling Psychologist, 19,* 157–176.

Fausto-Sterling, A. (2000). *Sexing the body: Gender politics and the construction of sexuality*. New York: Basic Books.

Fiske, S. T., & Glick, P. (1995). Ambivalence and stereotypes cause sexual harassment: A theory with implications for organizational change. *Journal of Social Issues, 51,* 97–115.

Grupo Gay da Bahia. (2009). *Relatório sobre crimes homofóbicos no Brasil* [Report about hate crimes in Brazil based on sexual orientation]. Grupo Gay da Bahia, Salvador: Grupo Gay da Bahia.

Glick, P., & Fiske, S. T. (1996). The Ambivalent Sexism Inventory: Differentiating hostile and benevolent sexism. *Journal of Personality and Social Psychology, 70,* 491–512.

Glick, P., & Fiske, S. T. (1997). Hostile and benevolent sexism: Measuring ambivalent sexist attitudes toward women. *Psychology of Women Quarterly, 21,* 119–135.

Glick, P., Fiske, S. T., Mladinic, A., Saiz, J. L., Abrams, D., Masser, B., et al. (2000). Beyond prejudice as simple antipathy: Hostile and benevolent sexism across cultures. *Journal of Personality and Social Psychology, 79,* 763–775.

Glomb, T. M., Richman, W. L., Hulin, C. L., & Drasgow, R. (1997). Ambient sexual harassment: An integrated model of antecedents and consequences. *Organizational Behavior and Human Decision Processes, 71,* 309–328.

Goering, L. (1997, April 4). Brazil's gay men appear singled out, attacked for living ordinary lives. *The Chicago Tribune*. Chicago, IL. Retrieved March 25, 2005, from http://www.familyresearchinst.org/FRI_EduPamphet4.html

Green, J. N. (1999). *Beyond carnival: Male homosexuality in twentieth-century Brazil*. Chicago: University of Chicago Press.

Herek, G. H. (2000). Sexual prejudice and gender: Do heterosexuals' attitudes toward lesbians and gay men differ? *Journal of Social Issues, 56,* 251–266.

Horowitz, J. L., & Newcomb, M. D. (2001). A multidimensional approach to homosexual identity. *Journal of Homosexuality, 42,* 1–19.

Instituto de Pesquisa e Cultura GLS [Institute of Research and Culture GLS]. (2000). 1o. Censo GLS do Brasil [First Census of GLS in Brazil]. São Paulo: GLS Planet. Retrieved June 8, 2009, from www.censogls.com.br

Kimmel, M. S. (1997). Masculinity as homophobia: Fear, shame, and silence in the construction of gender identity. In M. M. Gergen & S. N. Davis (Eds.), *Toward a new psychology of gender* (pp. 223–242). New York: Routledge.

Kitzinger, C., & Wilkinson, S. (2004). Social advocacy for equal marriage: The politics of "rights" and the psychology of "mental health." *Analyses of Social Issues and Public Policy, 4,* 173–194.

Klein, C. (1999). "The ghetto is over, darling": Emerging gay communities and gender and sexual politics in contemporary Brazil. *Culture, Health, & Sexuality, 1,* 239–260.

Lacerda, M., Pereira, C., & Camino, L. (2002). Um estudo sobre as formas de preconceito contra homossexuais na perspectiva das representações sociais [A study of prejudice forms against homosexuals anchored on social representations]. *Psicologia: Reflexão e Crítica, 15,* 165–178.

Larsen, R. J., & Buss, D. M. (2008). *Personality psychology: Domains of knowledge about human nature.* New York: McGraw Hill.

Lawrence v. Texas, 71 U.S.L.W. 4574 (2003).

Leis [Laws]. (2002). *Pride.* Retrieved May 25, 2009, from http://mixbrasil.uol.com.br/pride/direito/dh.htm

Low, K. S. D., Radhakrishnan, P., Schneider, K. T., & Rounds, J. (2007). The experiences of bystanders of workplace ethnic harassment. *Journal of Applied Social Psychology, 37,* 2261–2297.

Masser, B., & Abrams, D. (1999). Contemporary sexism: The relationships among hostility, benevolence, and neosexism. *Psychology of Women Quarterly, 23,* 503–517.

Mendes-Leite, R. (1993). A game of appearances: The "ambigusexuality" in Brazilian culture of sexuality. *Journal of Homosexuality, 25,* 271–282.

Mott, L. (2002). *O crime anti-homossexual no Brasil* [Crimes against homosexuals in Brazil]. Salvador: Grupo Gay da Bahia.

National Gay and Lesbian Task Force. (2008, July 31). *State nondiscrimination laws in the U.S.* Retrieved June 6, 2009, from http://www.thetaskforce.org/reports_and_research/nondiscrimination_laws

Noviski, I. F., Davoli, J. C., & Castro, R. C. (2000). *Assédio sexual: Questão que ultrapassa a categoria profissional do secretário executivo* [*Sexual harassment: A question beyond the category of a superior*]. Monografia de conclusão de curso. Universidade do Vale do Paraíba. São José dos Campos, São Paulo.

O mundo gay rasga as fantasias [The gay world tears up the costumes]. (1993, May 12). *Veja,* 52–57.

Parada Gay agita São Paulo neste domingo [Gay Parade stirs São Paulo this Sunday]. (2009, June 14). Retrieved June 16, 2009, from http://ultimosegundo.ig.com.br/brasil/2009/06/14/parada+gay+deve+receber+cerca+de+35+milhoes+de+pessoas+em+sao+paulo+6718909.html

Parker, R. (1991). *Bodies, pleasures, and passions: Sexual culture in contemporary Brazil.* Boston: Beacon.

Parker, R. (1999). *Beneath the equator: Cultures of desire, male homosexuality, and emerging gay communities in Brazil.* London: Routledge.

Parker, R. G. (1993). "Within four walls": Brazilian sexual culture and HIV/AIDS. In H. Daniel & R. Parker (Eds.), *Sexuality, politics and AIDS in Brazil: In another world?* (pp. 65–84). London: Falmer.

Pastore, J., & Robortella, L. C. A. (2003) *Assédio sexual no trabalho* [*Sexual harassment at work*]. São Paulo: Makron Books.

Prado, M. A. M., & Machado, F. V. (2008). *Preconceito contra homossexualidades* [Prejudice against homosexualities]. São Paulo: Cortez.

Resolução [Resolution] CFP # 001/99. (1999, March 22). Estabelecer normas de atuação para os psicólogos em relação à questão da orientação sexual [Standards of performance for psychologists concerning sexual orientation].

Rios, R. R. (2002). A homossexualidade e a discriminação por orientação sexual no direito Brasileiro [Homosexuality and discrimination due to sexual orientation in Brazilian law]. In C. Golin & L. G. Weiler (Eds.), *Homossexualidades, cultura e política* [Homosexuality, culture and politics] (pp. 15–48). Porto Alegre, Brazil: Sulina.

Rocha, K. B., Barbosa, L. H. R., Barboza, C. Z., Calvetti, P. U., Carvalho, F. T., Cerqueira-Santos, E., et al. (2009). Attention to health in Brazil based on transvestites, transsexuals and transgender's perception. Unpublished manuscript.

Sedgwick, E. K. (1990). *Epistemology of the closet*. Berkeley, CA: University of California Press.

Silva, L., & Barbi, H. (2005, February 25). *Seus direitos* [*Your rights*]. Retrieved May 25, 2009, from http://mixbrasil.uol.com.br/pride/seusdireitos/visto/visto.asp

Starks, T. J., Gilbert, B. O., Fischer, A. R., Weston, R., & DiLalla, D. L. (2009). Gendered sexuality: A new model and measure of attraction and intimacy. *Journal of Homosexuality, 56*, 14–30.

Werba, G. C., & Strey, M. N. (2001). Longe dos olhos, longe do coração: ainda a invisibilidade da violência contra a mulher [Out of sight, out of mind [lit. heart]: The continued invisibility of violence against women]. In P. K. Grossi & G. C. Werba (Eds.), *Violências e gênero: Coisas que a gente não gostaria de saber* [Violence and gender: Things we didn't want to know] (pp. 71–82). Porto Alegre, Brazil: Edipucrs, 2.

Whitam, F. L., Daskalos, C., Sobolewski, C. G., & Padilla, P. (1998). The emergence of lesbian sexuality and identity cross-culturally: Brazil, Peru, the Philippines, and the United States. *Archives of Sexual Behavior, 27*, 31–56.

Whitley, B. E., Jr. (2001). Gender-role variables and attitudes toward homosexuality. *Sex Roles, 45*, 691–721.

Chapter 9

Frequency Rates and Consequences of Peer Sexual Harassment: Comparing U.S. and International Students[1]

Eros DeSouza
Joy Chien

Although sexual harassment is widespread on U.S. college campuses, we know of no study that has examined the incidence of sexual harassment among international students. Thus, the purpose of the current study described in this chapter was to fill an important gap in the literature by comparing frequency rates and psychological consequences of peer sexual harassment between U.S.-born and international college students. The findings showed that female international students were at the greatest risk of experiencing peer sexual harassment and were the most bothered by these experiences. There was also a trend for sexually harassed international students, regardless of gender, to have lower self-esteem compared to sexually harassed U.S.-born students. These findings have important practical implications for university officials.

REVIEW OF THE LITERATURE

Hill and Silva (2005) reported findings from a recent national survey conducted by the American Association of University Women in which 62 percent of U.S. male and female college students indicated having been sexually harassed, most often by peers (80 percent); the most common form of sexual harassment was unwanted comments, jokes, gestures, and looks (53 percent). In addition, many scholars suggest that sexual harassment is about power rather than sexual desire (e.g., Cleveland & Kerst, 1993; Fineran & Bennett, 1999; Jones, 1996; Sandler, 1997). Power may rest on the harasser's gender, size, race, "or any number of other dominant characteristics the harasser possesses or is perceived to possess by society" (Strauss, 2003, p. 114).

DEFINING SEXUAL HARASSMENT

From a psychological perspective, sexual harassment is defined as "unwanted sex-related behavior at work that is appraised by the recipient as offensive, exceeding her resources, or threatening her well-being" (Fitzgerald, Swan, & Magley, 1997, p. 15). Sexual harassment is, then, a type of stressor that has deleterious effects on a target's health and psychological well-being. Although we are interested in psychological sexual harassment, it is worthwhile noting that the definition of sexual harassment varies cross culturally (DeSouza & Solberg, 2003) and from one individual to another due to the subjective nature of sexual harassment (i.e., sexual harassment is in the eye of the beholder).

According to Paludi (1997), sexual harassment in educational settings can be defined in legal terms and in behavioral terms. As a legal term, the U.S. Department of Education: Office for Civil Rights (2001) defined sexual harassment as:

> [u]nwelcome conduct of a sexual nature. Sexual harassment can include unwelcome sexual advances, requests for sexual favors, and other verbal, nonverbal, or physical conduct of a sexual nature. Sexual harassment of a student can deny or limit, on the basis of sex, the student's ability to participate in or to receive benefits, services, or opportunities in the school's program. Sexual harassment of student is, therefore, a form of sex discrimination prohibited by Title IX under circumstances described in this guidance. (p. 2)

As a behavioral term, sexual harassment "can also occur where no such formal differential exists, if the behavior is unwanted by or offensive to the individual" (Fitzgerald & Ormerod, 1993, p. 556).

Sexual harassment is illegal (Equal Employment Opportunity Commission, 2009; U.S. Department of Education, Office for Civil Rights, 2001). It can be classified into two categories: *quid pro quo* and hostile environment. In *quid pro quo* sexual harassment, the harasser typically has more organizational power than the target (Sandler & Shoop, 1997); that is, when the harasser is in a position to provide benefits for the target in exchange for sexual favors or to punish the target for not cooperating—for example, when a teacher gives an "A" grade to a student who does not deserve it but is open to sexual interactions, or when a teacher fails a student because he or she is not willing to participate in sexual behaviors.

The other type of sexual harassment is hostile environment, which is defined as an environment being so hostile that it interferes with an individual's ability to perform her or his tasks, such as attending classes (Sandler & Shoop, 1997). Examples of behaviors that fall under this category include, but are not limited to, sexual innuendos, sexual bantering, unwanted touching, grabbing and pinching, sexual obscenities, computer harassment, exposure to pornographic materials, and being asked out on a date repeatedly after having said no.

Often in situations of hostile environment, the harasser and the target are in an equal organizational position, such as both being students. This form of hostile environment is called peer sexual harassment. However, only a few studies focused directly on peer sexual harassment in educational settings (e.g., DeSouza & Ribeiro, 2005; DeSouza, Schneider, & Hubbard, 2005; Goldstein, Malanchuk, Davis-Kean, & Eccles, 2007).

One of the reasons for the lack of attention on peer sexual harassment in educational settings is that many sexual behaviors that match the peer sexual harassment definition have become normalized in society due to the culture's perception of gender roles. According to Woods (2007), one aspect for men to be masculine in the United States is to be sexual; in other words, men should be interested in sex all the time. For example, it is common to find a group of men judging women's appearance and body parts when women simply pass by, and it would be "naturally" argued that judging women is a way of "men being men."

Peer sexual harassment occurs due to societal status bestowed upon men (Fitzgerald & Ormerod, 1993). Thus, it is a form of gender-based dominance and control (Fineran, Bennett, & Sacco, 2001), in which young men show their masculinity by sexually coming on to women (Woods, 2007). Fineran and Bennett (1999) reported that in the United States, high school boys sexually harassed their peers more often than high school girls did, and adolescents' beliefs that men should be dominant were correlated with engaging in sexually harassing behaviors toward peers.

Although Hill and Silva's study as well as other studies that use their own behavioral checklists (e.g., American Association of University Women, 1993, 2001; Fineran & Bennet, 1999; Ivy & Hamlet, 1996) are informative, these studies are largely atheoretical. They generally use various definitions of sexual harassment and psychometric instruments, making generalizations problematic (Raver & Gelfand, 2005).

In the late 1980s, Fitzgerald et al. created a behavioral measure of sexual harassment called the Sexual Experiences Questionnaire (SEQ), which has become the most widely used and rigorous assessment of sexual harassment with content, construct, and criterion validity (Arvey & Cavanaugh, 1995; Fitzgerald, Gelfand, & Drasgow, 1995; Stark, Chernyshenko, Lancaster, Drasgow, & Fitzgerald, 2002). Fitzgerald et al. defined sexual harassment as a behavioral construct, comprising three related but distinct dimensions: *gender harassment* (insulting, hostile, or degrading sexist behaviors), *unwanted sexual attention* (verbal or nonverbal sexual behaviors that are offensive, unwanted, and unreciprocated), and *sexual coercion* (when better treatment or rewards are contingent on sexual cooperation, either subtly or explicitly). Note that the term "sexual harassment" is never mentioned in the SEQ.

Moreover, gender harassment and unwanted sexual attention parallel the legal definition of a hostile environment, whereas sexual coercion parallels the legal definition of *quid pro quo*. Research suggests that gender harassment is the most common type of sexual harassment, followed by unwanted sexual attention, with sexual coercion being the least common (Pryor & Fitzgerald, 2003).

DEMOGRAPHIC FACTORS RELATED TO THE INCIDENCE OF SEXUAL HARASSMENT

Sexual harassers usually choose individuals who do not have the power to reject behaviors that are unwelcome, degrading, offensive, or intimidating, and that violate standards of interpersonal respect (DeSouza, 2008). In addition, perpetrators of these acts are motivated to maintain or enhance their social status (Berdahl, 2007).

Survey studies have shown that female workers are much more likely to experience sexual harassment than male workers (e.g., U.S. Merit Systems Protection Board, 1981, 1988, 1995). In educational settings, although male students can and do become targets of peer sexual harassment, those who seem most vulnerable to be sexually harassed by their peers are female students (Goldstein et al., 2007; Hand & Sanchez, 2000), students of color (Goldstein et al., 2007), and "effeminate" male students. That is, women, sexual minorities, and racial/ethnic minorities have been traditionally viewed as being inferior in compassion to heterosexual men and whites.

Factors such as gender, sexual orientation, race, and social economic status reflect an individual's power in society. Moreover, these factors interface. For instance, sexism and racism have been historically and experientially intertwined (Murrell, 1996). In fact, some researchers concluded that racialized sexual harassment is a central factor in the harassment experience of women of color (e.g., Berdahl & Moore, 2006, 2005; Buchanan & Ormerod, 2002; Cortina, Fitzgerald, & Drasgow, 2002; Schneider, Hitlan, & Radhakrishnan, 2000; Texeira, 2002; Yoder & Aniakudo, 1995).

Concerning social economic status, DeSouza and Cerqueira recently examined frequency rates, as assessed by the SEQ, and consequences of sexual harassment in a sample of 376 poor women, who were employed as domestic workers in Brazil. Ninety-eight percent of these women earned about US $200 or less a month and 89 percent had less than a high school education. Twenty-six percent of this sample was sexually harassed at work during the past 12 months. Live-in workers (e.g., those residing at their employers' residence) were at a significantly greater risk of experiencing sexual harassment than those who resided in their own homes after controlling for participants' age, race, and social class. Women who lived in their employers' residence used more alcohol/drugs than their counterparts. Harassed women had significantly higher self-esteem impairment and anxiety-depression than nonharassed women. Nonharassed women who resided in their own homes had the best physical well-being. When asked about one's worst sexually harassing experience, respondents indicated that the perpetrators were typically men (75 percent), who also engaged in more severe types of sexual harassment than female perpetrators. The emotional reaction to such incidents was significantly worse when perpetrated by men than by women. Most sexually harassed domestic workers experienced some form of retaliation (social or work-related) after asking their harassers to stop.

DeSouza and Cerqueira concluded that the low social and economic status of domestic workers in Brazil might allow the perpetration of sexual harassment and other forms of mistreatment with impunity. That is, these workers may refuse to file a formal complaint with the police due to fear of being ridiculed by officials and not finding a new job, putting themselves and their families at risk of not surviving (e.g., not being able to pay bills).

Another factor that researchers have paid little attention to is one's nationality/citizenship. Welsh, Carr, MacQuarrie, and Huntley (2006) studied Filipina domestic female workers who emigrated to Canada without full citizenship status. The authors argued that citizenship status was one of the major components that put these women at risk of experiencing sexual harassment and the way they defined sexual harassment. The Filipina domestic workers in their study usually kept their sexual harassment experiences unreported, because they were afraid that if they complained about it, they would lose their right to stay in Canada.

Xie, Meng, and Yamagami (1995) investigated the experiences of international students from China who studied in Japan. The student visa of a Chinese student requires sponsorship by a Japanese organization. These Chinese students did not report their experiences of sexual assault to the police because they feared being deported. Welsh et al. and Xie et al. concluded that individuals who do not have full citizenship have less power in the host society. In addition, they are fearful to report their experiences to authorities because they might lose their legal right to stay in the host country.

According to Sandler, female international college students are more likely to be harassed than college students born in the United States, because the former are objectified as exotic and/or passive and, as suggested above, they have less power in society due to their gender and citizenship status. Unfortunately, none of the previous studies on peer sexual harassment or any other form of sexual harassment have investigated the experiences of international students enrolled in U.S. colleges and universities. This is troublesome because 623,805 international students studied in the United States during the 2007/2008 academic year, accounting for 3.5 percent of the student body (Institute of International Education, n.d.). Thus, it is important to investigate the experiences of international students with peer sexual harassment.

Moreover, targets of peer sexual harassment may end up in self-doubt, affecting their entire education experience and future career, as they may become afraid of attending classes or joining social events in order to avoid the harasser and may end up transferring to another institution or dropping out of college altogether (Sandler, 1997). Furthermore, sexual harassment is a stressor that can have negative psychological outcomes on the targets (e.g., DeSouza & Cerqueira, in press; Willness, Steel, & Lee, 2007). In addition, even relatively mild experiences with sexual harassment may lead to negative consequences in one's physical and psychological health (e.g., DeSouza & Cerqueira, in press; DeSouza & Fansler, 2003; Goldstein et al., 2007).

THE CURRENT STUDY

The purpose of the current study was to examine frequency rates and psychological consequences of peer sexual harassment in a sample of international and U.S.-born students enrolled in a large midwestern state university. We examined whether being female and an international student moderated both the frequency of peer sexual harassment and its consequences on the victims' psychological well-being. Specifically, we predicted that female international students would experience the most peer sexual harassment and would be most bothered by it because they have the lowest power in society due to their gender and citizenship status compared to both male and female students from the United States and international male students. We also predicted that female international students would fare worst psychologically (i.e., lower self-esteem and more anxiety-depression) compared to the other groups.

All international students ($n = 429$) enrolled in a large midwestern state university and 426 randomly selected U.S.-born counterparts, who were matched by age and gender, received an e-mail in the fall of 2007 asking them to participate in a Web survey about social-sexual behaviors between college students. Of these, 165 college students (69 international students and 96 U.S.-born students) completed the Web survey, yielding a response rate of 19 percent.

The age of the total sample ($N = 165$) ranged from 19 to 37, with the average age being 26; 55 percent were women and 61 percent were graduate students. Most U.S.-born students were European American/white (88 percent), whereas most international students were Asian (66 percent), followed by white (25 percent), black (6 percent), and Latino (3 percent). The vast majority of international students (90 percent) reported that English was their second language. Also, most international students (64 percent) reported to be studying in the United States for two years or less, with 36 percent studying in the United States for three years or more. All students completed the following measures in the order presented below. Items about psychological well-being preceded all sexual harassment items to minimize response bias.

DEMOGRAPHIC AND PERSONAL INFORMATION

We asked all students their age, gender, race/ethnicity, student status (undergraduate or graduate student), and whether or not they were an international student. If they were an international student, they were asked whether or not English was their native language and how long they have been in the United States.

PSYCHOLOGICAL WELL-BEING

Students completed 15 items that assessed their psychological well-being. First, they answered five items from the Mental Health Index (MHI), developed by Veit and Ware (1983), that measured anxiety-depression during the 12 months. These items are scored on a 6-point scale from 1 (*Never*) to 6 (*All the time*). We reversed the scores of two positively worded items. Then, we averaged all responses, so that higher scores represent higher self-reported levels of anxiety and depression. A sample item reads, "I have felt downhearted and blue." In the current study the internal reliability (Cronbach's alpha) of the MHI was .83, which indicates that it is a reliable measure of anxiety-depression.

Then, students completed the 10-item Rosenberg Self-Esteem Scale (RSES; 1986), which is scored on a 4-point scale from 1 (*Strongly disagree*) to 4 (*Strongly agree*). A sample item reads, "I certainly feel useless at times." The RSES is a widely used measure of global self-esteem, with sound construct validity and psychometric properties (Robins, Hendin, & Trzesniewski, 2001). The Cronbach's alphas for the RSES across various samples ranged from .77 to .88 (Blascovich & Tomaka, 1993; Rosenberg, 1986). According to Rosenberg's recommendation, the scores of five negatively worded statements were reversed. Then, all scores were averaged, so that higher scores represent higher reported levels of self-esteem. In the current study the internal reliability (Cronbach's alpha) of the RSES was .87, which indicates that it is a reliable measure of self-esteem.

Student-to-Student Hostile Sexual Harassment

Students completed a shortened version of the SEQ (Stark et al., 2002), containing 12 behaviors initiated by either male or female college students during the past 12 months that may constitute hostile sexually harassing experiences (a sample item includes, "told sexual stories or jokes that were offensive to you"). That is, since hostile sexually harassing behaviors are far more common than coercive ones (Pryor & Fitzgerald, 2003), and since we were interested in student-to-student sexual harassment, we eliminated four items that measure sexual coercion (e.g., "implied certain rewards or better treatment if you were sexually cooperative"), as these behaviors would be unlikely to be initiated by students to other students. As stated earlier, the validity of the SEQ has been well established (Arvey & Cavanaugh, 1995; Fitzgerald et al., 1995). Stark et al. (2002) reported reliability estimates (Cronbach's alphas) of .91 men and .92 for women for the 16-item SEQ.

In the current study, each of the 12 SEQ items branches out into two response sets. The first set measures incident frequency, whereas the second set measures the emotional reaction to the experience (i.e., how bothersome it was if it happened at least once). That is, for each item, students first indicated how often it occurred on the following 5-point scale: 1 (*Never*), 2 (*Once or twice*), 3 (*Sometimes*), 4 (*Often*), and 5 (*Many times*). We averaged these responses, so that higher scores represent higher reported frequency of sexually harassing experiences. The Cronbach's alpha for the frequency measure was .86, which is comparable to the 16-item SEQ described above.

Next, if students had experienced a sexually harassing behavior at least once, they were asked how bothersome it was on the following 5-point scale: 1 (*Not at all*), 2 (*Slightly*), 3 (*Somewhat*), 4 (*A lot*), and 5 (*Extremely*). We averaged these responses, so that higher scores represent higher reported levels of feeling bothered by such incidents. The Cronbach's alpha for the bothersome measure was .81, which indicates good reliability.

RESULTS AND DISCUSSION

Eighty-six percent of the total sample reported having experienced at least one sexually harassing behavior from peers during the past 12 months. This figure suggests that peer sexual harassment is widespread, supporting Hill and Silva's findings.

The data generally supported our predictions. First, female students ($M = 1.78$) experienced significant more peer sexual harassment than male students ($M = 1.50$; $F(1, 151) = 11.74$, $p < .01$. These findings are in keeping with past studies, which found that female students were much more likely to be targets of sexual harassment than were male students (e.g., Goldstein et al., 2007; Hand & Sanchez, 2000).

Second, female students ($M = 1.81$) were more bothered by these experiences than were male students ($M = 1.48$; $F(1, 151) = 14.06$, $p < .01$. These findings are also in keeping with past studies, which found that men perceived sexually harassing experiences as less severe, less upsetting, less inappropriate, less bothersome, and less threatening than did women (Berdahl, Magley, & Waldo, 1996; Cochran, Frazier, & Olson, 1997; Hurt, Maver, & Hoffman, 1999; LaRocca & Kromrey, 1999; Marks & Nelson, 1993). Recent studies also found that female college students were much more likely to perceive social-sexual behaviors between students as constituting peer sexual harassment than did male college men (DeSouza & Solberg, 2004; DeSouza, Solberg, & Elder, 2007).

Although the main effect for citizenship was not significant for either the frequency or bothersome measure, we found significant interactions between gender and citizenship for both the frequency measure, $F(1, 151) = 4.12$, $p < .05$, and the bothersome measure, $F(1, 151) = 3.93$, $p < .05$. These interactions were in the expected direction, which supported our predictions. That is, female international students ($M = 1.80$) experienced the most peer sexual harassment and male international students the least ($M = 1.25$), with female U.S. students ($M = 1 .75$) and male U.S. students ($M = 1.61$) scoring in between. A similar and significant pattern was found for the bothersome measure: Female international students ($M = 1.83$) were most bothered by these experiences and male international students the least ($M = 1.24$), with female U.S. students ($M = 1.78$) and male U.S. students ($M = 1.60$) scoring in between.

We did not find a significant interaction for either the self-esteem or anxiety-depression measure. However, there was a trend for harassed international students ($M = 3.19$) to score lower on self-esteem than did harassed U.S.-born students ($M = 3.37$), $F(1, 134) = 2.93$, $p = .089$. In addition, harassed women ($M = 2.61$) scored significantly higher on anxiety-depression than did harassed men ($M = 2.33$), $F(1, 134) = 5.16$, $p < .05$. The latter is in keeping with past research (e.g., DeSouza & Fansler, 2003).

CONCLUSION

The current study advances our understanding of sexual harassment by comparing its incidence and psychological consequences between U.S.-born students and international student. Female international students experienced the most peer sexual harassment and were the ones most bothered by these experiences, which seem to add to their acculturation stress in a new culture (Wadsworth, Hecht, & Jung, 2008).

Harassed international college students, regardless of gender, may even blame themselves for their victimization. Thus, their lower self-esteem, compared to harassed U.S.-born college students, evidenced in our study is easy to understand, because being sexually harassed implies low status, as noncitizens, and a sense of powerlessness, as they may fear losing their student visa if they complain to university officials and returning home in shame.

The above findings have important implications for university officials who are in a position to prevent sexual harassment in all its forms. According to Hill and Silva, "[t]he ramifications of sexual harassment can be serious. Sexual harassment can damage the emotional and academic well-being of students, provoke and exacerbate conflict among students, and contribute to a hostile learning environment . . . society as a whole is affected as graduating students bring their attitudes about sexual harassment into the workplace and beyond" (p. 4).

University officials have a duty to protect international students from sexual harassment. International students may need extra help understanding how sexual harassment is defined in the United States and what can be done to redress the situation. Residence hall assistants (RAs) are often the first resource for international students residing on campus. Thus, RAs may need additional training about how international students may have a different conceptualization of sexual harassment. For example, Brazilian laws define sexual harassment only as sexual coercion by superiors, that is, *quid pro quo* sexual harassment (Código Penal Brasileiro, 2001).

Limitations and Future Directions

One important limitation of our study is that our sample was from one midwestern university, limiting the generalizability of our findings. Another limitation is that our study was cross-sectional rather than longitudinal, which precludes an examination of the consequences of sexually harassing experiences over time. Thus, we cannot infer causality from our correlational study. Hence, future studies need to include longitudinal designs to test the causality of the relationships found in our study. Future research should also include qualitative approaches, such as in-depth interviews and focus groups, in order to contextualize the sexual harassment experiences of international students. Researchers (e.g., Lim & Cortina, 2005) suggest that sexual harassment does not happen in isolation, but rather in an environment permeated by generalized hostility. Hence, other types of mistreatment (e.g., bullying and incivility) should be simultaneously investigated in future studies.

NOTE

1. Preliminary findings were presented at 2008 meeting of the International Coalition Against Sexual Harassment and at the Association for Psychological Science.

REFERENCES

American Association of University Women. (1993). *Hostile hallways: The AAUW survey on sexual harassment in America's schools*. Washington, DC: Harris/Scholastic Research.

American Association of University Women. (2001). *Hostile hallways: Bullying, teasing, and sexual harassment in school*. Washington, DC: Author.

Arvey, R. D., & Cavanaugh, M. A. (1995). Using surveys to assess the prevalence of sexual harassment: Some methodological problems. *Journal of Social Issues, 51*, 39–52.

Berdahl, J. L. (2007). Harassment based on sex: Protecting social status in the context of gender hierarchy. *Academy of Management Review, 32*, 641–658.

Berdahl, J. L., Magley, V. J., & Waldo, C. R. (1996). The sexual harassment of men? Exploring the concept with theory and data. *Psychology of Women Quarterly, 20*, 527–547.

Berdahl, J. L., & Moore, C. (2006). Workplace harassment: Double jeopardy for minority women. *Journal of Applied Psychology, 91*, 426–436.

Blascovich, J., & Tomaka, J. (1993). Measures of self-esteem. In J. P. Robinson, P. R. Shaver, & L. S. Wrightsman (Eds.), *Measures of personality and social psychological attitudes* (3rd ed., pp. 115–160). Ann Arbor, MI: Institute of Social Research.

Buchanan, N. T. (2005). The nexus of race and gender domination: Racialized sexual harassment of African American women. In J. E. Gruber & P. Morgan (Eds.), *In the company of men: Male dominance and sexual harassment* (pp. 294–320). Boston: Northeastern University Press.

Buchanan, N. T., & Ormerod, A. J. (2002). Racialized sexual harassment in the lives of African American women. *Women & Therapy, 25*, 107–124.

Cleveland, J. N., & Kerst, M. E. (1993). Sexual harassment and perceptions of power: An underarticulated relationship. *Journal of Vocational Behavior, 42*, 49–67.

Cochran, C. C., Frazier, P. A., & Olson, A. M. (1997). Predictors of responses to unwanted sexual attention. *Psychology of Women Quarterly, 21*, 207–226.

Código Penal Brasileiro [Brazilian Penal Code]. (2001). *Lei 10.224, Art. 216-A*. Brasília.

Cortina, L. M, Fitzgerald, L. F., & Drasgow, F. (2002). Contextualizing Latina experiences of sexual harassment: Preliminary tests of a structural model. *Basic and Applied Social Psychology, 24,* 295–311.

DeSouza, E., & Fansler, A. G. (2003). Contrapower sexual harassment: A survey of students and faculty members. *Sex Roles, 48,* 529–542.

DeSouza, E., Schneider, K. T., & Hubbard, C. R. (2005, August). Sexual harassment among high school students of color. In A. J. Ormerod & L. L. Collinsworth (Chairs), *New issues in high school sexual harassment.* Symposium presented at the annual meeting of the American Psychological Association, Washington, DC.

DeSouza, E., & Solberg J. (2003). Incidence and dimensions of sexual harassment across cultures. In M. Paludi & C. A. Paludi, Jr. (Ed.), *Academic and workplace sexual harassment* (pp. 3–30). Westport, CT: Praeger.

DeSouza, E. R. (2008). Workplace incivility, sexual harassment, and racial micro-aggression: The interface of three literatures. In M. Paludi (Ed.), *The psychology of women at work: Vol 2. Obstacles and the identity juggle* (pp. 65–84). Westport, CT: Praeger.

DeSouza, E. R., & Cerqueira, E. (in press). From the kitchen to the bedroom: Frequency rates and consequences of sexual harassment among Brazilian domestic workers. *Journal of Interpersonal Violence.*

DeSouza, E. R., & Ribeiro, J. (2005). Bullying and sexual harassment among Brazilian high school students. *Journal of Interpersonal Violence, 20,* 1018–1038.

DeSouza, E. R., & Solberg, J. (2004). Women's and men's reactions to man-to-man sexual harassment: Does the sexual orientation of the victim matter? *Sex Roles, 50,* 623–639.

DeSouza, E. R., Solberg, J., & Elder, C. (2007). A cross-cultural perspective on judgments of woman-to-woman sexual harassment: Does sexual orientation matter? *Sex Roles, 56,* 457–471.

Equal Employment Opportunity Commission. (2009, March 11). *Sexual harassment.* Retrieved May 12, 2009, from http://www.eeoc.gov/types/sexual_harassment.html

Fineran, S., & Bennett, L. (1999). Gender and power issues of peer sexual harassment among teenagers. *Journal of Interpersonal Violence, 14,* 626–641.

Fineran, S., Bennett, L., & Sacco, T. (2001). Peer sexual harassment and peer violence: South African children at risk. *Social Work, 37,* 211–221.

Fitzgerald, L. F., Gelfand, M. J., & Drasgow, F. (1995). Measuring sexual harassment: Theoretical and psychometric advances. *Basic and Applied Social Psychology, 17,* 425–445.

Fitzgerald, L. F., Shullman, S., Bailey, N., Richards, M., Swecker, J., Gold, Y., et al. (1988). The incidence and dimensions of sexual harassment in academia and the workplace. *Journal of Vocational Behavior, 32,* 152–175.

Fitzgerald, L. F., Swan, S., & Magley, V. J. (1997). But was it really sexual harassment? Legal, behavioral, and psychological definitions of the workplace victimization of women. In W. O'Donohue (Ed.), *Sexual harassment: Theory, research, and treatment* (pp. 5–28). Boston: Allyn & Bacon.

Fitzgerald, L. F., & Ormerod, A. (1993). Sexual harassment in academia and the workplace (pp. 553–581) In F. L. Denmark & M. A. Paludi (Eds.), *Psychology of women: Handbook of issues and theories.* Westport, CT: Greenwood Press.

Goldstein, S. E., Malanchuk, O., Davis-Kean, P. E., & Eccles, J. S. (2007). Risk factors of sexual harassment by peers: A longitudinal investigation of African American and European American adolescents. *Journal of Research on Adolescence, 17,* 285–300.

Hand, J. Z., & Sanchez, L. (2000). Badgering or bantering? Gender differences in experience of, and reactions to, sexual harassment among U.S. high school students. *Gender & Society, 14,* 718–746.

Hill, C., & Silva, E. (2005). *Drawing the line: Sexual harassment on campus.* Washington, DC: American Association of University Women.

Hurt, J. L., Maver, J. A., & Hoffman, D. (1999). Situational and individual influences on judgments of hostile environment sexual harassment. *Journal of Applied Social Psychology, 29,* 1395–1415.

Institute of International Education (n.d.). *International students.* Retrieved May 12, 2009, from http://opendoors.iienetwork.org/?p=131531

Ivy, D. K., & Hamlet, S. (1996). College students and sexual dynamics: Two studies of peer sexual harassment. *Communication Education, 45,* 149–166.

Jones, C. (1996). *Sexual harassment.* New York: Facts On File, Inc.

LaRocca, M. A., & Kromrey, J. D. (1999). Perception of sexual harassment in higher education: Impact of gender and attractiveness. *Sex Roles, 40,* 921–940.

Lim, S., & Cortina, L. M. (2005). Interpersonal mistreatment in the workplace: The interface and impact of general incivility and sexual harassment. *Journal of Applied Psychology, 90,* 483–496.

Marks, M. A., & Nelson, E. S. (1993). Sexual harassment on campus: Effects of professor gender on perception of sexually harassing behaviors. *Sex Roles, 28,* 207–217.

Murrell, A. J. (1996). Sexual harassment and women of color: Issues, challenges, and future directions. In M. S. Stockdale (Ed.), *Sexual harassment in the workplace: Perspectives, frontiers, and response strategies* (pp. 51–65). Thousand Oaks, CA: Sage.

Paludi, M. A. (1997). Sexual harassment in schools. In W. O'Donohue (Ed.), *Sexual harassment: Theory, research, and treatment* (pp. 225–240). Needham Heights, MA: Allyn & Bacon.

Pryor, J. B., & Fitzgerald, L. F. (2003). Sexual harassment research in the United States. In S. Einarsen, H. Hoel, D. Zapf, & C. L. Cooper (Eds.), *Bullying and emotional abuse in the workplace: International perspectives in research and practice* (pp. 79–100). New York: Taylor & Francis.

Raver, J. L., & Gelfand, M. (2005). Beyond the individual victim: Linking sexual harassment, team processes, and team performance. *Academy of Management Journal, 48,* 387–400.

Robins, R. W., Hendin, H. M., & Trzesniewski, K. H. (2001). Measuring global self-esteem: Construct validation of a single-item measure and the Rosenberg Self-esteem Scale. *Personality and Social Psychology Bulletin, 27,* 151–161.

Rosenberg, M. (1986). *Conceiving the self.* Malabar, FL: Krieger.

Sandler, B. R. (1997). Student-to-student sexual harassment. In B. R. Sandler & R. J. Shoop (Ed.), *Sexual harassment on campus* (pp. 50–65). Needham Heights, MA: Allyn & Bacon.

Sandler, B. R., & Shoop, R. J. (1997). What is sexual harassment? In B. R. Sandler & R. J. Shoop (Ed.), *Sexual harassment on campus* (pp. 1–21). Needham Heights, MA: Allyn & Bacon.

Schneider, K. T., Hitlan, R. T., & Radhakrishnan, P. (2000). An examination of the nature and correlates of ethnic harassment experiences in multiple contexts. *Journal of Applied Psychology, 85*, 3–12.

Stark, S., Chernyshenko, O. S., Lancaster, A. R., Drasgow, F., & Fitzgerald, L. F. (2002). Toward standardized measurement of sexual harassment: Shortening the SEQ-DoD using item response theory. *Military Psychology, 14*, 49–72.

Strauss, S. (2003). Sexual harassment in K—12. In M. Paludi & C. A. Paludi, Jr. (Eds.), *Academic and workplace sexual harassment: A handbook of cultural, social science, management, and legal perspectives* (pp. 105–145). Westport, CT: Praeger.

Texeira, M. T. (2002). "Who protects and serves me?" A case study of sexual harassment in one U.S. law enforcement agency. *Gender & Society, 16*, 524–545.

U.S. Department of Education: Office for Civil Rights. (2001, January 19). *Revised sexual harassment guidance: Harassment of students by school employees, other students, or third parties.* Retrieved May 12, 2009, from http://www.ed.gov/about/offices/list/ocr/docs/shguide.html#Guidance

U.S. Merit Systems Protection Board. (1981). *Sexual harassment in the Federal workplace: Is it a problem?* Washington, DC: U.S. Government Printing Office.

U.S. Merit Systems Protection Board. (1988). *Sexual harassment in the Federal Government: An update.* Washington, DC: U.S. Government Printing Office.

U.S. Merit Systems Protection Board. (1995). *Sexual harassment in the Federal Government: Trends, progress, continuing challenges.* Washington, DC: U.S. Government Printing Office.

Veit, C. T., & Ware, J. E., Jr. (1983). The structure of psychological distress and well-being in general populations. *Journal of Counseling and Clinical Psychology, 51*, 730–742.

Wadsworth, B. C., Hecht, M. L., & Jung, E. (2008). The role of identity gaps, discrimination, and acculturation in international students' educational satisfaction in American classrooms. *Communication Education, 57*, 64–87.

Welsh, S., Carr, J., MacQuarrie, B., & Huntley, A. (2006). I'm not thinking of it as sexual harassment: Understanding harassment across race and citizenship. *Gender & Society, 20*, 87–107.

Willness, C. R., Steel, P., & Lee, K. (2007). A meta-analysis of the antecedents and consequences of workplace sexual harassment. *Personnel Psychology, 60*, 127–162.

Woods, J. T. (2007). *Gendered lives: Communication, gender, and culture.* Belmont, CA: Thomson Wadsworth.

Xie, L., Meng X., & Yamagami A. (1995). Chinese student victims of sexual assault in Japan. *International Medical Journal, 2*, 214–217.

Yoder, J. D., & Aniakudo, P. (1995). The responses of African American women firefighters to gender harassment at work. *Sex Roles, 32*, 125–137.

Chapter 10

In Women's Voices

Janet Boyce

When I began writing this, I had to take a step back and think about what feminism really means to me. I then began to ask female friends and family members what feminism means to them. Surprisingly, I don't think that any two women had the same response. However, there was one predominant underlying factor, and that was the right to be given equal treatment. Women just want to be treated as equal to their male counterparts. Although women have made great strides over the last 50 years, there is still a ways to go before women are viewed as equals to men.

Traditionally, women were expected to get married, have a family, and stay home to take care of them. This changed, in a sense, when women went to work outside of the home during wartime and began to experience the freedom associated with earning a paycheck. Many of these women were then replaced by men returning from war. It was at this time that women noticed the inequalities in the workplace both from an economic and social standpoint.

As the baby boomers came of age in the 1960s, many with college educations did not accept the economic and social inequalities being imposed on them. These are the women that paved the way for the generations to come. These women mirrored the way activists were able to lobby for equality with the Civil Rights Act of 1964 legally prohibiting race discrimination and gender discrimination. This was later amended by Title IX, which prohibited discrimination in education and athletics. Although legislation made it illegal to discriminate against a person based on their gender, the traditional biases were still there in the workplace and in education.

As a woman born in the early 1960s, my own experiences in school were proof of these lingering biases. One example of this was when I entered my senior year of high school and met with my guidance counselor to talk about college. I remember him asking me whether I had thought about colleges and what I wanted to do after graduation. I told him that I wanted to go to Penn State and major in accounting. I will never forget his response, and perhaps it is still an underlying factor in what drives me today. He told me that accounting is not a woman's field, and that I should consider teaching or attending the local community college to learn to be a secretary. I had never felt as dejected in my life as when I walked out of his office that day. I am sorry to say that I believed him and began to pursue a teaching degree. I hated it, so I left school and did what was expected—got married and raised a family. I did return to school more than 20 years later to pursue a degree in a field of my choice.

Because of the courageous women who became activists and fought for all women, I am glad that my daughter never had to feel that same dejection as I did. I am thankful to say that my daughter's guidance counselor did everything he could to help her get into the college of her choice and pursue the degree of her choice.

Although women have a come along way through the years, they still have barriers to overcome in the workplace. One such barrier is that of equal pay—where any two people doing the same job should earn the same wage regardless of their gender. According to the Department of Labor (2003), as of 2002, women earn, on average, 78 percent of the salary that their male counterparts do for the same job. This means that white women earn on average 78 cents for every dollar a man makes, while women of other races earn significantly less than that. Although the wage gap is closing, there is still significant ground to cover.

Because women still tend to be the primary caregivers in the family unit, if their workplaces offered more family-friendly programs and policies, the gap could be offset. Many women today are faced with the challenge of taking care of aging parents and their own children. Many women in this position would opt to take advantage of a program like this in exchange for a lower wage.

In conclusion, I am a realist and know that my daughter will probably still suffer from inequalities in the workplace. I do believe that the millennial generation will continue to push forward and equality will be attained. I am optimistic that by the time my granddaughter comes of age the playing field will be more level in the workplace.

REFERENCE

Department of Labor. (2003, October 16). Women's earnings 78 percent of men's in 2002. Retrieved June 12, 2009, from: http://www.bls.gov/opub/ted/2003/oct/wk2/art03.htm

Chapter 11

Bullying and Sexual Harassment of Adolescents

James Gruber
Susan Fineran

Interpersonal violence, whether defined as sexual harassment or bullying, frequently occurs in schools and is both experienced and observed by students and school personnel alike (Stein, 1999). Sexual harassment is defined as discrimination and is illegal, while bullying, although abhorrent, is not considered discriminatory. However, because sexual harassment and bullying have emerged from two different paradigms (employment law and criminal law), exploration of their impact on students has been very different.

SEXUAL HARASSMENT AND BULLYING: DEFINITIONS AND DIFFERENCES

Studies of bullying and sexual harassment have two different historical and theoretical roots. The problem of bullying was brought to international attention most prominently by Dan Olweus, a Norwegian researcher in the 1970s. Nansel et al. (2001) defined bullying in a manner that reflects the perspective developed and subsequently modified over the years by Olweus: "Aggression that is intentionally harmful, that is repeated, and centers on an imbalance of power." This asymmetry of power "may be physical or psychological, and the aggressive behavior may be verbal (e.g. name calling, threats), physical (e.g., hitting), or psychological (e.g. rumors, shunning/exclusion)" (p., 2094). School bullies have been described as children who use physical or relational aggression in a systematic and calculated way with a group of weaker peers (Crick, 1996; Olweus, 1993; Pellegrini, 2001; Schwartz, Dodge, Pettit, & Bates, 1997).

Formal theories and definitions of sexual harassment originated in the United States in the 1970s with the work of Catharine MacKinnon, who defined it as a form of sex discrimination (1979). While bullying has often been characterized as inappropriate or aggressive interpersonal behavior (between individuals or between a group and an individual ("mobbing"), sexual harassment was originally defined as behavior by males who used organizational power or cultural privilege to coerce sexual favors from women (*quid quo pro*). This initial formulation expanded both theoretically and legally over the decades to include gender- or sexually focused behaviors by men that made it exceedingly difficult for women to work (*hostile environment*), and more recently, same-sex harassment involving the use of sexual threats, taunts, or attacks (e.g., *Oncale v. Sundowners*, 1998). The definition of sexual harassment by the U.S. Department of Education parallels that of other state and local governments and government agencies insofar as it includes both unwelcome interpersonal behavior (e.g., date pressures, sexual contact) "that is sufficiently severe, persistent, or pervasive . . ." and hostile environment (1997, p. 12,038).

While bullying focuses on aggressive behavior that occurs between individuals or by a group against an individual, it does not acknowledge differences in gender or sexuality as significant factors in perpetration or victimization. Bullying research tends to focus on situational and interpersonal dynamics. Sexual harassment, in contrast, is theoretically linked to hegemonic masculinity and consequently focused on structural and culturally sanctioned roles and meanings (masculine-feminine, heterosexual-homosexual) that are key aspects of social stratification. The term "sexual bullying" has surfaced recently and has muddled the definition of both sexual harassment and bullying. Some researchers (Craig, Pepler, Connolly, & Henderson, 2001; Pellegrini, 2001) view school sexual harassment as an adolescent form of bullying. This is an unfortunate development for two reasons. First, bullying is constructed as an interpersonal problem, while sexual harassment is a legal issue. Consequently, many students and their parents who perceive sexual harassment as a form of bullying may not exercise their rights to have schools address the issue as they are *legally* mandated to do. Also, when sexually-based experiences are viewed as bullying and not identified specifically as sexual harassment, problems of victimization that stem from gender or sexuality may be interpreted as private or interpersonal troubles experienced by unfortunate students who are caught up in difficult situations. The fact that most bullies are male, that girls experience more harm than boys from sexual harassment, and that homophobic comments are used routinely (mostly by boys) to humiliate and control others (primarily other boys) misses the point about the power of culturally-based stereotypes (AAUW, 2001; McGuffey & Rich, 1999; Kimmel & Mahler, 2003). Two recent studies by Jessie Klein (2006a, 2006b) have highlighted the role that gender and sexual stereotyping played in school shootings—a fact that has escaped public scrutiny because of a focus on "bullying": Most of the school shooters targeted girls primarily; and the shooters, who fell well outside the range of acceptable masculine body types, had weathered attacks on their masculinity, including homophobic taunts, for months—and in some cases, years.

PREVALENCE OF SEXUAL HARASSMENT AND BULLYING IN U.S. SCHOOLS

Four national studies of student victimization—two on sexual harassment and two on bullying—provide the broadest statistics regarding these behaviors in U.S. schools in the last two decades. The earliest study on bullying in the United States, conducted in 1998 by the National Institute of Child Health and Human Development (Nansel et al., 2001) that used Olweus's theoretical construction found that one-third of early adolescent children were directly involved in bullying, with 10 percent as bullies, 13 percent as victims, and 6 percent as bully-victims. The U.S. Department of Education School Crime Supplement to the National Crime Victimization Survey (2003) reported that in 2001, 8 percent of middle and high school students were bullied (9 percent males, 7 percent females). The American Association of University Women (AAUW) conducted both national studies on sexual harassment, the first in 1993 and the second in 2001. The two studies showed similar results: 81 percent of students experienced some form of sexual harassment during their school years. Fifty-nine percent of students were harassed occasionally and 27 percent were targeted often (AAUW, 2001). In addition, 54 percent of students said they sexually harassed someone during their school years. One interesting contrast with bullying outcomes, which tend to decrease with age and grade level was that sexual harassment frequency increases with grade level: 55 percent of eighth and ninth graders and 61 percent of tenth and eleventh graders reported that they had been physically sexually harassed at school (Hand & Sanchez, 2000).

When these four national studies are compared, it appears that sexual harassment is a national disaster that affects nearly all school children. The statistical contrast is stark: Over 80 percent of students said they had experienced sexual harassment, while fewer than one of six reported being bullied. Even more interesting, more than half of students said they perpetrated sexual harassment, while only 10 percent reported bullying others; and students who reported being both harasser and harassed constituted 55 percent (AAUW, 1993) while those who were bullied or who bullied others were about a quarter of that figure (Nansel et al., 2001). At first glance, then, it appears that sexual harassment is much more common than bullying. But significant differences in measurement are largely responsible for these discrepancies. Because the issues of bullying and sexual harassment emerged from different paradigms (bullying as a criminal offense and sexual harassment as illegal discrimination), they have evolved with different methodologies. Research conducted on peer sexual harassment in schools uses a behavior scale that asks students to indicate the frequency of each of 14 different sexually harassing behaviors they experienced (AAUW, 1993, 2001). In contrast, bullying research inspired by Olweus has for the most part used only one or two questionnaire items which contained the word "bullying" along with a definition (e.g., Elsea, Menesini, Moore, & Morita, 2003; Nansel et al., 2001; Olweus, 1993; Williams, Connolly, Pepler, & Craig, 2005). It is likely that asking a single question (e.g., Have you ever been bullied?) that allows the respondent to decide whether the behaviors they experienced were "bullying" produces a significant underreporting of experiences that might otherwise be construed as bullying. Sexual harassment research is instructive in this regard. The use of multiple survey items (checklists) has been standard protocol since the mid-1980s and has allowed researchers to tap different dimensions of sexual harassment (e.g., Fitzgerald and her colleagues identified three forms of sexual harassment—gender harassment, unwanted sexual attention, and sexual coercion). It was discovered early in research endeavors that using the words "sexual harassment" resulted in significantly lowered estimates of experiences that could otherwise be deemed "sexual harassment" according to theoretical or legal definitions (Fitzgerald & Shullman, 1993; Gruber, 1990). In addition, most harassment surveys since the 1980s have asked respondents if they experienced "uninvited and unwanted sexual attention" with no mention of the term, "sexual harassment" (e.g., United States Merit System Protection Board [USMSPB], 1988, 1995). In line with that practice, the AAUW surveys ask adolescents "How often has anyone done the following [14] things to you when you did not want them to?"

Compounding the measurement problem, researchers have also used different time frames. Some researchers inquired whether respondents' experiences occurred during an entire school year, while others asked about behaviors that occurred during a short time span (e.g., past week or month. The AAUW (1993, 2001) surveys inquired whether students had ever had one or more sexual harassment experiences during their "school years", while the National Crime Victimization Survey asked about bullying experiences that occurred "during the last 6 months." In some victimization studies different time frames were used even when both phenomena were studied together. DeSouza and Ribeiros (2005) used "last 30 days" for bullying and "last 12 months" for sexual harassment. Similarly, Williams et al. (2005) framed bullying as experiences that occurred "during the last 2 months" and sexual harassment as "during the last 6 months." Another study comparing bullying and sexual harassment behaviors conducted by Holt and Espelage (2007), utilized AAUW (2001) questions with a one-year time frame ("during the last twelve months") and then included a 30-day time frame ("last 30 days") for their own bullying scale items. Perhaps not surprisingly, their results showed that 70 percent of the students had been harassed while a little more than half (54 percent) had been bullied. Based on this measurement conundrum, it would seem that sexual harassment is rampant in schools compared to bullying.

In an attempt to address these measurement issues, Gruber and Fineran (2008a) conducted a study comparing bullying and sexual harassment using experience checklists, one that asked students to indicate the frequency of sexually harassing behaviors they experienced (AAUW, 2001) and the second that inquired about the frequency of bullying behaviors (Holt and Espelage, 2007). Using an identical time frame and the same benchmark for determining whether or not victimization has occurred, bullying was revealed as a much more common experience than sexual harassment. More than half (52 percent) of students had experienced bullying during the current school year while approximately one-third (34 percent) were sexually harassed.

GLOBAL PREVALENCE OF SEXUAL HARASSMENT AND BULLYING

Internationally, bullying and sexual harassment are shown to be prevalent in many countries and reflect a wide range of incidence: 15 percent to 77 percent for bullying and 18 percent to 80 percent for sexual harassment. The ensuing overview of research highlights, although not exhaustive, shows the global prevalence of these issues and their damaging impact on victims.

A 1999 study by Olweus found that 15 percent of 150,000 Norwegian and Swedish students ages 7 to 16 were involved in bully-victim problems that occurred at least once a week (Olweus & Limber, 1999). A much larger study of students in seven countries *that used the same question format and same time* frame designed by Olweus in each country found incidence rates that parallel those of the United States that use the same methodology: Bullying perpetration did not exceed 17 percent, bully-victim incidences were less than 20 percent and bullying victimization rates were less than 25 percent (Elsea et al., 2003). Other European studies find somewhat higher incidence rates. In Great Britain, Stephensen and Smith (1989) estimated that 23 percent of children were involved in bullying either as bullies or as victims, and O'Moore and Hillery (1989) found that 34 percent of Irish students were occasionally bullied and 8 percent were bullied frequently. A South African study (Holan, Flisher, & Lombard, 2007) that used the Olweus model found that 8.2 percent were bullies, 19.3 percent were victims, and 8.7 percent were bully-victims.

Research that does not use the Olweus paradigm finds much higher rates of bullying or peer aggression. A national study on bullying in Israel found that 53 percent of elementary and middle school students and 30 percent of high school students reported being seized and shoved by schoolmates at least once during the previous month (Zeira, Astor, & Benbenishty, 2003). Other bullying behavior described by students included having their personal belongings stolen. Specifically, 45 percent of elementary and middle school students and 34 percent of those in high school reported being victimized in this manner. The study used a checklist of nineteen behaviors and asked students to indicate the frequency and severity of these. In other parts of the world, Brazilian and Japanese research on bullying report similar statistics.

DeSouza & Ribeiros (2005) used a bullying scale developed by Bosworth and found that 60 percent of Brazilian high school students bullied a classmate during the past month. Kobayoshi (1999) reports that 77 percent of Japanese sixth graders and 62 percent of eighth graders were involved in bullying incidents, either as a bully or as a victim of bullying behavior.

Similar to the prevalence of bullying world wide, sexual harassment also appears to be a major social problem for students, and unfortunately is as widespread. Bullying has been researched much more extensively than sexual harassment, but nonetheless there exists a number of studies showing that sexual harassment is rampant and affects students negatively as well. Studies in Sweden, South Africa, Brazil, and the Netherlands confirm that students consider a variety of behaviors in their schools to be problematic. A random sample of 540 female high school students in Sweden were surveyed in 2005 by researchers Witkowska and Menckel. They found that 49 percent of the female students identified verbal behaviors such as sexualized conversations, attractiveness rating, demeaning comments about gender, name-calling, and sexual personal comments as a problem present in their schools. Fineran, Bennett, and Sacco (2003) found that 78 percent of students in four South African high schools in Johannesburg reported experiencing sexual harassment. A survey of 2,808 Dutch students by Timmerman (2005) revealed that 18 percent had experienced unwanted sexual behavior. Boys reported more verbal incidents while girls reported significantly more physical incidents. Most of these studies examined only 'victimization, but DeSouza & Ribeiros (2005) inquired about perpetration of sexual harassment as well. Results showed that 24 percent of 400 high school students admitted to sexually harassing a classmate.

PEER SEXUAL HARASSMENT AND BULLYING PERPETRATION

The 1993 AAUW study inquired broadly about sexual harassment perpetration and found that 54 percent of the students admitted sexually harassing another student during their school years.

However, only two studies have focused specifically on the perpetration of bullying and sexual harassment (Pellegrini, 2001; Pepler et al., 2002). Pellegrini's (2001) longitudinal study of U.S. sixth- and seventh-grade students found that "bullies (who tended to be boys) also engaged in sexual harassment, and this relation was mediated by self-reported dating frequency. . . . That is, bullies who also estimated their frequency of dating to be high . . . tended to sexually harass their peers" (p. 131). Thus, as bullies became interested in opposite-sex dating, their proclivity to become perpetrators of sexual harassment increased as well. Pellegrini also found that sexual harassment behaviors at the end of seventh grade were predicted by bullying at the start of sixth grade. Pepler et al. (2002) studied four cohorts of students in Canadian schools grades five through eight and examined the relationship between aggressive behavior and substance use. They found that students who bullied others were at significant risk for substance abuse before entering high school. Their results also indicated that girls or boys who acknowledged sexually harassing others were between four and six times more likely to use alcohol than those who did not sexually harass their peers.

PEER SEXUAL HARASSMENT AND BULLYING VICTIMIZATION: GENDER

Nationwide, the AAUW 1993 and 2001 studies found that more than 50 percent of male and female students experienced sexual jokes, comments, gestures, or looks. More than 30 percent of students also experienced physical behaviors, such as being touched, grabbed, pinched, or brushed up against in a sexual way from schoolmates. In addition to physical and verbal harassment, Fineran and Bennett (1999) found that 43 percent of girls and 30 percent of boys reported unwanted sexual attention in the form of pressure for dates and sex, while a Connecticut study found a quarter of the girls and 5 percent of boys reported unwanted sexual attention (Permanent Commission [CT] on the Status of Women [PCSW], 1995). Gender differences in victimization are common with girls experiencing sexual harassment more frequently than boys and boys perpetrating sexual harassment more frequently than girls (AAUW, 1993, 2001; Fineran & Bennett, 1999; Hand & Sanchez, 2000; Lee, Croninger, Linn, & Chen, 1996; McMaster, Connolly, Pepler, & Craig, 2002; PCSW, 1995; Stratton & Backes, 1997; Trigg & Wittenstrom, 1996).

With regard to bullying, Nansel et al., (2001) found that males both bullied others and were bullied significantly more often than females. Results also showed that males reported being bullied by being hit, slapped, or pushed, while females were bullied more frequently through the use of rumors and sexual comments. A meta-analysis of studies examining peer victimization that occurred over the past twenty years, showed that bullied boys are four times, and girls eight times, more likely to be suicidal than their non-bullied peers (Hawker & Boulton, 2000).

PEER SEXUAL HARASSMENT AND BULLYING VICTIMIZATION: SEXUAL ORIENTATION

An annual school survey, The Massachusetts Youth Risk Behavior Survey (Commonwealth of Massachusetts, April 1998), compared gay, lesbian, and bisexual students to their peers. Results showed that sexual minority students were four times more likely to have attempted suicide, and five times more likely to have missed school because of feeling unsafe. Fineran (2002a) found that lesbian girls experienced significantly more sexual harassment than heterosexual girls. A recent follow-up to the Massachusetts Youth Risk Behavior Survey (Massachusetts Department of Education, 2007) reiterated many of its finds from their earlier study: Sexual minority students had higher suicide rates, were more apt to skip school because they felt unsafe, had been threatened with or injured by a weapon at school, and experienced more dating violence and non-consensual sex. Fineran (2002a) found in a study of 712 high school students that sexual minority students were physically assaulted and sexually harassed more frequently than heterosexual students. She also reported that heterosexual girls were significantly more upset and threatened by peer sexual harassment than their heterosexual male peers. According to Williams et al. (2005), gay and lesbian students also experienced *both* bullying and sexual harassment at higher levels than their heterosexual counterparts; and, according to Poteat and Espelage (2007), being the target of homophobic victimization had significant psychological and social consequences for students. A report on Michigan schools by the Gay, Lesbian and Straight Education Network [GLSEN], 2005) revealed that two-thirds of students in their sample were harassed because they were, or appeared to be, gay or lesbian, and more than 80 percent of these students reported hearing derogatory homophobic comments. In a recent study (Gruber & Fineran, 2008a), sexual minority adolescents not only had significantly higher rates of sexual harassment and bullying victimization but they also had poorer mental and physical health, more trauma symptoms, and higher levels of substance abuse as a result of victimization than did heterosexuals.

According to Thurlow (2004), however, most adolescents rate homophobic slurs as both more common and less serious than racial slurs. It appears, then, that homophobia may be a "normalized" means of categorizing and victimizing peers during adolescence that has devastating consequences for some teens, in particular, sexual minorities.

PEER SEXUAL HARASSMENT AND BULLYING VICTIMIZATION: CHILDREN WITH DISABILITIES

Most of the research on peer victimization and disability takes a bullying perspective rather than a sexual harassment perspective. That is, victimization is assessed in terms of aggression (hitting, kicking, etc.), social isolation (having few friends or being shunned), or verbal abuse (ridicule or parodying a disability). Only rarely is victimization determined by sexual behavior on the part of the perpetrators—for example, sexual touching or grabbing, spreading sexual rumors, or sexual name-calling ("fag," "queer," "slut").

The research on peer victimization ("bullying") suggests that disabled children experience a number of problems in school. A meta-analysis of research on children with learning disabilities found that they were rated by their peers as unpopular, socially incompetent, and socially isolated (Kavale & Forness, 1996). Learning disabled students reported more aggression and teasing than other students (Martlew & Hodson, 1991). A study in Great Britain found that almost two thirds of children with special needs were bullied compared to only one quarter of mainstreamed children (Thompson, Whitney, & Smith, 1994). Though research presents evidence of higher levels of peer victimization or bullying among disabled students, an unanswered issue is the impact of victimization on health and school outcomes. Research indicates that bullied children have more mental health problems (depression, psychosomatic symptoms) and school problems (problems concentrating, poor grades) than other students (see Gruber & Fineran, 2009, for a review). There is overall, however, a dearth of research on bullying outcomes among adolescents with disabilities.

There is even less research on sexual harassment experiences and their impact on students with disabilities. A small pilot study consisting of 26 disabled students conducted by Rousso (1996) showed that girls were more likely to be sexually harassed by non-disabled male peers, and both male and female students reported sexual harassment from the adults who care for them. Fineran (2002b) found that students with disabilities experienced significantly more sexual harassment in school from classmates than non-disabled students did. Bullying research on disabled students is also sparse. A study of eighth graders by Fineran and Gruber (2004) found while disabled and able students had similar levels of sexual harassment victimization, disabled students experienced more negative mental health outcomes as a result of these experiences. A more recent study (Gruber & Fineran, 2009) revealed that adolescents with disabilities who were harassed or bullied had lower self-esteem, weaker attachment to school, and lower satisfaction with school. Students with disabilities were sexually harassed more frequently than their peers, but their bullying experiences were comparable.

PEER SEXUAL HARASSMENT AND BULLYING VICTIMIZATION: RACE AND ETHNICITY

Research on differences in victimization among racial groups reveals inconsistent findings. Several recent studies (Nansel et al., 2001; Juvonen, Nishina, & Graham, 2006; Peskin, Tortolero, & Markham, 2006) found that black adolescents were bullied more frequently than white or Hispanic students. However, it appears that there are few differences in the types of bullying between race groups. Peskin and her colleagues found that verbal bullying (teasing and name-calling) did not vary between groups but physical bullying (hitting) did. In general, it appears that specific types of bullying (e.g., name calling, teasing) do not vary substantially in frequency across populations, whether racial, regional, or international (Borg, 1999; Demaray & Malecki, 2003; Rigby, 2000).

While there are studies of race differences in bullying victimization, research on adolescent sexual harassment victimization and race is fairly sparse. The largest study to look at racial differences was conducted by the AAUW (2001). Similar percentages of African Americans and whites of both sexes said that their school had "a lot" or "some" sexual harassment. Some types of harassment were more prevalent among blacks than whites: Having their clothes pulled off or down, being touched or grabbed in a sexual manner, or being forced to kiss someone (p. 24). The most common places where victimization occurred did not vary by sex or by race: In halls, in classrooms, and in the gym or on the playing field. In another study that looked at both bullying and sexual harassment, there were no racial differences in frequency for the former, but a small though statistically significant difference for the latter—blacks were harassed more often (Gruber & Fineran, 2008b).

AAUW (2001) found that blacks reported less emotional and behavioral impact than whites. This was true for both sexes. For example, a substantially larger number of white girls said that harassment made them feel self-conscious (49 percent), or made them feel less self confident (35 percent) compared to black girls (25 percent and 17 percent, respectively). The fact that peer sexual harassment victimization may have less impact for blacks than whites may be due to the fact that racism and racial discrimination play significant roles in the health and well-being of African Americans. This point is made well by African American focus group members in Welsh and her colleague's (2006) study of workplace harassment who said that sexual harassment was easier to deal with and less pressing than racial harassment (p. 98). In particular, they found that sexual harassment from black males was not defined as such while similar treatment from whites was (p. 99). Buchanan and Fitzgerald (in press) found that adverse job and health outcomes for African American women that resulted from workplace sexual harassment were exacerbated by racial harassment.

PEER SEXUAL HARASSMENT AND BULLYING VICTIMIZATION: HEALTH AND SCHOOL OUTCOMES

There have been a number of studies on bullying and sexual harassment that point to negative outcomes for mental and physical health and school performance. Nansel et al., 2001 states that research on bullies and those bullied has consistently found that "youth who are bullied generally show higher levels of insecurity, anxiety, depression, loneliness, unhappiness, physical and mental symptoms, and low self esteem" (p. 2095). The National Institute of Child Health and Human Development (Nansel, 2001) also reports that students who were bullied experienced greater difficulty making friends, had poorer relationships with classmates, and reported greater loneliness. In additional studies, Espelage and Holt (2001) investigated depression among children who were bullied and found that 20 percent of middle school victims scored within the clinical range on a standard depression and anxiety measure, while Boulton and Hawker (2000) found that bullied kids were five times more likely to be depressed. Hazler, Hoover, and Oliver (1992) reported that 90 percent of bullied students experienced a drop in school grades, while Kochenderfer and Ladd (1996) showed that bullying victimization was related to school absenteeism or dropping out.

When examining sexual harassment victimization, AAUW studies (1993, 2001) revealed student reports of negative psychosocial effects such as depression, loss of appetite, nightmares or disturbed sleep, low self esteem, and feelings of being sad, afraid, scared, or embarrassed (Hand & Sanchez, 2000; Lee et al., 1996). Similar to bullying victims, students also reported loss of interest in regular activities, isolation from friends and family, and loss of friends. School performance difficulties included absenteeism, decreased quality of schoolwork, skipping or dropping classes, poor grades, tardiness, and truancy (AAUW,

1993, 2001; Corbett, Gentry, & Pearson, 1993; Hand & Sanchez, 2000; Lee et al., 1996; Loredo, Reid, & Deaux, 1995; PCSW, 1995; Roscoe, Strouse, & Goodwin, 1994; Shakeshaft et al., 1995; Stein, Marshall, & Tropp, 1993; Stratton & Backes, 1997; Trigg & Wittenstrom, 1996). In addition, students also reported feeling afraid, upset, or threatened by the sexual harassment (AAUW, 1993, 2001; Fineran & Bennett, 1999; PCSW, 1995; Stein, Marshall, & Tropp, 1993).

SEXUAL HARASSMENT OF ADOLESCENTS AT WORK

An emerging area of litigation and policy development is sexual harassment of adolescents who hold jobs in the formal (wage) economy while attending school. Over the past ten years, litigation filed against employers by adolescents was uncommon. For example, during 2002, sexual harassment complaints filed by teenagers comprised approximately 2 percent of more than 14,000 suits filed nationwide. By 2005 that number had quadrupled to 8 percent—and these rates have continued to rise (Drobac, 2007). In 2005 alone, for example, the United States Equal Employment Opportunity Commission (EEOC) filed fifteen employment discrimination lawsuits on behalf of teenagers who were sexually harassed at their jobs. The descriptions of their experiences parallel those of many adults. The following lawsuits are recent examples of sexual harassment in the workplace that have been filed by teens. These cases reflect the extent of sexual violence that is, too often, not associated with sexual harassment. These are not in any way "fringe cases" but are representative of sexual harassment occurring to male and female teens who work.

A class action case filed in February 2005 by the EEOC involved teenage female employees who were subjected to sexual harassment by a male assistant manager. The girls described having their breasts grabbed, being backed against walls while having their shoulders rubbed, and being rubbed up against. The lawsuit states that although the female employees complained to management, no appropriate action was taken to correct the situation (*EEOC vs. GLC, Inc.*, 2005).

A second class action suit involved young men who were subjected to same-sex sexual harassment by a male supervisor. Behaviors experienced by the men included requests for sex, sexual remarks, and unwanted touching. One employee had his work hours cut in retaliation for opposing the sexual harassment (*EEOC v. Pand Enterprises, Inc.*, 2005). In both of these suits the EEOC asks the courts in Arizona and New Mexico (respectively) to order (both companies doing business as) McDonald's to provide the harassment victims with back wages, compensatory damages, and punitive damages and stop McDonald's from engaging in any practice that discriminates based on sex or retaliation.

Other cases recently settled have involved sexual assault, stalking, and verbal abuse. Successful lawsuit settlements have included payments of $150,000 to employees, along with letters of apology and a requirement that stores train employees regarding sexual harassment and post signs explaining employees' right to a workplace free of sexual harassment. Examples of teen work related sexual harassment lawsuits are listed on the EEOC website: http://youth.eeoc.gov/cases.html.

While there is much information known about the type of work teens perform, including the number of hours they work and their wages (e.g., Mortimer, 2005), the pervasiveness and impact of sexual harassment has received only minimal attention (Fineran, 2002a). It is quite apparent that research has not kept pace with growing legal and social concerns over this issue. Numerous studies of adult sexual harassment have been conducted over the past 20 years, but few studies have explored the problem among adolescents who work part time while attending school. Five studies documenting adolescent workplace sexual harassment have been conducted since 1981 (Fineran & Gruber, in press; Fineran & Gruber, 2009; Fineran, 2002a; Stein, 1981; Strauss and Espeland, 1992). Stein (1981) surveyed 22 female students attending a Massachusetts vocational high school. Eight students reported experiencing workplace sexual harassment that occurred while employed as babysitters, store clerks, or wait staff. Harassers were reported to be employers, customers, managers, and coworkers. All of the students eventually quit because of the harassment or were fired from their jobs for non-compliance.

A second survey conducted by Strauss and Espeland (1992) found that 30 percent of 250 female vocational students surveyed from four Minnesota school districts had been sexually harassed at work. This was similar to the findings by Fineran (2002a). In a sample of 712 high school students, 35 percent of the 332 students who worked part-time reported experiencing sexual harassment (63 percent girls; 37 percent boys). Findings showed that students experienced harassment from supervisors (19 percent), coworkers (61 percent), and unidentified others at work (18 percent). Girls reported being significantly more upset and threatened by the harassment than boys. None of these studies examined the impact of harassment on adolescent health or well-being.

Recently, research by Fineran and Gruber (in press) found that girls experienced a rate of sexual harassment that was higher than those typically found in samples of adult women. More than 52 percent of the girls reported that they had experienced some form of sexual harassment during the past year at their jobs. Harassed teens also faced problems similar to women in terms of work stress and alienation from coworkers and supervisors. An analysis of their "most upsetting" harassment experience revealed that more than half (56 percent) of the perpetrators were coworkers, while supervisors and vendors/customers accounted equally for the remainder. A large majority of the perpetrators were older than the girls, with nearly half (46 percent) described as older than 30.

Another study by the same authors (Fineran & Gruber, 2009) found that young adolescents (ages 13-15) were impacted significantly by sexual harassment. In particular, girls' health—self esteem, physical and mental health, and post-traumatic symptoms—and work attitudes and behavior were adversely affected more so than boys'.

CONCLUSIONS

Research conducted nationally and internationally on teen sexual harassment and bullying describes a problem of victimization that persists throughout adolescence and has a number of unhealthy effects. Despite the varieties of sample sizes, theoretical definitions, measurements, and time frames, several important generalizations can be gleaned from the research.

It appears at first glance that sexual harassment occurs at a much higher rate than bullying does. On closer inspection, it appears that a significant amount of this difference may be attributed to the ways in which these forms of victimization are measured. The only study to date (Gruber & Fineran, 2008a) that used similar measures and time frames found that *bullying* was more prevalent. A clearer understanding of victimization rates across time and space—e.g., comparing victimization in 2009 to 2001, or comparing rates between the United States and European Union nations—would result from the use of similarly-constructed measures (e.g., a listing of behaviors found in the AAUW studies) and similar time frames.

Across the globe, regardless of culture and language it is clear that victimization and perpetration are not random but are indeed highly predictable events. Boys are perpetrators and frequently victims; girls are victims but seldom perpetrators. Also, sexual minority children are at risk for bullying and sexual harassment victimization. Though there is less research on them, children with disabilities also seem to be frequent targets of victimization. The research on racial and ethnic differences in bullying and harassment is mixed. Most studies find few differences either in the overall incidence of victimization or in the specific types of victimization. Since most perpetration and victimization is an in-group phenomenon (e.g., blacks bully and harass other blacks), the dynamics of cross-race experiences remain a research issue for the future.

Research from across the globe clearly shows that bullying and harassment victimization is not a trivial event in children's lives. Despite popular claims that victimization is "just part of growing up" that most children experience and weather successfully, a plethora of studies suggest otherwise. There are clear health risks associated with victimization to children's psychological well-being (e.g., poor self esteem, high anxiety, depression, trauma symptoms, suicidal behavior) as well as to adjustment to and functioning within school. Victimized children enjoy school less, perform poorly, and harbor negative attitudes toward teachers. But these adverse health and school outcomes are not spread evenly across the student population. Some types of students suffer more. In particular, girls and sexual minorities experience significant harm as a result of victimization. The gender difference in harm seems to be the case whether the environment is school or a workplace.

We end our chapter on a cautionary note. Recently, bullying has become the *probleme de jour* both in the United States and the European Union. The number of research papers, articles in popular literature, and television specials devoted to the problem is quite phenomenal. The attention to bullying, while well-meaning and well-deserved, has diminished the attention that sexual harassment is receiving. The research we have conducted recently suggests that placing sexual harassment in the shadow of bullying does not serve our schools and our children well. Specifically, we found that sexual harassment poses greater health risks for boys and girls, and especially for sexual minorities. Our research on school outcomes, which remains unfinished at this point, suggests similar findings.

REFERENCES

American Association of University Women Educational Foundation. (2001). *Hostile hallways: Bullying, teasing and sexual harassment in school.* Washington, DC: Author.

American Association of University Women Educational Foundation. (1993). *Hostile hallways: The AAUW survey on sexual harassment in American schools* (Research Rep. No. 923012). Washington, DC: Harris/Scholastic Research.

Borg, M. (1999). The extend and nature of bullying among primary and secondary schoolchildren. *Educational Research, 41,* 137–153.

Boulton, M., & Hawker, D. (2000). Twenty years' research on peer victimization and psychosocial maladjustment: A meta-analytic review of cross-sectional studies. *Journal of Child Psychology and Psychiatry and Allied Disciplines, 41,* 441–455.

Buchanan, N., & Fitzgerald, L. (in press). The effects of racial and sexual harassment on work and the psychological well-being of African American women. *Journal of Occupational Health Psychology.*

Corbett, K., Gentry, C., & Pearson, W. (1993). Sexual harassment in high school. *Youth & Society, 25,* 93–103.

Craig, W., Pepler D., Connolly, J., & Henderson, K. (2001). Developmental context of peer harassment in early adolescence: The role of puberty and the peer group. In J. Juvonen & S. Graham, (Eds.), *Peer harassment in school: The plight of the vulnerable and victimized* (pp. 242–261). New York: Guilford.

Crick, N. (1996). The role of overt, relational aggression, and prosocial behavior in the prediction of children's future social adjustment. *Child Development, 67,* 2317–2327.

Demaray, M., & Malecki, C. (2003). Perceptions of the frequency and importance of social support by students classified as victims, bullies, and bully/victims in an urban middle school. *School Psychology Review, 32,* 471–489.

DeSouza, E., & Ribeiros, J. (2005). Bullying and sexual harassment among Brazilian high school students. *Journal of Interpersonal Violence, 20,* 1018–1038.

Drobac, J. (2007). I can't to I Kant: The sexual harassment of working adolescents, competing theories, and ethical dilemmas. *The Albany Law Review, 70,* 675–739.

EEOC v. GLC, inc., d/b/a/McDonald's Restaurant, CIV 05-0618 PCT PGR.

EEOC v. Pand Enterprises, Inc. d/b/a McDonald's Restaurant, Civil Action No. 05-CIV-204.

Elsea, M., Menesini, M., Moore, A., & Morita, Y. (2004). Friendship and loneliness among bullies and victims: data from seven countries. *Aggressive Behavior, 30,* 71–83.

Espelage, D., & Holt, M. (2001). Bullying and victimization during early adolescence: Peer influences and psychosocial correlates. In R. Geffner & M. Loring (Eds.), *Bullying behavior: Current issues, research, and interventions.* Binghamton, New York: Haworth Press Inc.

Fineran, S. (2002a). Sexual minority students and peer sexual harassment in high school. *Journal of School Social Work, 11,* 50–69.

Fineran, S. (2002b, August) *Sexual harassment and students with disabilities.* Paper presented at the annual meeting of the Society for the Study of Social Problems Annual Meeting, Washington, DC.

Fineran, S., & Bennett, L. (1999). Gender and power issues of peer sexual harassment among teenagers. *Journal of Interpersonal Violence, 14,* 626–641.

Fineran, S., Bennett, L., & Sacco, T. (2003). Peer sexual harassment and peer violence among adolescents in Johannesburg and Chicago. *International Social Work Journal, 46,* 391–405.

Fineran, S., & Gruber, J. E. (2009). Youth at work: Adolescent employment and sexual harassment. *Child Abuse & Neglect.*

Fineran, S., Gruber, J. E., & Rioux, J. (2009, May 20). Employed Maine teens and workplace sexual harassment. Presentation to the Maine Department of Labor.

Fitzgerald, L., & Shullman, S. (1993). Sexual harassment: A research analysis and agenda for the 1990's. *Journal of Vocational Behavior, 42,* 5–27.

Gay, Lesbian, and Straight Education Network. (2005). *Grading our schools: The national report evaluating our nation's schools and their progress on creating safe and affirming learning environments for gay and lesbian students and staff.* New York: Author.

Gruber, J. (1990). Methodological problems and policy implications in sexual harassment research. *Population Research and Policy Review, 9,* 235–254.

Gruber, J., & Fineran, S. (2008a). Comparing the impact of bullying and sexual harassment victimization on the mental and physical health of adolescents. *Sex Roles, 59,* 1–13.

Gruber, J., & Fineran, S. (2008b, August). *Race, bullying and sexual harassment: The impact on health outcomes of adolescents.* Paper presented at the annual meeting of the Society for the Study of Social Problems, Boston, MA.

Gruber, J. & Fineran, S. (2009, August). *Disability, bullying and sexual harassment: The impact on health and school outcomes for adolescents.* Paper presented at the annual meeting of the Society for the Study of Social Problems, San Francisco, CA.

Hand, J., & Sanchez, L. (2000). Badgering or bantering? Gender differences in experience of, and reactions to, sexual harassment among U.S. high school students. *Gender & Society, 14,* 718–46.

Hazler, R. J., Hoover, J. H., & Oliver, R. (1991). Student perceptions of victimization by bullies in school. *Journal of Humanistic Education and Development, 29,* 143–150.

Holan, L., Flisher, A. J., & Lombard, C. J. (2007). Bullying, violence, and risk behavior in South African school students. *Child Abuse & Neglect, 31,* 161–171.

Juvonen, S., Nishina, A., & Graham, S. (2001). Ethnic diversity and perceptions of safety in urban middle schools. *Psychological Science, 17,* 393–400.

Kavale, K. A., & Forness, S. R. (1996). Social skill deficits and learning disabilities: A meta-analysis. *Journal of Learning Disabilities, 29,* 226–237.

Kimmel, M., & Mahler, M. (2003). Adolescent masculinity, homophobia, and violence: Random school shootings, 1982–2000. *American Behavioral Scientist, 46,* 1439–1458.

Klein, J. (2006a). An invisible problem: Everyday violence against girls in schools. *Theoretical Criminology, 10,* 147–177.

Klein, J. (2006b). Sexuality and school shootings: What role does teasing play in school massacres? *Journal of Homosexuality, 51,* 39–62.

Kobayoshi, F. (1999). Bullying in Japanese schools. United States Department of Education, Educational Resources Information Center. Retrieved July 7, 2007, http://www.eric.ed.gov/ERICDocs/data/ericdocs2sql/content_storage_01/0000019b/80/15/e6/ba.pdf

Kochenderfer, B.J., & Ladd, G.W. (1996). Peer victimization: Cause or consequence of school maladjustment. *Child Development, 67,* 1305–1317.

Lee, V., Croninger, R., Linn, E., & Chen, X. (1996). The culture of sexual harassment in secondary schools. *American Educational Research Journal, 33,* 383–417.

Loredo, C., Reid, A., & Deaux, K. (1995). Judgements and definitions of sexual harassment by high school students. *Sex Roles, 32,* 29–45.

MacKinnon, C. (1979). *Sexual harassment of working women.* New Haven, CT: Yale University Press.

Martlew, M., & Hodson, J. (1991). Children with mild learning difficulties in an integrated and in a special school: Comparisons of behaviour, teasing and teachers' attitudes. *British Journal of Educational Psychology, 61,* 355–369.

McGuffey, C., & Rich, M. (1999). Playing in the gender transgression zone: race, class, and hegemonic masculinity in middle school. *Gender & Society, 13,* 608–627.

McMaster, L., Connolly, J., Pepler, D., & Craig, W. (2002). Peer to peer sexual harassment in early adolescence: A developmental perspective. *Development and Psychopathology, 14,* 91–105.

Massachusetts Department of Education. (2007). *2005 Youth risk behavior survey.* Malden, MA: Author.

Massachusetts Department of Education. (1998). *1998 Massachusetts youth risk behavior survey results.* Boston: Author.

Mortimer, J. T. (2005). *Working and growing up in America.* Cambridge, MA: Harvard University Press.

Nansel, T., Overpeck, R., Pilla, W., Ruan, P., Scheidt, K., & Simons-Morton, B. (2001). Bullying behaviors among U.S. youth: Prevalence and association with psychological adjustment. *Journal of the American Medical Association, 285,* 2094–2100.

Olweus, D. (1978). *Aggression in the school: Bullies and whipping boys.* Chichester, United Kingdom: Wiley.

Olweus, D. (1993). *Bullying at school.* Oxford, United Kingdom: Basil Blackwell.

Olweus, D., & Limber, S. (1999). *Blueprints for violence prevention. Bullying Prevention Program.* Boulder: Institute of Behavioral Sciences, University of Colorado.

O'Moore, A. M., & Hillery, B. (1989). Bullying in Dublin schools. *The Irish Journal of Psychology, 10,* 426–441.

Oncale v. Sundowner Offshore Services, Inc., 523 U.S. 75 (1998).

Pellegrini, A. (2001). A longitudinal study of heterosexual relationships, aggression and sexual harassment during transition from primary school through middle school. *Applied Developmental Psychology, 22,* 119–33.

Pepler, D. J., Craig, W. M., Connolly, J., & Henderson, K. (2002). My friends made me do it: Peer influence on alcohol and substance use in adolescence. In C. Wekerle & A. M. Wall (Eds.), *The violence and addiction equation: Theoretical and clinical issues in substance abuse and relationship violence.* Philadelphia: Brunner/Mazel.

Permanent Commission (CT) on the Status of Women. (1995). *In our own backyard: Sexual harassment in Connecticut's public high schools.* Hartford, CT: Author.

Peskin, M., Tortolero, S., & Markham, C. (2006). Bullying and victimization among black and Hispanic adolescents. *Adolescence, 41,* 467–484.

Poteat, V., & Espelage, D. (2007). Predicting psychosocial consequences of homophobic victimization in middle school students. *Journal of Early Adolescence, 27,* 175–191.

Rigby, K. (2000). Effects of peer victimization in schools and perceived social support on adolescent well-being. *Journal of Adolescence, 23,* 57–68.

Roscoe, B., Strouse, J. S., & Goodwin, M. P. (1994). Correlates of attitudes toward sexual harassment among early adolescents. *Sex Roles, 31,* 559–577.

Schwartz, D., Dodge, K., Pettit, G., & Bates, J. (1997). The early socialization of aggressive victims of bullying. *Child Development, 68,* 665–675.

Shakeshaft, C., Barber, E., Hergenrother, M., Johnson, Y. M., Mandel, L., & Sawyer, J. (1995). Peer harassment in schools. *Journal for a Just and Caring Education, 1,* 30–44.

Stein, N. (1981). *Sexual harassment of high school students: Preliminary research results.* Boston, MA: Massachusetts Department of Education. Unpublished manuscript.

Stein, N. (1999). Incidence and implications of sexual harassment and sexual violence in K–12 schools. Hamilton Fish National Institute on School and Community Violence. Washington, DC: George Washington University.

Stein, N., Marshall, N. L., & Tropp, L. R. (1993). *Secrets in public: Sexual harassment in our schools.* Wellesley, MA: Wellesley College Center for Research on Women.

Stephensen, P., & Smith, D. (1989). Bullying in the junior school. In D.P. Tatum & D.A. Lane (Eds.) *Bullying in schools.* London: Trentham Books.

Stratton, S., & Backes, J. (1997, February/March). Sexual harassment in North Dakota public schools: A study of eight high schools. *The High School Journal, 80,* 163–172.

Strauss, S., & Espeland, P. (1992). *Sexual harassment and teens.* Minneapolis: Free Spirit Publishing, Inc.

Thompson, D., Whitney, I., & Smith, P.K. (1994). Bullying of children with special needs in mainstream schools. *Support for Learning, 9, 103–106.*

Thurlow, C. (2004). Naming the "outsider within": homophobic pejoratives and the verbal abuse of lesbian, gay and bisexual high-school students. *Journal of Adolescence, 24,* 25–38.

Timmerman, G. (2005). A comparison between girls' and boys' experiences of unwanted sexual behaviour in secondary schools. *Educational Research, 47,* 291–306.

Trigg, M., & Wittenstrom, K. (1996). That's the way the world goes: Sexual harassment and New Jersey teenagers. *Initiatives, Special Issue: Sexual Harassment 57,* 55–65.

U.S. Department of Education, Office for Civil Rights. (1997). Sexual harassment guidance: Harassment of students by school employees, other students, or third parties. *Federal Register 62,* 12034–12051.

U.S. Department of Education, Office for Civil Rights. (2003). *School crime supplement to the National Crime Victimization Survey.* Washington, DC: Author.

U.S. Merit Systems Protection Board (USMSPB). (1995). *Sexual harassment in the Federal workplace: Trends, progress, and continuing challenges.* Washington, DC: U.S. Government Printing Office.

U.S. Merit Systems Protection Board. (1988). *Sexual harassment in the Federal workplace: An update.* Washington, DC: U.S. Government Printing Office.

Welsh, S., Carr, J., MacQuarrie, B., & Huntley, A. (2006). I'm not thinking of it as sexual harassment: Understanding harassment across race and citizenship. *Gender & Society, 20,* 87–107.

Williams, T., Connolly, J., Pepler, D., & Craig, W. (2005). Peer victimization, social support, and psychosocial adjustment of sexual minority adolescents. *Journal of Youth and Adolescence, 34,* 471–482.

Witkowska, E., & Menckel, E. (2005). Perceptions of sexual harassment in Swedish high schools: Experiences and school-environment problems. *European Journal of Public Health, 15,* 78–85.

Zeira, A., Astor, R. A., & Benbenishty, R. (2003). School violence in Israel: Findings of a national survey. *Social Work, 48,* 472–483.

Chapter 12

Great Is Our Sin: Pseudoscientific Justifications for Oppression in American Education

Jennifer L. Martin

If the misery of our poor be caused not by laws of nature, but by our institutions, great is our sin.

—Charles Darwin

The above quotation by Charles Darwin is still very relevant in contemporary American society. Not only the poor, but also those who experience disenfranchisement in a variety of forms, for example, gender, race, ethnicity, and so on, are subject to inequity on multiple levels: personal, interpersonal, institutional, and cultural. These levels of oppression are interactive, and it is easy to see how the majority viewpoint can subtly make its way into the cultural framework. For example, one's personal values, beliefs, and feelings can lead to interpersonal interaction (behavior), which can then lead to the creation of institutional rules and policies and then finally to cultural views involving the nature of beauty, truth, and right. It is frightening to examine our own history and the history of the American public education system in this light, but the same is true for both: personal values and beliefs were held that excluded and were detrimental to minority viewpoints. These racist and sexist beliefs were used to create a sociopolitical agenda that separated people into racial categories and promoted the "superiority" of the white race. In *Inheriting Shame: The Story of Eugenics and Racism in America* (1999), Steven Selden discusses how such personal values and beliefs led to institutional policy in the American school system, the repercussions of which are still with us.

Although most people associated with American education were not overtly radical racists, it is frightening when one considers that they nonetheless attached their names to philosophical ideas that were the basis for organizations that advocated for the segregation and sterilization of "undesirables." For example, G. Stanley Hall, developer of Child Study, which was highly influential on curriculum in the twentieth century, was a firm believer in biological determinism. He felt that nature defined "educability." He also advocated for a wide range of curricula to correspond to the wide range of abilities in individuals, which, not surprisingly, were more often than not based on racial and gender differences. Leta Hollingworth is still recognized today as a leading researcher and advocate for gifted and talented education, despite her alignment with the Eugenics Movement. As Selden states: "Educational policy, in Hollingworth's (1924) view, disregarded gifted children due to a misguided social philosophy that denied 'innate permanent, hereditary superiority'" (p. 101). Dr. Helen Putnam's eugenical ideas linked the National Education Association (NEA) with biological determinism. Dr. Putnam's report at the 1916 NEA conference, entitled "The New Ideal in Education—Better Parents of Better Children," advocated for the rationale that there was in fact a "superior" race: "'If humanity is to survive,' Putnam informed her audience of teachers and administrators, 'individualism and nationalism must conform to the laws of racial well-being'" (Putnam, quoted in Selden, p. 57). Putnam also expanded her platform of eugenical ideas to include programs of teacher education.

Interestingly, knowledge about the existence of the notion of eugenics and the Eugenics Movement in America is not widely known by most modern educators, or by the general public for that matter. Unfortunately, not having this knowledge allows similar ideas to reappear in contemporary society in more covert forms, for example, in the form of tracking students, having differential expectations based on gender, socioeconomic class, and so on. More shocking is when such racist notions appear quite overtly in society. For example, the racism justified by biological determinism emerged again recently with the publication of *The Bell Curve* (1994) by Charles Murray and Richard J. Hernstein. *The Bell Curve* presents pseudoscientific "evidence" of the genetic inferiority of blacks. As Macedo and Bartolomé state:

> This book has not only activated what had appeared to be a dormancy of racism in the United States after the enactment of the civil rights laws, but it also has resurrected an old form of intellectual lynching that, unfortunately, has been embraced by ever more powerful representatives of the far right and, with some exception, by liberals through a form of silence. (1999, p. 85)

Despite the fact that knowledge of the Eugenics Movement in America is not well known by most modern educators, it is easy to trace eugenical ideas in public education through science textbooks used during the period between 1914 and 1948. There was little scientific evidence to support eugenics in its infancy, but even when research suggested that there was absolutely no scientific basis for eugenical conclusions textbooks continued to promote individual differences based on hierarchical notions of race and biological determinism. In essence, textbook authors and publishers, such as George William Hunter, believed what they wanted to believe, despite evidence to the contrary. They used their beliefs to promote their own sociopolitical agendas: agendas of exclusion that promoted the continued privilege of whites. As Selden states:

> Programs of selective breeding were most frequently recommended to the high school reader: Positive eugenics, which called for the selective matings of those judged as society's best, was cited in 64.4% of the texts, and negative eugenics, which demanded the restriction of child-bearing by those judged socially inferior, appeared in 46.3% of the volumes. In addition, 19.5% of the texts recommended immigration restriction and 14.6% suggested policies of segregation and sterilization. (p. 68)

The influence of the Eugenics Movement on American education shows itself most clearly today in the form of the hierarchical system of tracking students by ability. As Selden states: "Eugenics promoted a concept of schooling as an open market in which individuals competed by means of their inherited traits for high scores—a scarce commodity indeed" (p. 37). "Compensatory education" has been a common practice in American public schools to deal with inequities in education. Proponents of this philosophy argue that educational inequity results from the failure of underachieving linguistic and ethnic minorities. Compensatory education programs rely on remediation in an attempt to get underachieving students up to the levels of their peers. The curriculum in compensatory education programs is reduced in content and in scope and is delivered at a slower pace. However, students placed in remedial tracks, for the most part, do not catch up to their peers. As Hugh Mehan states (1997): "Research has shown, however, that the schools' practices of tracking, ability grouping and testing contribute to inequality (Rosenbaum, 1978; Cicourel & Mehan, 1983; Oakes, 1985; Page & Valli, 1991; Mehan, 1992; Oakes et al., 1992)" (p. 116). Despite this research, the practice of tracking still continues, in one form or another, in the majority of schools in America.

It is alarming to recognize the degree to which science has been misused in the past and even today to justify existing social prejudices or as Tavris states: "to confirm the prejudice that some groups are assigned to their subordinate roles 'by the harsh dictates of nature'" (p. 24). Supposed biological differences between the races were used throughout history to justify oppression and maintain white privilege. Perhaps more alarming, is the fact that many do not question such studies because they are reported in academic publications and through the media as "science." Our sin is great, again as Darwin suggests, for our institutions perpetuate the misery of the disenfranchised and, to make matters worse, often pass this misery off as being caused by the laws of nature—and thus our responsibility is (or should be) greater. As educators we must promote awareness about our own past and present in order to create a better future *for all*. We must look with a questioning eye at policies and programs for their hidden biases and agendas. Perhaps then Margaret Mead's often quoted phrase would be cause for celebration: "Never doubt that a small group of thoughtful, committed citizens can change the world; indeed, it's the only thing that ever has."

REFERENCES

Macedo, D., & Bartolomé, L. I. (1999). *Dancing with bigotry: Beyond the politics of tolerance*. New York: St. Martin's Press.

Mehan, H. (1997). Tracking untracking: The consequences of placing low-track students in high-track classes. *Race, ethnicity, and multiculturalism: Policy and practice* (pp. 115–150). New York: Garland Publishing, Inc.

Selden, S. (1999). *Inheriting shame: The story of eugenics and racism in America*. New York: Teachers College, Columbia University.

Tavris, C. (1992). *The mismeasure of woman*. New York: Simon & Schuster.

Chapter 13

Discrimination, Harassment, and Women's Physical and Mental Health

Krystle C. Woods
NiCole T. Buchanan

Women's health is inextricably linked to their status in society. It benefits from equality and suffers from discrimination.
—World Health Report (World Health Organization, 1988, p. 6)

Women across the world bear the burdens of discrimination, harassment, poverty, and maltreatment (United Nations Population Fund [UNFPA], 2005). Unequal pay, lower workforce participation, and disparate access to health care place women at a disadvantage relative to men (Pratt, 1997; UNFPA, 2002), and contribute to women representing more than 75 percent of the world's poor (United Nations, 2005). Society's (mis)treatment of women contributes to their higher rates of certain forms of mental illness (e.g., depression, anxiety, and eating disorders) and their increased incidence of physical disability relative to men (Landrine & Klonoff, 1997; Nosek, Howland, Rintala, Young, & Chanpong, 2004).

Women's participation in paid employment determines their ability to combat both poverty and financial dependence, both of which put them at risk of being abused. Yet, for many women, the workplace is fraught with additional hazards that can place their financial, physical, and psychological well-being in peril. Specifically, gender discrimination and harassment are reported by approximately half of all working women in the United States (Ilies, Hauserman, Schwochau, & Stibal, 2003), with damaging effects on their mental and physical health (Willness, Steel, & Lee, 2007). Given the high toll women pay as a result of work-related gender discrimination and harassment, the specific negative mental and physical health outcomes associated with this mistreatment should be well understood.

DEFINING GENDER DISCRIMINATION AND HARASSMENT

Title VII of the Civil Rights Acts of 1964 and 1991 prohibits employment discrimination based on gender, race, color, religion, and national origin. Gender discrimination is divided into two forms: disparate treatment and disparate impact (Cleveland, Vescio, & Barnes-Farrell, 2005). *Disparate treatment* occurs when individuals are deliberately treated differently because of their gender. Examples include offering women lower starting salaries, posing different interview questions to male and female applicants (e.g., querying their intent to have children), or refusing to hire female applicants. *Disparate impact*, also referred to as adverse impact, occurs when ostensibly neutral workplace practices have an unnecessary negative effect on members of a protected class (e.g., women), thereby limiting the opportunities of that group. Gender-related examples of disparate impact frequently include the use of height, weight, or strength requirements for physically demanding jobs. For example, the Dial Corporation required a pre-employment test of physical strength that rendered 60 percent of female applicants, but only 3 percent of male applicants, ineligible for employment, including women who had already been successfully employed in the position. The ruling in *EEOC v. The Dial Corporation* asserted that a fair test should not screen out employees who successfully worked in the same position, therefore, the strength test had an unnecessary adverse effect on women.

Originally, the law protected against gender-based *discrimination*, but did not address sexual harassment until 1976 when the ruling in *Williams v. Saxby* legally recognized it as a form of sex discrimination in violation of Title VII (Equal Employment Opportunity Commission [EEOC], 1980). The legal definition of sexual harassment separates it into two categories: quid pro quo and hostile environment. *Quid pro quo* includes any attempt to coerce sexual interactions via job-related threats or promises of benefits based on one's sexual compliance (e.g., threatening termination or promising a promotion). A *hostile work environment* is created when an employee perceives the general workplace milieu as hostile as a result of unwanted gender-based comments or behaviors. Similarly, a hostile environment can be created when these behaviors negatively affect an employee's job performance, regardless of whether or not there are tangible or economic job consequences (Equal Employment Opportunity Commission [EEOC], 1980). As a psychological construct, sexual harassment is defined as unwanted gender-based or sexual comments and behavior that an individual appraises as offensive and a threat to her/his well-being (Fitzgerald, Swan, & Magley, 1997). There are three primary subtypes of sexual harassment (Fitzgerald et al., 1988; Fitzgerald, Gelfand, & Drasgow, 1995): *gender harassment* (negative non-sexual, gender-based comments and behaviors, such as sex-stratifying jobs as "men's work"); *unwanted sexual attention* (verbal and nonverbal sexual comments, gestures, or attempts at physical contact, such as asking someone on a date repeatedly or touching someone sexually); and *sexual coercion* (which is equivalent to the legal construct of quid pro quo).

HOW DISCRIMINATION AND HARASSMENT HARM PSYCHOLOGICAL WELL-BEING AND PHYSICAL HEALTH

Gender-based discrimination and sexual harassment exact a heavy toll on the psychological and physical health of women targeted for harassment.[1] According to the Transactional Model of Stress (Lazarus & Folkman, 1984), an experience becomes stressful when the individual appraises a situation as "exceeding his or her resources and endangering his or her well-being" (p. 21). Both sexual harassment and gender discrimination are frequently interpreted as such by targets and are likely to result in psychological and physical sequelae common to trauma (Avina & O'Donohue, 2002; Fitzgerald, Drasgow, Hulin, Gelfand, & Magley, 1997). The transactional model of stress also outlines several different factors that increase the extent to which an event will be perceived as stressful: the amount of harm done to the individual, the threat of negative outcomes in the future, the inability to predict and control the situation, the pervasiveness and frequency of the stressor, and its occurrence in settings where mastery was previously achieved. Gender discrimination and sexual harassment frequently include these characteristics that increase the likelihood that they will be stressful (Huerta, Cortina, Pang, Torges, & Magley, 2006; Langhout, Bergman, Cortina, Fitzgerald, Drasgow, & Hunter Williams, 2005). For example, gender discrimination and sexual harassment are often chronic stressors defined by their insidious onsets and their extended, unpredictable endpoint (Wheaton, 1997), which result in greater detriment to one's mental and physical health than single traumatic events (Green et al., 2000; Krupnick, Green, Stockton, Goodman, Corcoran, & Petty, 2004; McGonagle & Kessler, 1990). As these acts are perpetrated against women in their place of work, school, or residence, targeted women rarely feel that they have control over their occurrence, pervasiveness, or frequency. Further, discrimination and harassment often harm the individual's well-being at the present and have the potential for future negative consequences (e.g., being fired for refusing to comply or creating a hostile work environment that inhibits professional growth and learning). All of these factors increase the likelihood that gender discrimination and sexual harassment will be traumatic events that damage women's mental and physical health.

In addition to the nature of the experiences themselves, some theorize that experiences of gender-based discrimination and harassment can be more stressful than generic stressors (e.g., moving or starting a new job) because they are inherently personal and attack a social identity tied to an immutable personal characteristic (e.g., biological sex) (Landrine & Klonoff, 1997; Zucker & Landry, 2007). Compared to privileged group members, members of disadvantaged groups are more likely to experience discrimination, view prejudice against their group as pervasive and systemic, and perceive discrimination as uncontrollable, unavoidable, and a devaluation of a core social identity (Major & Crocker, 1993; Schmitt et al., 2002). Such experiences negatively impact one's perceptions of the views others have about their social group (i.e., public regard; Allport, 1979; Cartwright, 1950), which results in poorer physical and mental health. Further, these relationships are stronger when one holds a meritocracy worldview—that people are appropriately rewarded for their efforts and thus, can determine their own success (Major, Kaiser, O'Brian, & McCoy, 2007)—perhaps because recognition of maltreatment independent of one's personal efforts and abilities challenges one's basic understanding of the world and one's opportunity structure.

MENTAL HEALTH OUTCOMES RELATED TO DISCRIMINATION AND HARASSMENT

Meta-analytic reviews have found significant associations between gender discrimination, sexual harassment, and indicators of psychological well-being, such as depression, anxiety, posttraumatic stress disorder, disordered eating, nicotine use, and alcohol use (Cantisano, Dominguez, & Depolo, 2008; Chan, Lam, Chow, & Cheung, 2008; Willness et al., 2007). Moreover, studies have found that the negative effects of harassment can persist for more than ten years after the harassment has ended (Glomb, Munson, Hulin, Bergman, & Drasgow, 1999; Street, Gradus, Stafford, & Kelly, 2007). These relationships have been supported across a wide variety of populations, including former military reservists (Street et al., 2007), women in the U.S. (Bergman & Drasgow, 2003) and the Swedish (Estrada & Berggren, 2009) Armed Forces, female employees of the U.S. federal judicial circuit (Lim & Cortina, 2005), physicians (Shrier et al., 2007), police officers (Dowler & Arai, 2008), college women (Schmitt et al., 2002), women seeking counseling (Moradi & Funderburk, 2006), lesbian/bisexual women (Szymanski, 2005), and Latina (Cortina, 2004), Asian (Patel, 2008), and black women (Buchanan & Fitzgerald, 2008). Thus, the negative effects of gender discrimination and sexual harassment appear to be universal.

The strength of the relationship between discrimination and psychological well-being is affected by several factors (Fineran & Gruber, 2008) reflecting individual (e.g., age, self-esteem, and feminist identity) and experiential differences (e.g., appraisal, multiple forms of harassment occurring simultaneously). For example, younger working women appear to be more negatively impacted by harassment than their older counterparts, perhaps because they do not have the same job stability, seniority, and security (Chan et al., 2008). Collective self-esteem or perceptions of women in general and personal self-esteem both appear to moderate the relationship between discrimination, sexual harassment, and psychological distress (Fischer & Holz, 2007). For example, women with a strong and positive view of themselves may be better equipped to dismiss discrimination experiences than women who are unsure of their personal worth (Moradi & Subich, 2004) and those with more positive views of women in general (higher collective self-esteem) reported less depression and anxiety following harassment (Fischer & Holz, 2007).

Feminist consciousness is theorized to provide a framework for understanding gender discrimination, which can reduce self-blame associated with these experiences (Landrine & Klonoff, 1997). Feminist attitudes have been found to be protective against the negative effects of gender discrimination and harassment (Moradi & Subich, 2002), suggesting that women who endorse a more feminist consciousness may avoid internalizing blame by recognizing harassment as a manifestation of larger social injustices. Furthermore, feminist-identified women may feel more empowered to actively cope with discrimination, making them less vulnerable to negative outcomes (Sabik & Tylka, 2006). Notably, a feminist identity does not appear to be equally protective for all women. Whereas a feminist identity may help white women label their harassment experience as a social injustice instead of internalizing blame, Rederstorff, Buchanan, and Settles (2007) found that a higher feminist identity exacerbated the negative effects of harassment for black women. The authors attributed these findings to the double consciousness found among many multiply oppressed people where an increased awareness of oppression based on one salient identity increases awareness of one's vulnerability based on other salient identities. As a result, black women who endorsed more feminist attitudes were more likely to report higher levels of posttraumatic stress in the face of sexual harassment and discrimination. Another study of predominantly white lesbian and bisexual women found that participation in feminist activities (e.g., membership in feminist organizations, participation in feminist boycotts, marches, or rallies) buffered against psychological distress at low levels of harassment, but more severe sexual harassment was associated with significant psychological distress, regardless of feminist affiliation (Szymanski & Owens, 2009).

Women's subjective appraisal of the harassment (e.g., how disturbing, embarrassing, threatening, frightening, or offensive they perceived it to be) and the coping strategies they use to deal with it can buffer or exacerbate distress. According to cognitive theories of stress, the target's subjective appraisal of a potentially stressful situation impacts the level of distress they experience following a traumatic event (Lazarus & Folkman, 1984). Consistent with this theory, appraisal has been shown to mediate the relationship between sexual harassment and mental health outcomes (Langhout et al., 2005). Similarly, women who perceive harassment as pervasive in society or believe it is directed at them personally experience heightened psychological distress as compared to women who believed harassment was a relatively rare phenomenon and directed at women as a group rather than a personal attack (Dambrun, 2007; Foster & Dion, 2003; Schmitt, Branscombe, & Postmes, 2003).

Women are frequently told they should respond directly and assertively in the face of harassment, but such responses may run counter to their well-being. Women who utilize direct forms of coping, such as confronting the perpetrator or filing a complaint against the harasser often find that the work environment worsens and their social support from co-workers and peers wanes (Bergman, Langhout, Cortina, Palmieri, & Fitzgerald, 2002; Cortina & Magley, 2003). For example, sexual harassed black women in the U.S. Armed Forces who used contemplative strategies to cope with harassment (e.g., thinking about the event) reported significantly higher psychological well-being compared to women who filed a formal complaint (Buchanan, Settles, & Langhout, 2007).

Finally, the race of the target and the perpetrator can significantly influence the harassment experience and the extent to which it harms a woman's well-being. For example, being sexually harassed while separately experiencing racial harassment or experiencing racialized sexual harassment has been associated with increased psychological distress (Thomas, Witherspoon, & Speight, 2008). Black women report experiencing sexual racism and racialized sexual harassment (Buchanan, 2005; Texeira, 2002) as attacks that target their race and gender simultaneously (Buchanan & Ormerod, 2002; Mecca & Rubin, 1999; Yoder & Aniakudo, 1995, 1996, 1997). These behaviors call upon sexualized stereotypes of the black woman (i.e., being called a "black whore") and physical features thought to vary by race (i.e., commenting on her "large black behind"). Harassment that simultaneously attacks one's gender and race is perceived as more severe by victims (King, 2003) and may exacerbate harm because it targets two central and salient identities (Settles, 2006).

The relationship between racialized sexual harassment and psychological well-being is also mediated by avoidant coping, whereby black women who try to avoid and distract themselves from the negative harassment experience report worse psychological outcomes (Thomas et al., 2008). The use of an avoidant coping style is very prevalent among black women (Utsey, Ponterotto, Reynolds, & Cancelli, 2000), perhaps because of the pressure to uphold a façade of strength pro-scripted by gender role norms of black women (e.g., the Strong Black Woman archetype; Thomas et al., 2008). In addition, the race of the perpetrator mediates the relationship between sexual harassment and resulting distress. Among black college and working women, sexual harassment from an out-group (e.g., non-black) male was associated with more symptoms of posttraumatic stress than harassment from an in-group (i.e., black) male, because it was appraised more negatively by victims (Woods, Buchanan, & Settles, 2009).

DISCRIMINATION, HARASSMENT AND SPECIFIC FORMS OF MENTAL ILLNESS

Both daily records of sexist experiences and retrospective reports from harassed women indicate that depression, anxiety, eating disorders, and substance abuse are common sequelae following gender discrimination and sexual harassment (see Avina & O'Donohue, 2002; DeSouza & Fansler, 2003; Harned, 2000; Richman, Rospenda, Flaherty, Freels, & Zlatoper, 2004; Swim, Hyers, Cohen, & Ferguson, 2001; Zucker & Landry, 2007). In fact, some researchers suggest that the gender differences in conditions such as depression (women's rates are twice those of men; Kessler, 2003) are due in part to women's higher rates of discrimination and harassment (Klonoff, Landrine, & Campbell, 2000; Swim et al., 2001).

Some have also argued that because gender discrimination and harassment are often pervasive, chronic stressors, they can be catego-rized as traumatic events that result in posttraumatic stress (PTS) symp-toms (Avina & O'Donohue, 2002; Berg, 2006; Fitzgerald, Buchanan, Collinsworth, Magley, & Ramos, 1999). Both lifetime accounts and recent events of sexist discrimination perpetrated at work, school, and by strangers on the street are associated with posttraumatic stress (Berg, 2006). Researchers have argued that sexual harassment meets the criteria for a diagnosable trauma as defined by the *Diagnostic and Statistical Manual of Mental Disorders, Fourth Edition* (*DSM-IV*; American Psychiatric Association, 1994; Avina & O'Donohue, 2002; Murdoch, Polusny, Hodges, & Cowper, 2006). As evidence for this argument, sexual harass-ment experiences are associated with symptoms of posttraumatic stress in college women (Rederstorff et al., 2007), women in the U.S. Marines (Shipherd, Pineles, Gradus, & Resick, 2009), military reservists (Street et al., 2007), and female veterans of the Gulf War (Vogt, Pless, King, & King, 2005) and posttraumatic stress symptom severity increases as sexual harassment severity increases (Murdoch et al., 2006).

Sexual harassment is associated with eating pathology and distorted body image as a result of multiple processes. First, sexual harassment is associated with decreased self-esteem, particularly body-based self-esteem, which concomitantly increases the likelihood that the target will develop pathological eating behaviors (sexual harassment syndrome; Backhouse & Cohen, 1978; Larkin, Rice, & Russell, 1996). Another model proposes that sexual harassment increases anxiety, heightens bodily discomfort and scrutiny, and distorts one's body image, culminating in a heightened risk for disordered eating (Barker & Galambos, 2003; Frederickson & Roberts, 1997; Hofschire & Greenberg, 2002; Larkin & Rice, 2005; Larkin, Rice, & Russell, 1996). Finally, self-objectification theory proposes that when women's bodies are looked at, evaluated, and potentially objectified through experiences like sexual harassment, women may internalize these images (self-objectification), and engage in increased body monitoring (Frederickson & Roberts, 1997). Excessive body scrutiny can lead to shame, anxiety, and body image distortion, all of which negatively affect psychological well-being (Frederickson & Roberts, 1997). Further, research has demonstrated a direct relationship between self-objectification and restrictive eating, bulimic, and depressive symptoms (Fredrickson, Roberts, Noll, Quinn, & Twenge, 1998; Noll & Fredrickson, 1998; Joiner, Wonderlich, Metalsky, & Schmidt, 1995; McKinley, 1998; Stice, Hayward, Cameron, Killen, & Taylor, 2000).

Health-damaging behaviors, such as drug and alcohol use, take a significant toll on one's health (Centers for Disease Control and Prevention, 2004; National Institute on Drug Abuse, 2002). Sexual harassment has been associated with the use of alcohol and prescription drugs (e.g., sedatives, antidepressants; Zucker & Landry, 2005) and cigarettes (Richman et al., 1999). This may indicate that some women may use these substances to reduce stress, depression, anxiety, hostility, and a perceived lack of control associated with experiences of discrimination and harassment (Grunberg, Moore, & Greenber, 1998; Ragland & Ames, 1996; Richman & Rospenda, 2005). Longitudinal analyses and national samples of working adults (Rospenda, Richman, & Shannon, 2009) and female college students (Zucker & Landry, 2007) also demonstrated a relationship between harassment and alcohol misuse (Freels, Richman, & Rospenda, 2005; Rospenda, Richman, Wislar, & Flaherty, 2000).

PHYSICAL HEALTH OUTCOMES RELATED TO DISCRIMINATION AND HARASSMENT

In addition to psychological distress, gender discrimination and sexual harassment are sufficiently stressful to result in detriment to one's physical health, such as stress-induced physiological changes, suppressed immune system functioning, inflammation, gastrointestinal problems, fatigue, headaches, sleep problems, and back pain (Cleary, Schmieler, Parscenzo, & Ambrosio, 1994; Dansky & Kilpatrick, 1997; Smith, 2006; van Roosmalen & McDaniel, 1998). Meta-analyses indicate that a perceived lack of control, chronic stress, and threats tied to social identity are important in increasing levels of cortisol, which is an indication of stress (Dickerson & Kemeny, 2004; Michaud, Matheson, Kelly, & Anisman, 2008; Miller, Chen, & Zhou, 2007). Bodily systems that usually serve to adaptively cope with isolated stressors, like the hypothalamic-pituitary-adrenal axis and the sympathetic arousal system (Goldstein & McEwen, 2002; Sapolsky, Romero, & Munck, 2000), may become overtaxed with chronic stressors like discrimination, resulting in negative health outcomes (McEwen, 2000, 2003). In addition, pervasive discrimination and harassment may also lead one to engage in behaviors that are counter to positive health outcomes, such as neglecting self-care and health sustaining behaviors (e.g., exercise, healthy eating, and regular sleeping patterns), which may result in a plethora of health problems (Zucker & Landry, 2007).

Meta-analyses specific to harassment outcomes also support the association between harassment and negative physical health indicators (Cantisano et al., 2008; Chan et al., 2008). Similar to mental health, the relationship between sexual harassment and physical health is mediated by one's appraisal of the event and general psychological well-being (Langhout et al., 2005). Namely, sexual harassment and gender discrimination are associated with medical symptoms like gastrointestinal (stomach-ache, flatulence, diarrhea, heartburn, stomach pains), musculoskeletal (headaches, pain in joints, muscles, back, and neck), irritability, sleeping problems (fatigue, restlessness, sleep disturbances), cardiovascular symptoms (chest pain, tachycardia), headache, eye strain, skin problems, itching, and worry about health hazards (Bergman, 2003; Bildt, 2005; Estrada & Berggren, 2009; Langhout et al., 2005; Shipherd et al., 2009). These experiences are also associate with persistent and chronic diseases, such as hypertension, neurological disorders, diabetes, cardiovascular diseases, gastritis, cataracts, etc. (Keskinoglu, Ucuncu, Yildirim, Gurbuz, Ur, & Ergor, 2007).

Discrimination experiences and mood also influence stress-reactive physiological systems. As an example, women primed to feel angry or sad during a lab-induced discrimination event experienced changes in salivary cortisol levels (Matheson, Gill, Kelly, & Anisman, 2008). In particular, when primed to feel angry, they experienced sustained arousal levels throughout the discrimination experience and increases in systolic and diastolic blood pressure and heart rate persisted after the discrimination event ended. Extrapolating these findings to real world harassment and discrimination would suggest that negative, repeated and unpredictable discrimination events raise cortisol levels and arousal for extended periods of time, leading to negative health consequences (McEwen, 2003). Particularly, those discrimination events that evoke anger are associated with increases in heart rate and cardiovascular problems over time (Matheson et al., 2008). Thus, women's experiences of discrimination and harassment can result in significant detriment to their overall physical health and well-being over time.

CONCLUSION

Across the globe, working women are subjected to gender discrimination and sexual harassment at work, and an abundance of evidence supports that such experiences result in significant negative consequences for a woman's psychological well-being and physical health. With more than 40 percent of women reporting at least one such experience annually (DeSouza & Solberg, 2003), gender discrimination and sexual harassment may be the most common occupational hazard faced by working women today. The focus of this chapter has been on the negative effects of gender discrimination and sexual harassment on targeted women; however, the financial toll on companies is also extensive (Sims, Drasgow, & Fitzgerald, 2005). Increased awareness of these negative outcomes is necessary to encourage organizations to improve prevention efforts and promote anti-discrimination legislation, resulting in a more equitable work environment for all employees.

NOTE

1. Gender-based discrimination and sexual harassment are both perpetrated against men and women, however behavioral assessments of harassment and formal reports alleging both forms of discrimination and harassment are more commonly reported by women than by men (EEOC, 2009); as such, we will commonly refer to targets of harassment as women.

REFERENCES

Allport, G. (1979). *The nature of prejudice*. New York: Doubleday Anchor. (Original work published 1954)

American Psychiatric Association. (1994). *Diagnostic and statistical manual of mental disorders* (4th ed). Washington, DC: Author.

Avina, C., & O'Donohue, W. (2002). Sexual harassment and PTSD: Is sexual harassment diagnosable trauma? *Journal of Traumatic Stress, 15,* 69–75.

Backhouse, C., & Cohen, L. (1978). *The secret oppression*. Toronto: Macmillan.

Barker, E. T., & Galambos, N. L. (2003). Body dissatisfaction of adolescent girls and boys: Risk and resource factors. *The Journal of Early Adolescence, 23,* 141–165.

Berg, S. H. (2006). Everyday sexism and posttraumatic stress disorder in women: A correlational study. *Violence Against Women, 12,* 970–988.

Bergman, B. (2003). The validation of the women workplace culture question-naire: Gender-related stress and health for Swedish working women. *Sex Roles, 49,* 287–297.

Bergman, M. E., & Drasgow, F. (2003). Race as a moderator in a model of sex-ual harassment: An empirical test. *Journal of Occupational Health Psychology, 8,* 131–145.

Bergman, M. E., Langhout, R. D., Cortina, L. M., Palmieri, P. A., & Fitzgerald, L. F. (2002). The (Un)reasonableness of reporting: Antecedents and conse-quences of reporting sexual harassment. *Journal of Applied Psychology, 87,* 230–242.

Bildt, C. (2005). Sexual harassment: Relation to other forms of discrimination and to health among women and men. *Work, 24,* 251–259.

Buchanan, N. T. (2005). The nexus of race and gender domination: The racial-ized sexual harassment of African American women. In P. Morgan & J. Gruber (Eds.), *In the company of men: Re-discovering the links between sexual harassment and male domination* (pp. 294–320). Boston: Northeastern Univer-sity Press.

Buchanan, N. T., & Fitzgerald, L. F. (2008). The effects of racial and sexual har-assment on work and the psychological well-being of African American women. *Journal of Occupational Health Psychology, 13,* 137–151.

Buchanan, N. T., & Ormerod, A. J. (2002). Racialized sexual harassment in the lives of African American women. *Women & Therapy, 25,* 107–124.

Buchanan, N. T., Settles, I. H., & Langhout, R. D. (2007). Black women's coping styles, psychological well-being, and work-related outcomes following sexual harassment. *Black Women, Gender and Families, 1,* 100–120.

Cantisano, G. T., Dominguez, J. F. M., & Depolo, M. (2008). Perceived sexual harassment at work: Meta-analysis and structural model of antecedents and consequences. *The Spanish Journal of Psychology, 11,* 207–218.

Cartwright, D. (1950). Emotional dimensions of group life. In M. L. Raymert (Ed.), *Feelings and emotions* (pp. 439–447). New York: McGraw-Hill.

Centers for Disease Control and Prevention. (2004). Tobacco information and prevention source: Overview. Retrieved August 23, 2004, from http://www.cdc.gov/tobacco/issue.htm

Chan, D. K. S., Lam, C. B., Chow, S. Y., & Cheung, S. F. (2008). Examining the job-related, psychological, and physical outcomes of workplace sexual harassment: A meta-analytic review. *Psychology of Women Quarterly, 32,* 362–376.

Cleary, J. S., Schmieler, C. R., Parascenzo, L. C., & Ambrosio, N. (1994). Sexual harassment of college students: Implications for campus health promotion. *Journal of American College Heath, 43,* 3–10.

Cleveland, J. N., Vescio, T. K., & Barnes-Farrell, J. L. (2005). Gender discrimina-tion in organizations. In R. L. Dipboye & A. Colella (Eds.), *Discrimination at work: The psychological and organizational bases* (pp. 149–176). Mahwah, NJ: Erlbaum.

Cortina, L. M. (2004). Hispanic perspectives on sexual harassment and social support. *Personality and Social Psychology Bulletin, 30,* 570–584.

Cortina, L. M., & Magley, V. J. (2003). Raising voice, risking retaliation: Events following interpersonal mistreatment in the workplace. *Journal of Occupa-tional Health Psychology, 8,* 247–265.

Dambrun, M. (2007). Gender differences in mental health: The mediating role of perceived personal discrimination. *Journal of Applied Social Psychology, 37,* 1118–1129.

Dansky, B. S., & Kilpatrick, D. G. (1997). Effects of sexual harassment. In W. O'Donohue (Ed.), *Sexual harassment: Theory, research, and treatment* (pp. 152–174). Needham Heights, MA: Allyn & Bacon.

DeSouza, E., & Fansler, A.G. (2003). Contrapower sexual harassment: A survey of students and faculty members. *Sex Roles, 48,* 529–542.

DeSouza, E., & Solberg, J. (2003). Incidence and dimensions of sexual harassment across cultures. In M. Paludi & C. Paludi (Eds.), *Academic and workplace sexual harassment: A handbook of cultural, social science, management, and legal perspectives* (pp. 3–30). Westport, CT: Praeger.

Dickerson, S. S., & Kemeny, M. E. (2004). Acute stressors and cortisol responses: A theoretical integration and synthesis of laboratory research. *Psychological Bulletin, 130,* 355–391.

Dowler, K., & Arai, B. (2008). Stress, gender and policing: The impact of perceived gender discrimination on symptoms of stress. *International Journal of Police Science & Management, 10,* 123–135.

Equal Employment Opportunity Commission. (1980). Guidelines on discrimination because of sex. *Federal Regulations, 43,* 74676–74677.

Equal Employment Opportunity Commission. (2009). Sexual harassment charges EEOC & FEPAs combined. Retrieved June 13, 2009. http://www.eeoc.gov/stats/harass.html

Estrada, A.X., & Berggren, A.W. (2009). Sexual harassment and its impact for women officers and cadets in the Swedish Armed Forces. *Military Psychology, 21,* 162–185.

Fineran, S., & Gruber, J. (2008). Mental health impact of sexual harassment. In M. Paludi (Ed.), *The psychology of women at work: Challenges and solutions for our female workforce, Volume 3: Self, family, and social affects* (pp. 89–108). Westport, CT: Praeger Publishers.

Fischer, A. R., & Holz, K. B. (2007). Perceived discrimination and women's psychological distress: The roles of collective and personal self-esteem. *Journal of Counseling Psychology, 54,* 154–164.

Fitzgerald, L. F., Buchanan, N. T., Collinsworth, L. L., Magley, V. J., & Ramos, A. M. (1999). Junk logic: The abuse defense in sexual harassment litigation. *Psychology, Public Policy, and the Law, 5,* 730–759.

Fitzgerald, L. F., Drasgow, F., Hulin, C. L., Gelfand, M. J., & Magley, V. J. (1997). Antecedents and consequences of sexual harassment in organizations: A test of an integrated model. *Journal of Applied Psychology, 82,* 578–589.

Fitzgerald, L. F., Gelfand, M. J., & Drasgow, F. (1995). Measuring sexual harassment: Theoretical and psychometric advances. *Basic and Applied Social Psychology, 17,* 425–427.

Fitzgerald, L. F., Shullman, S. L., Bailey, N., Richards, M., Swecker, J., Gold, Y., et al. (1988). The incidence and dimensions of sexual harassment in academia and the workplace. *Journal of Vocational Behavior, 32,* 152–175.

Fitzgerald, L. F., Swan, S., & Magley, V. J. (1997). But was it really sexual harassment? Legal, behavioral, and psychological definitions of the workplace victimization of women. In W. O'Donohue (Ed.), *Sexual harassment: Theory, research, and treatment* (pp. 5–28). Needham Heights, MA: Allyn & Bacon.

Foster, M. D., & Dion, K. L. (2003). Dispositional hardiness and women's well-being relating to gender discrimination: The role of minimization. *Psychology of Women Quarterly, 27,* 197–208.

Frederickson, B., & Roberts, T. (1997). Objectification theory: Toward understanding women's lived experiences and mental health risks. *Psychology of Women Quarterly, 21,* 173–206.

Frederickson, B. L., Roberts, T. A., Noll, S. M., Quinn, D. M., & Twenge, J. M. (1998). That swimsuit becomes you: Sex differences in self-objectification, restrained eating, and math performance. *Journal of Personality and Social Psychology, 75,* 269–284.

Freels, S. A., Richman, J. A., & Rospenda, K.M. (2005). Gender differences in the causal direction between workplace harassment and drinking. *Addictive Behaviors, 30,* 1454–1458.

Glomb, T. M., Munson, L. J., Hulin, C. L., Bergman, M. E., & Drasgow, F. (1999). Structural equation models of sexual harassment: Longitudinal explorations and cross-sectional generalizations. *Journal of Applied Psychology, 84,* 14–28.

Goldstein, D. S., & McEwen, B. (2002) Allostasis, homeostats, and the nature of stress. *Stress, 5,* 5–58.

Green, B. L., Goodman, L. A., Krupnick, J. L., Corcoran, C. B., Petty, R. M., Stockton, P., et al. (2000). Outcomes of single versus multiple trauma exposure in a screening sample. *Journal of Traumatic Stress, 13,* 271–286.

Grunberg, L., Moore, S., & Greenberg, E. S. (1998). Work stress and problem alcohol behavior: A test of the spillover model. *Journal of Organizational Behavior, 19,* 487–502.

Harned, M. S. (2000). Harassed bodies. An examination of the relationships among women's experiences of sexual harassment, body image, and eating disturbances. *Psychology of Women Quarterly, 24,* 336–348.

Huerta, M., Cortina, L. M., Pang, J. S., Torges, C. M., & Magley, V. J. (2006). Sex and power in the academy: Modeling sexual harassment in the lives of college women. *Personality and Social Psychology Bulletin, 32,* 616–628.

Ilies, R., Hauserman, N., Schwochau, S., & Stibal, J. (2003). Reported incidence rates of work-related sexual harassment in the United States: Using meta-analysis to explain reported rate disparities. *Personnel Psychology, 56,* 607–631.

Joiner, T. E., Wonderlich, S. A., Metalsky, G. I., & Schmidt, N. B. (1995). Body dissatisfaction: A feature of bulimia, depression, or both? *Journal of Social and Clinical Psychology, 14,* 339–355.

Keskinoglu, P., Ucuncu, T., Yildirim, I., Gurbuz, T., Ur, I., & Ergor, G. (2007). Gender discrimination in the elderly and its impact on the elderly health. *Archives of Gerontology and Geriatrics, 45,* 295–306.

Kessler, R. C. (2003). Epidemiology of women and depression. *Journal of Affective Disorders, 74,* 5–13.

King, K. R. (2003). Racism or sexism? Attributional ambiguity and simultaneous memberships in multiple oppressed groups. *Journal of Applied Social Psychology, 33,* 223–247.

Klonoff, E. A., Landrine, H., & Campbell, R. (2000). Sexist discrimination may account for well-known gender differences in psychiatric symptoms. *Psychology of Women Quarterly, 24,* 93–99.

Krupnick, J. L., Green, B. L., Stockton, P., Goodman, L. A., Corcoran, C. B., & Petty, R. M. (2004). Mental health effects of adolescent trauma exposure in a female college sample: Exploring differential outcomes based on experiences of unique trauma types and dimensions. *Psychiatry: Interpersonal, and Biological Processes, 67,* 264–279.

Landrine, H., & Klonoff, E. A. (1997). *Discrimination against women: Prevalence, consequences, remedies.* Thousand Oaks, CA: Sage.

Langhout, R. D., Bergman, M. E., Cortina, L. M., Fitzgerald, L. F., Drasgow, F., & Hunter Williams, J. (2005). Sexual harassment severity: Assessing situational and personal determinants and outcomes. *Journal of Applied Social Psychology, 35,* 975–1007.

Larkin, J., & Rice, C. (2005). Beyond "healthy eating" and "healthy weights": Harassment and the health curriculum in middle schools. *Body Image, 2,* 219–232.

Larkin, J., Rice, C., & Russell, V. (1996). Slipping through the cracks: Sexual harassment, eating problems, and the problem of embodiment. *Eating Disorders, 4,* 5–26.

Lazarus, R. S., & Folkman, S. (1984). *Stress, appraisal, and coping.* New York: Springer.

Lim, S., & Cortina, L.M. (2005). Interpersonal mistreatment in the workplace: The interface and impact of general incivility and sexual harassment. *Journal of Applied Psychology, 90,* 483–496.

Major, B., & Crocker, J. (1993). Social stigma: The consequences of attributional ambiguity. In D. M. Mackie & D. L. Hamilton (Eds.), *Affect, cognition, and stereotyping: Interactive processes in group perception* (pp. 345–370). San Diego, CA: Academic Press.

Major, B., Kaiser, C. R., O'Brien, L. T., & McCoy, S. K. (2007). Perceived discrimination as worldview threat or worldview confirmation: Implications for self-esteem. *Journal of Personality and Social Psychology, 92,* 1,068–1,086.

Matheson, K., Gill, R., Kelly, O., & Anisman, H. (2008). Cortisol and cardiac reactivity in the context of sex discrimination: The moderating effects of mood and perceived control. *The Open Psychology Journal, 1,* 1–10.

McEwen, B. S. (2000). Allostasis and allostatic load: Implications for neuropsychopharmacology. *Neuropsychopharmacology, 22,* 108–124.

McEwen, B. S. (2003). Mood disorders and allostatic load. *Biological Psychiatry, 54,* 200–207.

McGonagle, K. A., & Kessler, R. C. (1990). Chronic stress, acute stress, and depressive symptoms. *American Journal of Community Psychology, 18,* 681–706.

McKinley, N. M. (1998). Gender differences in undergraduates' body esteem: The mediating effect of objectified body consciousness and actual/ideal weight discrepancy. *Sex Roles, 19,* 113–123.

Mecca, S. J., & Rubin, L. J. (1999). Definitional research on African American students and sexual harassment. *Psychology of Women Quarterly, 23,* 813–817.

Michaud, K., Matheson, K., Kelly, O., & Anisman, H. (2008). Impact of stressors in a natural context on release of cortisol in healthy adult humans: A meta-analysis. *Stress, 11,* 177–197.

Miller, G. E., Chen, E., & Zhou, E. (2007). If it goes up, must it come down? Chronic stress and the hypothalamic–pituitary–adrenal axis in humans. *Psychological Bulletin, 133,* 25–45.

Moradi, B., & Funerburk, J. R. (2006). Roles of perceived sexist events and perceived social support in the mental health of women seeking counseling. *Journal of Counseling Psychology, 53,* 464–473.

Moradi, B., & Subich, L. M. (2002). Perceived sexist events and feminist identity development attitudes: Links to women's psychological distress. *The Counseling Psychologist, 30,* 44–65.

Moradi, B., & Subich, L.M. (2004). Examining the moderating role of self-esteem in the link between experiences of perceived sexist events and psychological distress. *Journal of Counseling Psychology, 54,* 50–56.

Murdoch, M., Polusny, M. A., Hodges, J., & Cowper, D. (2006). The association between in-service sexual harassment and post-traumatic stress disorder among Department of Veterans Affairs disability applicants. *Military Medicine, 171,* 166–173.

National Institute on Drug Abuse. (2002). *Use of selected substances in the past month by persons 12 years of age and over, according to age, sex, race and Hispanic origin: United States, select years 1979–99.* Retrieved April 12, 2002, from http://www.cdc.gov/nchs/products/pubs/pubd/hus/tables/2001/01hus063.pdf

Noll, S. M., & Fredrickson, B. L. (1998). A mediational model linking self-objectification, body shame, and disordered eating. *Psychology of Women Quarterly, 22,* 623–636.

Nosek, M. A., Howland, C., Rintala, D. H., Young, M. E., & Chanpong, G. F. (2004). National study of women with physical disabilities: Final report. *Sexuality and Disability, 19,* 5–40.

Patel, N. (2008). Racialized sexism in the lives of Asian American women. In C. Raghavan, A. E. Edwards, & K. M. Vas (Eds.), *Benefiting by design: Women of color in feminist psychological research* (pp. 116–128). Cambridge: Cambridge Scholars Publishing.

Pratt, C. C. (1997). Ageing: A multigenerational, gendered perspective. *Bulletin on Ageing, No. 2/3.* New York: United Nations.

Ragland, D. R., & Ames, G. M. (1996). Current developments in the study of stress and alcohol consumption. *Alcoholism, Clinical and Experimental Research, 20,* 51A–53A.

Rederstorff, J. C., Buchanan, N. T., & Settles, I. H. (2007). The moderating roles of race and gender-role attitudes in the relationship between sexual harassment and psychological well-being. *Psychology of Women Quarterly, 31,* 50–61.

Richman, J. A., Rospenda, K. M., Flaherty, J. A., Freels, S., & Zlatoper, K. (2004). Perceived organizational tolerance for workplace harassment and distress and drinking over time. *Women & Health, 40,* 1–23.

Richman, J. A., Rospenda, K. M., Nawyn, S. J., Flaherty, J. A., Fendrich, M., Drum, M. L., et al. (1999). Sexual harassment and generalized workplace abuse among university employees: Prevalence and mental health correlates. *American Journal of Public Health, 89,* 358–363.

Rospenda, K. M., Richman, J. A., & Shannon, C. A. (2009). Prevalence and mental health correlates of harassment and discrimination in the workplace: Results from a national study. *Journal of Interpersonal Violence, 24,* 819–843.

Rospenda, K. M., Richman, J. A., Wislar, J. S., & Flaherty, J. A. (2000). Chronicity of sexual harassment and generalized work-place abuse: Effects on drinking outcomes. *Addiction, 95,* 1,805–1,820.

Sabik, N. J., & Tylka, T. L. (2006). Do feminist identity styles moderate the relation between perceived sexist events and disordered eating? *Psychology of Women Quarterly, 30,* 77–84.

Sapolsky, R. M., Romero, L. M., & Munck, A. U. (2000). How do glucocorticoids influence stress responses? Integrating permissive, suppressive, stimulatory, and preparative actions. *Endocrine Reviews, 21,* 55–89.

Schmitt, M. T., Branscombe, N. R., Kobrynowicz, D., & Owen, S. (2002). Perceiving discrimination against one's gender group has different implications for well-being in women and men. *Personality and Social Psychology Bulletin, 28,* 197–210.

Schmitt, M. T., Branscombe, N. R., & Postmes, T. (2003). Women's emotional responses to the pervasiveness of gender discrimination. *European Journal of Social Psychology, 33,* 297–312.

Settles, I. H. (2006). Use of an intersectional framework to understand Black women's racial and gender identities. *Sex Roles, 54,* 589–601.

Shipherd, J. C., Pineles, S. L., Gradus, J. L., & Resick, P. A. (2009). Sexual harassment in the Marines, posttraumatic stress symptoms, and perceived health: Evidence for sex differences. *Journal of Traumatic Stress, 22,* 3–10.

Shrier, D. K., Zucker, A. N., Mercurio, A.E., Landry, L.J., Rich, M., & Shrier, L.A. (2007). Generation to generation: Discrimination and harassment experiences of physician mothers and their physician daughters. *Journal of Women's Health, 16,* 883–894.

Sims, C. S., Drasgow, F., & Fitzgerald, L. F. (2005). The effects of sexual harassment on turnover in the military: Time-dependent modeling. *Journal of Applied Psychology, 90,* 1,141–1,152.

Smith, T. W. (2006). Personality as risk and resilience in physical health. *Current Directions in Psychological Science, 15,* 227–231.

Stice, E., Hayward, C., Cameron R. P., Killen, J. D., & Taylor, C. B. (2000). Body-image and eating disturbances predict onset of depression among female adolescents: A longitudinal study. *Journal of Abnormal Psychology, 109,* 438–444.

Street, A. E., Gradus, J. L., Stafford, J., & Kelly, K. (2007). Gender differences in experiences of sexual harassment: Data from a male-dominated environment. *Journal of Consulting and Clinical Psychology, 75,* 464–474.

Swim, J. K., Hyers, L. L., Cohen, L. L., & Ferguson, M. J. (2001). Everyday sexism: Evidence for its incidence, nature, and psychological impact from three daily diary studies. *Journal of Social Issues, 57,* 31–53.

Szymanski, D. M. (2005). Heterosexism and sexism as correlates of psychological distress in lesbians. *Journal of Counseling & Development, 83,* 355–360.

Szymanski, D. M., & Owens, G. P. (2009). Group-level coping as a moderator between heterosexism and sexism and psychological distress in sexual minority women. *Psychology of Women Quarterly, 33,* 197–205.

Texeira, M. T. (2002). "Who protects and serves me?" A case study of sexual harassment of African American women in one U.S. law enforcement agency. *Gender & Society, 16,* 524–545.

Thomas, A. J., Witherspoon, K. M., & Speight, S. L. (2008). Gendered racism, psychological distress, and coping styles of African American women. *Cultural Diversity and Ethnic Minority Psychology, 14,* 307–314.

UNFPA (United Nations Population Fund). (2002). *Population aging and development. Social, health and gender issues.* Population and Development Strategies Series, Number 3. New York: UNFPA.

UNFPA (United Nations Population Fund). (2005). *State of World Population 2005. The Promise of Equality. Gender equality, Reproductive Health and the Millennium Development Goals.* New York: UNFPA.

United Nations. (2005). *The Millennium Development Goals Reports.* New York: Author.

Utsey, S. O., Ponterotto, J. G., Reynolds, A. L., & Cancelli, A. A. (2000). Racial discrimination, coping, life satisfaction, and self-esteem among African Americans. *Journal of Counseling and Development, 78,* 72–81.

van Roosmalen, E., & McDaniel, S. A. (1998). Sexual harassment in academia: A hazard to women's health. *Women & Health, 28,* 33–54.

Vogt, D. S., Pless, A. P., King, L. A., & King, D. W. (2005). Deployment stressors, gender, and mental health outcomes among Gulf War I veterans. *Journal of Traumatic Stress, 18,* 115–127.

Wheaton, B. (1997). The nature of chronic stress. In B. H. Gottlieb (Ed.), *Coping with chronic stress* (pp. 43–74). New York: Plenum.

Willness, C. R., Steel, P., & Lee, K. (2007). A meta-analysis of the antecedents and consequences of workplace sexual harassment. *Personnel Psychology, 60,* 127–162.

Woods, K. C., Buchanan, N. T., & Settles, I. H. (2009). Sexual harassment across the color line: Experiences and outcomes of cross- vs. intra-racial sexual harassment among Black women. *Cultural Diversity and Ethnic Minority Psychology, 15,* 67–76.

Yoder, J. D., & Aniakudo, P. (1995). The responses of African American women firefighters to gender harassment. *Sex Roles, 32,* 125–137.

Yoder, J. D., & Aniakudo, P. (1996). When pranks become harassment: The case of African American women firefighters. *Sex Roles, 35,* 253–270.

Appendix: Feminist and Women's Rights Organizations Worldwide

Susan Strauss
Michelle Strand
Michele A. Paludi

We have compiled a listing of resources dealing with feminism and women's rights internationally. We believe this listing is a good starting point for seeking additional information about women's issues and support groups on issues including women and mental health, physical health, employed women, legal rights, political advocacy groups, reproductive health and rights, violence against women, and women and education. Please recognize that this listing is neither complete nor exhaustive.

GENERAL ORGANIZATIONS

African Feminist Forum
http://www.africanfeministforum.org

Association for Women's Rights in Development
http://www.awid.org

Center for Global Justice
http://www.globaljusticecenter.org

Centre for Development and Population Activities
http://www.cedpa.org

Equality Now
http://www.equalitynow.org

Feminist Activist Resources on the Net
http://www.women.it

Feminist Majority Foundation: Global Feminism
http://feminist.org/global

Global Fund for Women
http://www.globalfundforwomen.org

Global List of Women's Organizations
http://www.distel.ca/womlist/womlist.html

International Alliance of Women
http://www.womenalliance.org/

International Women's Organizations
http://www.africa/upenn.edu/burundiwomen/international.htm

MADRE
http://www.madre.org

Ms. Foundation for Women
http://www.ms.foundation.org

National Council for Research on Women
http://www.ncrw.org

National Council of Women's Organizations
http://www.womensorganizations.org

National Organization for Women
http://www.now.org

PDHRE
http://www.pdhre.org/rights/women.html

Regional Network on Arab Women
http://www.aucegypt.edu/src

Sudan Women's Alliance
http://www.sarah@acs.aucegypt.edu

Third Wave Foundation
http://www.thirdwavefoundation.org

United Nations Commission on the Status of Women
http://www.un.org/womenwatch/daw/csw

United Nations Division for the Advancement of Women
http://www.un.org/womenwatch/daw/

United Nations Population Fund; Gender Equality
http://www.unfpa.org/public/publications/pubs_gender

Women and Gender Studies Web Sites
http://libr.org/wss/wsslinks/

Women for Women International
http://www.womenforwomen.org

Women Peace and Security Network, Africa
http://www.ajws.org

Women's Human Rights Resources Programme
http://www.law-lib.utoronto.ca/diana

EMPLOYED WOMEN

All Business Network
http://www.all-biz.com

Association for Women in Science
http://www.awis.org

Business and Professional Women's Organization
http://www.bpwusa.org

Center for Leadership and Change Management
http://leadership.wharton.upenn.edu

Center for Women and Work, Rutgers University
http://www.cww.rutgers.edu

Center for Women and Work, University of Massachusetts, Lowell
http://www.uml.edu/centers/women-work

Centre for Families, Work and Well-Being
http://www.worklifecanada.ca

Center for Stress Management
http://www.managingstress.com

Employee Assistance Professional Association
http://www.eapassn.org

Equal Employment Opportunity Commission
http://www.eeoc.gov

Families and Work Institute
http://www.familiesandwork.org

Feminist Majority Foundation
http://www.feminist.org

International Network of Women Engineers and Scientists
http://www.inwes.org

National Institute for Occupational Safety and Health
http://www.cdc.gov/niosh

National Institute of Mental Health
http://www.nimh.nih.gov

National Partnership for Women and Families
http://www.nationalpartnership.org

Occupational Safety and Health Administration
http://www.osha.gov

Office Politics
http://www.officepolitics.co.uk/frame.html

The Coaching and Mentoring Network
http://www.coachingnetwork.org.uk/

Third World Organization for Women in Science
http://www.twows.org

Work and Family Connection
http://www.workfamily.com

HEALTH

American Association of People with Disabilities
http://www.aapd-dc/org

American Association on Intellectual and Developmental Disabilities
http://www.aamr.org

American Psychological Association
http://www.apa.org

Black Women's Health
http://www.blackwomenshealth.com

Breast Cancer Information Network
http://www.cancernetwork.com

Canadian Women's Health Network
http://www.cwhn.ca

Disability Rights Education and Defense Fund
http://www.dredf.org

Disabled Peoples' International
http://v1.dpi.org

EngenderHealth
http://www.engenderhealth.org

Feminist Women's Health Center
http://www.fwhc.org

International Women's Health Coalition
http://www.iwhc.org

World Association of Persons with Disabilities
http://www.wapd.org

World Health Organization
http://www.who.int

World Institute on Disability
http://www.wid.org

LEGAL RIGHTS

The Legal Research and Resource Center for Human Rights
lrrc@frco.eun.eg

Women in International Law
http://www2lib.uchicago.edu/llou/women.html

POLITICAL ADVOCACY GROUPS

Center for American Women and Politics
http://www.cawp.rutgers.edu

Center for Asia-Pacific Women in Politics
http://www.capwip.org

Centre for Advancement of Women in Politics
http://www.qub.ac.uk/cawp/

Council of Women World Leaders
http://www.womenworldleaders.org

Emily's List
http://www.emilyslist.org

European Women's Lobby
http://www.womenlobby.org

International Women's Democracy Center
http://www.lwdc.org

League of Women Voters
http://www.lwv.org

National Foundation for Women Legislators
http://www.womenlegislators.org

National Women's Council of Ireland
http://www.nwci.ie

National Women's Political Caucus
http://www.nwpc.org

Political Parties in Africa
http://www.idea.int/africa/pp.cfm

Women in Politics
http://www.ipu.org

REPRODUCTIVE HEALTH AND RIGHTS

American Pregnancy Association
http://www.americanpregnancy.org

Australian Reproductive Health Alliance
http://www.arha.org.au

Center for Reproductive Rights
http://www.reproductiverights.org

EC/UNFPA Initiative for Reproductive Rights in Asia
http://www.asia-initiative.org

Family Care International
http://www.familycareitl.org

Federation of Family Planning Associations Malaysia
http://www.ffpam.org.my

Fertility Awareness and Natural Family Planning
http://www.FertilityUK.org

Global Action Network
http://www.globalactionnetwork.org

Health Action Information Network
http://www.hain.org

Interact Worldwide
http://www.interactworldwide.org

International Women's Health Coalition
http://www.iwhc.org

MySistahs
http://www.mysistahs.org

National Healthy Mothers, Healthy Babies Coalition
http://www.hmhb.org

National Latina Institute for Reproductive Health
http://www.latinainstitute.org

National Organization for Women
http://www.now.org

Pathfinder International
http://www.pathfind.org

World Health Organization
http://www.who.int/reproductive-health/

VIOLENCE

American Bar Association Commission on Domestic Violence
http://www.abanet.org/domviol/home.html

American Domestic Violence Crisis Line
http://www.awoscentral.com

Antistalking Web Site
http://www.antistalking.com

A Safe Passage
http://www.asafepassage.info

Asian and Pacific Islander Institute on Domestic Violence
http://www.apiahf.org/apidvinstitute

Battered Women's Justice Project
http://www.bwjp.org

British Columbia Institute Against Family Violence
http://www.bcifv.org

Canadian Association of Rape Crisis Centres
http://www.casac.ca/english/avcentres/avcentres.htm

Canadian National Clearinghouse on Family Violence
http://www.hc-sc.gc.ca/hpb/family violence

Clearinghouse on Abuse and Neglect of the Elderly
http://db.rdms.udel.edu:8080/CANE/index.jsp

Coalition Against Trafficking of Women
http://www.catwinternational.org

College Violence
http://youthviolence.edschool.virginia.edu/violence-in-schools/college
campus.html

Communities Against Violence Network
http://www.cavnet2.org

Domestic Violence Clearinghouse and Legal Hotline
http://www.stoptheviolence.org

Family Violence Prevention Fund
http://www.endabuse.org

HPP Earth: International Domestic Violence Information
http://www.hotpeachpages.net

International Society for Research on Aggression
http://www.israsociety.com

Management of Imminent Violence
http://www.psychiatry.ox.ac.uk/cebmh/guidelines/violence/violence_
full.html

Men Can Stop Rape
http://www.mencanstoprape.org

Nation to Nation: Promoting the Safety of Native Women
http://toolkit.ncjrs.org/default.htm

National Center for Missing and Exploited Children
http://www.missingkids.com

National Center for Victims of Crime
http://www.ncvc.org/ncvc/Main.aspx

National Center on Domestic and Sexual Violence
http://www.ncdsv.org

National Center on Elder Abuse
http://www.elderabusecenter.org

National Coalition Against Domestic Violence
http://www.ncadv.org

National Domestic Violence Hotline
http://www.ndvh.org

National Latino Alliance for the Elimination of Domestic Violence
http://www.dvalianza.org

National Network to End Domestic Violence
http://www.nnedv.org

National Organization for Men Against Sexism
http://www.nomas.org

National Organization for Women
http://www.now.org/index.html

National Resource Center on Domestic Violence
http://www.nrcdv.org

National Sexual Violence Resource Center
http://www.nsvrc.org

New York Model for Batterer Programs
http://www.nymbp.org

Nursing Network on Violence Against Women International
http://www.nnvawi.org

Office of Violence Against Women, U.S. Department of Justice
http://www.ojp.usdoj.gov/vawo

Partnerships Against Violence Network
http://www.pavnet.org

Rape, Abuse and Incest National Network
http://www.rainn.org

Security on Campus
http://www.securityoncampus.org

Stop Family Violence
http://www.stopfamilyviolence.org

Tibet Justice Center
http://www.tibetjustice.org

U.S. Department of Health and Human Services
http://www.4women.gov/violence/index.cfm

U.S. Department of Justice's Victims of Crime
http://www.usdoj.gov/crimevictims.htm

Violence Against Women
http://www.vaw.umn.edu

Violence Against Women in American Indian/Native American and
Alaska Native Communities
http://www.vawn.edu

Womenslaw
http://www.womenslaw.org

WOMEN AND EDUCATION

American Association of University Women
http://www.aauw.org

Canadian Congress for Learning Opportunities for Women
http://www.nald.ca/litweb/other/cclow

Central European Centre for Women and Youth in Science
http://www.cec-wys.org

International Federation of University Women
http://www.ifuw.org/index.shtml

About the Editor and Contributors

Michele A. Paludi, PhD, is the Series Editor for Women's Psychology for Praeger Publishers. She is the author/editor of 33 college textbooks and more than 160 scholarly articles and conference presentations on sexual harassment, campus violence, psychology of women, gender, and sexual harassment and victimization. Her book, *Ivory Power: Sexual Harassment on Campus* (1990) received the 1992 Myers Center Award for Outstanding Book on Human Rights in the United States. Dr. Paludi served as Chair of the U.S. Department of Education's Subpanel on the Prevention of Violence, Sexual Harassment, and Alcohol and Other Drug Problems in Higher Education. She was one of six scholars in the United States to be selected for this Subpanel. She also was a consultant to and a member of former New York State Governor Mario Cuomo's Task Force on Sexual Harassment. Dr. Paludi serves as an expert witness for court proceedings and administrative hearings on sexual harassment. She has had extensive experience in conducting training programs and investigations of sexual harassment and other EEO issues for businesses and educational institutions. In addition, Dr. Paludi has held faculty positions at Franklin & Marshall College, Kent State University, Hunter College, Union College, and Union Graduate College, where she directs the human resource management certificate program. She teaches in the School of Management.

Janet Boyce graduated from Adirondack Community College in August 2006 with an Associate in Applied Science Degree in Business Administration. In May 2008 she graduated from SUNY Plattsburgh State University with a Bachelor of Science Degree in Management. She is currently enrolled in the MBA and Human Resource Management Certificate programs at Union Graduate College, with an anticipated graduation date of spring 2010.

NiCole T. Buchanan, PhD, is an Associate Professor in the Department of Psychology at Michigan State University (MSU) and a core faculty affiliate in MSU's Center for Multicultural Psychology Research, Center for Gender in Global Context, and the Violence against Women Research & Outreach Initiative. Her research examines the intersection of race and gender in harassment, racialized sexual harassment, health, coping, and resilience among women of color. Dr. Buchanan received the 2008 International Coalition Against Sexual Harassment Researcher Award; the 2008 Carolyn Payton Early Career Award for research making "a significant contribution to the understanding of the role of gender in the lives of black women;" the Association of Women in Psychology's 2007 Women of Color Award for empirical research contributions; Michigan State University's 2007 Excellence in Diversity Award in the category of "Individual Emerging Progress" for outstanding research and teaching accomplishments in the areas of diversity, pluralism, and social justice; and two Clinical Faculty Awards from the National Institutes of Health (NIH). Representative publications include: The effects of racial and sexual harassment on work and the psychological well-being of African American women, *Journal of Occupational Health Psychology*; Comparing sexual harassment subtypes for Black and White women: Double jeopardy, the Jezebel, and the cult of true womanhood, *Psychology of Women Quarterly*; Sexual harassment across the color line: Experiences and outcomes of cross- vs. intra-racial sexual harassment among Black women, *Cultural Diversity and Ethnic Minority Psychology*; and Racialized sexual harassment in the lives of African American Women, *Women & Therapy*.

Elder Cerqueira-Santos, **PhD,** received his PhD in psychology from Federal University of Rio Grande do Sul, Brazil. He is currently adjunct professor at the Federal University of Sergipe, Brazil; consultant for the World Childhood Foundation; and a member of the Center for at Risk Children in Brazil. His main research interest is the relationship between risk-taking behavior and religiosity among youth in Brazil. He is also interested in sexual harassment and sexual development (gender and sexual orientation identity). As of August 2009, he has written six book chapters and 13 scholarly articles; he has also co-authored 72 papers presented at conferences.

Joy Chien received her Bachelor of Science degree from Illinois State University.

Lillian Comas-Diaz, PhD, is the Executive Director of the Transcultural Mental Health Institute, a clinical psychologist in private practice in Washington, DC, and a Clinical Professor at George Washington University School of Medicine. The former director of the American Psychological Association's Office of Ethnic Minority Affairs, Dr. Comas-Diaz also directed the Yale University Department of Psychiatry Hispanic Clinic. The author of more than a hundred publications, Dr. Comas-Diaz's writings focus on women's issues, culture, ethnicity, social class, spirituality, and creativity. She is the co-editor of the textbooks *Clinical Guidelines in Cross Cultural Mental Health*; *Women of Color: Integrating Ethnic and Gender Identities in Psychotherapy*; and *WomanSoul: The Inner Life of Women's Spirituality*. She currently serves as an Associate Editor of the *American Psychologist*.

Eros DeSouza, PhD, is currently a professor of psychology at Illinois State University. He earned his PhD in community psychology from the University of Missouri at Kansas City. He has carried out qualitative and quantitative research on sexuality and gender issues, including sexual orientation and sexual harassment from a cross-cultural perspective. As of August 2009, he has written nine book chapters and more than 40 scholarly articles; he has also co-authored 115 papers presented at conferences.

Nancy Felipe Russo, PhD, is Regents Professor of Psychology and Women's Studies at Arizona State University. Founding director of the Women's Programs office of the American Psychological Association, she is author or editor of more than 200 publications related to the psychology of women and women's issues; current editor of the *American Journal of Orthopsychiatry*; and a former editor of the *Psychology of Women Quarterly*. Dr. Russo is a Fellow of the New York Academy of Sciences, the American Psychological Association (including divisions: 1-General, 9-Social Issues, 26-History, 34-Population and Environment, 35-Psychology of Women, 38-Health, 45-Ethnic Minority Issues, and 52-International Psychology), and the American Psychological Society. Dr. Russo's involvement in international issues as a leader, researcher, and policy advocate has spanned four decades. In these roles she has worked to increase and apply psychological knowledge related to women's lives and circumstances, and to forge links between scientists, policy makers, and the public concerned with diverse women's mental health. In doing so she has been a pioneer in the development of a multicultural feminist psychology of women. She has been awarded the Distinguished International Psychologist Award by APA's Division of International Psychology, the Denmark-Gunvald Award for significant contributions to the psychology of women and gender by the International Council of Psychologists, and the American Psychological Association's Award for Distinguished Contributions to Psychology in the Public Interest. Other honors include a Carolyn Wood Sherif Award and a Heritage Award for Contributions to Public Policy from APA's Division 35. She has been identified among "Trailblazing Women in Community Psychology" by APA Division 27's Committee on Women, received a Distinguished Career Award from the Association for Women in Psychology, and was recognized by APA's Board of Ethnic Minority Affairs for contributions to ethnic minority issues.

Susan Fineran, PhD, is an associate professor at the University of Southern Maine School of Social Work and Women and Gender Studies. Her professional career includes clinical experience in the areas of aging, substance abuse, child and family treatment, sex discrimination, and women's issues. Her research interests include peer sexual harassment and bullying in schools and the mental health implications for children and adolescents. Dr. Fineran joined the University of Southern Maine School of Social Work in 2002 after teaching on the social work faculties of Boston University and the University of Illinois at Chicago. Her education includes an MSW (1981) from the Catholic University of America, and a PhD (1996) from the University of Illinois at Chicago.

James Gruber, PhD, has published research on sexual harassment for 25 years. He was among the first researchers to conduct studies of workplace sexual harassment in the early 1980s and cross-national studies in the 1990s. His work on the experiences of women in male-dominated occupations resulted in a recent book, *In The Company of Men: Male Dominance and Sexual Harassment* (2005), co-edited with Phoebe Morgan. Since 2002, Drs. Gruber and Susan Fineran have presented conference papers and published journal articles on bullying and sexual harassment among adolescents in schools. Two recent publications with Dr. Fineran studied that the effects of bullying and sexual harassment at school: "The Impact of Bullying and Sexual Harassment on Health Outcomes of Middle and High School Girls," published in *Violence Against Women* (2007), and "Comparing the Impact of Bullying and Sexual Harassment Victimization on the Mental and Physical Health of Adolescents" (*Sex Roles*, 2008). He has also co-authored a publication in *Child Abuse & Neglect* (in press) that examines the effects of workplace sexual harassment on adolescent girls.

Paula Lundberg-Love, PhD, is a professor of psychology at the University of Texas at Tyler (UTT) and the Ben R. Fisch Endowed Professor in Humanitarian Affairs for 2001–2004. Her undergraduate degree was in chemistry, and she worked as a chemist at a pharmaceutical company for five years prior to earning her doctorate in physiological psychology with an emphasis in psychopharmacology. After a three-year postdoctoral fellowship in nutrition and behavior in the Department of Preventive Medicine at Washington University School of Medicine in St. Louis, she assumed her academic position at UTT where she teaches classes in psychopharmacology, behavioral neuroscience, physiological psychology, sexual victimization, and family violence. Subsequent to her academic appointment, Dr. Lundberg-Love pursued postgraduate training and is a licensed professional counselor. She is a member of Tyler Counseling and Assessment Center, where she provides therapeutic services for victims of sexual assault, child sexual abuse, and domestic violence. She has conducted a long-term research study on women who were victims of childhood incestuous abuse, constructed a therapeutic program for their recovery, and documented its effectiveness upon their recovery. She is the author of nearly 100 publications and presentations and is co-editor of *Violence and Sexual Abuse at Home: Current Issues in Spousal Battering and Child Maltreatment* as well as *Intimate Violence Against Women: When Spouses, Partners, or Lovers Attack.* As a result of her training in psychopharmacology and child maltreatment, her expertise has been sought as a consultant on various death penalty appellate cases in the state of Texas.

Jennifer L. Martin is the department head of English at a public alternative high school for at-risk students in Michigan and a lecturer at Oakland University where she teaches graduate research methods in the department of Educational Leadership, Feminist Methods and Introduction to Women and Gender Studies in the Department of Women and Gender Studies. She is not only a feminist teacher, but a feminist activist. She has volunteered as an assault responder and engaged in political action for feminist causes. Currently, she is the Title IX Education Task Force Chair for the Michigan National Organization for Women to advocate for Title IX compliance in Michigan's schools. She has conducted research and written articles on the topics of peer sexual harassment, teaching for social justice, service learning, and the at-risk student.

Avigail Moor, PhD, is a feminist clinical psychologist who specializes in the treatment of women in general and survivors of sexual violence in particular. She heads the Women Studies program at Tel Hai College in Israel and is also on the faculty of the Psychology and Social Work programs. In addition, she serves as a psychological consultant to several rape crisis centers in Northern Israel. Her past and present research focuses primarily on the social context of sexual violence against women and its psychological sequelae. She has also written articles on treatment issues with survivors of this type of violence. Other research interests concern the psychology of women and the effects of gender-based power imbalances on women's mental health.

Kevin L. Nadal, PhD, is a professor, psychologist, performer, activist, and author, who received his doctorate in counseling psychology from Columbia University in 2008. As an assistant professor of mental health counseling and psychology at John Jay College of Criminal Justice–City University of New York, he has published several works focusing on Filipino American, ethnic minority, and LGBTQ issues in the fields of psychology and education. He is the author of the book *Filipino American Psychology: A Handbook of Theory, Research, and Clinical Practice,* and his current research on microaggressions, or subtle forms of discrimination towards oppressed groups, has been published in the *American Psychologist* and other journals. He was named one of *People Magazine*'s hottest bachelors in 2006, he was a guest on Fox News Channel's "The O'Reilly Factor," and he has been featured on The Filipino Channel, the History Channel, *Philippine News*, and *Filipinas Magazine*

Dorota Wnuk Novitskie is a third-year doctoral student in the Clinical PhD program at Fairleigh Dickinson University. Her research interests include cross-cultural studies, domestic violence/interpersonal violence, and family violence.

Joy Rice, PhD, Clinical Professor of Psychiatry and Emerita professor of Educational Policy Studies and Women Studies at the University of Wisconsin–Madison, received the *Woman of the Year Award* from the American Psychological Association (APA), Section for the Advancement of Women in Counseling Psychology at the annual APA meeting in Boston in August 2008, for "significant contributions and promotion of the status of women in psychology, leadership and activism on behalf of women, and research that has significantly advanced knowledge of women's concerns in counseling psychology." Dr. Rice's pioneering work on gender issues in psychotherapy dates from the early 1970s when she began the first women's studies course on women and therapy at the University of Wisconsin. Her 1973 paper in the *American Journal of Psychiatry* was one of the first articles to address key issues of gender discrimination in psychotherapeutic theory and practice. She was co-chair of the task force that worked for seven years in developing the *APA Guidelines for Psychological Practice with Girls and Women.* It was passed by APA and published in the *American Psychologist* in 2007. Dr. Rice also co-chaired the APA Resolution on *Gender and Cultural Awareness in International Psychology* passed by APA in 2004. Active in state, federal, and international advocacy for mental health parity, she currently serves as co-chair of the Wisconsin Lieutenant Governor's Task Force on Women and Depression and is the International Council of Psychologists representative to the World Federation of Mental Health. Her most recent book, *Women and Leadership: Transforming Visions and Diverse Voices* (John Wiley, 2007), explores feminist models of leadership that embrace collaboration, inclusion, and social action. Dr. Rice is a recipient of the Educational Press Association Distinguished Achievement Award and an APA Fellow of four divisions.

Janet Sigal, PhD, is a Professor of Psychology at Fairleigh Dickinson University. She received her PhD in Social Psychology from Northwestern University. She has more than 100 presentations, and several articles and chapters primarily in the area of women's issues, including intimate partner violence and sexual harassment. She is currently conducting a

12-country study on perceptions of intimate partner violence (IPV). She is a Fellow of the American Psychological Association and a member of the APA UN Team.

Lindsey Speach graduated from Siena College in May 2007 with a BS in Marketing Management and a minor in Sociology. She is enrolled in the Certificate of Human Resources program at Union Graduate College and plans to join the MBA program. Lindsey is currently the Recruiting Coordinator for the Northeast region of KeyBank N.A.

Michelle Strand received her Bachelor of Arts degree in Psychology and Criminology in 2006 from Wilkes University in Wilkes-Barre, Pennsylvania. While at Wilkes, she also minored in Business Administration and Sociology. Michelle was a student in Union Graduate College's Masters in Business Administration program and graduated in June 2009. Her specialization being Human Resources (HR), Michelle has been a co-op at General Electric in the HR department since November 2007. It was there that she was able to put her studies to real life situations, and became more acquainted with a variety of aspects in the field of business. Michelle's co-op experience takes place within GE's manufacturing plant for steam turbines and generators in Schenectady, New York. While there, she has planned, designed, and implemented a salaried new hire orientation, assisted in interviewing and on-boarding 300+ production positions, coordinated work/life balance on-site seminars, along with many other experiences in Human Resources. Michelle is a member of the Society for Human Resources Management and the Capital Region Human Resources Association. She has attended several conferences around the country to improve her business knowledge, including the National Association for Women in MBA, and the International Coalition Against Sexual Harassment. She also took a 10-day tour of Shanghai, China, in December 2008 to learn about the country's distinctive business strategies and developments. Michelle is also an avid volunteer in her local community. She has helped build a house for the Habitat for Humanity, taught at an elementary school for Junior Achievement, and walked dogs at the Society for the Prevention and Cruelty of Animals, including several other volunteering activities.

Susan Strauss, RN, EdD, is a national and international speaker, trainer, and consultant. Her specialty areas include harassment and workplace bullying, organization development, and management/leadership development. Her clients are from business, education, health care, law, and government organizations from both the public and private sector. Dr. Strauss has authored book chapters, articles in professional journals, written curriculum and training manuals, as well as authored the book, *Sexual*

Harassment and Teens: A Program for Positive Change. Susan has been featured on *The Donahue Show, CBS Evening News,* and other television and radio programs as well as interviewed for newspaper and journal articles such as the *Times of London, Lawyers Weekly,* and *Harvard Education Newsletter.* Susan has presented at international conferences in Botswana, Egypt, Thailand, Israel, and the United States, and conducted sex discrimination research in Poland. She has consulted with professionals from other countries such as England, Australia, Canada, and St. Maarten.

Bethany Waits is a graduate student in clinical psychology at the University of Texas at Tyler. She anticipates graduation in May of 2010 and plans to pursue the Licensed Professional Counselor designation upon completion of her degree. Ultimately, she would like to work as a therapist for a nonprofit community organization, such as a crisis center. In May 2007, she obtained her BA in psychology from UT-Tyler, graduating Summa Cum Laude. She was accepted as a lifetime member of Psi Chi, the national honor society in psychology, and Alpha Chi, a national college honor society. While an undergraduate, she participated in a student panel addressing issues related to sexual assault on campus. In addition, she has worked with several professors on various research projects.

Jessica Wilmot earned her BS in Business Administration from Le Moyne College in Syracuse, New York, in 2007. Afterward she took some time away from school and traveled to Europe to spend a few months volunteering in England at a Surrey Women's Aid, a not-for-profit women's shelter. She then returned home to continue her education and is currently a MBA student at Union Graduate College in Schenectady, New York. As well as her MBA, she is working on her HR Certificate with Dr. Paludi and will be graduating June 2010. Currently Jessica is an intern at General Electric on the Pension Team and has enjoyed learning about corporate America.

Krystle C. Woods's research examines the influence of perpetrator race on sexual harassment outcomes, racialized sexual harassment, and depression in African American women. Ms. Woods is a clinical doctoral candidate in the Department of Psychology at Michigan State University. She was the 2005 recipient of the Michigan State University Enrichment Fellowship "recognizing academic achievement, research goals, contribution to a diverse educational community and a record of overcoming obstacles."

Index